D0794343

PITT THE YOUNGER

Pitt the Younger

A Life

Michael J. Turner

Hambledon and London
London and New York

Hambledon and London

102 Gloucester Avenue
London, NW1 8HX

175 Fifth Avenue
New York
NY 10010

First Published 2003

ISBN 1 85285 377 8

Copyright © Michael J. Turner 2003

The moral rights of the author has been asserted.

All rights reserved.
Without limiting the rights under copyrights
reserved above, no part of this publication may be
reproduced, stored in or introduced into a retrieval system,
or transmitted, in any form or by any means (electronic, mechanical,
photocopying, recording or otherwise), without the prior
written permission of both the copyright owner and
the above publisher of the book.

A description of this book is available from the
British Library and from the Library of Congress.

Typeset by Carnegie Publishing, Lancaster,
and printed in Great Britain by Cambridge University Press.

Distributed in the United States and Canada
exclusively by Palgrave Macmillan,
a division of St Martin's Press.

Contents

Illustrations

Introduction

On 27 January 1806, the House of Commons assembled for an eagerly awaited debate on whether or not to accord William Pitt the Younger, the recently deceased prime minister, funeral honours at the public expense. The motion in favour of full honours referred to Pitt as 'that excellent statesman' and dwelt on 'the public sense of so great and irreparable a loss'. Many MPs in the chamber, however, took a different view.

Naturally Pitt's former colleagues and supporters approved of the motion in the strongest terms. To them Pitt had been the saviour of the constitution, the architect of sound public finances and general prosperity, and the guardian of the nation's vital interests. They spoke of his 'eminence and splendour', his 'transcendent merits' and 'virtues and extraordinary talents'. He had been an 'illustrious' and 'magnificent' leader, 'so able, so eminent, so distinguished and disinterested', a man who 'exhausted his life in serving his country to the best of his great abilities'. Time and again MPs rose to commend 'the vigour and sagacity of his measures', his 'exalted character', and his 'enlarged views', 'personal purity' and 'indefatigable patriotism'.

But there were some speakers who made a distinction between Pitt's earlier career, which they admitted had been admirable, and his later career, which they deplored. They claimed that Pitt had left the nation in an appalling condition. Although they meant no personal slight against him, they doubted the propriety of full public honours.

Pitt's most resolute and intractable political opponents went much further. They could not accept any motion that referred to Pitt as an 'excellent statesman', and found the idea of funeral honours wholly objectionable on public grounds. Pitt's methods and priorities, they argued, had been pernicious throughout his career, not just in its later stages, and he was completely unworthy of the tribute that had been proposed.

At the close of the debate, the motion for public honours was carried by a large majority (258 to 89 votes).[1] The opinions expressed during the debate are instructive. They point to some of the reasons why, during and after Pitt's lifetime, there was heated disagreement about his career and legacy. The debate was not just about funeral honours. It was an opportunity for

Pitt's friends and foes to validate themselves and their politics. Some tried to vindicate the departed premier, others to discredit him. To a considerable extent, therefore, the debate was about the ownership of history, the imposing of a pattern on the recent past, the shaping of memory. It was about claiming the right to influence future interpretations of Pittite government.

Even today Pitt's historical significance is a matter on which there are widely differing points of view. Towards the end of the twentieth century there was a notable increase in the number of publications dealing directly with the man who had dominated British politics two hundred years previously. This reflects an enduring interest in William Pitt the Younger among readers of all kinds, and the return of British political history to school and university curricula after a period of relative decline. By far the most important contribution to Pitt studies has been John Ehrman's trilogy, completed in 1996 (volumes one and two were published in 1969 and 1983). Shorter and more focused treatments include the 'Lancaster Pamphlet' written by Eric Evans (1999), and the 'Profile in Power' of Michael Duffy (2000). There have been scholarly monographs, such as Jennifer Mori's *William Pitt and the French Revolution* (1997), and in 1998 an entire volume of *History*, the journal of the Historical Association, was devoted to Pitt.[2] He also features prominently in works that re-examine the politics of the late eighteenth and early nineteenth centuries.[3]

This book will draw recent scholarship together in order to assess the current state of play. It will also offer a sensitive portrayal of the man himself and the times in which he lived. The basic purpose is to answer perennial questions about Pitt and his career. How did he become prime minister at such an early age (twenty-four), and only two years and ten months after first entering parliament? What were his political priorities and methods? Who were his chief associates and supporters, and why did they follow him? What were his assets as prime minister? Did they outweigh his shortcomings as a politician and leader? How did Pitt respond to revolution and war in Europe? Was he more successful as premier in peacetime than in war? Why did he remain prime minister for so long, and why did he eventually resign? How does his second administration (1804–6) compare with his first (1783–1801)?

In addressing these questions I will allow Pitt, and those who knew and observed him, to speak for themselves. This book seeks to combine the best features of traditional political biography (lucid, coherent narrative and strong reliance on speeches, correspondence, reminiscences and the like) with the insights provided by modern historical research. Due attention will be paid not only to the words and deeds of Pitt, but also to the nature of the state and growth of government activity, the evolution of the cabinet and office of prime minister, and the political influence of the crown. There will be full discussion of controversies surrounding such issues as economical reform, constitutional change, public order, trade and foreign policy. Public opinion and popular political participation will be analyzed, as will the image, rhetoric, principles, motives and goals of elite politicians in late eighteenth- and early nineteenth-century Britain.

After an examination of Pitt's early life, his arrival in the House of Commons and rise to the premiership, and a general discussion of the political system in which he operated, I will try to elucidate central themes in his career – particularly Pitt's reforms, their rationale, nature and reception, and Pitt's accomplishments and limitations as a leader. His relationships with king, cabinet, parliament and public will be explored in depth, for they shaped his leadership style in decisive ways. I will also discuss the impact of the French Revolution and subsequent war, before bringing all of these topics together in an analysis of Pitt's later career. Circumstances in the early 1800s were certainly not what they had been in the mid-1780s, and the causes and effects of Pitt's decline will be explained along with the changing contexts within which questions of reform, leadership and war had to be addressed.

The picture that emerges is one of a practical man of affairs whose ideas, methods and aspirations were largely determined by prevalent conditions. This study will show that Pitt must not be judged primarily as a reformer, a political thinker, the creator of the early nineteenth-century Tory party, an archetypal nationalistic war leader, the first modern prime minister, or the facilitator of cabinet government. There may be a strong case for advancing any of these (and indeed other) descriptions to indicate the essence of Pitt. But we must not confuse intentions with consequences. Pitt was really a creature of his times and a pragmatic leader for whom immediate needs and available expedients mattered more than apparent consistency. At the same time, he cared about posterity's verdict. He hoped and expected to be remembered in a certain way and to leave behind some lasting achievements. Pitt's natural inclination was to seek and exercise power, and there was little in his life above and beyond politics. He saw himself as a patriotic public servant. Yet his self-definition presents a difficulty. Opinions still differ about Pitt's reputation and legacy, and questions are still asked about his personal qualities: was he talented or lucky, a genius or a good technician, naturally brilliant or forced into extraordinary acts by external pressures? Pitt genuinely tried to live up to the expectations that attached to a pre-existing 'patriotic' vocation, but in doing so he crafted an image to suit himself and his environment.

For
Steve and Sandra
and
Bill and Jackie

Acknowledgements

I am grateful to Martin Sheppard, Tony Morris and Eva Osborne at Hambledon and London, and to the excellent staff at university libraries in Newcastle, Reading and Sunderland, the Bodleian Library, Oxford, and the British Library.

As ever, Catherine, Grace and Jill have been good-humoured and wonderfully supportive, and my debt to them is immeasurable. I would also like to thank the rest of the family across Britain and America for many kind words of encouragement. Special mention must be made of friends at Bethshan and the Mission, the members of Bethshan FC, colleagues at Sunderland and (for help and advice at various times) John Belchem, Michael Bentley, Jeremy Black, David Eastwood, Theo Hoppen, John Stevenson, Stewart Weaver and Chris Williams.

Any errors or shortcomings in this book are entirely my own responsibility.

July 2002   Gosforth

1

Beginnings

William Pitt the Younger was born on 28 May 1759, at Hayes Place, Kent. He was the second son of William Pitt the Elder and Hester Grenville, and the fourth of five children born between 1755 and 1761. At an early age he became aware that he belonged to a distinguished and well-connected family. Both the Pitts and Grenvilles had a long record of office-holding and political commitment, and Pitt's own father was one of the most famous men of his generation. In 1759, the year of Pitt's birth, his father was at the height of his power and popularity. As a child Pitt idolized him, conscious of his father's special status in the recent history of Britain and indeed the world, and in turn Pitt was his father's favourite, a son in whom the Elder Pitt was determined to instill some of his own greatness and upon whom, in consequence, he lavished his attention.

By the mid-eighteenth century the Pitts had been respectable landowners and office holders for several generations, with property in Dorset and Hampshire. Their fortune had been established by Thomas Pitt, an East India merchant who became governor of Madras and was known to posterity as 'Diamond Pitt' (he acquired a large and valuable diamond in India). He died in 1726. Most of his children married into the nobility. His eldest son Robert married Lady Harriet Villiers in 1703 (she was the grand-daughter of the fourth Viscount Grandison in the Irish peerage, and sister of the first Earl Grandison). Robert Pitt was MP for several constituencies between 1705 and 1727 (Old Sarum, Salisbury and Okehampton, where the family had electoral interests), and served as clerk of the household of the Prince of Wales, who succeeded as King George II in 1727. Thomas Pitt's second son, also named Thomas, was created Earl of Londonderry in 1718. The title subsequently passed to his sons, but became extinct in 1765 through lack of heirs. Lucy, the daughter of 'Diamond Pitt', married the soldier and politician James Stanhope in 1713 (he was created Earl Stanhope in 1718 and served as prime minister between 1717 and 1720).[1]

The family's reputation and status were further enhanced during the time of William Pitt the Elder, the fourth of Robert Pitt's seven children, who was born in Westminster on 15 November 1708. His elder brother Thomas

was MP for Okehampton and then Old Sarum. His two elder sisters were
Harriet, who married Sir William Corbet, and Catherine, who married
Robert Needham (whose family had held an Irish peerage since 1625).[2] One
of his younger sisters, Ann, served in the royal household as maid of honour
to George II's consort, Queen Caroline. William Pitt the Elder became a
Member of Parliament in 1735. He sat in the House of Commons for over
thirty years before his elevation to the Lords as Earl of Chatham.[3]

Pitt the Elder was of striking appearance, tall and erect, with keen eyes,
a thin face and long, hooked nose. His dress and conduct were dignified,
his conversation pedantic. He was a brilliant but flawed personality. As a
public figure he came to be known as the protector of constitutional liberties
at home and architect of British power abroad. Talented, courageous and
decisive, in his prime he was also extraordinarily popular. He became an
inspirational war leader, and basked in his reputation as an honest and
patriotic public servant. But he was arrogant and vain. He loved pomp
and ostentation. Relying on his own judgment, he showed scant respect
for those who disagreed with him and antagonized almost everyone he
ever worked with in politics.

A man of uncommon ability and enormous ambition, William Pitt the
Elder held junior government offices from 1746 and was appointed secretary
of state and leader of the House of Commons in 1756. He rose to become
the dominant figure in the cabinet nominally led by the first Duke of
Newcastle from June 1757. He gained prestige and popularity for British
victories in the Seven Years War (1756–63), but resigned in 1761 because
some of his colleagues, the new king, George III (who succeeded in October
1760), and the king's political allies were pressing for peace. The Elder Pitt's
resignation seemed to many a proud and selfish act. It tarnished the reputation he had cultivated as an honest and devoted patriotic leader, and his
'Great Commoner' image – rooted in his virtue and independence – was
further damaged when he accepted a pension (£3000 a year for his own
lifetime and that of his wife and eldest son John) and a peerage for his
wife.

The early part of George III's reign was marked by prolonged ministerial
instability. The king, seeking a reliable premier who could command a
parliamentary majority, eventually turned to Pitt the Elder in July 1766.
Pitt served as chief minister until October 1768, but this was not a successful
administration. There were cabinet divisions and Pitt was continually
absent through illness. Indeed, rather than serve as first lord of the treasury,
which was by now the office normally held by the prime minister, he
took the less demanding post of lord privy seal. In addition, he was
no longer the 'Great Commoner' and spokesman for popular causes. In

August 1766 he was created Viscount Pitt of Burton Pynsent and Earl of
Chatham. Elevation to the House of Lords contributed to his weakness as
prime minister, for the Commons had been his power base and was the
dominant branch of the legislature, and his peerage alienated many of
the extra-parliamentary groups that had previously regarded him as their
champion.

Despite serious illness and his disappointing premiership, in the 1770s
Chatham retained influence as a respected elder statesman. During the
American crisis he recommended a negotiated settlement and deplored the
outbreak of war against the colonists. He argued for concessions to heal
the breach, unable to accept the prospect of American independence (which
would negate many of his previous policies and break up the empire he
had helped to construct). His conciliatory approach, however, did not accord
with opinion in parliament and out of doors.

Away from his public duties the Elder Pitt enjoyed a happy marriage and
home life, though inherited physical and mental disorders (he was increasingly afflicted by gout and depression) took a heavy toll.[4] When a bachelor
he resided at South Lodge in Enfield, Middlesex. He purchased Hayes Place,
near Bromley in Kent, after marrying Hester Grenville in 1754. The house
was subsequently rebuilt and the grounds extended as he pursued one of
his principal hobbies, landscape gardening. From 1759 to 1761 Pitt kept a
house in St James's Square, London, but gave it up after resigning from
the government. He decided to reside at Hayes exclusively. In January 1765
he found that he was a beneficiary of Sir William Pynsent, whom he had
never met, and took possession of the estate of Burton Pynsent near Langport
in Somerset, valued at £40,000. The deceased baronet had evidently been
impressed by Pitt's public character and achievements; and, although a
disgruntled relative disputed the will, Sir William Pynsent's wishes prevailed.
Pitt later erected a column in the grounds (the 'Burton steeple', 140 feet
high) in memory of his benefactor. He moved the family to Somerset and
sold Hayes Place, but, as his health deteriorated, he came to believe that
only the air at Hayes could help. He therefore bought it back late in 1767,
by which time he was Earl of Chatham, and it remained his favourite
residence.

The property at Hayes was significantly extended and improved. Eventually there were gardens, farms, pasture, stables, a dairy, orchards and a
fenced park. The house had twenty-four bedrooms. The accommodation
was substantial, though not sumptuous by eighteenth-century aristocratic
standards. The improvements at Burton Pynsent were even more striking.
Chatham embarked upon a series of building, landscaping and planting
projects, laid new roads and completely altered the estate's appearance. He

indulged his passions with no thought of the financial implications, and ran up heavy debts. By the 1770s his liabilities were numerous, and it was left to his wife to manage the family's resources as best she could. Hayes Place was sold in 1785, seven years after Chatham's death. Lady Chatham lived on the estate at Burton Pynsent until her death, when that too was sold.

Chatham died at Hayes on 11 May 1778. He was buried in Westminster Abbey, with full public honours. The funeral was attended by all the leading opposition peers and MPs. With Chatham's eldest son absent on military service abroad, William Pitt the Younger served as chief mourner.

Hester Grenville survived her husband by almost twenty-five years. She had been born in Wotton, Buckinghamshire, on 8 November 1720. The Grenvilles were a well-established Whig clan. Hester's father was Richard Grenville, who like many of his relatives had entered the House of Commons to pursue a public career.[5] Her mother was Lady Hester Temple, who succeeded (by special licence) to the viscountcy of her brother, Lord Cobham, and was created Countess Temple in her own right in 1749.

Hester was their only daughter. She married William Pitt the Elder on 16 November 1754. He was forty-six. She was thirty-four, tall and graceful, with auburn hair. She was reputed to have an amiable manner and a fondness for country life. Two of her brothers, Richard Grenville-Temple (the first Earl Temple) and George Grenville, served with Pitt in the Newcastle government of 1757 to 1761. They later broke with Pitt, and George Grenville was himself prime minister from 1763 to 1765. Pitt restored his relationship with Temple in 1774 at the prompting of his wife and his nephew Thomas Pitt, later first Baron Camelford. Another of Hester's brothers, James, was appointed to a lordship of the treasury in December 1756 (but never held cabinet office). Hester herself was created Baroness Chatham in October 1761 in recognition of her husband's public services. The unfavourable response to his acceptance of this title and a pension led to her being lampooned as 'Baroness Cheat'em'. She was devoted to her children and sustained her husband through thick and thin, never doubting his greatness, nursing him through sickness, tolerating his tantrums and financial improvidence, sharing in his political interests. She died on 3 April 1803, aged eighty-two, and was buried with her husband in Westminster Abbey. The barony of Chatham passed to her eldest son, John, second Earl of Chatham.[6]

The first child of Pitt the Elder and Hester Grenville was a daughter, Hester, who was born in October 1755. In December 1774 she married Charles Stanhope, Lord Mahon (subsequently third Earl Stanhope).[7] They had three daughters.

John Pitt was born in October 1756. He married Lady Mary Elizabeth

Sydney in 1783. She died in 1821. They had no children. John Pitt joined the army in 1774. As a lieutenant in the 39th regiment of foot, and subsequently a captain in the 86th regiment, he took part in the siege of Gibraltar (1779–83). Although he never distinguished himself on active service, he was promoted to the rank of colonel in 1793, commanded a brigade in Holland in 1799 (and was wounded), and was made up to lieutenant general in 1802. In physical appearance he resembled his father. His manner was cold and reserved, but he remained on good terms with King George III, which probably helps to explain his army promotions and government appointments. He was a long-serving cabinet minister, and as the second Earl of Chatham his political career was closely linked to that of his younger brother William. He held several ministerial offices between 1788 and 1810, in the administrations of Pitt (1783–1801), Addington (1801–4), Pitt (1804–6), Portland (1807–9) and Perceval (1809–12).[8] His real ambition in life, however, was to win military glory. In 1808 he pressed his claims to the commandership-in-chief of British forces in the Peninsula, and was annoyed to be passed over (the post went to Arthur Wellesley, later Duke of Wellington). Possibly as compensation, he was given command of the Walcheren expedition in 1809. The goal was to capture Antwerp and destroy French ships and arsenals on the Scheldt. The operation was a dismal failure. Chatham was partly to blame, for he lacked the talent and energy needed for so important a mission, but other disadvantages were equally serious: no effective assistance was given by the Royal Navy, and political support for the expedition was shaky owing to a cabinet split on war strategy. Chatham's reputation suffered, though this did not prevent his promotion to the rank of general in 1812. He also served as governor of Plymouth from 1805 to 1807, Jersey from 1807 to 1820, and Gibraltar from 1820 until his death in 1835.

The third child of Pitt the Elder and Hester Grenville was Harriot, born in April 1758. She married Edward James Eliot, son of Baron Eliot, in September 1785.[9] The fourth child was William, born in May 1759. The fifth child was James Charles Pitt, born in April 1761. He became an officer in the Royal Navy. Before the age of twenty he was captain of his own sloop, the HMS *Hornet*.

Despite the political influence of his father and the eminence of his wider connections, William Pitt the Younger's rise and success as a public figure were hardly inevitable, and in his youth and early career he had to contend with serious disadvantages. The family finances were in a parlous state because of his father's habitual extravagance and constant indebtedness, and Pitt the Elder's political decline during the 1760s and 1770s also created obstacles for the son who hoped to follow in his footsteps. The Elder Pitt had made enemies and lost position, reputation and support, and hence the family link was less of an asset to his son than it might otherwise have been. The Pitt motto 'By benign providence' (*Benigno numine*) was therefore quite apt,[10] for Pitt the Younger's progress would require good luck as well as his own exertions and a careful exploitation of the positive aspects of his father's legacy. When he embarked upon a public career the Younger Pitt was to find that important opportunities opened up for him at just the right times.

As a child William Pitt the Younger was educated privately at home. From 1765 his tutor was the Rev. Edward Wilson, a graduate of Pembroke Hall, Cambridge. A home-based education was necessitated by Pitt's poor health,[11] but it also accorded with his father's preferences. The Elder Pitt had hated his years at Eton (1719–26) – a stultifying and brutal place, he thought – and wanted to guide the intellectual development of his son along the lines most appropriate for a life in politics. In particular, Pitt the Younger received a rigorous training in oratory. Instructed by his father, he would recite passages from Shakespeare and Milton to improve his elocution, and verbally translate sections from Greek and Latin texts, which exercised his mind and broadened his vocabulary. If family anecdotes offer any guide, there were early signs of attainment. In 1772 Pitt's mother noted the 'fineness' of his mind, and recorded that he seemed to be developing much faster than other children of the same age. Family acquaintances also remarked upon the extent to which he was excelling his elder brother in intelligence and conversation.[12] His boyhood fascination with politics was obvious. He expressed a wish at seven years old to serve the nation as his father had done, and composed a political play at the age of thirteen to be performed by the Pitt children at home.

Pitt was a precocious youngster. For his tutors the Rev. Wilson, the most amazing thing about him was his memory; he seemed to *recollect* rather than learn.[13] His father insisted on a secure grounding in the classics, mathematics and English history and literature, while the regular instruction in debate and elocution added to Pitt's longing for a life in politics and sense of involvement in his father's career. He copied his father, began to share his tastes, and it was from the Elder Pitt that he picked up his lifelong enthusiasm for landscape gardening. It should also be noted that, like his father, Pitt cared little about financial prudence. He may have seen in his father's extravagance the appropriate lifestyle for a great man.

From 1773 Pitt was a student at the University of Cambridge, though illness prevented regular attendance at Pembroke Hall until 1776.[14] Awarded the degree of Master of Arts without examination in the spring of 1776, he formed a lasting friendship with his tutor, the Rev. George Pretyman.

Between 1776 and 1779, during which time his restored health allowed him to remain in Cambridge, Pitt became an accomplished classical scholar (relying heavily on Latin and Greek, Pretyman's programme included no modern literature or languages and only a little mathematics). He also read philosophy and English history. Pretyman later recalled that Pitt was never idle. He devoted himself to his books, paid close attention to style and expression, and continued his habit of extemporaneous translation. He liked to compare arguments on opposite sides of an issue, noting how protagonists answered the key points in each other's case. Pitt did not subsequently expand upon the education he received in these years. He mastered what he enjoyed – composition, translation, the practical application of what he had read – but in other fields of knowledge he showed little interest. The intellectual influences that shaped him before he left Cambridge were not added to in later life.

Meanwhile, Pitt's political interests led him often to parliament, where he could meet prominent MPs and listen to debates. On one occasion he was introduced to Charles James Fox, an outspoken critic of the government of Lord North, who was impressed by his eager and informed remarks about recent proceedings.[15] Enthralled as he was by his father's legend, Pitt enjoyed nothing better than to dine and talk politics with Chatham's old colleagues. He was present on 7 April 1778 when his father addressed the House of Lords for what proved to be the last time. Chatham collapsed while trying to speak, and Pitt helped to carry him from the chamber. His father's death just over a month later (11 May) was a huge blow. Pitt, not yet twenty, had to steel himself for the ordeal of Chatham's funeral. He was grateful for the marks of esteem that were shown, but noted a lack of respect on the part of George III and his allies. He wrote to his mother (9 June 1778):

> The sad solemnity has been celebrated so as to answer every important wish we could form on the subject. The Court did not honour us with their countenance, nor did they suffer the procession to be as magnificent as it ought; but it had notwithstanding everything essential to the great object, the attendance being most respectable, and the crowd of interested spectators immense.[16]

The years at Cambridge and immediately after were significant for two other reasons. For recreation and emotional succour, the normally shy and reserved Pitt depended on a small group of friends, notably Edward Eliot (subsequently his brother-in-law), John Jeffreys Pratt (son of the first Earl Camden), George Henry Fitzroy (Lord Euston, son of the third Duke of Grafton), Charles Manners (Lord Granby, grandson of the third Duke of Rutland), William Lowther (who belonged to one of the leading political families in northern England), Charles Long (a future secretary to the treasury), Richard Pepper Arden (a lawyer, fourteen years older than Pitt) and William Wilberforce. (The group took a keen interest in contemporary affairs, and each of its members went on to enter public life.) Though Pitt could be humorous and highly engaging in an intimate circle, he was not gregarious and it seems that he often found it difficult to relax in wider social settings. In later life he continued to prefer the closed society of old and familiar companions, and he never had many women friends.

Another tendency to survive from Pitt's youth was his habitual consumption of strong drink. This began on medical advice. The Chatham family physician Dr Anthony Addington, whose clients also included George III, had recommended a bottle of port a day to combat gout. Pitt followed this advice, but it brought further medical complications in its wake, and these became increasingly apparent as Pitt the statesman was exhausted by public service. (Addington also offered advice about diet and exercise. At Cambridge Pitt kept a horse and rode every day.)

Though Pitt was determined to enter parliament and pursue a political career, he needed an income and a respectable profession when he left Cambridge and decided to train as a lawyer. This course had probably been discussed previously with his father. His elder brother was in the army, his younger brother had joined the navy, and it appears that his father considered the law an appropriate standby in case Pitt's political career failed to take off. He briefly resided at Lincoln's Inn during 1780 and 1781, and he witnessed at first hand the Gordon Riots of June 1780, the most serious disorders in London during the whole of the eighteenth century. He wrote to tell his mother that 'religious mobs' (protesting against concessions to Roman Catholics) had set fire to property around Lincoln's Inn, but that the danger had soon passed.

> The only objects of resentment seem to have been public characters and the residences of Roman Catholics or felons. None of those you are particularly interested for have been exposed to any inconvenience or apprehension, or anything else than the disagreeable and disgraceful sight which such uncontrolled licentiousness exhibits.

(It is evident that this experience reinforced Pitt's suspicions about popular agitation while also reminding him how controversial religious matters could be.) Called to the Bar on 12 June 1780, Pitt joined the western circuit in August. He did not practise law for very long, but enjoyed the company of other barristers and seems to have made a favourable impression upon them. During the summers of 1780 and 1781 Pitt took on several cases and did well at the Exeter assizes.[17]

Even at this relatively young age Pitt had great confidence in his own abilities. A striking demonstration of his self-assurance was recorded by James Bland Burges (later an under-secretary at the foreign office). Among the guests at a dinner in Lincoln's Inn were Pitt and the historian Edward Gibbon, author of the acclaimed *The Decline and Fall of the Roman Empire* (published in six parts between 1776 and 1788). The learned Gibbon was more than twenty years Pitt's senior, but Pitt got the better of him in 'a very animated debate' that was 'conducted with great talent and brilliancy on both sides'. Pitt did not rate Gibbon's work very highly, and disliked his politics (Gibbon had held a junior post at the board of trade in North's government). As Gibbon took charge of the conversation at dinner, offering his thoughts on foreign and political topics, Pitt intervened. In 'a deep-toned but clear voice', he 'very calmly and civilly' disputed Gibbon's statements.

> The historian, turning a disdainful glance towards the quarter whence the voice proceeded, saw, for the first time, a tall, thin, and rather ungainly-looking young man, who now sat quietly and silently eating some fruit. There was nothing very prepossessing or very formidable in his exterior, but, as the few words he had uttered appeared to have made a considerable impression on the company, Mr Gibbon ... thought himself bound to maintain his honour by suppressing such an attempt to dispute his supremacy ... At length the genius of the young man prevailed over that of his senior, who, finding himself driven into a corner from which there was no escape, made some excuse for rising from the table and left the room. He refused to return, declaring: 'That young gentleman is, I have no doubt, extremely ingenious and agreeable, but I must acknowledge that his style of conversation is not exactly what I am accustomed to, so you must positively excuse me'. And away he went, in high dudgeon.

Back in the dining room, Pitt proceeded 'very tranquilly with the illustration of the subject from which his opponent had fled, and which he discussed with such ability, strength of argument, and eloquence, that his hearers were filled with profound admiration'.[18]

Pitt's prospects were certainly enhanced by his intellectual confidence and verbal dexterity, but lack of money remained a problem. The Elder Pitt left debts amounting to about £20,000 when he died in 1778. Although these were paid by the state as a mark of respect, the family income was limited. The Pitts had property, but it was mortgaged. They had the Chatham title, the pension that had been granted with the barony in 1761, and a parliamentary grant (as well as paying off Chatham's debts in 1778, parliament established an annuity of £4000 to go with the Chatham earldom). But the family could not sustain a high aristocratic lifestyle. Pitt the Younger even lacked the means to pay his way at Cambridge. From his late teens he was in debt, and would be so for the rest of his life.[19]

A major drain on his resources at this time was the accommodation he took at Lincoln's Inn. He could not afford the rooms, but went ahead anyway. The inevitable consequences of living beyond his means seem not to have disturbed him. This is surprising, perhaps, in view of the fact that Pitt had to assist in settling his father's affairs (in the absence of his elder brother John) and cannot have been unaware of the dangers of insolvency. Lady Chatham tried to pay back most of the loans that had been made to her husband, and the parliamentary grants helped, but that of 1761 was in arrears and Pitt had to press for its prompt and regular payment. His mother could just about afford to continue living at Burton Pynsent after Chatham's death. Pitt and his siblings, however, had to wait for any benefit from their assigned shares in Chatham's property and incomes. Only the sale of Hayes Place in 1785 brought some relief. Pitt received around £4400 after the sale. Previously, on leaving Cambridge, he had been obliged to live on an annual grant of £600 from his elder brother (half of this came from the money the second Earl of Chatham paid to his mother, but she made it over to William). This sum was not sufficient for Pitt's purposes; his borrowing continued.

If in his political calling and messy personal finances Pitt imitated his father, in his physical features and character traits he resembled his mother and her family. The Grenvilles were certainly as proud and ambitious as the Pitts, but less brilliant and creative, and more calm, conventional and methodical. As he reached manhood Pitt was tall and thin with lively eyes, brown hair and angular features (his long face and pointed nose were gifts to political cartoonists as Pitt's notoriety increased). To many who met him he seemed awkward, aloof and imperious, an impression typified by the celebrated artist George Romney's remark that Pitt's nose was 'turned up at all mankind'. But there was also a vague sadness in Pitt's make-up. Perhaps his father's decline and death, the family's financial straits and his own health problems contributed to this gloomy disposition. Nor was he untouched by personal tragedies. Pitt's sisters Hester and Harriot both died in their twenties after childbirth, Hester on 18 July 1780, Harriot on 24 September 1786. His younger brother James died at sea (off Barbados) aged only nineteen on 13 November 1780. The emotional and psychological impact of these events can only be guessed at, but they probably made Pitt feel more lonely and isolated, and reinforced such character traits as his reserved manner and occasional melancholia. Pitt's continuing reliance on a small circle of close friends may be partly attributable to his lack of a closely-knit family. By the time he was twenty-seven, his only surviving sibling was his brother John.[20]

In view of these personal troubles, Pitt's determination in his early twenties, as his public career began in earnest, is all the more remarkable.

Clearly his willpower, sense of calling and confidence in his own abilities, and the influence of his education and training, made him believe that he could reach the goals he set himself. His political ambitions must have increased, moreover, as he reflected not only upon the achievements of his father and the political activities of his uncles and cousins, but as parliamentary and extra-parliamentary pressure on the government of Lord North made possible a change of ministry. A period of political excitement would almost certainly present opportunities for advancement after years of relative ministerial stability.

Following a series of short-lived ministries during the 1760s, George III had appointed North as prime minister in 1770. The king had been brought up to believe that his grandfather and predecessor, George II, had allowed royal prerogatives to be appropriated by the great aristocratic clans that dominated parliament. The idealistic George III sought to ensure that the crown could play a more decisive role in government, and this led to heated controversy, as the political leaders of the time either worked with the king or resisted his pretensions. According to George III, politicians had to recognize the crown as the source of executive authority, respect the monarch's free choice in making cabinet appointments, and accept that important policy decisions ought to be implemented only with royal knowledge and approval. The king and his supporters believed that these basic principles were quite in keeping with established constitutional practice. To their opponents, however, it appeared that George III was attempting to overturn constitutional conventions. Any increase in royal power, it was claimed, would endanger liberty. This argument was advanced most forcefully by the Rockingham Whigs.

The failed expedients and frequent ministerial changes of the 1760s made it obvious that, in order to survive, a government needed both royal support and a secure parliamentary majority. North's ministry met these requirements during the 1770s. North respected George III's wish to participate in the political process, enjoyed royal confidence as a result, and strengthened his administration with a shrewd use of executive patronage and by developing his own skills as a parliamentary manager. To his enemies, though, he was the corrupt ally of the court, a man who had joined in with the king's scheme to subvert the constitution. Various groups in opposition to the government took full advantage of its apparent mismanagement of the American war. Military failures in the colonies (and alarm prompted by the involvement of France and Spain on the Americans' side) coincided with economic problems and social tension at home. There were growing calls for peace and reform, aided by the expanding press and extra-parliamentary organizations that stimulated new levels of political engagement and informed discussion. By the end of the 1770s Britain was facing crisis. North was no war leader. As his position deteriorated and his morale faded, he asked George III to let him resign. The king refused more than once, intent on fighting to the finish in America in order to uphold the principle of parliament's legislative authority over the colonists, and reluctant to surrender to the Rockingham Whigs, the dominant section of the parliamentary opposition.[21]

These were the circumstances in which Pitt the Younger prepared to begin his public career. His lack of money was a hindrance, and a seat in the Commons would not help in this regard because MPs did not receive a salary. But he had regular payments from his brother, and he borrowed money, his hope being to rise quickly and secure a paid government office. At a time when patronage and connection determined most elections and appointments, Pitt's expectation was not unrealistic. He was the son of a famous father and had well-placed relatives. Indeed, the Pitt name was becoming more useful: as criticism mounted against the government, Chatham's reputation was rising again. Chatham had been a successful war leader between 1757 and 1761, and had subsequently argued for a non-military solution to the dispute with the American colonists (inevitably, the merits of this position were more likely to be recognized now that the American war was going badly). By 1780 Chatham was widely remembered as the public-spirited patriot, while North's regime was discredited. The Younger Pitt saw in this situation an opening for himself.[22]

From the summer of 1779 Pitt's letters to his mother and others were full of comment about contemporary affairs. He followed the course of the American war, hoping that 'there may still be spirit and resources in the country sufficient to preserve at least the remnant of a great empire'. He wondered about the ability of North's government, which he frequently condemned, to maintain its position in parliament, and hoped that opposition leaders really had the public good in view. He welcomed the movement in the counties, beginning with Yorkshire, to organize petitions on economical reform.[23] Pitt was sure that he would soon be in the Commons; he could live out his destiny nowhere else.

Yet he placed himself under a burden. He not only sought to match his father's accomplishments in public life, and in so doing help permanently to restore Chatham's reputation, but also wanted to achieve these things and serve his country on his own terms. The role he cast for himself was the acclaimed 'patriot': virtuous, independent and disinterestedly devoted to useful service. Pitt hoped to conduct himself as a 'patriot', but it was also essential for him to be *seen by others* in this light. He knew that

Chatham's former status as a successful patriotic leader had been lost by the time of his death. In taking up the principles he associated with his father, therefore, he had also to avoid his father's errors.

It was not easy for Pitt scrupulously to adhere to these patriotic standards. One of his key concerns was to maintain his political independence, without which the vocation of 'patriot' would be false and empty. He wanted a public office, but it had to be a responsible one, not simply a sinecure, and independence meant that he could not rely for advancement on party or connection. A seat in the Commons was Pitt's for the taking if he chose to accept offers of help from his cousins the second Earl Temple (George Nugent Temple Grenville succeeded to this title in 1779) and Thomas Pitt, both of whom had influence in several boroughs. But at the general election of September 1780 Pitt presented himself as a candidate in Cambridge University, a relatively 'open' constituency more in keeping with the identity he wished to fashion. The electorate consisted of doctors and masters of arts who had graduated at Cambridge. They numbered about 500 in 1780, rising to 800 by the end of the eighteenth century. Pitt had been canvassing hard in Cambridge during the late 1770s, hoping that the time would soon arrive when he could claim (as he put it in July 1779) 'a seat of all others the most desirable, as being free from expense, perfectly independent, and I think in every respect extremely honourable'.[24]

Unfortunately for Pitt, in 1780 he came bottom of the poll (in fifth place with 142 votes, less than 14 per cent of the votes cast); the Cambridge University seats were taken by James Mansfield, a government supporter, with 277 votes, and John Townshend, an opposition candidate, with 247 votes. In truth Pitt's chances had been slim. Mansfield was one of the sitting MPs for the constituency, and had recently been appointed solicitor general. Townshend had only narrowly been beaten by Mansfield in a previous election, and as a Rockingham Whig he was able to gather the bulk of opposition support.

Pitt had no choice but to accept a seat made available by Sir James Lowther (Earl of Lonsdale from 1784), who controlled one of the leading electoral interests in the northern counties. Lowther had been returned for both Carlisle and Appleby at the general election. He decided to represent Carlisle, and nominated Pitt for Appleby. Pitt was returned unopposed at a by-election on 8 January 1781. His Cambridge friend Lord Granby, who had succeeded as the fourth Duke of Rutland in 1779, had recommended him to Lowther, and the latter's respect for Chatham prompted him to look favourably upon Chatham's son. For his part, Pitt did not feel that his independence had been compromised. Lowther imposed no specific conditions, and it was agreed that Pitt would vacate the seat should he disagree with Lowther on any important public question. Yet this was hardly the opening for which Pitt had hoped. He was no doubt relieved that a semblance of patriotic independence could be preserved, but the fact was that he owed his seat to an old university friend and a notorious borough-monger. He could not manage without connection and influence after all. Appleby, moreover, was not exactly an 'open' constituency. A small market town in Westmorland, it was a burgage borough (in which the right to vote attached to ownership of property) and there were only about 250 electors. Lowther was the unchallenged patron. The most recent contest in Appleby had been in 1754; no subsequent election in the borough was contested before it was disfranchised by the Great Reform Act of 1832.[25]

Nevertheless, as he contemplated his election Pitt was able to put the best possible interpretation upon what had been arranged. He wrote to his mother:

> I can now inform you that I have seen Sir James Lowther, who has repeated to me the offer he had before made, and in the handsomest manner. Judging from my father's principles, he concludes that mine would be agreeable to his own, and on that ground – to me of all others the most agreeable – to bring me in. No kind of condition was mentioned, but that if ever our lines of conduct should become opposite, I should give him an opportunity of choosing another person. On such liberal terms I could certainly not hesitate to accept the proposal, than which nothing could be in any respect more agreeable. Appleby is the place I am to represent, and the election will be made (probably in a week or ten days) without my having any trouble, or even visiting my constituents. I shall be in time to be a spectator and auditor *at least* of the important scene after the holidays.[26]

The deal with Lowther was a lucky break for Pitt. He had lost in Cambridge. It was not clear when the next vacancy would occur in a desirable 'open' borough, and besides, he lacked the money to finance an election in such a constituency. Appleby was available immediately, at no cost to Pitt, and he was not bound to any particular line of conduct by its patron (which was unusual for Lowther, who generally liked his MPs to do as they were told).

North's ministry strengthened its position at the 1780 general election. Better news from America about the military situation, along with the usual executive influence and inducements, brought an apparently secure majority. When Pitt entered the Commons he sat on the opposition benches (as his father had done on becoming an MP), and it was expected that he would co-operate with the remaining Chathamites, who were led by the second Earl of Shelburne.

Pitt delivered his maiden speech on 26 February 1781 in support of a

Rockingham Whig proposal to regulate the civil list. Economical reform was a burning issue in this period. It involved public retrenchment and a weakening of royal influence. Rockingham Whigs sought to divert money from the crown for public purposes, convinced that the power of the king and his advisers was the root cause of political corruption. Pitt agreed that civil list reform would help to curb improper influence, but the main focus of his speech was on the relationship between monarch and people. The proposed measure, he said, would demonstrate the king's sensitivity to the nation's sufferings in a time of war, hardship and heavy taxes. By setting an example of retrenchment, the king would be sharing in the sacrifices made by his subjects and 'abating from magnificence what was due to necessity'. The dignity of the crown should not depend on useless and unnecessary expenditure, Pitt declared, and the crown would gain more respect and real power by giving up some of the ostentation and grandeur that for so long had consumed the nation's resources. Pitt attacked ministers for failing to introduce the type of retrenchment plan now proposed by the opposition. Since the government had not done its duty voluntarily, he argued, it was up to the House of Commons to insist that changes be made. North's majority remained intact, however, and the motion was defeated by 233 to 190 votes.

His father's name had ensured him a hearing, but Pitt's speech was generally praised as forceful and eloquent, regardless of comparisons with Chatham. The opposition leaders Charles James Fox and Edmund Burke, and even the prime minister North, expressed admiration for Pitt's performance and recognized in him a man of promise. By June 1781 Pitt was receiving plenty of publicity and his friend William Wilberforce wrote that 'he comes out as his father did a ready-made orator, and I doubt not but that I shall one day or other see him as the first man in the country'.[27]

2

Inheritance

Pitt the Younger had eagerly embraced the political world, and would soon make it his own. But in order better to understand his career, it is first necessary to pay more detailed attention to the nature and development of the eighteenth-century British political experience, to questions of trade and empire, to the forces that had shaped the system of government, and in particular to the part that Pitt's father had played in influencing the course of events.[1]

Success in war, the growth of the empire, and expansion of trade made Britain the world's first superpower, and although this position was not achieved until 1815, the foundations were laid during the eighteenth century. Britain's international ascendancy mirrored England's dominance within Great Britain: England was economically more advanced than Wales, Scotland and Ireland, and political control was exercised from London (the legislative union with Scotland had been accomplished in 1707, and the Declaratory Act of 1720 had formally established the British parliament's right to legislate for Ireland). The assertion of power at home developed into an acquisitive policy overseas. Imperial expansion was to a large extent commercially driven. Colonies were important markets and suppliers of raw materials. They also had strategic value and added to Britain's prestige, and empire was quickly given religious significance as well (many people assumed that Britain had been entrusted with a holy mission to secure and spread Protestantism). Empire became a fixture of the national identity and popular culture; it signified the decent and robust national virtues of courage, enterprise, liberty and public spirit.[2] Success in war fed elite and popular enthusiasm for the growth of British wealth and liberty, extending across the globe, with colonies as bulwarks of trade, prosperity and naval strength.

Naval manpower rose from about 45,000 men in 1748 to 107,000 in 1783, and, with maritime supremacy guaranteed by the Royal Navy, trade and empire developed in tandem. During the first half of the eighteenth century there was a rapid increase in the volume and value of British overseas trade and in the size of the merchant marine. British shipbuilders flourished during the eighteenth century. By 1785 British merchant tonnage was double that of France, four times that of the Dutch, and ten times that of Spain. In addition, the merchant marine provided a pool of trained seamen for the navy, and without this resource it would not have been possible to sustain the large wartime fleets.

Commercial intercourse with the colonies far exceeded that with Europe, and was growing at a faster rate (as demand from the older markets diminished, colonies became even more necessary as outlets and suppliers). Profitable trade fostered business confidence and prosperity at home. In turn, government revenues were enhanced. Merchants, manufacturers and financiers became more influential. When they formed pressure groups to alter policies or pursue other specific goals, parliament had to pay attention. Eighteenth-century governments generally tried to promote trade. They also regulated it, mainly through tariffs and navigation acts, and made sure that Britain had the appropriate naval and military power to safeguard advantageous imperial arrangements. In due course Pitt the Younger would adopt and establish even more firmly the priorities of trade, revenue and imperial defence.

Britain's chief rival was France, and, as a result of the long series of wars from the late seventeenth to the early nineteenth centuries, Britain emerged as the imperial and economic victor. Britain was at war (against imperial rivals and rebels within the empire) for fifty-five of the seventy-seven years between 1739 and 1815. A huge amount of manpower was required, and a huge amount of money (which is the main reason for government growth in this period – the state had necessarily to develop the administrative and financial capacity to fight wars). Britain's expenditure on war rose from £95,500,000 in 1739–48 to £236,500,000 in 1776–83. The long war against France of 1793 to 1815 cost a staggering £1,657,900,000.

Britain became the most heavily taxed nation in Europe. The tax burden in France between 1793 and 1815 was only a third of Britain's (in 1756 the French and British burdens had been about equal). The nation was able to pay for the great wars of the eighteenth century, and the acceptance of heavy taxation further underlines the enthusiasm for trade and empire. The proportion of government revenue provided by indirect taxation – that is, from taxes on a broad range of articles of consumption, rather than property or income – rose from about 65 per cent to over 80 per cent during the century, which helped to secure public acceptance. So did the removal of the most unpopular burdens, the central government's delegation of assessment and collection tasks to local officials, and the scrutiny of expenditure as performed by parliament and the press. In gaining parliamentary and public sanction, moreover, the government enhanced its ability to borrow money. This prevented the tax burden from exceeding acceptable levels because the state did not have to cover all wartime expenses immediately (the interest on loans became the most pressing item). The state borrowed £29,700,000 during the war of 1739 to 1748; loans amounting to about £440,300,000 were needed between 1793 and 1815. The national debt rose enormously, and controversially, as a result of all this borrowing. For most of the century, however, concern about the cost of Britain's wars was kept in check by the desire for glory and expansion.

Of pivotal importance was the Seven Years War, which began in 1756. Empire, war, trade and patriotism all came together in a more aggressive spirit personified by William Pitt the Elder, who focused the nation's efforts and attention on extra-European operations – in North America, India and the Caribbean. His primary goal was to capture French colonies, especially those that were economically valuable. But after the Seven Years War there was trouble in North America as colonists objected to the British government's efforts to raise money for defence. That the Americans eventually rebelled suggests not only that the relationship between parliament and the recalcitrant colonies had been mismanaged, but also that success in war was a mixed blessing (among its drawbacks were the increased national debt, and the extra administrative and defence responsibilities across the globe), and that the core British concept of unitary sovereignty could no longer be carelessly imposed upon the periphery by the centre. Policies had to change if authority was to be preserved. Subsequently there were new measures to deal with Ireland, India and Canada. (It was Pitt the Younger who presided over the most significant changes in the nature of British imperial rule before the mid-Victorian era.)

In the oligarchical system of government of eighteenth-century Britain, political power rested mainly with the landed aristocracy. Noble families and their connections controlled parliament, and their presence in the House of Commons – the elected chamber – made up for the fact that the House of Lords was gradually losing ground to the Commons, the dominant estate of the realm. Cabinets, to which the crown's chief advisers were appointed, were mainly aristocratic in composition. The nobility also exercised enormous electoral influence. As wealthy property owners, employers, landlords and local patrons, aristocrats had direct control over a large number of constituencies and could by various means determine the results in many others. It was easy to exert influence when voting was open, particularly in constituencies with small electorates.

General elections did not offer voters a choice between two national parties with clear programmes. Governments tended to call elections when they wanted to confirm their position in the Commons. The Septennial Act of 1716 set the maximum duration of parliaments at seven years, and in many constituencies electoral contests were unusual. Between 1707 and 1800 the number of seats in the Commons was 558. Only 60 were contested at the general election of 1747. In 1754 the number rose to 66, falling to 54 in 1761. There were 83 contests in 1768, but even this represented less than 15 per cent of the total. In order to avoid the trouble and expense of a contest, the dominant families in many localities agreed to share the representation.[3]

From 1710 the property qualification required of MPs was an annual income of at least £600 for a county representative, and £300 for a borough representative. By a statute of 1430, the voting qualification in English and Welsh counties was possession of freehold property valued at 40 shillings a year. In practice 'freeholds' could be land, offices in church and state, or cash incomes. By the eighteenth century the value of money had declined, so the 40-shilling freeholder franchise was relatively wide. County constituencies varied considerably in the number of voters, which in turn bore little relation to their size and populations. In 1761 Yorkshire had over 15,000 electors and Rutland 609, but they both returned two MPs.

English and Welsh boroughs varied greatly in size and voting qualification. In 1761 only about forty of England's 202 boroughs had electorates of over 1000. Twenty-two had between 600 and 1000 voters each, eleven had around 500, and seventy-seven had fewer than 100 voters. Many of the small boroughs were 'rotten' or 'pocket' boroughs, controlled by a patron or the government. Different franchises operated from place to place. In 'potwalloper' or householder boroughs, the right of voting was vested in inhabitant householders who owned a fireplace and were not receiving poor relief. In 'scot and lot' boroughs the vote was given to householders who paid local rates and were not on poor relief. In 'freeman' boroughs the right to vote was vested in the freemen of the borough; 'freedom' could be obtained by inheritance, marriage, apprenticeship or purchase. In 'corporation' boroughs the vote was confined to members of the corporation. In 'burgage' boroughs (like Appleby, Pitt the Younger's first constituency) the right to vote was linked with ownership of land within the borough. In 'freeholder' boroughs the right of voting lay with the freeholders.

In most counties the main aristocratic families controlled parliamentary representation, and many boroughs were also open to elite influence. It has been estimated that in 1761 fifty-one peers had 102 borough seats at their disposal. Taking the peerage as a whole, and their electoral activities throughout England and Wales, more than ninety MPs were directly nominated by peers and a further 120 were elected though the influence of peers during the 1790s.

In Scottish counties the franchise belonged to most freeholders who possessed land worth 40 shillings a year, and owners of land valued at £400

Scots (that is, about £35 sterling). Scottish boroughs – burghs – were grouped together for the purpose of returning MPs by a process of indirect election. In effect, MPs were nominated by the small burgh councils.

These various qualifications meant that only a small proportion of the adult male population of Britain could vote (about 3 per cent in 1800). The representative system was also partial in that the distribution of seats favoured the rural south of England. Many areas that had risen in wealth and population did not have their own MPs. More than half of all borough constituencies were situated south of a line between the Wash and the River Severn. About a third of all English boroughs were old seaports, many of which were already in decline by the mid-eighteenth century. Five counties in the south west of England, with their respective boroughs, returned about 25 per cent of the House of Commons. More than 40 per cent of MPs represented county and borough constituencies south of a line between London and Bristol.

As the eighteenth century progressed there were increasing demands for electoral reform, and organized agitation from the 1760s onwards focused upon voting rights and the distribution of seats as its primary targets. Many leading politicians also came out in favour of reform (including both William Pitts, father and son). But for most contemporaries, the supposed flaws in the system did not invalidate the values and assumptions upon which it rested. The vote was thought to be a trust, not an entitlement, and property was regarded as the appropriate basis for rights and influence. MPs were meant to represent not places but broad interests in the community; and the variety of voting qualifications ensured that all social groups could play a part in the electoral process. Parliament's essential duties were to represent interests and check executive power, and the general consensus was that, in the main, it performed these tasks satisfactorily.

The aristocratic elite also played an important role in local government. Peers served, for example, as lords lieutenant in their home counties. The power of property owners at local as well as national level was enhanced by co-operation between the nobility and gentry. The gentry provided the majority of magistrates and MPs. Peers and gentry normally ruled their own districts quite independently, while central government dealt with the most pressing affairs of state: public finance and foreign policy. In most towns the trading and professional elites had at least a share of power; in some urban areas they ran local government. At manor and parish level, institutions were open to smaller landowners, tenants and rate-paying house-holders. The whole administrative structure, from top to bottom, operated according to the values that underpinned social hierarchy and the rights of property. In addition, religious conformity was a prerequisite for most forms of office holding (although, as will be shown, this did not completely exclude non-Anglicans).

Central government was always concerned with the political reliability as well as the propertied status of those who oversaw local affairs. For most of the eighteenth century, the ascendancy of a particular party or connection in parliament was mirrored in the political complexion of the county magistracy. In some areas, however, men of substance were appointed without much regard to their political affiliation (most obviously between about 1760 and 1790, in an attempt to calm party feeling). The development of industry also led to a gradual increase in the appointment of manufac-turers as magistrates; many of them could satisfy the property qualification (set in 1732) of £100 a year. Central government's control over appointments meant that, as well as influencing local politics, it could promote admin-istrative efficiency, but control had to be exercised carefully because blatant interference in local matters tended to provoke a backlash.

In urban areas administrative duties were vested in lords of the manor and their appointees, elected bodies, corporations (many of which were dominated by local cliques that reproduced themselves by co-option) and officers of the parish. There was no uniformity. The strength of local government organs varied from place to place. Complaints rose about corruption, exclusivity and incompetence in local government, and the confusion produced by overlapping jurisdictions, but real improvement was a long time coming.

Parliament determined the basic functions of local government, and contacts between the centre and localities were maintained informally (through political and personal networks, for example) as well as formally (as in matters of public order or revenue collection). In times of crisis central government intervened directly in local affairs, but generally it chose not to be closely involved. At the same time, parliament became more important as a point of contact between central and local government. During the eighteenth century parliamentary sessions grew longer, more business was transacted, and for many peers and MPs regular attendance became the norm. Although parliament's main concerns continued to be public finance and matters of state, it also attended to an increasing number of local issues. Individuals and groups applied for local acts dealing with such things as enclosures, roads, canals, civic amenities and street improve-ments. Parliament's accessibility, indeed, was widely appreciated (another reason why the unreformed electoral system was accepted for so long). It appeared that laws and institutions could be altered, and problems tackled, in line with what influential local people wanted.

Aristocrats and their allies and clients used patronage networks and the perks of office to retain political control and thereby protect their own interests. As a result, taxes on consumption increased as burdens on the land were lightened, and the law courts defended ever more rigorously the rights of property owners. Although society was changing, ownership of land remained the basis for influence, and only slowly did membership of parliament begin to reflect the broader developments associated with the early stages of the industrial revolution. By 1761 perhaps sixty MPs (less than 11 per cent of the Commons) were drawn from commercial and manufacturing backgrounds.

Many issues gave rise to political contention between the main aristocratic connections in parliament (and, increasingly, their supporters out of doors). The major wars of the eighteenth century, for example, prompted discussion of goals, strategy and resources. Following the War of the Grand Alliance (1688–97), Britain fought the War of the Spanish Succession (1701–13), the War of the Austrian Succession (1739–48) and the Seven Years War (1756–63). Success in these wars, and the resulting expansion of Britain's trade and empire, undermined those who opposed government policy, but war matters were endlessly disputed, and invariably, at the end of each conflict, there were protracted arguments about peace terms. Defeat in the American War of Independence (1775–83) increased the political tension, as well as damaging British prestige abroad, and there were recurrent fears about the possibility of hostile landings on the mainland and Britain's colonies across the globe, especially by the French.

Other causes of instability related to social, political and religious divisions in Scotland and Ireland, with which the central government did not always find it easy to deal, and the labouring poor's not infrequent resort to violent protest, most notably at times of high food prices and heavy taxation. Ministers were often troubled by these problems, and by difficulties in managing parliament and the king. In these respects Pitt the Younger's career in office would follow a familiar pattern.

Religious contention remained intense during the eighteenth century. In Scotland the Episcopalians struggled with Presbyterians. In Ireland the Catholic majority was bitterly conscious of its subjection to the small Protestant minority. With respect primarily to England, some historians have written of a 'confessional state' to emphasize the importance of approved religion. England had one official faith, Anglicanism, upheld and enforced by the law, and a national church with unique privileges and status. But this church did not have supremacy over its own affairs, since its structure and practices were decided in parliament, and it was vulnerable to criticism because of glaring inefficiencies. Concerns were expressed about clerical absenteeism and non-residence, massive disparities in clerical incomes, and the failure to halt a perceived decline in religious observance. The church's response to the growth of the towns was too slow. Its teachings became more moderate and rational as senior churchmen abandoned the zeal and expansionism of former times. Opposition from Catholics and Protestant Dissenters, meanwhile, became more open and vigorous; they resented the church's special role in state and society.

Yet this role did not preclude the growth of religious pluralism. By engaging in 'occasional conformity', for instance, Dissenters could evade legal obstacles and hold public offices. In practice there was no Anglican monopoly. The Whigs made use of the church to buttress their political ascendancy (ecclesiastical appointments invariably went to reliable Whigs), but were not much interested in reforming the church or helping it to defend itself against its enemies. The Whig commitment to legal toleration for Dissenters may have been principled, but it was no less a matter of political calculation for all that. Accepting religious pluralism (and even apathy) was a means of defeating Toryism.

Another source of controversy was the dynastic question, though this became much less significant after the failed Jacobite rebellion of 1745. By the Glorious Revolution of 1688 an attempt had been made to end the religious and constitutional crises of the seventeenth century. The crown was prevented from abusing its prerogatives, the privileges of parliament were extended and the Protestant faith protected (the established church continued to enjoy special status). These gains were reinforced by the Hanoverian succession of 1714, when the crown passed to George I, the elector of Hanover. But the new dynasty did not win unanimous support. The most dangerous threat came from the Jacobites, who regarded James Francis Edward Stuart, the son of King James II, as rightful monarch. James II had been forced into exile and deposed in 1688 after seeking to increase royal power and, it had been feared, restore Catholicism. Nevertheless, according to the rules of hereditary succession, his son had a stronger claim to the throne than did George I. Jacobitism drew together many interests (including families who had lost influence and property under the new order, Catholics and others who wanted greater religious toleration, and Scots who resented the legislative union between England and Scotland of 1707), and the cause was aided by Britain's enemy France. The failure of the 'Forty-Five' was decisive, however, and the Jacobite threat rapidly declined.

Before the Glorious Revolution two distinctive political parties had emerged. Their names, 'Whig' and 'Tory', were originally insults: Whigs were militant Scottish Presbyterians, Tories were Irish robbers. In terms of policy and principle, Whigs stood for parliamentary rule, ministerial responsibility and Protestantism, and they regarded the Glorious Revolution as a party triumph. Tories favoured the Church of England, supported the royal prerogative, and believed in divine right monarchy and hereditary succession (many became Jacobites). Whigs were mostly willing to engage in an active and interventionist foreign policy, while Tories relied on a strong navy and the 'blue water' strategy. Those Whigs who held office for long periods became accustomed to the exercise of power and exuded a pride, dignity and even arrogance that set them apart. Their vital constitu tional function, as they understood it, was to remind the monarch of limitations upon his political role, but they also accepted the crown's right to be consulted and on many important points the king had the final say. Although he mistrusted some of them and disliked their cliquishness, George II (who reigned from 1727 to 1760) accepted them because they had repudiated Jacobitism, were loyal to his dynasty, and offered good service as competent managers of government business in parliament. These and other basic Whig characteristics would subsequently be extended and trans- formed – in line with the circumstances of a new age – by Pitt the Younger's rise to ascendancy.

After backing the wrong side in the Glorious Revolution and losing power to the Whigs in 1714, Tories became the natural opposition. The Whigs had outmanoeuvred them, the first two Georges never trusted them, and the Jacobite slur, together with the Tories' association with conservative Anglicanism, divine right monarchy and other discredited doctrines, made easier their removal from central and local government. Nevertheless, Toryism survived as a distinctive political force. Proscription from office and the long years in opposition created a keen sense of identity, as did traditional political attachments and staunch Anglicanism. George I and George II were Lutherans, not Anglicans; they favoured toleration for Protestant Dissenters and found the Tories' rigidity on religious subjects appalling. The Whigs, although they were certainly ready to defend the established church, were also willing to legislate in order to extend toler- ation. This was anathema to Tories who believed that nothing should be done to encourage non-Anglican sects.

The Tories did not lose their local and regional concentrations of support, and although their numbers declined in the Commons (from about 200 in 1715 to 106 in 1754), they had considerable cohesion as a parliamentary unit. In some counties and boroughs they managed to step up their electoral organization and propaganda. As the Whigs divided into different groups (on account of personal or family differences and policy disagreements), individual Tory leaders explored the possibility of combining with particular Whigs. This became a serious possibility in 1744, but in the event no terms for co-operation could be agreed. Nevertheless, the refusal of the vast

majority of Tories to join in the Jacobite rebellion of 1745 indicated acceptance of the changes wrought by the Glorious Revolution and a recognition
that the only way back for Toryism was in parliament. Tories became less
strident in their pronouncements about religious matters, the Hanoverian
dynasty, executive corruption and the government's abuse of power. Pitt
the Elder began to coax some Tories away from open opposition. He was
not an 'old corps' Whig and not disinclined to work with Tories, and they
liked his populist, patriotic style. They backed him from 1757 as he directed
war policy during the Seven Years War.

The 'Whig' and 'Tory' labels probably had less currency after 1714, as the
Whigs monopolized power. Different Whig factions vied for office while
many Tories were excluded from public life because of their supposed
hostility towards the Hanoverian regime. But George III, who became king
in 1760, wanted to end the dominance of 'old corps' Whigs, so the Tories
enjoyed a resurgence. Proscription was discontinued, political affiliations
altered. The use and meaning of party names continued to change during
the late eighteenth century (a development for which Pitt the Younger was
partly responsible). They were widely employed at the 1807 general election,
by which time it was generally understood that Whigs were advocates of
civil and religious liberty, and that Tories were defenders of the crown,
church and established institutions. There were serious clashes of opinion
between Whigs and Tories on Catholic emancipation, parliamentary reform,
finance and administration, foreign policy, the royal prerogative, ministerial
conduct and public order. Neither Whigs nor Tories, however, belonged
to monolithic, tightly organized or stable political parties; they were more
like loose alliances. Indeed, although some candidates at election time made
plain their adherence to Whig or Tory causes, they more often presented
themselves as supporters of ministry or opposition. For much of the eighteenth century the Whig versus Tory divide did not matter at local level, or
even in parliament, except on particularly sensitive issues. Still, the fact that
there was heated conflict on these issues indicates the strength of underlying
party bonds and the personal, familial, local, ideological, pragmatic and
traditional impulses that sustained them. In the right circumstances they
quickly came to the fore.

Nevertheless, it should be noted that, despite the virulent party feeling
that often surfaced, issues were resolved within the established political
framework and the constitution survived intact. Conflict was contained.
The content of politics remained largely personal and local, and indeed,
with the Whigs in control of affairs for so long, there was little prospect
of fundamental change.

At the same time, politics *were* becoming more participatory. Leading

politicians had actively appealed for support outside as well as inside parliament, and popular scrutiny of public men was both a cause and effect of press
comment, open meetings and other occasions for informed debate. New
political habits and expectations were taking shape. Parliament's accessibility
and willingness to attend to local business, as mentioned above, helped to give
rise to this participatory political culture, along with the expansion of the press
and right of public assembly. The wars of the eighteenth century accelerated
the politicization process (the outbreak of the Seven Years War, for example,
increased newspaper sales by 25 per cent); almost everybody wanted to
discuss the costs involved, the economic consequences, the government's
war management. Voluntary associations also contributed: commercial interests, lobbying groups, societies for the reformation of manners, charities,
educational bodies and many others. On one specific issue, slavery, a large
and well-organized agitation was mobilized in the late eighteenth century,
setting new standards for canvassing, fundraising and propaganda.

General respect for the constitution prevented political conflicts from
straying beyond conventional forms and channels. There was broad acceptance
of aristocratic rule, executive control over parliament, and – from 1714 to 1760
– exclusively Whig government. Stability was also reinforced by the sense
of common interests that held the ruling elite together, and by the opening
up of opportunities for political involvement lower down the social scale.
The containment of political contention was greatly assisted, in addition, by
economic developments. Over the eighteenth century as a whole, standards
of living rose and there was generally a fortuitous balance between wages,
prices and population growth. (Although there were serious disorders during
the eighteenth century – most notably food riots, machine breaking and the
destruction of tollbooths on turnpikes – these popular protests were triggered
by specific immediate grievances and not usually directed against the system
of government.) Those with modest means and property were doing well.
The expansion of the respectable professions satisfied the gentry, and increasing trade brought prosperity to many (not to mention more revenue
for the government). The availability of employment and profits reinforced
the idea that established institutions were worth supporting. More and more
people had a stake in the existing order, and plenty to lose if it succumbed
to crisis. Even diehard Tories, proscribed and stigmatized for more than a
generation, had made their peace with the Hanoverian regime by 1745.

The dominant values in eighteenth-century British society were conservative and hierarchical. They were rooted in respect for monarchy, church,
aristocratic rule, the land, patriarchy, privilege and constitutionalism.
But this is not to suggest that society was static. Change was perceptible.
The population of Britain increased from 6,500,000 in 1701 to 10,500,000

in 1801 (the decadal rate of increase during the second half of the eighteenth century was 7 per cent). Towns were growing. Industry was developing. A related change was the rise of the commercial middle classes. Another was the political assertiveness of Dissenters and reformers. In fact, British society mixed old and new. Along with the mainstream values of political conservatism and social hierarchy, there were new and often challenging modes of thought and behaviour. The ruling elite eventually had to adapt. Old institutions had to be modified, different interests accommodated.

During the period of Whig ascendancy after the Hanoverian succession, the dominant political figure was Robert Walpole, who served as first lord of the treasury (in effect prime minister) from 1721 to 1742. Walpole provided stability and continuity. Trusted by both George I and George II, he was a shrewd manager of cabinet and parliament, avoided expensive wars in order to keep taxes at an acceptable level, and strengthened his position by making effective – if controversial – use of executive patronage. Although his preference was for peace, Walpole could not prevent British involvement in the War of the Austrian Succession. The ministry lost support as opinion turned against its management of the war, and Walpole's Commons majority was reduced at the 1741 general election. He resigned in February 1742.

After Walpole there was ministerial instability. Political realignment and changes in policy and personnel continued as a result of ongoing personal rivalries, arguments about the cost of the war and the apparent subordi-nation of British interests to those of Hanover, and George II's meddling (the king continued to consult his favourite Lord Carteret, for example, even when Carteret was not a member of the government). Unease was increased by the Jacobite rebellion of 1745.

Relative stability returned under Henry Pelham and his brother the first Duke of Newcastle, former associates of Walpole. From 1746 they developed an efficient working relationship with the king. They ended the war (1748) and passed several reforms (including the adoption of the Gregorian calen-dar), and Henry Pelham's financial policies won the confidence of parliament and businessmen alike. Newcastle had established himself as a master manipulator of patronage, and he built up the parliamentary support on which his more talented brother relied. Pelham died in 1754, and Newcastle (previously a secretary of state) became first lord of the treasury.

It was at this point that William Pitt the Elder rose unmistakably to the fore. Having entered the Commons in 1735,[4] he made his mark as an opponent of the Walpole ministry. Although he had not been born into one of the 'old corps' governing families, he quickly formed a close association with the influential 'Cobham cousinhood'.[5] Pitt was among those opposition MPs who collected around (and pinned their hopes for advancement upon)

George II's heir, Frederick, Prince of Wales. After urging the Commons to establish a generous annuity for the prince, Pitt became a groom of the bedchamber in the latter's household (September 1737). His hostility to the government did not pass unnoticed at court, where George II began to nurture a grudge against him.

The Elder Pitt emerged as one of the foremost orators of the age. His speaking was passionate, forceful and eloquent, and his strong voice and ebullient style invariably captured attention. Yet he rarely prepared his speeches. Nor did he offer sustained argument, or seek to establish himself as an expert on trade and finance, parliamentary rules, or indeed any of the topics on which he spoke. He preferred to enunciate principles rather than focus on details. (The Younger Pitt may not always have been able to match his father's passion and bombast in speaking, but he certainly had a better command of facts and figures.)

As the Elder Pitt rose to prominence in the Commons he successfully courted extra-parliamentary popularity, and created for himself a lasting reputation for patriotism and virtue. He denounced those who used their public offices to enrich themselves, and declared that he would never seek to gain personally from any position of trust. He spoke repeatedly about the national interests, and especially the need to expand trade and strengthen the empire. There had to be a final reckoning with France and Spain, he believed, because they would seek to frustrate Britain's imperial pursuits. The main prize at stake was the enormous wealth available in North America, the Caribbean and India. Britain had to claim it and deny it to others. These were his obsessions, and, though he did not offer a comprehensive programme, his general goals were clearly and unequivocally stated at every opportunity. What he longed for was the chance to guide policy and act upon the ideas he had been expressing.

Walpole's resignation early in 1742 seemed to open the way, but Pitt was left out of the new administration in which the king's favourite, Carteret, competed for control with Pelham and Newcastle. Pitt continued his attacks on Walpole and accused Carteret of sacrificing British interests by truckling to Hanover. George II was deeply annoyed, but Pitt's popularity soared (to pay Hanoverian troops with English money, it was claimed in the press and on the platform, was disgraceful).

After Carteret's fall at the end of 1744, Pitt made plain his readiness to combine with Pelham. But George II could not forgive Pitt for his disrespectful remarks about Hanover and condemnation of foreign subsidies. Although some of his friends were brought into the ministry, Pitt was again excluded. Nevertheless, Pitt offered the government his assistance (having resigned from Prince Frederick's household), and Pelham repeatedly tried to persuade the king to accept him. Still the king refused. In fact, George II wanted to bring back Carteret (now Earl Granville). He dismissed Pelham and Newcastle, only to find that no viable ministry could be formed without them. He had to reappoint them, and reluctantly agreed that Pitt should be offered the junior post of vice treasurer of Ireland (February 1746).

Pitt's impressive speeches bolstered the government's position. He even supported the employment of Hanoverian troops in Flanders. In May 1746 he was promoted. He became paymaster of the forces and a member of the privy council, though remaining outside the cabinet. Pitt lived up to his rhetoric of probity and service, taking only his official salary and, unlike most public men of the time, refusing to use his position to seek other personal benefits. This helped him to retain public confidence, notwithstanding his change of mind on the question of foreign subsidies.[6]

On Pelham's death in March 1754 the Elder Pitt expected a promotion. Instead, he was obliged to remain outside the cabinet as paymaster. He considered this an affront, and, with international tension rising and another war likely, began openly to express dissatisfaction with the trend of policy. As before, he questioned the payment of subsidies to German princes (in return for which they promised to safeguard Hanover). Newcastle tried to mollify him, but Pitt insisted on a senior place in the cabinet, and drew closer to the Leicester House interest of the Princess of Wales and her son, the future George III (Prince Frederick had died in 1751). Pitt was dismissed from office in November 1755.

Britain and France had been competing for trade and colonies for several generations, and by the mid-eighteenth century their rivalry across oceans and continents was intense. In Europe, meanwhile, there was a reversal of previous alliances after some rapid diplomatic manoeuvres. Finding that Austria was no longer willing to defend Hanover, Newcastle had tried to come to an understanding with Russia. This alarmed Prussia, whose ruler Frederick the Great decided to seek a treaty with Britain, even though he had previously been the ally of France. By concluding a pact (for co-operation in Germany) with Prussia early in 1756, Britain alienated the Russians, who had been planning an attack on Prussia, and the Austrians, who wanted to regain Silesia, seized by Prussia in 1740. Both Russia and Austria now sided with France.

Britain declared war on France in May 1756. Early setbacks made Newcastle's government vulnerable, and, as Pitt the Elder continued his assault on ministers, the cabinet's authority and cohesion collapsed. At the end of the year Pitt became secretary of state and took over as effective head of the government (though nominally it was led by the fourth Duke of Devonshire).[7] George II did not take to Pitt, despite the latter's assurances that he appreciated the need to protect Hanover, and Newcastle and his supporters were eagerly plotting to regain the initiative. Pitt did not have a majority in the Commons. In addition, his opponents took full advantage of his absences through illness. The king removed Pitt in the spring of 1757, but a wave of popular demonstrations (especially in London), and repeated tributes to Pitt's energy and patriotism, made Newcastle realize that he would have to work with him. The Elder Pitt's patriotic image was an invaluable asset. He had shown himself to be a man of virtue who put the nation's needs before those of any faction, who condemned incompetence and greed in public life, and who had held aloof from the discredited connections that had previously controlled the government.

Newcastle returned as first lord of the treasury in June 1757, with Pitt as secretary of state and director of war policy. George II accepted the arrangement, knowing that no other combination would be stronger in parliament or in the nation. The new ministry immediately set about gathering the money and political support needed in this time of emergency, although at first there were no decisive victories against France. High prices, heavy taxes and the mounting public debt increased agitation at home, and there were riots against the Militia Act of 1757 (to the suspicion that recruits might be sent abroad against their will was added resentment about the practice of allowing the well-off to pay for exemption from service). Gradually the situation improved, however, and Pitt the Elder's war leadership was crowned with a string of successes: the conquest of Quebec, the capture of commercially lucrative and strategically important sugar islands in the West Indies, and British advances in India and West Africa. Pitt planned to continue the war. With more victories and conquests, he thought, Britain would be in a position to dictate peace terms. But parliament and nation were tiring of the war, and growing friction between Pitt and Newcastle reflected serious divisions within the cabinet. The cost of the war was particularly alarming. There were doubts about the nation's ability (and willingness) to continue paying heavy taxes, and much comment about the massive borrowing that was pushing the debt up to unconscionable levels.

George II died in October 1760. George III did not share his predecessor's attachment to Hanover and wanted peace. He also brought his favourite, the third Earl of Bute, into the ministry as a secretary of state, in March 1761. This alarmed Newcastle and the 'old corps' Whigs, who sensed correctly that the new king wished to end their political dominance. The Elder Pitt, meanwhile, was pressing for a declaration of war against Spain, to prevent the Spanish from helping France. Although he was a national hero, he could not get the cabinet to agree and resigned in October 1761. In fact, war with Spain soon broke out. Then Newcastle resigned, in May 1762, because Bute and George III wanted to end the subsidy to Prussia and thereby abandon Britain's main ally. Bute was appointed first lord of the treasury.

The king, Bute and their associates favoured moderate peace terms as the only means by which to foster international goodwill and reduce the risk of future conflict. Pitt completely disagreed. He argued that Britain must drive a hard bargain. Only by remaining strong, he thought, could Britain counter the threat posed by the Bourbon family compact between the ruling dynasties of France and Spain (and offering generous peace terms would not remove this threat). The Treaty of Paris, concluded in February 1763, met with a storm of protest. Pitt was vociferous in his condemnation of the abandonment of Prussia and handing back of British conquests. Important gains had been given up – Caribbean islands, bases in India, fishing rights off Newfoundland – and nothing obtained from France in return. Although in the long run the Seven Years War promoted Britain's continued rise to global influence, extended the empire and increased British trade, initially the peace settlement came as a profound disappointment to many contemporaries, and in Pitt they found their most effective spokesman. After so many dangerous and unnecessary concessions, he warned, France would soon recover and Britain's vital interests would again be in jeopardy.

The Elder Pitt posed as the defender of all that Britain had achieved since the late seventeenth century in the long (and unfinished) struggle against France. Important as his war leadership was between 1757 and 1761, however, British victories during the Seven Years War cannot be explained solely with reference to Pitt. He was not responsible for building up the navy before the war, for example, and the navy was essential to Britain's success. An added bonus was that the French had allowed their armed forces to fall below full strength during the early 1750s. Other advantages enjoyed by Britain during the Seven Years War included the neutrality of Spain for most of the war, and the fighting capacity of Prussia. Frederick the Great engaged the bulk of the enemy's forces in Europe, exhausting French resources and rendering French colonies more vulnerable than they would otherwise have been.

As for the aspects over which Pitt had direct influence, it is clear that his general policy worked well, based as it was on a shrewd estimation of what was appropriate and possible, given the prevailing circumstances. He protected British interests and weakened French power. But much of the strategy was already in place, and details were settled pragmatically (not in deference to some elaborate scheme of Pitt's devising). Pitt could have done little, moreover, without the assistance of Newcastle. He needed Newcastle to raise money, manage parliament, solidify the government's support, and retain George II's co-operation.

Nevertheless, Pitt the Elder's contribution was considerable. His confidence, energy, devotion to duty and impressive oratory inspired others, and they followed his lead. His unrivalled reputation as a patriot increased his authority; his utter determination to beat France rubbed off on contemporaries in parliament and out of doors. He saw the importance of trade to Britain's wealth and security, and established this as an axiom for all time. He promoted naval and military commanders on merit, in a significant break with tradition, and drove them on to victory. Pitt also linked together the different theatres of conflict. He hoped to trouble the enemy in several theatres at once. Action in Germany would assist the cause in North America, he decided, and a blockade of the French coast would prevent reinforcements from reaching the West Indies. Indeed, the Seven Years War was the first conflict that Britain fought mainly outside Europe, and Pitt's basic method was relentless aggression – striking the enemy in many places at once. This range of simultaneous attacks was unprecedented. Mistakes and defeats in one theatre were masked by successes elsewhere, and Pitt kept the momentum going by advancing on all fronts. True, his arrogance and impatience alienated his colleagues, his fixations damaged his health and personal relationships, and he laid himself open to the charge that he was too fond of war and cared nothing about its cost. But to his admirers and supporters – and a thankful public (at least temporarily) – there was no doubting his greatness, and it is not difficult to understand why Pitt the Younger's image of his father would remain entirely positive.

It could also be argued that the Elder Pitt was no less responsible than Newcastle for the construction of a political consensus. Without Pitt there could have been nothing like a government of national unity, and Pitt was the only man who could have led the dominant parliamentary coalition consisting of his own 'patriot' supporters (who were more used to being in opposition), Newcastle and the 'old corps' Whigs (formerly Walpole's party), and those Tories who were prepared to trust Pitt on account of his 'blue water' preferences.

After his resignation in 1761, George III offered Pitt various rewards for his services (probably in an attempt to undermine his popularity). Pitt refused to take any sinecures, and had no wish for a colonial governorship, but he did accept a pension and title for his wife. He managed to counter at least some of the bad press his decision received by publicizing his reasons for resigning and explaining the true nature of his negotiations with the king. Pitt's gout was now seriously debilitating, but he remained a formidable figure and lost none of his debating skill. His speeches in the Commons were as impressive as ever, and during the 1760s, a time of frequent ministerial changes and bitter political discord, competing factions tried to enlist Pitt's support. When George III asked for his advice in 1763, he declared that the only way to restore stability was to bring back Newcastle and the 'old corps' Whigs, but the king was unwilling to do this. (Pitt subsequently distanced himself from Newcastle and decided that he would never work with him again.)

Despite his ill health Pitt was invited to join the government led by the second Marquess of Rockingham (1765–66). He agreed with the Rockingham Whigs' general policy ideas, but did not join the ministry. It is likely that sickness was now affecting his judgment. Certainly his physical and mental ailments became increasingly severe during his time as prime minister between July 1766 and October 1768. His departure from the Commons and acceptance of a peerage damaged his popularity. Now the Earl of Chatham, he proved too weak to impose a pattern on the divided ministry, and his insensitive outbursts prompted those Rockingham Whigs who had joined him to resign. His health collapsed early in 1767. He stayed away from parliament and hardly communicated with anybody, let alone his cabinet colleagues, for over a year. Parliament was unruly, policies were confused, and the government continued to lack direction and cohesion. Chatham left office with his political credit much lower than it had been for years. But his career was not over.

As mentioned above, the Seven Years War was followed by a mounting crisis in relations between the British political establishment and the 'thirteen colonies' in North America. The colonists had long enjoyed considerable political, economic and religious freedom, but after 1763 British governments, backed by the majority in parliament, began a process of reorganization – the central purpose of which was to raise revenue to pay for imperial defence. The Seven Years War had almost doubled the national debt (to £140,000,000), and the cost of defending the North American possessions, including Canada, was estimated at £300,000 a year. But the American colonists disputed parliament's right to tax them, and feared that, if they gave up this point of principle, there would be further interference with their affairs in future. The removal of the French threat in North America encouraged them to resist imperial policies that they disliked. As well as their stand on taxation, for example, they resented Britain's attempt to prevent colonists from moving westwards to settle on lands held by the native tribes, although this policy made perfect sense in view of the need to limit defence costs. British opinion turned against the Americans. They could not be allowed to question parliament's sovereignty, it was thought, and should pay a share of colonial expenses. There was also a suspicion that the Americans had not done enough previously to defend themselves against the French (and it was known that many had continued to trade with the French even during the war).

American protests became more confrontational, while British political leaders disagreed about whether to conciliate or take a hard line (the ministerial instability of the 1760s did not make for consistency in colonial policy). By the time of Lord North's appointment as first lord of the treasury in 1770, some Americans had resorted to violence and others, by adopting non-importation agreements, had tried to damage the interests of British merchants and manufacturers. At the 'continental congress' in Philadelphia in September 1774, the colonists' leaders declared that the only solution to the crisis lay in a redefinition of the imperial parliament's powers in America. This was unacceptable to George III, North's ministry, parliament and indeed the whole of the British political establishment. North insisted that parliament's legislative supremacy was not a matter for discussion, though he was willing to offer more rights to the colonial assemblies. It was too late. Clashes in April 1775 between armed colonists and British troops sparked off the American War of Independence.

More than anything else, it was the American question that kept the Earl of Chatham in politics. During the 1760s he had argued that American protests were justified. He was sure that parliamentary supremacy should not be compromised, but maintained that it did not include a right to tax the colonists without their consent. This was a matter of constitutional liberty. After his serious indisposition of the late 1760s, Chatham recovered sufficiently to attend the House of Lords intermittently from 1770 to 1772. He took up his familiar themes of national defence and the need for a stronger navy, accused North's ministry of incompetence and misconduct, and upheld the cause of liberty at home and in America. Another prolonged absence followed. Then in May 1774, disappointed by the continuing dispute with the colonists, he returned to recommend measures of reconciliation.

Chatham's mental and physical condition deteriorated quickly, but he managed to make several more appearances in the Lords. In May 1777 he called for an end to hostilities in America, and by the end of the year he was arguing for a peace settlement that would persuade the colonists to remain as subjects of the crown. He disagreed with the Rockingham Whigs, who were willing to accept American independence. After a stroke in 1777, and against medical advice, Chatham arrived at parliament on 7 April 1778 to reject the Rockingham solution. Wrapped in flannel and resting on crutches, he was led to his place by his son, William Pitt the Younger, and his son-in-law Lord Mahon. The peers were hushed in anticipation. Chatham gave a short and barely audible speech against the dismemberment of the empire. As the debate proceeded he tried to rise and speak again, but suffered a fit and fell back. He was carried from the chamber (the debate was immediately adjourned). A few days later Chatham was carried back to Hayes Place, where he died.

Britain was not able to put down the American rebellion. Lack of pre-paredness for war and the early failure to take the initiative put Britain's policy makers and naval and military commanders at a disadvantage. The great distance between Britain and the colonies made communication and supply extremely difficult, and the British were naturally reluctant to employ ruthless terror tactics against fellow free born subjects of the crown. It was hoped that the American rebels would quickly see the error of their ways and come to a negotiated settlement. This hope may have been indulged for too long; the British also erred in failing to make better use of the large number of loyalists in America who did not join in the rebellion. Other significant problems were posed by Britain's diplomatic isolation at this time (Prussia had not been persuaded to renew the former alliance, despite Chatham's efforts between 1766 and 1768), and by French and Spanish involvement in the war as allies of the Americans. In addition, North was not suited to war leadership. He did raise the loans and tax revenues that were needed to finance the war, and retained the confidence of both George III and the majority in parliament until the war was almost over. A skilled political manager, he also broadened the basis of his authority by winning over former opponents with favours, offices and other rewards. But he had no coherent strategy for winning the war, and lacked the energy and charisma evinced by Chatham twenty years earlier. He never imposed himself upon government colleagues or military commanders. He could not inspire others. He lost heart as the war dragged on, and repeatedly asked the king to accept his resignation.

This was the situation in 1781 when Pitt the Younger entered the House of Commons as MP for Appleby. He had studied the nation's political history; he had made himself aware of how and why things had happened. Now he observed North's failing administration, contemplated the impend-ing loss of the American colonies, and sensed that a political crisis was inevitable. Most of all, perhaps, he reflected on his father's later career. It had been full of disappointments, yet to Pitt his father's glory was un-dimmed. Chatham remained his idol. What is more, Chatham had passed public responsibilities on to his favourite creation. The continuity was tangible. Chatham had died in the same bedroom at Hayes Place where Pitt the Younger had been born, and tradition has it that his last words were to his devoted son: 'Leave your dying father', he instructed, 'and go to the defence of your country.'

3

Arrival

Acutely conscious of his father's legacy (and personal commission), and driven on by his own ambition, Pitt the Younger sought to confirm his early rise to prominence in the House of Commons. He wanted to assert himself and serve the nation, a yearning that was reinforced by the discomfiting trend of events. Britain was in decline; somebody had to meet the challenge and restore the nation to greatness.

On 12 June 1781 Pitt made an impressive speech in support of a motion for peace. Chatham had been mentioned unfavourably during the debate, and Pitt defended his father and declared that the unjust and expensive American war had brought the nation nothing in return for all the misery it was causing. The government won the division by 172 to 99 votes, but, as Pitt informed his mother Lady Chatham, the debate was 'a triumph to opposition in everything but the article of numbers'. Pitt had not intended to speak. The remarks about his father forced him to rise, though, and he was 'very favourably and flatteringly received' as he replied to speakers

> who chose to say that my father and every other party in the kingdom who had objected only to the internal taxation of America, and had asserted at that time the other rights of this country, were accessories to the American war. This I directly denied, and expressed as strongly as I could how much he detested the principle of the war. I gave several general reasons that occurred to me for the necessity, in every point of view, for an inquiry into the state of the war ... but avoided saying anything direct on the subject of independence, which at that stage of the business I thought better avoided.[1]

Pitt put his debating skills and famous name to good use in these early months of his parliamentary career, but the route to high office was blocked while North remained in place. Fortunately for Pitt, North's government began to lose control of parliament as the American war dragged on towards its ultimately unsuccessful conclusion. On 28 November 1781 Pitt was loudly applauded for his speech condemning the government's war record. News of the surrender of British forces at Yorktown (19 October) had arrived in London on 25 November. Two days later, at the opening of the new session, the king's speech referred to 'the late misfortune' that 'calls loudly for your firm concurrence and assistance, to frustrate the designs of our enemies'. When the Commons considered an address of thanks for the king's speech, opposition MPs criticized its description of the war as 'just and necessary'. Pitt added his voice to these complaints. He called the address of thanks 'hypocritical and delusive', attacked it as degrading both to the crown and to parliament, and suggested that the king had been misled by his advisers. The war was ruining the nation and must be ended, Pitt said, and since ministers could offer no clear explanation of how they now intended to prosecute the war, MPs should not approve the address. The members of North's government were divided and desperate. How could they be trusted by parliament, indeed, when they did not even trust each other?[2]

By early 1782 Pitt was emerging as one of the leading young talents in opposition to the government. On 27 February 1782 the Commons passed a motion against the continuation of the war, and on 15 March North only narrowly survived two motions of no confidence. The prime minister had been longing to resign for some time. Though George III again pressed him to remain in place, North finally announced his resignation on 20 March. He saw clearly that he could not serve a king who wanted to continue the war when the Commons majority wanted to end it.[3]

The final weeks of North's premiership were marked by increasingly bitter contention as opposition leaders sought to bring down and replace a government that had been in power for over twelve years. At this time Pitt was not closely attached to any of the main political factions, for he was anxious to maintain his independence, but he did have allies, including his Cambridge friends Eliot (MP for St Germains), Henry Bankes (MP for Corfe Castle) and Wilberforce (MP for Hull). Other influential friends were the lawyer Pepper Arden and banker Robert Smith (both of whom were later raised to the peerage, in 1801 and 1796 respectively, as a result of their association with Pitt). He was also on good terms with Lowther and Rutland, and with the sons of men who had formerly supported Chatham, most notably J. J. Pratt, MP for Bath, and Lord Euston, MP for Thetford.

Pitt wanted high office, but was ready to wait until the time was right for him to make his move. The more experienced parliamentarians of the day knew that Pitt would soon have to be reckoned with. Indeed, in view of his name, debating power and friendships there had been talk of him joining North's ministry, to shore it up just before its collapse. The ambitious Pitt was aware that he might be courted, and he made a remarkable statement on 8 March 1782, before North's departure, when he told the Commons that 'I could not expect to form part of a new administration; but were my doing so more within my reach, I feel myself bound to declare that I would never accept a subordinate situation'. This temporarily weakened his chances, for many observers thought him arrogant and presumptuous to speak in such terms. He may not have meant to make so bold a revelation; perhaps the excitement of the occasion got the better of him. On the other hand, Pitt's former tutor at Cambridge, George Pretyman, who became his secretary and subsequently one of his first biographers, recorded that Pitt's statement accurately reflected the course he intended to pursue.

Among modern historians, Michael Duffy argues that Pitt made the mistake of overplaying his hand, while Eric Evans seems not to agree. As well as highlighting Pitt's confidence, Evans comments, the statement of 8 March also indicates his shrewdness. He knew that George III did not want North to go and that the king hated the Rockingham Whigs, who were likely to form the next ministry. Lord Shelburne would probably be included too, and competition between Shelburne and C. J. Fox would seriously divide the new cabinet and bring about its rapid demise. According to Evans, Pitt concluded that his own reputation and future would be damaged if he associated himself with a doomed ministry. There may be something to this thesis, though it is difficult to believe that everything could have been so clearly foreseen as Evans thinks. The truth of the matter is that Pitt was unwilling to enter into bargains until he had some idea of the consequences for himself and his 'patriot' agenda. In the spring of 1782, when many things seemed possible as a result of North's impending departure, even a presumptuous statement by a relative newcomer – such as that of 8 March – would not necessarily blight his prospects for long.[4]

After North's resignation George III was forced to take the Rockingham Whigs into government. The Marquess of Rockingham, as leader of the largest opposition group, set about constructing an administration. He was formally appointed as first lord of the treasury on 27 March 1782. The Rockingham Whigs were not strong enough to govern alone, however, and were obliged to co-operate with Shelburne and his followers. The partners in this coalition did not trust each other and never cohered as an effective team. The king's obvious preference for Shelburne and detestation of Fox (who had made his name as an outspoken critic of royal influence) made matters worse, not least because it appeared that Shelburne's patronage requests and policy suggestions would carry greater weight at court than those of the Rockingham Whigs. As an old ally of Chatham, and one of the two secretaries of state in the new cabinet (Fox was the other), Shelburne was in a position to facilitate the Younger Pitt's rise. But he needed to persuade others of Pitt's worth, and, more importantly, he could only help Pitt after more urgent claims for preferment had been dealt with.

As negotiations concerning appointments proceeded, Pitt was mentioned as a candidate for the minor office of vice treasurer of Ireland (which had been his father's first office in 1746). Pitt needed the salary, but saw that it would be inconsistent for him to take the post after what he had told the Commons, and decided that to accept the salary would be to weaken his stance as a virtuous patriot. Shelburne had other associates to satisfy, and could do no more for Pitt, and some of the Rockingham Whigs considered him too young and inexperienced for government office. It is possible that Pitt would have accepted a more senior post than the one offered, but he knew that his time had not yet arrived, and by remaining outside the Rockingham-Shelburne government he gained real advantages. He preserved his freedom of manoeuvre, raised the value of his support, and though he might choose to give the ministry *independent* backing, he would not be directly involved in any of its difficulties.[5]

Pitt enhanced his profile further by presenting himself as a spokesman for the burgeoning parliamentary reform movement. Pressure for reforms had been building up for many years, and featured prominently in the agitation against North's government from about 1778 onwards. The American war had become a focus for discontent. Hardship and disappointments associated with the war, its huge cost, and the apparent ineptitude of Britain's rulers and generals prompted insistent calls for change, and one of the key requirements was a more representative system of government. Reformers wanted to curb corruption, remove anomalies that had developed within the constitution, and promote greater efficiency and accountability in government. Many MPs sympathized with these ends, and extra-parliamentary bodies were organized as reformers from both the respectable propertied classes and the labouring population readied themselves for an energetic campaign. The lead was taken by the Rev. Christopher Wyvill and the Yorkshire Association. Wyvill, a conservative parson, advocated economical reform and moderate parliamentary reform, and made contact with reform associations in other regions and sympathizers in parliament. The movement proved impossible to unite, however, because for all their general agreement on the need for change, reformers continued to disagree on specifics.

As for Pitt, he was committed to reform because he thought it would facilitate constitutional balance and efficient administration. His father had also favoured reform, regarding it as essential for the preservation of political liberty. In January 1770, for example, Chatham had recommended an increase in the number of county MPs as a means of counteracting the influence of rotten boroughs.[6] Influenced by his father's example, Pitt engaged in long discussions with fellow aristocratic reformers, particularly Lord Mahon (who had married his sister), Shelburne and the third Duke of Richmond. Wyvill was also consulted as definite plans took shape during the spring of 1782. In order to test opinion in the Commons, it was decided that Pitt should propose the establishment of a select committee to consider the representative system.

Pitt introduced his motion in a ninety-minute speech on 7 May 1782. He recommended a mild reform to tackle obvious anomalies and shortcomings, but offered no detailed scheme because the purpose of his motion was simply to encourage an examination of relevant issues. These included royal power, the duration of parliaments, distribution of seats, existence of rotten boroughs, and public concern about high taxes and the partial, unsatisfactory nature of representation. Pitt's motion was defeated by just twenty votes (161 to 141), which encouraged many reformers to feel confident about future attempts. The defeat did not harm Pitt. He had delivered yet another highly regarded speech, placed himself at the forefront of the reform movement as one of its leading advocates in the Commons, and cultivated some influential extra-parliamentary supporters (who began a national petitioning campaign in the hope that Pitt would try again in the next session). Pitt's reformist credentials were reinforced when he voted for shorter parliaments on 17 May (this motion was defeated by 149 to 61 votes), and for a bill to check bribery and electoral irregularities on 19 June (the bill was withdrawn after its main provisions were rejected by 66 to 40 votes).[7]

With no government office or income, Pitt thought of returning to the western circuit to practise law. Personal rivalry and policy disagreements within the Rockingham-Shelburne cabinet, meanwhile, and especially a clash between Fox and Shelburne on peace negotiations with America and France, made possible further ministerial changes. Pitt wanted to involve himself in any new arrangement. His chance came sooner than he might have anticipated. Rockingham died of influenza on 1 July 1782 and the breach between the two sections of the administration opened the way for Pitt's advancement. Rockingham Whigs attempted to install their own choice, the third Duke of Portland, as prime minister, but George III asked Shelburne to succeed Rockingham. Fox had expected to dominate Portland, and resigned rather than serve under Shelburne. Some of his friends followed him into opposition. Shelburne had to replace those who resigned, and urgently needed talented speakers in the Commons to combat Fox, so he offered Pitt a seat in the cabinet as chancellor of the exchequer. Pitt accepted on 6 July.

This was undoubtedly an important promotion, and several associates of Pitt were also given government posts. Pepper Arden became solicitor general, Eliot a junior official in the treasury, and Pratt a member of the admiralty board. Though Pitt now had the high ministerial rank he had been seeking, his was not a strong position. He was offered the exchequer only after others had refused it, and it was not yet the vital office it became in the Victorian period. Indeed, Shelburne controlled financial policy as first lord of the treasury. Pitt found it difficult to gain influence: he and Shelburne were not personally close, and the government had trouble attracting support and establishing itself in power. The new prime minister was clever but widely considered to be devious and untrustworthy, and the manner in which he handled the tortuous peace negotiations with the Americans provoked arguments within the cabinet and great controversy in parliament and nation. Shelburne often acted without consulting his colleagues, and since the role of the cabinet was to some extent limited, the authority that Pitt might have accumulated there could make little difference. Although the ministry had royal backing, this may have been less decisive at a time when George III's prestige had been dented by defeat in the American war (in which he had invested a great deal of his political credit) and by the resignation of his chosen adviser North and subsequent instability in high politics.[8]

It was customary for a Member of Parliament to stand for re-election after joining the government, in order for his constituents to register their verdict on his acceptance of an employment under the crown. Pitt was returned unopposed at the Appleby by-election of 5 August 1782.[9] At this time the largest groups in the Commons were those led by Shelburne (about 140 MPs), Fox (about 90) and North (about 120). There were also many unattached independents who attended irregularly and whose votes had to be actively solicited. Some were willing to side with the government because they were habitual supporters of the king's ministers, or because they expected Shelburne to last and to deliver what they wanted (whether political stability, a peace treaty, retrenchment or parliamentary reform). The balance of forces in the Commons, however, meant that the Shelburne administration had to win over some adherents of North or Fox in order to secure a reliable majority. Shelburne hoped to bring them in without their chiefs (evincing the old Chathamite aversion to bargaining with organized parties). As George III urged North to back the ministry and tried to counteract the influence of Fox, Pitt hoped that there would be no alliance with North. Not only were North and Pitt on opposing sides of the parliamentary reform question, but Pitt had decided that he could not possibly work with the man he held responsible for his father's decline during the 1770s. He blamed North for the loss of America, which had undone some of Chatham's achievements during the Seven Years War, and believed that the crisis in America was partly responsible for his father's death, that is, that Chatham had worn himself out protesting against North's American policy. Pitt also subscribed to the idea that North had employed the powers of the crown to corrupt parliament, bringing public men into disrepute and undermining the political process.

Pitt supported Shelburne's proposals for reorganizing the national debt, customs duties, taxation, public loans, official salaries and departmental business and accounting. Shelburne also favoured parliamentary reform. Like Chatham before him, he thought of increasing the number of county MPs, because they were widely thought to be independent in character and county electorates were larger and less amenable to improper influence than those of boroughs. Reform societies stepped up their agitation, and Pitt's discussions with Wyvill continued into 1783.

Shelburne's policy ideas were not well received among the conservative followers of North, however, and the peace terms he arranged with the Americans were generally condemned. He had intended to allow the colonists limited home rule, his main concern being to bind Britain and America more closely together so that they could pursue co-ordinated foreign and economic policies. American negotiators did not accept Shelburne's proposals. He offered them more territory as a means of enlarging the market for British goods, but Fox accused him of making too many concessions, and many MPs, merchants, manufacturers and others questioned his faith in the wealth-creating potential of freer trade. There was an outcry when the peace terms were finally revealed. Even cabinet ministers were unable to appreciate the premier's wider aims for the expansion of British wealth and power, for he had worked too much on his own.

To Pitt the original peace preliminaries that had ended the war in America implied British recognition of the colonists' full independence, and this could not be withheld no matter what the shape of the final treaty. George III disagreed, but Pitt refused to change his mind even though the king insisted that he could do so with honour. Pitt's position was improving. The king considered him an indispensable barrier against Fox, and, in view of the government's vulnerability in the Commons, Shelburne came to value his debating skills all the more. Pitt became an essential prop to the faltering cabinet. Shelburne listened to his advice when new attempts were made to expand the ministry's basis of support. In the wake of resignations over the peace terms, Pitt's ally Rutland was promoted to the cabinet early in February 1783 as lord steward of the household. Shelburne made overtures to members of North's connection, but Pitt insisted that North himself must be excluded, and his followers refused to join the government without their leader. When Pitt met with Fox to discuss the possibility of a juncture, Fox declared that the prime minister must resign as a precondition for the formation of a new coalition ministry. 'I did not come here to betray Lord Shelburne', Pitt retorted, and the talks were broken off. Fox and Pitt were never again to meet in private.[10]

Fox and North then combined (rancorous enemies in the past, now that the war was over they apparently had less to quarrel about), and the Commons passed a motion of censure against the peace terms by 207 to 190 votes on 22 February 1783. Much to the king's annoyance, Shelburne resigned two days later. If he could find no alternative George III knew that he would have to appoint a government led by Fox, the crown's principal opponent, and North, who had abandoned the king less than a year earlier.

Pitt had been in office for only eight months, but he had gained valuable executive experience and played a significant role in such government initiatives as the revision of customs duties and reorganization of public offices. Here was an early indication of one of his abiding political priorities, administrative efficiency, involving the elimination of waste to save public money and the remuneration of officials on the basis of their actual service rather than political favouritism. The fall of Shelburne was a crucial event in Pitt's early career, and he knew it. He tried to make the best of the government's collapse, demonstrating that he could stand alone politically as a self-styled 'independent Whig' who, though he had been loyal to Shelburne, was determined not to sink with him.

On 21 February, in a collected and confident speech of nearly three hours, Pitt defended the peace terms as the best that were possible under the circumstances, and attacked the Fox-North coalition as an unnatural and self-seeking venture. Its promoters were not acting on some principled objection to the peace, Pitt argued; they just wanted to oust Shelburne and take office in his place. Pitt praised Shelburne's record and then described his own principles in detail. His creed was one of disinterested public service, as practised by his father, and he would always eschew words and deeds that could be deemed corrupt or selfish. Pitt said that his ambition was to do all he could for the nation. If he could not be in office himself, he would seek to assist any government that put the national interests first. In this bold statement of political consistency and rectitude, Pitt gave notice that he aspired to be (and be seen as) an even more uncompromising patriot leader than Chatham had been. Pitt's political opponents admitted that he had given an excellent performance (North remarked upon his 'amazing eloquence') and would emerge with credit from the Shelburne administration. Pitt announced his resignation on 31 March, describing himself as 'unconnected with any party whatever'. No longer allied with Shelburne, he had expertly detached himself from the former premier without criticizing him or damaging his own reputation, and was increasingly regarded as a premier-in-waiting.[11]

Shelburne had already suggested to George III that Pitt could succeed as prime minister, and the influential political manager Henry Dundas, who had served North and Shelburne while building up a formidable patronage machine in Scotland, agreed. Pitt's relative youth and independence were high recommendations, because he was not tarnished by recent struggles and not closely bound to any other political leader. Unlike most of them, Dundas thought, he had not aroused the resentment that would prompt objections to his appointment as premier. The king invited Pitt to head the government, but Pitt was cautious. Despite his desire to lead, he realized that he would not be able to command a Commons majority. He chose to wait for a better opportunity. The advice he received from some well-disposed veterans confirmed him in this decision. Camden, for example, warned that to accept the premiership in prevalent conditions would make him too dependent upon the court. Pitt discussed the parliamentary arithmetic with Dundas and saw that in order to govern he would need the support of North's friends, which would probably not be forthcoming. Even if it were, everyone would be aware that Pitt's ministry rested upon the Northites for its survival, and Pitt's continuing antipathy towards North made him unwilling to serve on these terms.

Convinced that his virtuous reputation was at stake, and that there would be no honourable way of ensuring the security of his administration, Pitt informed the king that he could not accept the premiership (25 March). This came as a huge disappointment to George III, desperate as he was to frustrate Fox and North. But, as John Ehrman stresses, Pitt's judgment was sound: the time was not right. Not only is this episode significant in that it highlights Pitt's self-restraint even when the highest office of all was within his reach, but it also elucidates his interpretation of his father's famous mantra of 'measures not men'. Pitt's reluctance to work with North might suggest that personal enmity took precedence over the national interests, and Michael Duffy accuses Pitt of failing to live up to his own patriotic rhetoric. In fact, Pitt was not contravening the 'measures not men' principle. Certain men were associated with particular measures, and it was North's 'measures' that Pitt disliked, as well as the man himself. It was also unlikely, had they been obliged to co-operate politically, that Pitt would have found North and his connection sympathetic to the policies he wished to implement. Therefore Pitt was objecting to North both on public grounds *and* as a result of private animosity.[12]

Negotiations continued as George III tried to find an alternative to the Fox-North coalition. Pitt became stronger because it was clear that nobody else had the talent and pedigree to stand up to Fox in the Commons. The crisis was prolonged by George III's refusal to send for the Duke of Portland (nominal head of the Fox-North coalition), Portland's admission that the coalition partners were already quarrelling about appointments and patronage, and rumours that Pitt might still be persuaded to take the premiership if a large number of independent MPs entreated him to end the instability. In the event no such appeal was made to Pitt, and the Foxites and Northites patched up their differences. Finally the king saw that he had no option but to accept Portland as prime minister and Fox and North as the two secretaries of state. The appointments were made on 2 April 1783.

Pitt emerged from the confusion with influential new allies, particularly Dundas and the Marquess of Carmarthen (a former supporter of North who had risen to prominence as an opposition peer after 1780), and many of Shelburne's supporters now looked to him as their leader. He attracted further attention by pushing for Shelburne's programme of administrative improvement and by repeating the call for parliamentary reform. On 7 May he introduced a plan to combat bribery at elections, disfranchise corrupt boroughs and add their voters to the appropriate county electorates, and increase the representation of the counties and London. The proposal was heavily defeated, by 293 to 149 votes. But once again Pitt had demonstrated his attachment to reformist principles. Some of his opponents were quick to commend his reason and moderation, and reformers were gratified that he was keeping the issue alive. As he wrote to his mother on 15 May: 'My defeat on the parliamentary reform was much more complete than I expected. Still, if the question was to be lost, the discussion has not been without its use.' Pitt was also able to embarrass the coalition ministry. Fox spoke in favour of Pitt's motion, in order to avoid charges of incon-sistency. Since 1780 Fox had been MP for the prestigious constituency of Westminster, where a wide scot and lot franchise made popular opinion unusually influential, and Fox had therefore been identifying himself more closely with reform causes. But his new colleague North opposed parliamentary reform, and Fox could not afford to alienate him. So in May 1783 Fox was inconvenienced by Pitt's initiative and equivocated. Some Foxites abstained from the division, while North's connection and the court interest (or 'king's friends') voted against Pitt. On 2 June Pitt followed up by introducing a bill to correct abuses in public offices. It was passed by the Commons, but defeated in the House of Lords. Again Pitt gained credit for his performance.[13]

Although the Fox-North government had a reliable majority, its longevity was far from assured. Most informed observers knew that George III would not rest until a new ministry had been installed. Indeed, he openly and deliberately refused to grant peerages or any marks of royal approval to the coalition, attempting thereby to convince others that since it would not be in office for long, it was hardly worth their support. George III was outraged by the financial settlement promoted by Fox for the king's wayward son

George, Prince of Wales, who had long delighted in offending his father and uniting with opponents of the king's chosen ministers. Economy-minded MPs were uneasy about the grants given to the extravagant, dissolute prince, and North was angered to find Fox unmoved by his warnings about antagonizing the king unnecessarily.

The ministry faced other problems. Having condemned Shelburne's peace terms, the coalition partners now ratified them with the claim that they were impossible to alter.[14] This acceptance of terms so recently rejected provoked charges of inconsistency and selfish ambition. Ireland also gave cause for concern. The Irish volunteer movement, originally a response to defence needs during the American war, had been demanding constitutional change as a means of safeguarding Ireland's trade and liberty. Although there was a parliament in Dublin, ultimate authority resided with the British parliament in London, and resentment within Ireland against this lack of autonomy had prompted the Rockingham-Shelburne ministry to entrust the Dublin parliament with more control over internal affairs during the spring of 1782. Ireland's legislative and judicial independence was confirmed by the 1783 Renunciation Act. It was hoped that a sense of common interest would prompt the Irish to agree to commercial and other regulations likely to benefit the empire as a whole, but the formal relationship between Ireland and the imperial power was still in dispute, as were the means of co-ordinating the actions of the two parliaments. Tension persisted because some Irish leaders did not think that the new independence went far enough, and because Irish politics and society were controlled by the Anglo-Irish Protestant elite, when the vast majority of the population was Catholic and excluded from public life. Fox and North had no clear idea about how to proceed, and their procrastination threatened to make matters worse. Another matter demanding their attention was the administration of India. The dominant political and commercial force in British India was the East India Company. It was in crisis. Financial difficulties, wars, disrupted trade and factional struggles within the company created a need for government intervention. The remedy concocted by Fox and his friend Edmund Burke, an India expert, proved to be the coalition ministry's undoing.[15]

In opposition, with the Fox-North government apparently secure in parliament, Pitt's options were limited. Some contemporaries considered that the appointment of the coalition left Pitt, in the words of treasury secretary George Rose, 'extinguished nearly for life as a politician'.[16] But it is not clear that Pitt had really given up hope. He left England for a visit to France in September 1783, and from late October lived in his brother's London residence at Berkeley Square, where he contemplated a return to the legal profession. Yet he had previously been in discussion with several of the government's most dangerous opponents (including the former lord chancellor Baron Thurlow, one of George III's closest allies, as well as Dundas and the second Earl Temple), and in July 1783 Pitt had clearly expressed a willingness to involve himself in some new ministerial arrangement provided it was consistent with his reputation and principles. What he really needed, and what George III, Thurlow and the other conspirators were longing to engineer, was a major controversy that would destroy the Fox-North coalition.

On 13 November Pitt rebuffed a Foxite attempt to draw him into the government. On 18 November Fox introduced the government's bill to reorganize the administration of India. One of its effects would have been to transfer the considerable patronage capabilities of the East India Company to Fox and his party. Lacking royal approval, Fox saw Indian patronage as a more than adequate substitute. But the bill raised a storm of indignant protest. Pitt described the government's measure as cynical, scandalous and unconstitutional, and, though the ministerial majority in the Commons made the bill safe there, a favourable verdict in the Lords was no foregone conclusion.[17] Powerful pressure groups outside parliament agitated against the India Bill, led by the East India Company and other business interests in the City (where there was growing concern about stock values and utter fury at the government's attempted interference with chartered rights). Public opinion was stirred by the controversy, and Fox's attempt to create a party ascendancy stimulated hostile comment in the press. As the excitement increased, George III's confidants Thurlow and the third Duke of Chandos met Pitt's associates Richmond and Temple, and Dundas made contact with North's former political manager John Robinson, who as a secretary to the treasury had manipulated the electoral system on North's behalf and delivered the ministerial majority of 1780. It was concluded that the India Bill could be defeated in the Lords, and the coalition forced from office, if George III allowed the plotters to use his name. Thurlow and Temple composed the necessary written statement and Thurlow explained the situation to the king at the end of November.

Historians have disagreed about the nature and extent of Pitt's role in this scheming. In response to those who deny that Pitt had any knowledge of the Thurlow-Temple plan it has been argued that Pitt was directly involved as the main mover. Another view is that Pitt was not the chief but an assistant who was involved and persuaded by others, although it has also been pointed out that Pitt rarely allowed himself to be led by anyone. Pitt knew that the defeat of the coalition would make the premiership available to him on much better terms than in March. He also saw, as did

Thurlow, Temple and the others, that the plot could not get far without his participation. George III agreed, and wanted to be sure that Pitt would not again refuse the premiership: hence the king's request for clarification on this point before proceeding with the Thurlow-Temple plan. In addition, Thurlow and Temple would probably not have approached the king in the first place had Pitt not been their willing accomplice. If Pitt was not the most active of the conspirators, the reasons are clear enough. To involve himself more directly would have been to risk alerting Fox, North and their allies. Pitt was also jealous of his patriotic image. His reputation for probity and disinterested public service would have been difficult to sustain had he directed the plot himself and been discovered doing so.[18]

Fox's India Bill represented an excellent opportunity for Pitt. Agitation against the measure allowed him to oppose the government without seeming selfish or factious, and he could reasonably claim that he and his backers were concerned only to serve the public's best interests. John Robinson's analysis of the Commons early in December indicated that the Fox-North majority was steadily fading away and would be completely overturned at a general election. Pitt continued to communicate with the court through intermediaries. By 10 December 1783, when he met Temple, Richmond, Thurlow and the second Earl Gower (a veteran servant of the crown),[19] it had been settled that the king's name would be used to stiffen opposition to the India Bill in the House of Lords. This was a better option than George III's immediate dismissal of the ministry, because it gave time to assess opinion in parliament and the nation and to organize influential public petitions against the coalition. Pitt hoped that the government would disintegrate by itself after the defeat of its India Bill, making further machinations by him, George III and their accomplices unnecessary.

In due course the king permitted Temple to make it known that he would consider any peer voting for the India Bill as his enemy, and the Lords rejected Fox's measure by 95 to 76 votes on 17 December. Instead of demoralizing the ministers and prompting their resignation, however, the vote caused pandemonium as the Fox-North coalition retaliated. Pitt had envisaged an easy transfer of power, but this was now impossible. His designs were therefore jeopardized. Though he was determined to be prime minister, it was important for him to remove any impression that he was a tool of the court, dependent on the king's allies and in place only as the beneficiary of a plot against the coalition. He had to sustain his 'independent Whig' identity, allowing the crown its proper role in politics while defending the constitution against royal encroachment and demonstrating the executive's purity and efficiency (hence his concerns about the *composition* of a new cabinet).

In the aftermath of the Lords vote on the India Bill, it was not clear if or how Pitt could bring all this about. The House of Commons condemned the manner in which king's name had been used to influence the Lords' decision. A Foxite motion to this effect on 17 December, attacked by Pitt as 'frivolous and ill-timed', was passed by 153 to 80 votes. Fox declared that men who took office in these circumstances would be mere puppets. They would have to take responsibility in parliament for decisions made elsewhere, by 'reptiles who burrow under the throne'. In other words, real power would be exerted by the secret advisers surrounding George III. Fox did not hide his scorn for the youthful Pitt.

> Boys without judgement, without experience of the sentiments suggested by the knowledge of the world, or the amiable decencies of a sound mind, may follow the headlong course of ambition thus precipitately, and vault into the seat while the reins of government are placed in other hands. But the minister who can bear to act such a dishonourable part, and the country that suffers it, will be mutual plagues and curses to each other.

Unmoved, and annoyed that the ministers would not resign, George III notified Portland, Fox and North of their removal from office on 18 December. On the following day, with the Commons in uproar, it was announced that Pitt would be the new first lord of the treasury, with Temple as foreign secretary and Gower as lord president. Almost at once the new ministry was dubbed a 'mince pie administration'; it was not expected to last beyond Christmas.[20]

The constitutional propriety of George III's actions was and long remained open to question. Foxites maintained that the king had flagrantly contravened accepted constitutional practice by interfering with the Lords vote on the India Bill and removing ministers who were backed by a Commons majority. Having previously undertaken to respect parliament's independence, George III had seemingly gone back on his word. Yet many commentators believed in this time of crisis that the ends justified the means, for they saw in the India Bill an unacceptable abuse of power. As for the king, he was certain that he had done right.[21]

The task now was to strengthen Pitt's government as quickly as possible. Initially Pitt hoped that moderate supporters of Fox and North would give him a fair trial. The signs were not encouraging, for many office-holders resigned when they heard of the dismissal of their principals. As he struggled to put together a viable cabinet Pitt even thought of an accommodation with Fox, and asked the second Earl Spencer (a friend of Portland and Burke) to explore this possibility on his behalf. But Fox declared that he would not desert North, and Pitt had already vetoed North's inclusion in the cabinet. Pitt badly misjudged the situation if he really thought that an arrangement was possible with Fox. He may not have thought any such thing. It should be noted, however, that the two men *had* previously been on the same side, notably on parliamentary reform and in opposition to North before 1782, and that in Temple's brother (and Pitt's cousin) Thomas Grenville, as well as Spencer, Pitt had potentially useful channels of communication with the Foxite leadership. Perhaps it was not completely beyond the realms of possibility for Pitt and Fox to co-operate. This was evidently the opinion of those who pressed Pitt to make the attempt.

In fact, Pitt and Fox were already separated by personal differences and discordant political priorities. In December 1783 Pitt insisted on the premiership. Fox would not accept a subordinate position, and Pitt knew this. His probable motive in sending Spencer to deal with Fox was simply to make a gesture that might convince the uncommitted that he was genuinely trying to restore political order and construct a strong cabinet. Pitt could not have worked cordially with Fox, and the king was not prepared to take Fox back into office at this time. Fox's goal after the events of 17–19 December 1783, and the abiding fixation throughout the rest of his life, was to reverse what had happened and force George III publicly to accept a Foxite interpretation of constitutional propriety. Obviously the king would do all he could to resist Fox and vindicate himself. Pitt could not allow Fox to win either, because his own career and reputation were at stake. Pitt was willing to co-operate with the king, while Fox regarded the king as an enemy. The king hated Fox and favoured Pitt. Fox was an ally of North, whom Pitt had always opposed. As these preferences and associations became stronger during 1782 and 1783, it was obvious that Pitt and Fox would find themselves in conflict.[22]

Pitt's survival in office seemed unlikely at first. He lacked a parliamentary majority and found it difficult to fill cabinet offices with men of real talent (Bland Burges commented that Pitt 'hastily patched together an administration composed of men wholly inadequate to the work before them'). His situation was all the more desperate because a land tax bill, essential to the revenue, had been postponed by the Fox-North coalition once it became clear that the India Bill might fail in the Lords. No government could operate without the necessary funds, and postponing the land tax bill was the coalition's way of hampering any attempt to form a new administration. Pitt could not dissolve parliament in the hope of overturning the coalition's majority because the government needed money without delay and there was no time to arrange a general election.

In order to persuade a hostile Commons to approve the land tax, therefore, Pitt had to make concessions. He ruled out an immediate dissolution, and agreed that Temple should resign from the cabinet. George Rose recorded that Pitt was 'led almost to despair' by Temple's departure, but Pitt must have been aware that the government had a better chance without him. A central figure in the plot against the India Bill, Temple was certain to be singled out for opposition attack and by remaining he would have increased the government's vulnerability.[23] Interpreting Pitt's concessions as a sign of weakness, Fox allowed the land tax bill to pass (22 December) and looked forward to further tests of strength after the Christmas break, if indeed the Pitt ministry lasted that long. Fox was particularly insistent that there should be no dissolution. The parliament elected in 1780 still had more than three years to run, and Fox planned to use the existing House of Commons to drive Pitt out. Pitt and his allies had debated the pros and cons of a dissolution at great length. They wanted a swift general election, but the land tax issue presented complications, and there was no point in dissolving before the new ministry had a chance to attract support and work out an election strategy.[24]

After Temple's departure the cabinet was reorganized. Apart from Pitt, its most influential members were probably Gower, Thurlow (who returned as lord chancellor), and Richmond (master general of the ordnance). Pitt's friend Rutland became lord privy seal, Viscount Howe (from 1788 Earl Howe) first lord of the admiralty, Lord Sydney (from 1789 the first Viscount Sydney) home secretary, and Carmarthen foreign secretary. Several of these senior appointments were intended to be temporary, as was the case with some non-ministerial appointments. Pitt recognized at this early stage that he must use the offices and favours at his disposal to cement alliances with various aristocratic families, especially those that controlled votes in the Commons. Before parliament reassembled on 12 January 1784 Pitt and his associates did all they could to strengthen themselves, and in this they were assisted by the king, but as the remaining posts were filled opposition leaders mocked Pitt's government for its ramshackle appearance. It consisted of a loose amalgam of Pitt's friends, erstwhile supporters of Shelburne and others who had opposed the North ministry before 1782, adherents of the court, and former Northites who preferred office to opposition. Pitt was unable to persuade many experienced figures to join the government and this made even starker his forced reliance on mediocrities.

Despite the lack of talent in his ministerial line-up, however, Pitt refused to take just anyone who happened to be available. He had not invited the discredited Shelburne to join the administration. He also left out John Robinson and another astute political manager, Charles Jenkinson, formerly North's secretary at war, who was close to the king (and later ennobled as the first Earl of Liverpool). These omissions indicate Pitt's desire to distance himself from the executive manipulation and corruption that had characterized previous regimes. Yet they failed to make much difference early on. Pitt continued to feel uncomfortable because, for all his patriotic rhetoric about virtue and disinterestedness, he had come to power as the result of underhand scheming and could not remain in office without the grubby bargaining he affected to despise. Most independent MPs, moreover, as well as borough patrons and patronage-seekers of all kinds, were reluctant to offer their support until they could be sure that Pitt would last. Here, in fact, was the key to Pitt's success. Too many of his political opponents underestimated his capacity for survival. They considered him a young upstart, unqualified for the premiership, and they soon realized their mistake as he began to show his mettle. He drew attention away from his relative youth by combining with older, established elite politicians, and he also made plain his determination to be the real *leader* of his government (this was one of the reasons why he made no overture to Shelburne). Although doubts about Pitt persisted, and even the favourably disposed wondered if he had the character and talent to lead, it only took a few months for him to prove his detractors wrong.[25]

On 12 January 1784, to embarrass Pitt further and put off a dissolution, Fox moved for a committee on the state of the nation. During the debate Pitt was accused of relying on 'secret influence'. He defended himself well, though was less than frank. Pitt denied that he had intrigued with the king, rejected claims against his personal integrity, and asserted that he would never allow behind-the-scenes advisers to control his government. But Fox won the division by a margin of thirty-nine votes (232 to 193). Pitt was worried about the strength of his opponents, though he resisted the king's suggestion that there should be a quick dissolution and tried to remain positive in spite of frustrating reversals. The Commons majority condemned the unconstitutional use of the king's name, declared against an early dissolution, and called for the appointment of a ministry in which parliament and public could have full confidence. More encouraging was a division of 16 January. During a debate on the king's right to choose and appoint ministers, Fox argued that in exercising this right the king had to respect the dominant opinion in the Commons. The opposition's majority in this division fell to twenty-one. Pitt also took advantage of a debate on parliamentary reform to emphasize his record on this question, and reinforced his previous statements against corruption and 'secret influence'. Another welcome development was the City of London's decision to organize a petition in favour of George III's removal of the Fox-North government.

Meanwhile, Pitt and his colleagues had been hoping to seize the initiative with their own plan of Indian reform. It was clear that something had to be done about the administration of India, and Pitt consulted East India Company directors, political allies and bureaucratic experts in order to frame a workable reform and address likely objections before anything was put to parliament. Designed to check misrule in India and punish corrupt company servants, Pitt's measure (largely the work of Dundas, who held the junior office of treasurer of the navy from January 1784) involved the transfer of political and military power to a board of control appointed by the crown. Instead of attempting to engross patronage for his own purposes, as Fox had done, Pitt was content to leave most patronage in the hands of the company directors, and he presented his bill as a means of tackling abuse without increasing executive influence or interfering excessively with chartered privileges.

Much to Pitt's dismay, the measure was lost in the Commons on 23 January. The margin was only eight votes (222 to 214), which was some consolation, but here was further proof that ministers could not secure a majority without a general election. George III, and others, again recommended dissolution. The king was impatient to break the opposition Whigs. If unchecked, he feared, they would overturn the constitution by using the Commons to demolish the rights of the crown. On the morning of 4 February 1784, the king wrote to Pitt:

> The whole conduct of Opposition confirms the opinion I gave very early of its dangerous intentions of going step by step as far as the House of Commons can be led, avoiding if possible any avowed illegality of conduct; but not looking to the spirit either of the Constitution or of justice … If the two only remaining privileges of the Crown are infringed – that of negativing Bills that have passed both Houses of Parliament, or that of naming the Ministers to be employed – I cannot but feel, as far as regards my person, that I can no longer be of any utility to this country, nor can with honour continue in this island.

Pitt was still concerned to protect his reputation, however, and sensitive about his statement to the Commons of 22 December (that there would be no early dissolution). He decided, and the cabinet agreed, that there was insufficient time to hold an election and assemble a new parliament before 25 March, when the Mutiny Bill (essential for the discipline and control of the armed forces) came up for its annual renewal. Therefore Pitt carried on as before. If he could frustrate and divide his opponents, this would encourage more opposition MPs to change sides and possibly convince independents that he offered the best hope for stable and efficient government. There would have to be an election before too long, Pitt knew, but not until the government was ready.[26]

In the circumstances Pitt did well. He made good use of patronage to secure support (the king helped with peerages and promises), and enhanced his reputation as a disinterested, independent patriot by refusing to accept a lucrative sinecure. The clerkship of the pells would have brought Pitt a handsome income (£3000 a year), but he gave it instead to an old ally of Shelburne, Isaac Barre, and in return Barre gave up his pension. Pitt and his supporters made much of this saving to the nation.[27] The prime minister's growing popularity was confirmed on 28 February 1784 when he received the freedom of the City of London at the hall of the Grocers' Company. As he left the ceremony his coach was surrounded by an unruly mob, quite close to Brooks's Club (known to be frequented by opposition politicians), and this prompted many expressions of sympathy and outrage.[28] In these weeks extra-parliamentary bodies were encouraged to petition the crown in favour of the ministry, and there was a positive response: by March over 200 petitions and addresses had been presented.[29]

Gradually Pitt's influence in the Commons grew and the opposition's majority shrank. Initially over fifty, by March, in certain divisions, the margin was less than ten votes. Pitt was proving himself. His debating talent was a crucial weapon in this period of adversity. Though in Commons debates he could rely on the assistance of Dundas and a few other friends, the main government speaker was always Pitt himself (all the other leading members of the cabinet sat in the Lords). Pitt won respect, gained confidence, and made full use of his reputation for political virtue, repeatedly contrasting his patriotic creed with the selfish designs of an ambitious and factious opposition. His father's name was useful too, for Chatham could be associated with national greatness and Pitt warned that, thanks to the selfishness of the Fox-North coalition, national greatness was being forfeited. By such means Pitt exploited the mounting sense of crisis and presented himself as the only leader who could provide a way out.

Independent MPs called for talks between government and opposition to end the confusion. A damaging deadlock would continue indefinitely, they perceived, while the ministry, though backed by the crown and enjoying popular support, was unable to transact business in the Commons. They encouraged all sides to compromise so that Pitt, Portland and Fox might be brought together in a broadly based cabinet that could restore stable government. On 2 February a motion demanding the appointment of 'a firm, efficient, extended, united administration', as required by the 'present arduous and critical situation of public affairs', was passed by the Commons without a division. Pitt made his position clear shortly after this. He was determined to remain in place, and although he lacked a majority he did not consider himself constitutionally obliged to resign. The power of dismissal did not belong to the Commons, he stressed, and the Commons could not claim that a ministry was unworthy of its confidence unless it made specific charges.[30]

Pitt had no intention of taking second place in any reconstructed government, but to buy time he expressed a willingness to negotiate. Fox and Portland insisted that he must resign before they could agree to serve with him. They hoped thereby to force Pitt and George III to admit the invalidity of the removal of the previous ministry. Prime minister and monarch refused to countenance any such precondition, however, and the negotiations ended. Pitt emerged stronger. He stigmatized Fox as an obstacle to political stability, deplored the manner in which the Commons majority was being used for party purposes, and accused his opponents of ignoring the wishes of king and people. Pitt also predicted serious consequences should the Commons refuse to grant supply. Public order and the safety of established institutions would be in doubt, he said, if the king's government could not be carried on through lack of money. The Foxites argued that no supply could be allowed until George III responded to a previous address that had urged him to remove his ministers.

By now opinion in the Commons was turning, and many independent MPs had no wish to deepen the crisis by withholding supply. As Fox toned down his remarks, Pitt became more assertive. He gambled that his opponents would eventually give way. He also believed that he could deflect continuing pressure from independents for the formation of a new and more inclusive cabinet. Some of Fox's supporters questioned the wisdom of resorting to the refusal of supply – it was too extreme for them – and Fox had to accept that Pitt and George III were not going to back down. As the days passed and important issues were pressed to a division, Pitt was able further to erode the opposition's majority. On 1 March it sank to twelve. Fox still favoured the stopping of supply at this stage, and Pitt again accused him of endangering the peace and order of the country. Fox continued to rail against royal influence, but a popular rally on 7 March in his constituency of Westminster turned out to be less impressive than a rival meeting organized by friends of Pitt. On 8 March, annoyed by George III's refusal to employ royal powers as the Commons majority wished, Fox proposed that the king should be issued with a firm remonstrance. This motion was only carried by a single vote. On the following day opposition peers and MPs decided that they would have to allow the supplies and the Mutiny Bill to pass. This was the vital breakthrough for Pitt and the king. Parliament was dissolved on 25 March.[31]

Having retained the king's backing, made himself stronger in the Commons, and built up considerable extra-parliamentary support, Pitt looked forward to the general election with confidence. The detailed predictions made by experienced electoral managers Rose and Robinson suggested that the government would win a decisive victory. Treasury influence was used to great effect, as was pro-court propaganda. There was money from Pitt's allies in the East India Company and other private interests. Favours, bargains and bribes were all familiar electoral inducements, and Pitt benefited from the reaction against Fox's India Bill. Many voters disliked this attempt to control Indian patronage for party purposes. They may also have been attracted by Pitt's known sympathy for reforms, or by his status as an 'independent Whig' who put patriotic appeal above faction. Pitt was known to be the king's choice, another asset in certain quarters. The government won a majority of about 120 at the 1784 general election. The Foxites and Northites lost 100 seats between them.[32]

This was the most dramatic general election of the eighteenth century. In an era marked by electoral continuity in many counties and boroughs, a low number of contested seats and a restricted franchise, the extent of the change in terms of government gains and opposition losses was remarkable. Historians have argued at length about the reasons for Pitt's electoral success in 1784. Some attribute it to executive influence and constituency manipulation, others to popular support and voter choice. It is probable that in most constituencies, though to varying degrees, all these forces played a part.[33]

Relieved as he was to see his government secure a convincing majority, Pitt must also have been highly gratified to be returned at the top of the poll in Cambridge University. He had tried unsuccessfully to win a seat there in September 1780. Now he and his friend Lord Euston were the victorious candidates, with 355 and 299 votes respectively (it was not unhelpful to have Euston's father, the Duke of Grafton, as chancellor of the university at this time). The men elected in 1780, Townshend and Mansfield, supporters of the Fox-North coalition, were both unseated. They gained 278 and 181 votes respectively.[34] Pitt's arrival as an imposing political presence was confirmed when his ministry easily came through an initial test of strength in the new parliament. His opponents tried to amend the address of thanks for the king's speech at the opening of the session (24 May 1784). Pitt resisted and the government won the division by 282 to 114 votes.[35]

4

Reform

Electoral victory was not enough to ensure longevity in office and competent government. Pitt saw that measures of reform were necessary both to improve the workings of the British state, and to strengthen his own position and that of his ministry. Reforms to mitigate abuses and anomalies would make government function more efficiently and thereby serve Pitt's general purpose of providing reliable, cost-effective administration. Reforms would also assuage grievances and attract for Pitt and his colleagues considerable extra-parliamentary support. Policies that promoted real financial, administrative, economic and social progress were bound to be popular in a nation that had just lost a war and was still suffering the effects of war burdens, widespread discontent and political instability. Pitt could reasonably expect that his remedial agenda would win the approval of many influential groups, whether or not they were particularly reformist in opinion. In addition, reforms were important to Pitt personally because they were likely to reinforce his patriotic image and reputation for principled public service, and develop further his positive rapport with the people.

On coming to the premiership, Pitt had to address difficult problems without delay. It was a case of swim or sink. With limited administrative experience, he relied heavily on the best available advice and information. In time he demonstrated remarkable resourcefulness, evolved his own distinctive practices and preferences, and brought to the tasks of government a creed of thorough executive action.

One of his earliest priorities was to tackle the India question. Pitt's India Act of 1784, based on his previously defeated bill, was shaped by Dundas and, to a lesser extent, Robinson and Jenkinson. Daniel Pulteney, MP for Bramber and an adherent of the Duke of Rutland, observed in July 1784 that of the government's speakers on India, Dundas 'made the greatest figure'.[1] The main provision of the India Act was to establish a board of control, consisting of six privy councillors appointed by the king. Two of these would be government ministers. The board was to supervise East India Company affairs, while the company retained its control of patronage and appointments in India, subject to royal veto. The company would still control commerce, but it was not to make military alliances with any Indian state or involve itself in India's internal politics. Ministers of the crown were now the dominant partners in relations between government and company, though company negotiators had won concessions and obviously preferred to deal with Pitt rather than Fox. By strengthening the directors of the East India Company against the court of proprietors, extending the powers of India's chief administrators and subjecting the whole system to government oversight, Pitt hoped that company affairs would be stabilized and British power in India enhanced and purified.

In the Commons Fox attacked the government's policy, claiming that it would perpetuate rather than remove abuses. According to Pulteney, Pitt agreed to modify his plan 'in order to accommodate all parties', but not because of Fox. The opposition was so weak, in fact, that Pitt's alterations were made *ex gratia*, as a matter of choice. Pitt's system proved durable. It provided a framework for regulation of Indian affairs that lasted into the 1850s. By itself, however, the legislation of 1784 did not provide a complete settlement. Pitt was forced to make additional changes in 1786 and 1788 in order to clarify the powers of the governor general in India and the remit of the board of control. The Declaratory Act of 1788 was particularly controversial, and its passage through the Commons far from easy (one of its aims was to establish a permanent military force in India, for which the East India Company would have to pay). The situation was not helped by some ill-judged remarks by Pitt at the outset of the relevant debate. Various accounts suggest that he was unwell or suffering from a hangover. He baldly pointed out that he wanted further to reduce the powers of the East India Company, which immediately stirred its directors and their allies in parliament. This was unusual for Pitt, for he generally said no more than he had to when broaching delicate subjects. William Wyndham Grenville (Pitt's cousin, then joint paymaster general) subsequently reported to his brother the Marquess of Buckingham, lord lieutenant of Ireland, that an Indian debate had gone badly for the ministry because

> Pitt, who had reserved himself to answer Fox, was just at the close of a very able speech of Fox's taken so ill as not to be able to speak at all, so that the House went to the division with the whole impression of our adversaries' arguments in a great degree unanswered. I had spoken early in the debate, and Dundas just before Fox. I think this is the most unpleasant thing of the sort that has ever happened to us.

Indian affairs continued to vex the government. In May 1787 articles of impeachment were approved against former governor general Warren Hastings. Proceedings began in February 1788 and lasted for seven years. Pitt was sure that the trial should go ahead, not least because of the financial irregularities in which Hastings appeared to be involved, but the cabinet was divided on the matter and Thurlow – not to mention George III – strongly disagreed with Pitt's stance. The Foxites pressed for impeachment, as did the 'Saints', a group of evangelical Christian MPs led by Wilberforce, and Pitt shared some of their concerns about Indian abuses. Foxites were really hoping that the Hastings trial could be used against Pitt's government, to discredit its India policy and attach to ministers the stigma of corruption, but in the long run Pitt's political opponents failed to damage him. They simply began to argue amongst themselves (there was a breach, for instance, between Fox and Burke). Hastings was acquitted in 1795 and the directors of the East India Company, after negotiating with the board of control, awarded him a pension of £4000 a year. He was also given a loan of £50,000, for his trial had ruined him financially. The Hastings affair may have been useful to Pitt in reminding the ruling faction within the company that it was no longer its own master, a message also underlined by the Declaratory Act of 1788. Nevertheless, Pitt preferred compromise to confrontation, and Indian problems became less controversial as a result. As other matters commanded his attention, indeed, Pitt tended to leave India to Dundas. Although the home secretary Sydney was nominal head of the board of control until 1790, and was succeeded by Grenville, Dundas was the government's India expert and he managed the board for Pitt, becoming its first salaried president in June 1793. As Pitt told the Commons in July 1784, the end in view was a system

> which should at once confirm and enlarge the advantages derived to this country from its connections with India, render that connection a blessing to the native Indians, and at the same time preserve inviolate the essence and spirit of our own constitution from the injuries to which this connection might eventually expose it.

His attitude to India was always based on this general premise.[2]

Pitt's early achievement in carrying the Indian reform was accompanied by a number of reverses. The ministry was defeated in the spring of 1785, for example, on the Westminster scrutiny. This was an attempt to nullify the Westminster result at the 1784 general election. Had it succeeded, Fox would have been prevented from sitting as MP for this popular constituency to which attached great prestige in reform circles (it had the largest borough electorate in Britain). Evidence of electoral malpractice was not conclusive, and Foxites accused Pitt of vindictive scheming against his chief adversary. Perhaps Pitt's motives were indeed personal. It would have been useful to damage Fox's reputation and deprive him of his important constituency.

Yet Pitt also believed the scrutiny to be necessary on public grounds, and he championed electoral purity as a means of preparing the way for a parliamentary reform bill. The scrutiny was abandoned on 3 March 1785, however, when the government lost a division by thirty-four votes. Pitt's defeat was significant because he was engaged in vital parliamentary manoeuvres at this time, particularly with respect to Irish reform, and the scrutiny proved particularly embarrassing because opposition spokesmen pointed out that the malicious attack on Fox put the lie to the myth of Pitt's virtuous and disinterested character. Pitt never forgot this damaging episode. In subsequent years he became much more tactically adroit, and developed a keener awareness of prevalent sentiment in the Commons. There was another early disappointment for Pitt in March 1785 when the government was forced to revise its ordnance estimates. Pitt's opponents successfully appealed to MPs' desire for retrenchment, and this was followed by the rejection (27 February 1786) of a plan to fortify the dockyards at Plymouth and Portsmouth. The Commons division ended in a tie, but the Speaker, Charles Wolfran Cornwall, gave his casting vote against the government.[3]

Pitt's vision and talent came to the fore in fiscal and commercial matters. Reorganization of public finance was set in motion by the budgets of 1784 to 1787 in line with Pitt's general intentions to increase British trade with Europe and offset the loss of the American colonies, restore confidence in the financial system, and stimulate economic development after an expensive war and a period of political instability. Obviously much was beyond government's direct control, but in time trade, investment and industry did recover, and Pitt's measures helped to promote this revival. Nevertheless, there was still a great deal of scepticism about new economic ideas, and even within the ministry Pitt had to accept that some of his commitments were not shared by colleagues. Inevitably these obstacles imposed limits on what Pitt tried to do, especially during the early years of his premiership. His new taxes, moreover, sometimes had untoward consequences. Those on windows, linen and cotton retarded the glass and textile industries. Pitt learned quickly, and several burdens were withdrawn soon after their introduction. At the same time, circumstances were not altogether unfavourable to Pitt's cautious experimentation, for his predecessors had already adopted new methods of financial and economic management. North had initiated reforms at the treasury, for example, and reorganized stamp duty and the customs and excise. A statutory commission had been set up to examine public accounts in 1780. Shelburne continued this trend of financial and administrative reform (assisted by Pitt), and the Fox-North coalition also joined in, instituting an inquiry into the problem of smuggling (which deprived the state of essential revenue). From 1784 Pitt was able to take advantage of this previous work. He studied reports of the public accounts commission, and regularly consulted specialists and allies as he framed his own policies. Among those who advised him were his secretary George Pretyman and cousin William Wyndham Grenville, his former brother-in-law Mahon, the financial expert Jenkinson, senior officials like George Rose at the treasury and Richard Frewin of the customs department, the Cambridge mathematician George Atwood, and the reformer Richard Price, a friend of Shelburne who had developed a sinking fund scheme to facilitate repayment of the national debt.[4]

The national debt now stood at over £213,000,000, having been virtually doubled by the American war. Interest charges represented the largest item of government expenditure (60 per cent of the total) and added to an annual deficit of about £10,000,000, which in turn increased the debt on which charges had to be paid. Such indebtedness undermined confidence and retarded investment and enterprise. If this situation was to change, Pitt urgently needed to increase government revenue. There were new taxes, despite complaints that burdens were already heavy, and he secured better terms for government loans. But these were temporary expedients. Pitt saw that the only way to repair the finances permanently was to lower the debt and extend trade. He established a sinking fund in May 1786 in order gradually to pay off the debt, expecting that a budget surplus would make available £1,000,000 a year for the fund. Commissioners would use this to buy government stock, interest on which would be used to purchase more stock so that compound interest could be applied to reduce the debt (in this way the annual investment in the fund would rise from £1,000,000 to £4,000,000 within twenty-eight years). Pitt also decreed that his sinking fund, unlike earlier such funds, would not cover temporary financial needs. It would be wholly devoted to debt redemption. This measure was passed without much difficulty, for parliament and the propertied classes recognized its necessity. The only significant attack came in the House of Lords from Mahon, now third Earl Stanhope, who argued that more should be done to protect the value of government stock, and that greater precautions were needed to prevent ministers from raiding the sinking fund. Pitt amended the operation of the fund in 1792, partly along the lines suggested by Stanhope, and in its new form it survived into the 1820s. Pitt's sinking fund was at the core of his long-term financial strategy; many other policies depended upon its success. By committing the state to a rational plan of debt repayment, Pitt wanted to convince people that they could be confident about public solvency and their own economic future. The elimination of debt became a sign of Britain's prosperity and strength. To Pitt this had

vital political as well as financial and economic implications, and he became
bolder as he sought to create the conditions within which his goals could
be realized. In April 1787 all the duties imposed by Pitt and his predecessors
were consolidated into a single fund. Previously this money was applied to
different purposes, for which separate accounts had to be kept, but Pitt
now arranged for the consolidated fund to meet the government's financial
obligations in order of priority – first came the interest on the national
debt, second was the civil list, and third was the current annual expenditure
approved by parliament. It was a huge task to implement this reform.
Nobody had ever tried it before.[5]

Although Fox never matched Pitt's understanding of financial questions,
he raised objections to some of the prime minister's statements in the
Commons. There was a notable skirmish in April 1785. Denying that he
wanted to make the government unpopular by forcing it to increase taxation,
Fox questioned Pitt's confidence about a revenue surplus and the reduction
of the national debt. Circumstances were worse than Pitt was prepared to
admit, said Fox, and the prime minister could not be trusted to do what
was necessary to reduce the debt.[6] Most MPs were unimpressed by these
warnings, and Foxites were not able greatly to undermine parliamentary
approval for Pitt's sinking fund. Not only was the scheme commendable
in itself; it was also associated with some promising efforts to increase
revenue and save public money. Pitt moved cautiously at first, aware that
too rapid or innovative an approach would play into the hands of his
political opponents and create problems for the government in parliament.
Nevertheless, it was difficult to argue against his calm and logical doctrine
of necessity. Pitt invariably reiterated this doctrine when presenting his
financial, commercial and administrative reforms for deliberation.

In order to ensure a budget surplus Pitt tried to cut costs. The armed
forces were scaled down after the American war, there were efforts to
combat government waste (a stationery office was established in 1786, for
example), and opening loans to competitive tender, rather than a few
privileged subscribers, enabled Pitt to get better terms from public creditors.
Reducing or abolishing pensions and sinecures also brought savings, though
this activity provoked some resistance. Pitt dedicated himself to imposing
checks, where possible, on government spending. A statutory body for
auditing the public accounts was established in 1785, the role and duties of
specific officials were redefined, and Pitt's desire for financial rectitude
within government departments was indicated by the appointment of a
privy council committee on fee taking. The problem of smuggling was
addressed directly as Pitt sought to enhance the revenue (at this time perhaps
a fifth of all imports came into the country illegally). His continual lowering

of commercial duties helped in this respect because, as he predicted, losses to the government were rapidly outweighed by increased income from legitimate trade and rising consumption. Pitt raised money from loans and a national lottery (established in 1784), as well as taxation. The new taxes introduced in the mid-1780s, however, yielded less than Pitt expected (some were expensive to collect, easy to evade, and too complicated in operation) and, as indicated above, the outcry against certain imposts prompted their repeal. The shop tax of 1785, for instance, was discontinued in 1789. Taxation generally followed a familiar pattern. The orthodoxy was that all social ranks should be liable to tax, but that the poor should not be heavily burdened and the rich should pay more for their luxuries. Pitt followed traditional forms of assessment and relied heavily on indirect taxes, using more direct forms (on property, occupations and necessities) as required.

Along with the new taxes, Pitt ensured a more efficient collection of existing taxes. He strengthened the powers of and simplified procedures in the customs department. The excise department, one of the more competent revenue bodies, was given wider responsibilities. Assessed taxes were grouped together and administered by a new tax board, and local collectors and inspectors were subjected to closer supervision. On 17 February 1792 Pitt told the Commons that annual revenue, under £13,000,000 in 1783, had been increased by about £4,000,000 (subsequent commentators have suggested that the actual increase may have been greater than Pitt thought, perhaps as much as £6,000,000). Growing prosperity and burgeoning trade accounted for about half of the increase, Pitt said, while new taxes had brought in about £1,000,000 and the reduction of fraud and smuggling a similar amount. Government policy was partly responsible for this healthy balance sheet, but Pitt also paid tribute to the commercial spirit of the people, without which the accumulation of capital, revival of credit and rapid expansion of trade would not have been so remarkable. With a surplus of £400,000, Pitt decided, the time was right to reduce taxation, and he also planned to lower naval expenditure and pay off about £25,000,000 of debt over the next fifteen years.[7]

By the early 1790s Pitt had also set in motion a programme of economical reform and administrative improvement. Fox, Burke and their followers had been concerned most to restrict the crown's capacity for political mischief, but Pitt scrutinized all aspects of public spending, however uncontroversial. His thorough approach won the approval of economy-minded MPs as well as the nation's taxpayers. Pitt's gradual abolition of sinecures assisted in the work of retrenchment, and was of constitutional importance because it closed up former avenues for corruption. Pitt was determined to overhaul government departments; and though some of the ideas and methods had been in operation for years, it was Pitt who successfully implemented them. Efficiency was not an end in itself, however. Nor was probity. The wider political purpose was to justify aristocratic rule at a time when popular attacks on 'Old Corruption' were undermining the authority of the governing elite. Therefore tax reform, retrenchment, administrative reorganization, elimination of abuses and other attempts to purify government were all, at least in part, responses to outside pressure. Pitt tried to demonstrate that inefficiency and corruption were no longer prevalent in order to make aristocratic rule less objectionable. Gradually the elite sanitized government and by the 1830s the critique of 'Old Corruption' had lost much of its force.[8] Pitt's role in this development was to create an environment within which charges of greed and abuse would be weakened. This was important because the high cost of the American war, and the fact that Britain had been defeated, focused attention on the debt, heavy taxation, and the opportunities presented for aristocratic connections to live off the public wealth. Elite depredations and government extravagance became dominant political issues, taken up out of doors by independent country gentlemen, who wanted to pay less tax, and by metropolitan and provincial radicals, who linked 'Old Corruption' with misgovernment and (to them) reprehensible disparities in wealth, status and influence. Pitt saw that criticisms of the state could only be removed if there were substantial financial and administrative improvements. There was much to be gained. Faith in public men would increase; the state would become more efficient and respected, without weakening central government or changing the political system; and reform from within would diminish pressure from without and confirm Pitt's reputation for integrity. Yet the critique of 'Old Corruption' did not collapse. Pitt was a cautious economical reformer. Unwilling to risk controversy and obstruction, and keen for the executive to retain control over the reform process, he could not allow the Commons or extra-parliamentary agitators to interfere. Though he was ready to respond to criticisms, he did so as and when he chose. Then the massive increase in expenditure after 1793, necessitated by the French war, made it impossible for him to reduce the size of government or carry forward the retrenchment programme. Complaints about 'Old Corruption' therefore revived, undermining Pitt's image as the public-minded steward.[9]

The process of economical reform was too slow for many observers (radicals turned increasingly to parliamentary reform as the only means by which government could be forced to respond to the people's will), and Pitt was unable permanently to weaken resentment against the aristocratic state. Indeed, in some respects his relationship with the people remained uneasy. Although he sought popular support he also believed in a salutary limit to the public's influence over its rulers. To reformers, meanwhile, it was clear that politicians should no longer expect to operate in isolation from extra-parliamentary pressures, and that Pitt's government must take account of the development of reform movements, goals and vocabulary, as promoted by social and economic change (press, public opinion, urban growth, industrialization). Another complication for Pitt was that 'Old Corruption' involved more than just the state. Condemnation of the wealth and privileges of the Established Church, for example, suggested that elite politicians would find it difficult to preserve their authority if they attended only to the better management of administrative institutions. In this respect the commitment to moral reform at the end of the eighteenth century takes on greater significance. The anti-corruption cause helped to stimulate a campaign for the reformation of manners. In addition to religious and social concerns (sin, crime, poverty, moral decline), campaigners focused upon the loss of political virtue because it appeared that Britain's rulers were placing private desire before the public good.[10] The elite had to be persuaded to set a better example. Pitt's economical reforms were all the more important, therefore, in view of their social and moral as well as political meaning.

After a review in 1786 Pitt reorganized the civil list. He also provided for a more profitable management of crown lands and woods (given up by George III on his succession). None of this raised difficult constitutional questions or arguments about the royal prerogative; in a time of relative political stability, the extension of parliamentary control over royal finances seemed unobjectionable. Pitt carried on the reform of government departments, forcing officials to work harder and subjecting them to new standards of proficiency. He wanted government to be respected for its professionalism but proceeded slowly, for improvements effected in one department were not necessarily possible or useful in another. Change was uneven, and probably more the result of financial policies than direct administrative reform. Pitt continued to replace fees with official salaries, though again this was a slow process because of the trouble and expense involved. A rapid change to payment by salary would create extra charges, not least because those affected would expect compensation. Many of Pitt's supporters still thought of office as a type of property, and he had to respect their point of view. So fees could not be abolished completely. In 1788 they still represented over a third of the remuneration received by customs officials. On sinecures Pitt did not force the pace. He simply kept a record of unnecessary offices and, as their holders died, refrained from appointing successors. Some sinecures were abolished by legislation, but Pitt much preferred the gradual method. His *reputation* for probity was perhaps more

significant than his actual *achievements* in administrative and financial reform; many improvements were postponed because the approach was
essentially conservative.[11] Yet Pitt's reorganizations were sometimes striking.
In 1789 alone, for example, 765 revenue offices were abolished. Another 196
were abolished in 1798. Government gradually lost the capacity to use these
offices as political rewards (as a result peerages and other honours became
even more significant). Pittite reforms were therefore of long-term political
as well as administrative importance. The drive for efficiency changed the
patronage system and reduced the political power of the crown. A monarch
could no longer exert influence as in the past. Though the Foxite claim that
the Commons should approve and remove ministries had been discredited
in 1783 and 1784, this became the accepted practice before George III's death
in 1820. Royal patronage would no longer be sufficient to support a prime
minister who did not have parliament's backing.

Pitt's measures for economical reform and administrative improvement
further hampered the Foxite opposition, for (as with the national debt and
tax and tariff reforms) it was difficult to condemn the ends he had in view.
Fox could only point to relatively minor details during Commons debates,
which gave him few opportunities to challenge Pitt's authority. As Pitt
proposed reforms or reported on their beneficial effects, Fox ran out of
criticisms and alternative suggestions. In February 1785 Pitt spoke about
new accounting procedures in government departments, stricter financial
management, and the disappearance of unnecessary offices (he preferred
public office to be regarded as a trust rather than a property). In response
Fox weakly claimed that governments of which he had been a member had
done more useful work than Pitt in these fields, in a shorter period of time,
and that emoluments prescribed in a grant from the crown could not
properly be meddled with because they were a species of freehold property.[12]
Ultimately resistance to Pitt's proposals for retrenchment and efficiency
achieved little, and the government won the vital parliamentary divisions
on these matters.

Customs reform signified Pitt's ongoing concern for efficiency. The aim
was not only to increase trade; cheaper and more competent government
was also in view. So was an elimination of fraud, an inevitable problem
while departmental business lacked order. Under Pitt, customs offices were
amalgamated, and the old practice of securing government loans on separate
items of duty was ended. Even Fox and Burke welcomed the establishment
of the consolidated fund in 1787, and the new ranking of government
spending (with interest on the national debt accorded priority status)
reassured public creditors that their money was safe. Another advantage
of the single fund was that official salaries charged upon it were rendered

more secure. Though several items of revenue and expenditure were not included in Pitt's reorganization, his reform was thorough by the standards of the time (and notwithstanding his preference for traditional and cautious methods, he has been regarded as the founder of modern tax procedure).[13] As has already been suggested, financial reorganization remained pragmatic. Pitt did not carry it too far because he had no wish to create new political complications, and his usual approach was not to levy new taxes but to increase the yield from existing ones.

Pitt's financial and administrative reforms represent a constructive if preliminary response to problems associated with what has been termed the 'fiscal-military state'. By the 1780s Britain had spent almost half of the preceding century at war, and the need to fight and finance wars had prompted a massive increase in taxation, greater government borrowing and the growth of public administration. This transformation gave rise to a struggle to limit government power, cut expenditure, make institutions more accountable, and slow down the expansion of bureaucracy. In practice the struggle made the state even stronger, it has been argued, for scrutiny reduced peculation, and parliamentary consent (given in return for more accountability) legitimized government action. But as government became bigger and more expensive, there were complaints of the kind noted above with reference to 'Old Corruption'. While some contemporaries condemned the 'fiscal-military state', others found ways of exploiting it. Early eighteenth-century interest groups had mobilized in opposition to specific measures. By the 1780s, perhaps encouraged by Pitt's willingness to reform, competing interests were urging government departments to be more active and looking for the advantages to be gained by dealing with (rather than opposing) the state.[14] The effects and wider reception of Pitt's reforms were therefore linked to attitudes toward government growth. Much depended on the extent to which elements of the 'fiscal-military state' could be run down during peace. Pitt began to explore this option before 1793, and it had important implications both for the role of parliament and for relations between government and people. Those who were able to benefit from government growth would have been predisposed against some of Pitt's peacetime policies. Competition between special interests (especially in commerce, manufacturing and finance) also revealed that inability to come to an accommodation with the reforming state could bring serious disadvantages. The social impact of the 'fiscal-military state', meanwhile, was most severe on the poor, since indirect taxation rested heavily upon the lower classes, and many landlords were able to transfer the burden of direct taxation to their tenants. These circumstances no doubt increased popular pressure for reforms and brought into question the state's readiness

to adjust to broader social and economic changes. Although differing interpretations of the 'fiscal-military state' and its consequences are possible,[15]
it is clear that Pitt's quest for a smaller, cheaper and more efficient state
before 1793 can be viewed in a wider context. His methods and priorities were
partly shaped by contemporary concerns about the nature of government
and the points of contact between state and public opinion.

Sometimes Pitt framed his policies in the light of favoured dogmas rather
than (or as well as) pragmatic utility. He hoped, for example, to free trade
as prescribed in Adam Smith's *Inquiry into the Nature and Causes of the
Wealth of Nations*, published in 1776 (Smith's ideas had also influenced
Shelburne, while Fox once admitted that he had never even read Smith, let
alone evaluated his propositions). Free trade principles inspired many of
Pitt's commercial reforms. According to old mercantilist doctrine, there was
a limited amount of wealth available in the world and it was up to each
nation to protect and increase its own share. Convinced of the wealth-
generating propensities of free trade, Pitt rejected the mercantilist nostrum.
Ideologically he favoured the simplification and consolidation of customs
and excise, the lowering of duties on many goods to encourage consumption
and check smuggling, and tariff reforms designed to secure greater access
to raw materials for British manufacturers and wider markets for their
finished products. Pitt believed that cumulative prosperity would inevitably
accrue from a greater volume of trade.

These ideas influenced his plan for new Irish commercial arrangements.
The measure introduced in February 1785 provided for freer trade between
Britain and Ireland, and was intended to promote closer relations between
the two and assist Ireland's economic development. Pitt knew that the earlier
grant of legislative independence had created the problem of co-ordinating
the actions of the parliaments in Dublin and Westminster. Ireland's separ-
ateness had to be respected, yet Ireland could not be permitted to adopt
policies that did not suit British interests. Pitt was sure that freer trade would
foster prosperity and cordial Anglo-Irish relations. In return for measured
autonomy the Irish would have to accept the supremacy of the British
government and pay towards imperial defence. Economic advantages would
be added to previous concessions in order to reconcile Ireland to these
conditions. But Pitt went further. He wanted permanent benefits and a
settled pattern for future policy. His strategy became too complex, however,
as he tried to counter every possible objection and effect a lasting solution
to the Irish question. Even his colleague Grenville saw that Pitt's elaborate
scheme was doomed: so many requirements and provisions simply could
not hold together in one all-embracing plan.[16]

Fox denounced the scheme and asserted that Ireland would gain too much under the proposed system of commerce. The Irish themselves had made much of the facility they would acquire to supply British markets and turn Ireland into an emporium of trade. The Fox-North government had hoped to attend to Ireland, Fox continued, but would never have proposed the excessive changes now advocated by Pitt. The practice of keeping Ireland happy with continual concessions was highly objectionable, and nothing could justify the intended 'surrender' of Britain's commerce and navigation.[17]

There was also protest from manufacturers and merchants in the Midlands, Lancashire and the West Riding, who formed a Great Chamber of Manufacturers to resist Pitt's policy. Freer trade would bring ruin, they claimed, and their propaganda stressed that Irish labour costs were considerably lower than those in England. In free competition Irish products would be that much cheaper. Another concern was that admittance to external trade would enable the Irish to import foreign sugar, harming the British West Indies and merchants engaged in the British carrying trade. Panic spread, and Pitt's parliamentary opponents took full advantage. He amended his plan in May 1785. Then the Dublin parliament condemned the modified proposals in August, and a dejected Pitt withdrew the whole project (17 August).[18] This was probably his most serious defeat in the early years of his premiership. It was a heavy personal blow, for Pitt had involved himself fully in the Irish question and invested much of his time, energy and reputation. After due reflection, he wrote to Rutland (lord lieutenant of Ireland from February 1784 to November 1787):

> we have the satisfaction of having proposed a system which I believe will not be discredited even by its failure; and we must wait times and seasons for carrying it into effect ... Let us meet what has happened, or whatever may happen, with the coolness and determination of persons who may be defeated, but cannot be disgraced, and who know that those who obstruct them are greater sufferers than themselves.[19]

Pitt's proposal for a commercial treaty with France met with a different fate, partly because he consulted merchants and industrialists beforehand. They were in two minds about freer trade with France. Some expected profitable business, while others, notably the producers of silk, paper and leather, were strongly protectionist. If most manufacturers had opposed the Irish plan, there was considerable support for the French project, though Foxites relied on traditional anti-French sentiment to create difficulties for Pitt in parliament. The prime minister gave William Eden, who was later raised to the peerage as Baron Auckland, special responsibility for negotiations with the French (his adherence indicates Pitt's growing ability to win over former opponents, for Eden had been a junior minister under North and a supporter of Fox's India Bill). The Anglo-French treaty was concluded in September 1786. Duties on a range of products were reduced and a system of reciprocity was established. Pitt explained the benefits to the Commons in February 1787. In response to the claim that the treaty was flawed, just as the Irish propositions had been, he argued that manufacturers were the best judges of their own interest. They had opposed the Irish plan, but there had been no clamour against the French treaty. Pitt extolled 'relative' commerce, the exchange of staples for staples, and strongly recommended a bargain that would open France to British exports by allowing French goods easier access to Britain. Pitt won the parliamentary divisions on the treaty, and he also won the argument. Many of Fox's objections were weak or irrelevant. Even his valid point about Pitt's tendency to rush measures through, which had caused so much trouble with the Irish scheme, made little impression on the Commons majority. In allowing French and British subjects free access to each other's country and opening navigation and trade between French and British colonies, as well as lowering tariffs on many items, the Anglo-French Commercial Treaty was a notably thoroughgoing reform.[20]

Freer trade made sound sense to Britain as the industrial revolution brought a clear competitive advantage, and many merchants and manufacturers applauded Pitt's efforts to provide new commercial opportunities. Yet the success in concluding a treaty with France could not mask the failure of other negotiations with foreign governments. Indeed, Pitt did not want to give up too much in return for the concessions he sought abroad. He continued to protect British shipping, colonies and industries, which annoyed other trading states. The commercial treaty with France was the only such agreement he managed to secure, and there were special reasons why the talks with France went well. Pitt needed a high-profile success to make up for the defeat of his Irish scheme, Eden wanted to revive his own political career, and the French government hoped to ward off a financial crisis at home by expanding trade with Britain.[21] Any benefits that Britain gained from the treaty were soon lost. The French Revolution destabilized the economy and external relations of France, and in February 1793 Britain and France went to war.

The merits of Pitt's financial, administrative and economic reforms might be questioned on other grounds. Though in general his measures helped to restore financial confidence, debt was not permanently reduced because the war with France brought an increase in government spending. Budget surplus became growing deficit. Pitt did not suspend the sinking fund, because he was optimistic about the war's duration and outcome. Money was borrowed at high interest to reduce the debt at a lower rate of interest, a policy that provoked enormous indignation in later years.[22] To be successful, the sinking fund required an excess of revenue over expenditure. Pitt achieved this in peacetime (mainly due to higher customs yields), but war frustrated his plans. On the other hand, his policy was useful in political and social terms. Pitt had signified an intention to solve the state's revenue problems and halt the growth of the debt and its interest. He deemed this a matter of honourable public service. In return MPs, voters and taxpayers trusted him, most of the time, to look after public money carefully and responsibly. This helped to calm political and social tensions, and Pitt became more concerned about these wider problems than about his own record as a reformer.

Even before the war he had decided that he could not press his reforms much further. Though he was in a position to do more, he may have judged that the political costs would be too high. Perhaps the obstacles to change within government departments were simply too strong. In any case Pitt was never as enthusiastic a reformer as some of his supporters hoped, as some of his opponents complained, and as Pitt himself – for his own political purposes – sometimes chose to appear. Though he had responded positively to the findings of the public accounts commission, in 1787 he decided it could be dissolved. The privy council committee on fees was dissolved two years later, having completed less than half of its projected work. Its reports were shelved. The assault on sinecures, discussed above, remained slow and uneven. Any assessment of Pitt's impact as a financial reformer must also recognize that he was not always the originator of policy. He sought the advice of colleagues and experts, and in implementing as well as framing measures he relied on a group of talented senior officials. Pitt had noticed their promise, promoted them to positions of responsibility, and encouraged them to develop their own techniques and ideas. His sinking fund owed much to others, notably Richard Price and the public accounts commissioners. Shelburne had already made moves towards freer trade. The attack on government waste was partly inspired by the revenue frauds committee. The practice of opening government loans to tender had already been followed in the ordnance and victualling departments, and previous governments had embarked on a course of economical reform and administrative improvement. In office Pitt pushed this work forward more quickly than he needed to, and more thoroughly than his predecessors and even some of his closest political allies apparently thought possible or appropriate. This is probably where the real significance of his contribution lies: he had the political will, command of detail, influence in cabinet and parliament, personal inclination and energy, fresh ideas and combination of boldness and pragmatism that were needed to make things happen. Pitt committed himself to efficiency and retrenchment before becoming prime minister, and though his reforms owed a great deal to earlier ideas and examples, and often were not carried through as they might have been, it cannot be denied that his premiership represents a watershed in financial and administrative practice.[23]

Pitt's achievements in other spheres were less remarkable. On parliamentary reform (as with the Irish commercial propositions) he had to accept that he could not carry the Commons with him. Nor was respectable opinion out of doors totally behind the prime minister. There was also the problem of George III's hostility, and many MPs took a similar line to the king, preferring Pitt to the Foxites but not necessarily sharing the prime minister's commitments. Pitt persuaded the king to allow him to introduce a parliamentary reform bill, knowing that the court would not promote its passage. The best Pitt could hope for was that George III would remain neutral.[24] In the spring of 1785 Pitt proposed that thirty-six rotten boroughs should be disfranchised, the relevant interests compensated for their loss, and the seats transferred to London, Westminster and the counties. The county franchise would be extended to admit 40 shilling copyholders and some leaseholders. This scheme affected neither the total number of MPs nor the duration of parliaments. The redistribution of seats would not threaten private rights (Pitt respected borough patronage), and the franchise would only be moderately extended. Pitt envisaged a process of parliamentary reform that would be gradual and voluntary. He considered this process necessary, wanted to reward reformers who had given him support inside and outside parliament, and may also have expected to improve the government's electoral position with a modest redistribution of seats. By carrying his proposals, moreover, he thought he could reconcile independents to the general idea of reform. All these developments would be useful for the future. Dundas assisted in soliciting support for Pitt's measure, stressing its moderation and the manner in which Pitt had sought to appease 'those who are adverse to a spirit of innovation'.[25]

Pitt told the Commons that he would not try to convert those who believed the constitution to be perfect. Instead, he recommended his reform to those who admitted that defects existed but feared the consequences of any attempt to remove them. Pitt said that he revered constitutional custom and wanted no unnecessary or speculative changes. His would be a final plan, with a clear principle and identifiable limits. Though he had been defeated twice before in the Commons on parliamentary reform, he wanted to try again because this was a new house, elected the previous year, which had not yet considered the question. Pitt's premise was that there should be a closer bond between parliament and public. This made adequate representation essential. Through history the system had been amended when necessary. Electoral arrangements had evolved gradually as political and social conditions changed, and their flexibility was most evident with respect to decayed boroughs (some of which, though they had previously returned MPs, no longer did so on account of their loss of wealth and population). The constitution contained within itself the means to grant or transfer elective rights as appropriate. Change was an established feature of the constitution, Pitt insisted, and to deny this would be to ignore experience and reason. What was needed was a settled reform process, and Pitt's specific proposals were intended to set one in motion.[26]

Many MPs disliked the plan, as did the king and some of Pitt's ministerial colleagues. It had to be proposed by Pitt in his individual capacity, much to his regret, for he had hoped to make parliamentary reform government policy. Opposition leaders also raised objections. North pointed to the lack of support in the country, and rejected the 'extraordinary' idea that 'the people of England were to be supposed to wish really for an alteration in the state of parliamentary representation, when they did not ask for it'. Fox insisted that the franchise was a trust, not an entitlement or possession, and that it was outrageous to offer compensation to owners of corrupt boroughs. (Pitt's view was that compensation would allay hostility to reform by acknowledging customary rights.) Fox voted for Pitt's motion, to demonstrate consistency as a reformer, but added that the nation wanted more than the limited and gradual change offered by Pitt.[27]

On 18 April 1785, when Pitt sought leave to introduce his reform bill, he was defeated by 248 to 174 votes. Though the majority against him was down to 74, compared to 144 in 1783, Pitt was now leader of the government and probably expected to do better. He realized that George III disapproved of parliamentary reform, however, and accepted the verdict of the Commons (as in 1782 and 1783). Pitt was a realist. After 1785 he decided to let the matter rest. Many reformers understood why he was reluctant to press it, and continued to regard Pitt, not Fox, as the best hope for parliamentary reform, at least until the French Revolution. But opinions continued to differ about the need for parliamentary reform, and Pitt himself moved towards a more conservative position. In truth the defeat of 1785 made parliamentary reform more unlikely. If a moderate plan proposed by one of the dominant figures in parliament could be defeated so easily, what hope was there for other plans or advocates? Indeed, despite the efforts of campaigners such as Wyvill, Pitt's plan failed to attract much interest or support out of doors. More stability and competence in government, and an improving economic situation, meant that pressure for change was dwindling. Besides, the electoral system was not as iniquitous as its detractors claimed (there was always a tendency to exaggerate its flaws in order to foment agitation). The electorate was slowly expanding as population increased, giving more influence to craftsmen, shopkeepers and others of the middling sort who resided in boroughs that had comparatively wide franchises. The system lacked uniformity and was not as representative as some contemporaries wished, yet the general belief was that it served at least one of its purposes remarkably well: the representation of interests (rather than fixed places or social classes). Levels of politicization and participation rose in the later eighteenth century. Undue influence at elections remained a grievance, but as well as corruption, intimidation and deference, relations between patrons and voters were shaped by persuasion and mutual dependence. Perhaps a third of all boroughs were quite open in this respect, and even when seats were uncontested there was still a need for vigorous canvassing and electoral negotiation, if only to prevent a future rupture between voters and their landlords or employers. The complexities of negotiation can also be seen in arguments about the extent to which MPs should take instruction from their constituents.[28]

Many politically active and informed people in 1785 were not prepared to back Pitt's reform bill. The House of Commons was against it, the court was not for it, and there were no loud calls for reform out of doors. Measures for regulating elections were subsequently introduced by Stanhope in 1786 and 1788, but both efforts failed, and the annual reform motions of the radical MP John Sawbridge were repeatedly defeated. Neither in the government nor in opposition was there clear agreement on the pros and cons of parliamentary reform, and public opinion was also divided. It never became an issue that affected the fate of Pitt's ministry. As for the premier himself, he was always more cautious on constitutional questions than on fiscal and administrative matters. He respected the existing order. If changes were needed, he thought, they should not go beyond the salutary removal of obvious anomalies. The purpose was not to create a new system but to make the existing one run more smoothly. As more advanced and impatient reformers, especially those out of doors, came to understand Pitt's position more clearly, they attacked him for disappointing the high hopes of the early 1780s. But from the beginning his view had always been that reforms should only be implemented if they were shown to be necessary, and as prime minister he decided that necessity was not the sole criterion. One also had to consider what parliament would sanction and what the propertied classes in society really wanted. Pitt was impressed by the fact that his reform motion of 1783 had been backed by thirty-five petitions. Only twelve were submitted in support of his 1785 effort, so it is not surprising that he reconsidered his stance on parliamentary reform. The apparent need for constitutional change disappeared, moreover, as parliament and nation were satisfied by *other* measures (notably Pitt's financial and administrative improvements). By 1787 Wyvill was admitting that, for many people, the question of parliamentary reform had become an irrelevance.[29]

Pitt was still genuinely committed to a mild reorganization of the electoral system, but rather than propose measures himself he expressed support, when he deemed it appropriate, for proposals advanced by others. Again, though, he noted that reform was losing its appeal. Stanhope's bill of 1788 for the registration of county freeholders was widely criticized on the grounds of expense and inconvenience (even by voters themselves), and parliament received twenty-four petitions against it. Nevertheless, Pitt followed up his earlier support for the regulation of polls and scrutinies (in 1785 and 1786) with an attempt to win approval for Stanhope's measure. In April 1788 he urged the master of the rolls Sir Lloyd Kenyon (shortly to be appointed lord chief justice and raised to the peerage as Baron Kenyon) to assist in this effort. As Pitt explained: 'I consider the object itself of diminishing the expense and trouble of election as a very important public object, if it can be obtained.' Kenyon's advice was also needed on the legal questions involved in Stanhope's projected reform. It was passed after substantial amendment, but repealed in 1789 before it came into operation.[30]

Pitt lost enthusiasm for parliamentary reform, and during the mid-1780s he decided that he had more important and interesting problems to attend to. In future, he thought, he could only countenance plans that had necessity, moderation and usefulness to commend them, that attracted general support, and that did not offend George III or other influential figures. The French Revolution finally convinced Pitt that the time was not right for parliamentary reform. The rapid growth of popular radicalism, the demand for democratic rights and talk of manhood suffrage were too much for him, because in the midst of such excitement the basic issues at stake could not be discussed in a calm and constructive way. On certain points, moreover, there could be no flexibility. Pitt's view of representation was the orthodox view: the vote was a trust, not a right, and a democratic franchise had never been part of the British constitution and never could be, for the system was not meant to represent numbers but communities, interests and property. This is why, in 1785, he had recommended the addition of copyholders to county electorates, why he never wanted greatly to extend the franchise, and why in seeking to make the system more representative he looked to an increase in the proportion of relatively 'open' constituencies.

After the outbreak of the French Revolution many reformers accused him of betrayal, yet his purpose all along had been to reinforce the most efficient parts of the existing constitution, not to replace it with something else (certainly not a system designed along French or American lines). Revolutionary violence abroad also confirmed Pitt's opinion that constitutional reform at home should only be implemented if it had the consent of those who already enjoyed political rights and influence. During the 1790s it did not seem that this consent would be given, and when the Foxite MP Charles Grey introduced reform proposals in 1793 and 1797 he was heavily defeated. In this context Pitt argued that few people wanted reform, that there were unanswerable objections to the nature and timing of such proposals, and that any concession would encourage extremists and destabilize state and society.[31]

Pitt's general tests of necessity, approval, timing and usefulness meant that in certain circumstances he could still be found framing or pressing for significant constitutional change, though in the era of revolution and war this was more true of imperial than domestic affairs. The Canada Act of June 1791 demonstrates that Pitt was quite prepared fundamentally to alter systems of government. He had reorganized the administration of India in the 1780s, and in some respects the Canadian reform, on which he worked closely with his cousin Grenville (home secretary from June 1789 and then foreign secretary from June 1791), was an equally bold and substantial undertaking.[32] Clearly the French Revolution did not prompt Pitt to abandon reform completely (in fact, it could be said to have made certain types of reform more necessary). The Canada Act was designed to create a system of government that would promote order, hasten economic progress, and lower the tension between British and French sections of the population. Political, religious, social, ethnic and cultural differences between the two groups could not be allowed to endanger the security of Canada, Pitt argued, or prevent Canada's further integration into imperial commercial structures (Canada was an important market for British and colonial products and a supplier of raw materials).

The solution was to divide Canada into two provinces. Upper Canada was mainly British, Lower Canada mainly French. Each was to have representative institutions, but these would be based on a narrow franchise and (as in the British parliamentary system) the elected chamber would be balanced by an upper chamber, membership of which was hereditary or for life. The Canada Act also provided for the appointment of a governor general who would oversee the new system, an added precaution indicating Pitt's concern to discourage radicalism and ensure continuity. Ultimate authority over Canadian affairs was retained by the British government, which answered to parliament. Though the new arrangements did not bring lasting peace to Canada, they did survive until 1840. More immediately, the debates on the ministry's proposals during 1791 were remarkable for a serious breach in the parliamentary opposition. Fox had warmly welcomed the French Revolution, and refused thereafter to alter his positive opinion of it, while Burke pessimistically warned that French ideology and practice would inevitably threaten order and liberty. When Fox attacked the government's Canadian reform, claiming that the new assemblies would not be sufficiently representative, Burke insisted that any such change had to be guided by experience, not speculative, irreverent or democratic urges as in revolutionary France.[33]

Another weighty constitutional matter was religious toleration. For some time the propriety and necessity of penal limits imposed on non-Anglicans by the Test and Corporation Acts, which dated from the seventeenth century, had been hotly contested. Pitt himself never expressed or demonstrated any firm religious convictions. Wilberforce opined that his friend was too preoccupied with politics to give much time or attention to matters of theology. On 25 January 1806, shortly after Pitt's death, Wilberforce expressed deep regret that he had never been able to speak frankly to Pitt about the Christian faith:

> There is something peculiarly affecting in the time and circumstances of poor Pitt's death. I own I have a thousand times (aye, times without number) wished and hoped that a quiet interval would be afforded him, perhaps in the evening of life, in which he and I might confer freely on the most important of all subjects. But the scene is closed – for ever.[34]

For the Church of England Pitt had deep respect, because he appreciated its usefulness as a public institution, but no personal affinity, and in some respects he was less than complimentary (he found the sensitive issue of ecclesiastical preferment extremely irritating, and believed that the Anglican clergy's right to tithes impeded agricultural advances). The extension of civil and religious liberty, meanwhile, was a permanent and defining cause for the Foxites. Fox persistently advocated full toleration for Catholics and Protestant Dissenters. In comparison Pitt's record was mixed. He thought that the need for disabilities to protect church and state had virtually passed away, and that non-Anglicans posed no serious threat to the established order. Sympathizing with arguments about justice and inclusiveness, Pitt supported the extension of rights to Catholics in England in 1791 (many disabilities were removed at this time, but Catholics were still excluded from parliament and other civil offices),[35] and by the end of the 1790s he was in favour of Catholic emancipation as part of his scheme for a legislative union with Ireland.

But as with other constitutional changes, so with religious toleration Pitt's keen sense of pragmatism set a limit to what he was prepared to propose and support. Impressed by his image as a youthful, energetic reformer, and conscious that in 1772 his father had supported a bill to remove restrictions on their clergymen and schoolmasters,[36] Protestant Dissenters backed Pitt strongly in the early 1780s only to be disappointed later on. Pitt resisted their efforts to repeal the Test and Corporation Acts in 1787, 1789 and 1790. By this time many Dissenters were taking up public offices, especially in local government, without much hindrance, for parliament passed annual indemnity acts to suspend legal penalties. If the Test and Corporation Acts imposed no significant burden in practice, however, campaigners still objected to the principle of disabilities based on religion, and many commentators asserted that legal penalties were not in keeping with the libertarian spirit of the constitution.

To Pitt the real issue here was the role of the national state church, and he insisted that its status and influence should not be undermined. He opposed repeal as inexpedient, a danger to the Church of England, and – in view of the fact that practical toleration was already broad – unnecessary.[37] Parliament ought to preserve its discretion in this matter, he thought, and this was also George III's view. Pitt was reluctant to annoy the church, the court and their adherents. When he consulted the bishops in 1787, he had already decided that he would not back repeal unless the church agreed to it (he had no strong views on the matter initially). At a meeting attended by sixteen bishops, only two favoured repeal. Such considerations shaped Pitt's general rule on ecclesiastical matters: anything that was of fundamental concern to the 'church party', but relatively unimportant to Pitt and the government, was best left alone. There was nothing to be gained by needlessly causing trouble. As well as opposing repeal of the Test and Corporation Acts, therefore, Pitt abandoned a plan to commute tithes to a money payment when the bishops objected. He lost the support of many Dissenters, but the grateful church was a useful prop to his regime during the difficult 1790s, promoting loyalty and obedience, assisting in the wartime 'Church and King' mobilization, and offering solid support for the government's anti-French and anti-radical policies.[38]

Pitt gave his clearest statement on the Test and Corporation Acts in March 1790 when the Commons debated a repeal motion introduced by Fox:

The important question at issue was simply and plainly this: whether the house ought or ought not to relinquish at once those acts which had been adopted by the wisdom of our ancestors, to serve as a bulwark to the church, whose constitution was so intimately connected with that of the state, that the safety of the one was always liable to be affected by any danger which might threaten the other? He, for one, was clearly convinced that we ought not to relinquish those great and fundamental principles upon which the prosperity of the state so much depended.

Pitt explained that, though he favoured toleration, he did not understand toleration to mean equality. Rather, it meant freedom of worship and opinion, the protection of the laws, the enjoyment of liberty and property, and the ability to educate one's children as one wished. But 'the indispensable necessity of a certain permanent church establishment, for the good of the state, required that toleration should not be extended to an equality; for that would inevitably endanger such an establishment'. While nobody should be punished for their religious beliefs, in public life there had to be some security, and with respect to civil appointments it was necessary to test for loyalty and obedience. Pitt emphasized his own sense of special responsibility: 'to guard against danger to the constitution, however distant, was the indispensable duty of every member of that house, but of none more than of a person in the situation he had the honour to hold, with whom the safety of his country ought ever to be his principal object'.[39]

On the slave trade, another controversial issue of this time, Pitt was more clearly in the reform camp. Genuinely committed to abolition of the slave trade, he also expected to reap political and parliamentary benefits by involving himself closely with a popular cause. His concern to be seen as a patriotic leader with a clear mandate and wide approval in the nation led him to express himself unequivocally in favour of measures to end the British slave trade. He shared the view of abolitionists that the trade was objectionable on moral and economic grounds. But he had to be careful. Abolitionism was not a cause that enjoyed much favour at court or among some of Pitt's colleagues and supporters. Nevertheless, in May 1788, when his friend Wilbeforce was too ill to take the lead in a vital Commons debate on the issue, Pitt stepped in. He noted that over a hundred petitions had been submitted in support of repeal, and urged parliament to respond.

In these years the anti-slave trade agitation gathered impressive backing out of doors. It was well organized, with a central London committee co-ordinating the activities of many local bodies in the provinces. Agents and speakers moved from place to place, informing, advising and mobilizing, and full use was made of press, petition and public meeting in order to shape opinion. Pitt's open encouragement helped the movement and in return the prime minister could claim to enjoy popular approval. He made important speeches in support of abolition in 1789 and 1791, and his speech of 2 April 1792 (after parliament had received over five hundred petitions carrying about 400,000 signatures in all) ranks as one of most accomplished and celebrated speeches of his whole career.[40]

On 2 April 1792 Pitt denounced the slave trade as 'the greatest stigma on our national character which ever yet existed' and 'the greatest practical evil that has ever afflicted the human race'. The necessity and justice of abolition were generally admitted, he said, and the main point now was to decide on its timing and manner. Arguing against some of his government colleagues, Pitt denied that the merits of gradual outweighed those of immediate abolition. In response to those who believed that a cessation of the trade would be impossible to enforce, Pitt pointed to the success of other efforts to combat smuggling. He then rejected arguments about expediency, claiming that there was no need for more slaves to be taken from Africa to the West Indies. The slave population in Britain's colonies was reproducing itself – births outnumbered deaths, and the previous imbalance of the sexes was being mitigated. The labour force could be maintained without the slave trade, therefore, and abolition would also prompt the better treatment of slaves.

Some speakers had argued that the growth of the slave population told against the abolitionists' accusations about cruel and harsh treatment. Other MPs, in order to justify the continuation of the slave trade, had stated that the slave population was decreasing. Either way, Pitt declared, the case against abolition was ill founded. If the population was rising, as he believed, there was no need for the slave trade to carry on, and if the population was decreasing, bad treatment was a cause of this, and abolition would force planters to act more humanely. There was no shortage of evidence, Pitt explained, to indicate that the most hard-working slaves were those who were treated well. Improved conditions for slaves, moreover, would create a shared interest between workers and masters and render the British colonies safer in terms of internal order and security against foreign aggression. Slave rebellions would continue until the slave trade was curtailed, said Pitt, not least because it tended to be newly imported slaves who caused the most trouble. Abolition would benefit the masters in other ways. Slaves were expensive, and many masters were heavily in debt. If the trade was stopped they could save money and concentrate on getting the best out of the existing labour force. Abolition would not be ruinous, Pitt stressed, but, even if losses did result, parliament might be persuaded to offer compensation (provided planters could present a convincing case).

Pitt next addressed the objection that since the planters' property had been guaranteed by parliament, abolition would rob them of their legal and patrimonial rights. This objection, which applied to gradual as well as immediate abolition, made little sense. Just because the slave trade had received parliamentary sanction in the past, Pitt declared, parliament had not thereby given up jurisdiction over it for all time. As with any branch of commerce, previous rules might be altered in the light of new circumstances, and such rules invariably affected individual property. The stated objection was therefore erroneous, and parliament could not be expected to prolong a trade that was an outrage upon justice: 'As well might an individual think himself bound by a promise to commit an assassination.' Whether one considered law, morality, expediency or so-called pledges of good faith, Pitt saw no good reason to decide against immediate abolition of the slave trade.

Towards the end of his speech he focused on Africa. There had been enormous suffering there because of the slave trade, and the need to rectify this was 'the ground on which I rest'. The British had carried misery instead of happiness to Africa: 'False to the very principles of trade, misguided in our policy, and unmindful of our duty, what astonishing – I had almost said, what *irreparable* mischief, have we brought upon that continent'. The slave trade had retarded Africa's economic development and deprived Africa of the blessings of civilization. Britain must now atone for this national sin. It had been argued that the slave trade was too well established for British withdrawal to make much difference. But Pitt insisted that Britain should abolish its slave trade regardless of the policy of other nations. In time, Pitt was sure, they would be impressed by Britain's example, and they too would end their involvement with this evil traffic. Certainly it would be scandalous for parliament to justify delay by concluding that Britain should wait for other nations to make the first move.[41]

After the debate Wilberforce recorded that Pitt had spoken in an 'extraordinary' and 'inspired' fashion, 'with more energy and ability than were almost ever exerted in the House of Commons', and leaders of the parliamentary opposition admitted that Pitt had given an astonishing performance. Abolitionists soon published the speech as a cheap pamphlet, in order for Pitt's remarks to be disseminated as widely as possible. But the purpose of Wilberforce's motion (immediate repeal) was frustrated when Dundas carried a proposal for gradual abolition. A disappointed Pitt told the Commons:

> Every year in which you continue this abominable trade, you add thousands to the catalogue of misery, which if you could behold in a single instance, you would revolt in horror from the scene; but the size of the misery prevents you from beholding it ... I feel the infamy of the trade so heavily, the impolicy of it so clearly, that I am ashamed I have not been able to convince the house to abandon it altogether – to pronounce with one voice the immediate and total abolition.

In fact Pitt had misgivings about continuing to press for immediate abolition. He was coming under pressure from George III and cabinet colleagues, and feared that support out of doors was waning. He had tried to persuade Wilberforce to modify his motion before 2 April 1792, to give it a better chance of success, but Wilberforce had refused and Pitt felt obliged to support him.[42]

Worse was to follow the Dundas amendment. Although the Commons had sanctioned a gradual abolition of the slave trade, this was subsequently blocked in the Lords. Pitt remained sympathetic to the abolitionist cause, upholding it again in the Commons in February 1795, but he accepted that parliament was unwilling to end the trade. Reluctant to alienate George III and members of the government by persisting, and mindful of the political realities of wartime and a growing hostility towards reformers, Pitt no longer contemplated full abolition. But he did what he could. During the French wars, and partly justified as war measures, he by-passed parliament and restricted the traffic in slaves to conquered and re-conquered colonies by orders in council of 1798 and 1805.[43]

Pitt's reforming ventures in administrative, economic, financial and con- stitutional spheres – however limited their consequences, and notwithstanding his habitually cautious approach (indeed, for some his moderation was his chief recommendation) – added to his reputation as a responsible national leader and helped him to develop a politically useful rapport with public opinion. During the 1780s, when his progressive posture was at its most convincing, he could confidently rely not only on the assistance of dedicated reformers, but also the support of many people who, though not reformers themselves, could appreciate the potential benefits of the improvements he was trying to deliver. This was vital to Pitt. To survive, of course, his government needed the king's favour and a secure parliamentary majority. But Pitt valued his wider popularity too. His leader- ship style and aspirations, and patriotic identity, necessitated a popular mandate, and Pitt's presentation of himself as a sensible, conscientious reformer helped him to claim and make use of this mandate. As he estab- lished himself in power after the general election of 1784, people saw in him a leader who wanted to serve the nation rather than himself, the court or a party, and one determined to do what was necessary to improve state and society. Pitt's oft-expressed disdain for corrupt influence and factional manoeuvre further enhanced his credibility. His quest for legitimacy, facili- tated by useful reforms and patriotic rhetoric, indicated his belief that support in the nation would be an indispensable platform for political ascendancy. Indeed, the popularity gained during the 1780s became even more of an asset in the 1790s, when the domestic and external pressures of war raised the value of the government's ability to shape opinion out of doors. These developments also limited the influence of Pitt's opponents. They persistently sought popular backing too, but in the battle for the hearts and minds of the British people Pitt continued to have the upper hand.

Even before his appointment as premier Pitt had openly and directly appealed to the public. In his celebrated speech of 21 February 1783, as the Fox-North coalition prepared to replace Shelburne's administration, Pitt eschewed party spirit and 'the malice of faction', and declared that virtue mattered more to him than success. One of the foundations of political virtue, Pitt said, was fidelity to the public. Hence 'I will never engage in political enmities without a public cause. I will never forego such enmities without the public approbation'. Knowing that he would shortly be leaving office, Pitt announced that 'I can say with sincerity, I never had a wish which did not terminate in the dearest interests of the nation', and he stressed that if he was ever obliged to hold power without honour and dignity, he would give it up,

> triumphant in the conviction that my talents, humble as they are, have been earnestly, zealously and strenuously employed to the best of my apprehension, in promoting the truest welfare of my country; and that, however I may stand chargeable with weakness of understanding, or error of judgement, nothing can be imputed to my official capacity which bears the most distant connection with an interested, a corrupt, or a dishonest intention.[44]

During the crisis over Fox's India Bill, and especially at the 1784 general election, Pitt again appealed for popular approval in the knowledge that it could bestow and confirm political success. Before becoming prime minister, however, he was a relatively unknown figure. He did not even represent an 'open' or popular constituency, but sat in the Commons for the rotten borough of Appleby. Determined to raise his profile and cultivate a suitable image, he was fortunate to gain quick notoriety as an advocate of parliamentary reform. This won Pitt some useful allies, notably Wyvill and his movement, and as prime minister Pitt made much of his willingness to attend to the demands and complaints of influential groups in society. In making a case for moderate parliamentary reform in April 1785, he stressed the need for greater sympathy between politicians and people and the way in which reform would restore public respect for parliament.[45]

Pitt saw that a popular mandate could be almost as important as a parliamentary majority. Indeed, the former found expression in the latter, and at the same time Pitt's dominance in parliament impressed opinion out of doors. A favourable verdict from electors had symbolic as well as practical uses, especially in larger 'open' constituencies like the counties of Yorkshire and Middlesex, where Pitt's supporters did well from 1784 onwards. The twelve county and borough seats available in the London area were also important to Pitt, and he devoted a lot of effort (and government money) to winning and retaining them. The government took nine of the twelve at the general election of 1784, eight in 1790, and eight in 1796. By such means Pitt hoped to be seen as the nation's choice as well as the king's choice. This projection of himself as a patriotic and representative leader may also explain his attitude towards the Westminster scrutiny after the 1784 election: he wanted a popular success, and if he could gain it by damaging his rival Fox, so much the better. There were further hectic contests in Westminster in subsequent years, as government and opposition vied to control this prestigious constituency with its 12,000 voters. Pitt finally came to an arrangement with the opposition in 1790, after which the representation was shared.[46]

Apart from electioneering, Pitt cultivated his relationship with the public by encouraging and commending petitions to parliament. In this way he could make himself a spokesman for particular causes, and petitions also helped him to press for parliamentary action when he wanted it. In speaking for parliamentary reform in 1785 and slave trade abolition in 1788, he deliberately pointed to the number of popular petitions on these issues. Though Pitt became uneasy about the expansion of political participation, he balanced this concern with his continuing desire for popularity. Even when implementing the wartime repression, designed to protect the established order against radical subversives, Pitt never denied that the people had a constitutional right to petition parliament. As he told the Commons on 10 November 1795:

> no one would venture to deny the right of the people to express their opinions on political men and measures, and to discuss and assert their right of petitioning all branches of the legislature; nor was there any man who would be farther from encroaching on that right than himself. It was undoubtedly a most valuable privilege, of which nothing should deprive them.

In addition to petitions, at various times Pitt took advantage of addresses to the crown. Early in his career supporters gave him valuable assistance by rallying opinion all over the country and organizing formal addresses on such matters as Fox's India Bill, the appointment of Pitt as prime minister, and the dissolution of parliament in March 1784. Later addresses fortified Pitt and his ministry during the regency crisis (1788–89) and the disturbed 1790s, and the influence of these addresses was considerably increased when they were published in metropolitan and provincial newspapers.[47]

Pitt thought he had a clear idea of what the public wanted and deserved in its leaders. In this he followed the example of his father, whom he regarded as a model of political virtue. Indeed, Pitt wholeheartedly adopted the Chathamite goal of raising the tone of public life. His concern about reputation and character sprang naturally from this source, as did his much-vaunted reluctance to profit personally from office. Pitt appeared not to be interested in pensions or titles. His lifestyle was relatively modest. He had no lavish residences and was continually in debt, yet he studiously, even ostentatiously, avoided taking any course that might undermine his patriotic independence and make him liable to imputations of corruption. His decision not to accept the clerkship of the pells in 1784 was well received in parliament and nation. In 1788, during the regency crisis, when it seemed that he might have to give up the premiership, he refused to accept a subscription of £100,000 from City merchants and was apparently willing to return to the law in order to support himself. He had also politely declined the king's offer of financial assistance. In 1790 George III wanted to award him the Order of the Garter, but Pitt could not be persuaded to accept. The king subsequently acceded to Pitt's request that the honour should be bestowed upon his brother John, second Earl of Chatham (this was done, wrote the king, as 'a public testimony of my approbation, which will be understood as meant to the whole family'). Not until 1792 did Pitt accept a significant mark of distinction. At the king's insistence he became Warden of the Cinque Ports. This appointment was worth about £4000 a year and brought with it an impressive residence at Walmer Castle, near Deal in Kent. The money was welcome in view of Pitt's debts, but his chief motive in accepting the post may have been political, for explicit tokens of royal favour were useful to him as premier.[48]

Despite his carefully crafted reputation for probity and disinterested service, Pitt had to play the game of political bribery just like everyone else. Indeed, for many of his relatives, colleagues and supporters, political success meant personal gain, and Pitt could not strengthen himself as prime minister without responding to their expectations. In the early months of his premiership the king's willingness to listen to his patronage requests was a huge advantage. Two of Pitt's cousins were among the beneficiaries: Thomas Pitt was raised to the peerage as Baron Camelford in January 1784, and the second Earl Temple (who like most of the Grenvilles was known for his acquisitiveness) gained a promotion in the peerage in December 1784 when he was created Marquess of Buckingham. Accusations of selfish interest and arrant nepotism were not out of place, but this was how politics worked. All eighteenth-century governments built networks of support by employing the gifts and favours at their disposal. It was not unusual for Pitt to seek rewards for his cousins, moreover, in view of their political assistance. Temple had become one of his chief allies by the time he took the premiership, while Thomas Pitt was also an active politician. Though never close politically to Chatham, Thomas Pitt had risen to prominence as a supporter of Shelburne and critic of North, and in March 1783 – when George III had sought an alternative to the Fox-North coalition – he was spoken of as a serious candidate for the posts of secretary of state and leader of the Commons.

Patronage remained an essential feature of politics in this period, and Pitt's efforts to clean up the most flagrantly venal and disreputable aspects of public life indicate (among other things) his awareness of popular resentment. His hope was that, beneath a sanitized veneer, bargains that served his government could carry on relatively undisturbed, and it was important that he personally had little direct involvement with the routine business of patronage. This could be left to such deputies as Dundas, an accomplished political fixer. For much of Pitt's career, therefore, the purity of his own motives and character was rarely questioned out of doors. He managed to remain untainted. Even while his colleagues were indiscreetly feathering their own nests, Pitt was somehow excluded from the public outcry against corruption in high places. In time, however, this situation would change. Pitt's reputation was damaged by a scandal surrounding Dundas in 1805, for example, and there were ever-louder complaints that the prime minister had not pushed his economical reforms further during the 1780s and early 1790s. On the other hand, in assessing the supposed 'corruption' of Dundas (or of Pitt's regime as a whole), it is important to remember that the values and methods of the late eighteenth century subsequently fell out of favour and that later commentators have inevitably been influenced by a different agenda. The most remarkable thing about Dundas is not that he adopted any new or unique practices, but that he used the *existing* political machinery better than anyone else. He was indispensable to Pitt as a troubleshooter who did not mind getting his hands dirty and who could master the minutiae of patronage dealings and government influence.[49]

Apart from his stance as a sensible reformer, his patriotic integrity and capacity for hard work, the other main component of Pitt's public image was his relative youth. Obviously this attracted more comment during the 1780s than in later years. In cartoons and other media, the prime minister was 'Billy Pitt' and 'Master Billy'. His youth probably contributed to his celebrity as a reformer (and made him seem more progressive than he really was). Unlike other political leaders, he was free of the stigma of past failures and could present himself as a new man with energy and fresh ideas.[50]

During the 1790s some negative comment surfaced about Pitt's increasing consumption of alcohol, but characterizations of his main political opponent, the dissolute Fox, were usually far more condemnatory. At a time when the press was expanding rapidly, and when demand for information about public men and affairs reached unprecedented levels, journalists and caricaturists enjoyed a heyday. Pitt saw that good publicity and visual representations would bolster his image as patriot and reformer. Printed material had growing influence over the public mind, and for himself and his regime Pitt saw the need to manipulate the media as best he could. He soon began to enjoy cartoons about himself. Many were displayed on the walls of Holwood House, the residence near Bromley in Kent (not far from Hayes Place) purchased by Pitt in August 1785. One of the foremost caricaturists of the time, James Gillray, was awarded a pension in 1797 in recognition of his services to the government.[51]

Pitt made himself a popular politician by speaking for, taking up and implementing a range of reforms. But how genuine and thorough a reformer was he? The preceding discussion has shown that in most cases his desire was for continuity rather than change. Though there were some important innovations, Pitt's approach was generally cautious and piecemeal. He *was* a committed reformer, but on his own terms. In seeking popularity, indeed, there was always the proviso that he should not appear to be the tool of public opinion, and he was willing to risk losing support when convinced that a particular measure (such as an increase in taxation) was necessary. There was more to Pitt's concept of patriotic independence and virtue than devoted service from his side. In return, influential segments of the British public should not expect him to do everything they wanted. Free from the control of king and party, Pitt also had to be free from the dictates of extra-parliamentary opinion. This was precisely why many people trusted him.

Others, of course, were annoyed by his failure to respond to their demands (there were tax riots during 1785, for example, and Pitt's coach was stoned in November of that year). If Pitt respected public opinion, he also pointed out that the people could not expect to dominate their representatives in parliament. This would not be in keeping with the constitution. In January 1798, noting the protests against his decision to raise assessed taxes, Pitt declared that the nation's long-term interests mattered more than the changing likes and dislikes of the people.[52] These elitist attitudes were premised on Pitt's notion that political authority should be exercised from the top down. His viewpoint was essentially that from the government's front bench in the Commons. During his career he was not in opposition for long, and rarely did he experience the force and excitement of popular politics. His first constituency was the rotten borough of Appleby, whose 250 electors were controlled by Sir James Lowther. From the general election of 1784 until his death in 1806, Pitt sat for Cambridge University. This was a more independent constituency, but hardly 'open', and, again, sheltered from the pressures of popular electioneering.[53]

As the years passed Pitt's position on reform became more equivocal, and he lost interest in several progressive causes with which he had previously associated himself. This disappointed many who had supported him in the early part of his career, but it would be inappropriate to blame Pitt alone for any lack of achievement in particular areas of reforming activity. Though he had the will of a reformer, and demonstrated this repeatedly before the outbreak of war in 1793, political conditions did not always favour his tactics and goals, and some of his improvements were blocked or failed to work as intended. Even during the 1780s he faced opposition within the cabinet, most notably from lord chancellor Thurlow and home secretary Sydney, who were against parliamentary reform, abolition of the slave trade and various other measures contemplated by Pitt. George III was also unsympathetic. Pitt had no ally in the cabinet who was strong enough to help him overcome these obstacles. The likeliest prospect was Richmond, but though a keen reformer he proved unreliable.

Serious disagreements on policy threatened the government's unity, which made it even more important for Pitt to choose his moment and method carefully. Quarrels developed not only because of what Pitt wanted, but also because of his attempts to make other ministers co-operate. In 1785 Thurlow and Sydney used their influence in the Lords to stop a measure to regulate county elections. In the following year the measure was re-introduced. This time Thurlow was absent through illness, and Pitt provoked deep resentment by pressing Sydney to let it through. In 1788 Pitt backed Sir William Dolben's bill to improve conditions for slaves on the 'middle passage' from Africa to the Americas. Thurlow and Sydney obstructed the bill, but Pitt insisted that if it were lost he would not feel able to serve in the same administration as anyone who opposed it. He got his way, but again there was considerable ill feeling.[54]

The abandonment of some of Pitt's initiatives, and much slower pace of change from the late 1780s, might indicate that Pitt was not a committed reformer. Perhaps the French Revolution and subsequent wars turned him – like so many others – against reform, which could not remain the priority (if indeed it ever had been) when the watchwords had to be security and order. Certainly the impact of revolution and war abroad, and radical agitation and new political challenges at home, should not be under-estimated. But nor can we ignore Pitt's authentic desire for useful and moderate emendation. Reform continued even after the French Revolution became more violent and unstable during the summer of 1792, and the war between Britain and France may have inhibited Pittite improvements, but it did not halt them completely.

To the Foxites and their successors, Pitt cynically turned his back on reform because he had to satisfy the corrupt interests controlling court and government, and sought above all to maintain his personal grip on power. He created alarm about the spread of French revolutionary ideas, and needlessly prolonged the war against France, in order to extinguish liberties and silence his political opponents. According to this version of events, Pitt cannot have been genuine about reform. The Foxite analysis offers a salutary reminder that contemporary and subsequent commentators saw in Pitt what they wanted to see. Naturally his rivals were quick to seize on any evidence of inconsistency or, even better for them, apparent betrayal of causes (like parliamentary reform). Among reformers who had pinned their hopes on Pitt, meanwhile, there was disagreement. Some were reluctant to admit that they had been wrong about him and preferred to focus on what he achieved rather than on what was left undone. Others decided that there was more of the reactionary than the reformer in Pitt. Whatever the preferred explanation, the idea spread that Pitt had somehow changed, and the fact that the reforming will of his early career had faded by the 1790s was admitted even by some of his friends and supporters. Wilberforce believed that the prime minister's closer association with less idealistic politicians prompted him to lose interest in reform: his character and motives were brought down to their level as he immersed himself in government business and the exercise of power.[55]

Pitt's position has sometimes been misjudged because various critics have had their own axes to grind. In assessing Pitt's performance in the light of their particular principles or designs, they fail fully to appreciate the context in which he operated. Pitt had little in common with the radicals of his own day or the *laissez-faire* liberals of a later generation. He was a reformer on his own terms. His methods and aspirations were those of the 'patriot', as defined on eighteenth-century lines (especially those laid down by his father). In calm times it was appropriate to introduce moderate measures, Pitt thought, with the aim of correcting obvious abuses. In his view there was no need fundamentally to change society, economy or the constitution, but a responsible leader ought to try and make them function better and, if any major flaw emerged, respond with a suitable plan of action. The preference was always for preservation and improvement rather than change. Pitt wanted to protect established frameworks and was usually content to work within them. Too much can be made of his early commitment to parliamentary reform. This was only one issue among many, and Pitt's record depends on the sum of his efforts in several fields, not merely the constitutional.

At the same time, his views on parliamentary reform are worth reconsidering because they accurately reflect the patriot agenda. Pitt never suggested that the constitution was basically unsound. The problem was that some of its components had been corrupted. Specifically, the faltering relationship between parliament and people had to be repaired. Pitt admired the constitution as the foundation of national greatness, but he saw that all its parts had to be brought into a proper harmony if it was to facilitate political stability, social peace and economic prosperity. Hence his point in May 1783, that he wanted not to rearrange but to restore vigour to the constitution, and his remarks of May 1791 and April 1792 about the propriety of mild and gradual reform – the only way to enhance purity and balance within the constitution. In fact, the constitution had its own self-correcting mechanisms, and reform was needed only to put these to good use so that inadequacies relating to the electoral system and government accountability could be safely addressed.[56]

If Pitt was a cautious reformer by political conviction, personal temperament also played its part. He disliked anomalies and inefficiency, and was a natural improver, constantly thinking about how to make things run more smoothly. Pitt indulged this fascination in his hobbies of architecture and landscape gardening, but in public life he knew that improvements had to be attempted in a measured, uncontroversial manner, and he developed a clear sense of necessity and timing. He could become very enthusiastic about a project, but also quick to drop it. This stop-start method and the uneven pace of activity reflect both the limits of his approach to reform, and the limits imposed by contemporary political conditions. Pitt often encountered difficulties because of his habit of devoting himself entirely to one big problem. Other business that required action was often sidelined (much to the annoyance of Pitt's allies and officials, who found themselves competing for his attention). Pitt preferred to concentrate on matters that really moved him, and everything else was neglected while this fixation lasted. Even immediate needs could be forgotten: payment of a wartime subsidy to Prussia was delayed during the spring of 1794 because Pitt was preoccupied with an official investigation of radical associations, and he was slow to respond to a crisis in the Irish administration of early 1795 because the ministry was then being pressed to open peace negotiations with France.[57]

Pitt had no blueprint for government. Rarely did his reforming work reveal any system or focus, and he tended to take up issues and formulate proposals according to his own fancy. When obstructed he was normally willing to alter or abandon chosen policies, and as a reformer he remained pragmatic and flexible. He was not tied to any special dogma. His commitments were conditional. He liked to examine both sides of an issue. On sinecures, for instance, he recognized the need to respond to pressure for retrenchment while also seeing in sinecures a necessary reward for loyal public service. Another important feature of Pitt's character was his longing to lead, his need to feel that he could superintend the main activities of the government. Paradoxically, this may have increased confusion at the centre of power because his attention span could be short. He continually moved about from issue to issue. If an important matter arose and required government action, Pitt set about framing a response. If trouble surfaced in one area, he turned to another. He tried constantly to clarify issues in his own mind. The patriotic minister, he believed, had to define, examine and solve the nation's problems. But he found that public affairs could not always be managed in this fashion.

Pitt knew that no reform could work as intended unless circumstances were favourable. Often they were not. In the late eighteenth century, most improving ventures came up against the strong respect for tradition. The very nature of aristocratic government also created difficulties. Elite and institutional inertia, the scramble for patronage, the lack of specialist staff and information, and a predilection for order and stability made reform of almost any kind seem an inconvenient disturbance. In addition, Pitt did not have direct authority over all parts of the government, only those connected to or dependent upon the treasury. Some of his colleagues ran their departments quite independently (and, strictly speaking, they answered to George III, not to Pitt, and it was the king who appointed them). Averse to wrangling and discord, Pitt had to be wary when proposing reforms. For his main task, restoring the public finances, there was general approval. Many of Pitt's other reforms were organized around this core goal, but they could not be rushed. To attempt too much too quickly, Pitt realized, would be self-defeating.

Difficulties in one sphere of reforming activity often created new problems elsewhere. In the mid-1780s, when Pitt introduced a scheme for mail coaches and higher postal charges (in line with his drive to increase efficiency and raise revenue), there was resistance within the post office. This led to the dismissal of one of the postmasters general, and an embarrassing public discussion of post office abuses.[58] In turn, Pitt fell out with the comptroller of the navy, Sir Charles Middleton. Pitt had worked closely with Middleton, and in 1787 resisted the efforts of Viscount Howe, first lord of the admiralty, to have Middleton removed. Howe disliked Middleton's reforms, and this was one of the reasons why he resigned from Pitt's cabinet in 1788. Then

Middleton resigned in 1790, when Pitt delayed the publication of an official report on the navy. Pitt was holding back all such reports because they were likely to rekindle inconvenient arguments about the post office. (Another consideration was that George III would expect to be consulted about matters affecting the navy, and Pitt thought it best not to burden him so soon after the serious illness that had caused the regency crisis.) The post office dispute also led Pitt to shelve the reports of the committee on fees, which he had intended to refer to the privy council.[59]

The French Revolution and subsequent wars greatly changed the political environment. Pitt accepted that the methods and duties of a reforming prime minister were shaped by the course of events, and that the needs and opportunities of wartime would not be the same as those of peacetime. But it is important to remember that the pace of reform had already declined before the French Revolution. Britain's return to international influence meant that Pitt began to attend more to foreign policy, and between 1787 and 1790 he was involved in several international disputes. Domestically there were other developments demanding Pitt's attention, especially the regency crisis and a lengthy struggle to oust the obstructive lord chancellor Thurlow (not resolved until 1792). In February 1793 Britain went to war with revolutionary France. It was therefore impossible for Pitt to devote much time and energy to reform in these years, even had he planned to, and though he was still eager to promote useful improvements, circumstances obliged him to deal with more urgent matters. Nevertheless, he played a leading role in efforts to abolish the slave trade in the late 1780s and early 1790s, helped to reform the government of Canada, and defended and when possible extended his financial reforms. He was able to improve the sinking fund system in 1792, paying £400,000 directly into the fund, adding £200,000 to the regular annual payment into the fund, and arranging that 1 per cent of each new loan would automatically go towards paying back that loan. There were further efforts to ensure a more efficient collection of duties (the responsibilities of the excise department were extended in 1789 and 1790) and to combat smuggling (at the end of the 1790s Pitt created the Thames river police and enclosed the London docks). The management of crown lands continued to improve during the 1790s, and the reports of the committee on fees were finally referred to the privy council. Some of their recommendations were adopted after 1793 in the treasury, post office, home and foreign offices, navy board, admiralty and victualling department.[60]

Problems associated with the war and domestic unrest limited opportunities for reform. Pitt necessarily became more restrained. Innovation was inadvisable: the time was not right, and there was no groundswell of opinion pressing for it. Pitt's task, therefore, was to keep government on a steady course. By the mid-1790s the prime minister was apparently thinking more about repression than reform.[61] But it is safe to assume that different political conditions would have seen him pursue different policies. In any case, though war did make it more difficult to formulate, justify and implement reforms, significant change continued. Arrangements for freer trade were included in the treaty of amity, commerce and navigation (the 'Jay treaty') concluded with the United States in November 1794,[62] and Pitt's desire for a closer supervision of public expenditure did not abate one jot. If anything, government growth and the huge cost of the war made Pitt even more anxious about financial probity and administrative efficiency.

The increase in government activity during the war inevitably generated more fees, and there was a terrific public outcry as officials profited while the people struggled to pay heavier taxes. Pitt's modest economical reforms had to be pushed forward. In 1797 all fee taking by officials in the war office was curtailed and Pitt persuaded the Commons to set up a select committee on public finance. The latter manoeuvre was really an attempt to temporize. MPs were pressing for more, and Pitt thought that he could deflect pressure by offering a committee. He also agreed to establish a privy council committee on the coinage in order to dissuade parliament from taking up the question. Yet he did not fail to act when he felt he could, as when he extended the remit of the tax office, and even his temporizing techniques could have positive consequences, for there was eventually a marked improvement in the quality of the coinage. In spite of all this, however, it cannot be denied that the cost and scale of the war made more rapid and far-reaching changes impossible; and, although Pitt had done much to reorganize the administrative system, abuses, jobbery and inefficiency remained.[63]

Pitt's reforming activity became less pronounced after the French Revolution for two main reasons: his commitment to reforms had always been conditional, and the political world in which he had to operate was changing. Therefore a dichotomy between the 'reformer' of the 1780s and 'reactionary' of the 1790s is far too crude and simplistic. The only cause clearly abandoned by Pitt was parliamentary reform, and as far as he was concerned his stance on this issue was perfectly logical. He had concluded by about 1790 that conditions were not suitable for parliamentary reform. The revolution in France, with all its turmoil and uncertainty, could not be imitated to the slightest degree in Britain, and to allow the question to be repeatedly agitated in parliament and out of doors would inevitably destabilize society, with possibly catastrophic results. Pitt knew that most of the informed, influential and propertied men who generated respectable public opinion were not

ready for parliamentary reform. Nor could he forget that his own mild and
piecemeal proposals had been blocked in the Commons. Pitt openly stated
that when circumstances altered, he would be willing to try again. As he
reiterated to the Commons in March 1790, parliamentary reform was a
cause 'to which, after the most mature deliberation, he continued to be as
firm and zealous a friend as ever'. But it was not useful or appropriate to
press the matter in a period of revolution and war, and by May 1797 Pitt
had convinced himself that there was no serious practical grievance against
the electoral system.[64]

On constitutional affairs, therefore, his tone grew increasingly conservative. Nevertheless, the nature of government did change during the war,
partly because war necessitated certain innovations. New departments were
created (such as the aliens office and transport board), and a new cabinet
post – that of secretary of state for war – to which Dundas was appointed
in July 1794.[65] Indeed, despite Pitt's aversion to fundamental change, his
test of necessity prompted two highly controversial reforms during the war:
the introduction of income tax in 1799 and the legislative union with Ireland
of 1801. The war did not rule out substantial reform, though it did mean
that Pitt's formerly wide-ranging interests were narrowed. There could be
no rapid or general moves, and none were attempted. Instead, Pitt focused
on financial and administrative problems that were closely related to the
management of the war. If he lost support in some quarters because of his
apparent reluctance to reform during the 1790s, he gained much more by
responding in a responsible 'patriotic' manner to the national emergency.

5

Leadership

Significant as it was, Pitt's rapport with public opinion was only one of several determinants of his leadership style. His relationship with the king, dealings with cabinet colleagues and position within the government, and relationship with and influence in parliament, were all of more immediate importance to a political leader who knew that survival and success depended on closeness to the sources of real power and mastery of the techniques of employing and increasing that power.

George III's backing was an essential asset at a time when the crown was still a considerable political force and, in fact as well as constitutional rhetoric, the source of executive power. During the first twenty-three years of his reign George III had appointed nine prime ministers, including Pitt's father (who led the government as lord privy seal from July 1766 to October 1768). If Pitt benefited from the residual popularity of his father's name and principles in the nation, this association was a potential disadvantage at court, for George III remembered Chatham as assertive and arrogant. The king was slow to forgive a perceived affront, indeed, and resented Pitt the Younger's refusal to accept the premiership in March 1783. Pitt also had misgivings about the king, believing that quarrels with the court had damaged his father's health and effectively ruined his career. Schooled in the Whig tradition, Pitt held that the crown's political influence should be limited. He recognized that the crown had a role to play, and was willing to facilitate this, but deemed any attempt to increase royal power as a threat to constitutional balance. Crucially, Pitt was not prepared to govern as the creature of improper executive influence, and took great pains to demonstrate that as prime minister he remained the independent patriot (hence his eagerness to exclude some notorious allies of the court from the cabinet). Even while defending and justifying the king's prerogatives, Pitt was suspicious of royal power.[1] This seems paradoxical, but in fact his position is not difficult to understand. Shrewd and pragmatic, he was not merely fighting his father's battles. Pitt adapted his own goals and methods as various needs arose and new political situations unfolded. Conditions had changed since Chatham's day.

It was not long after Pitt entered parliament that his driving ambition and self-confidence took over. He wanted to be premier and was sure he could govern well. He accepted that George III would exert influence, in the manner suggested by constitutional convention. The king wanted no more than this. George III was a highly conscientious monarch. Although he was determined to express his views on policies and personnel, and to shape government activity in the service of his subjects, he had no wish to overstep the proper boundaries. On this general point George III and Pitt occupied common ground. On particulars there could be friction, however, since some of the boundaries were not fixed. Much depended on the working relationship between king and chief minister. Pitt and George III were never close personally, but they respected and valued each other, not least because they knew that any breach between them would strengthen their political opponents. After the vicissitudes of 1782 and 1783, both men had good reason to combine in pursuit of ministerial stability. George III realized that Pitt was a leader he could deal with, and a barrier against Fox. Pitt was grateful for the king's confidence, knew that his administration would not last without George III's help, and saw that royal goodwill had to be cultivated and could not be taken for granted.

It took time for Pitt's relationship with the king to become settled and secure. Initially Pitt's opinions, background and relative inexperience made him awkward in his dealings with George III, while the king and his allies (notably Thurlow and Robinson) were uneasy about Pitt's adherence to Chathamite ideas and commitment to parliamentary reform. George III was by now an adept politician. In view of this Pitt had to tread carefully. He was also aware that the king had powerful supporters in parliament and government, and that disagreement on questions of special concern to the court – especially parliamentary reform, the slave trade and foreign policy – could easily develop into a struggle that might bring his ministry down. Pitt quickly learned how best to handle the king. He was flexible and patient, and repeatedly managed to take advantage of favourable opportunities. George III was more dogmatic than Pitt, preferring to see things in black and white, which meant that the successful working relationship between king and premier rested mainly upon Pitt's temperament. In negotiations with George III Pitt was rather more disciplined than his father had been, and knew when not to demand his own way. Pitt was also assisted by the miscalculations of Fox. By maintaining that royal power was at the root of all political evil, and engaging in a personal battle with the king, Fox ensured that George III would value Pitt even more highly as adviser and defender. The king soon grasped that he could trust Pitt. What need was there for the crown to interfere? Pitt could be left free to govern on the well-founded assumption that as prime minister he would respect the crown's position and avoid any departure from established constitutional practice.[2]

Knowing that a split could bring disaster, and equally committed to the raising of standards in public life, George III and Pitt exercised self-restraint and when necessary agreed to disagree on particular matters. The king did not try to prevent Pitt from pursuing reforms, although he occasionally stipulated that Pitt should do so in his individual capacity, as a private member, and that the measures in question should not become government policy. Pitt proposed this arrangement himself on parliamentary reform early in 1784. He knew that George III and the 'king's friends' opposed parliamentary reform, and they decided that it was safer to let Pitt take charge of the subject rather than leave it to extra-parliamentary radicals. Pitt may have hoped to persuade the king to instruct his allies in parliament to vote for a mild reform. He told George III that, even though it would not be a government bill, its rejection might undermine general confidence in the ministry, especially if it was defeated 'by the weight of those who are supposed to be connected with the government'. This 'would render every future effort in your Majesty's service but too probably fruitless and ineffectual'. Pitt knew he could not force the king to agree, however, and the home secretary, Sydney, confirmed to George III that ultimately Pitt would not act against the king's wishes. So the king could bargain from a position of strength. He suggested that if Pitt honestly thought parliamentary reform to be necessary, he should go before parliament to explain himself and the king would not get involved, but Pitt should not try to use his position as premier to compel anyone to vote for reform. Of course it was widely known that the king opposed parliamentary reform, and his silence was no help to Pitt. Allies of the court were mostly conservative anyway. They voted with the majority against Pitt on 18 April 1785, and his motion for leave to bring in a parliamentary reform bill was defeated.[3] Pitt's level-headed acceptance of this defeat impressed George III and reinforced his confidence in the premier. Pitt's fidelity to the constitution, as the king understood it, was further demonstrated when the prime minister argued against repeal of the Test and Corporation Acts in 1787, 1789 and 1790, and against parliamentary reform during the 1790s.

Many of Pitt's administrative and financial reforms gained a sympathetic reception at court. The king backed his programme for national recovery after the American war and shared his desire for peace and prosperity. George III expressed approval for Pitt's tax reforms and sinking fund, the commercial treaty with France, and the gradual reorganization of public revenue and expenditure. These areas of policy did not directly affect the crown, and the king's limited understanding of complicated financial and economic questions hardly qualified him to raise objections. Arguments were far more likely to arise on matters relating to patronage and the royal family.[4]

George III employed the crown's rights and status as political patron to their fullest extent. He kept himself informed of all the lobbying for appointments, bargains and favours, and either in person or through willing agents headed some of the networks of reciprocal obligation upon which the system of government rested. Though Pitt often complained about the need to accommodate individuals or groups who might otherwise turn against him, he had no choice but to attend to them and knew how important patronage was to his ministry's survival. The Fox-North coalition had been seriously handicapped in 1783 because the king had deprived it of patronage, and when the regency crisis began in 1788 Pitt tried to ensure that, if his opponents toppled him, they would lack the necessary patronage capabilities to establish themselves in government. He therefore proposed that the Prince of Wales, as regent, should only be granted limited powers (there would be no royal household appointments, grants of crown property or reversions to offices; no peerages, except to royal princes when they came of age; and most of the other appointments at the regent's disposal were only to be held during the crown's pleasure, that is, they could easily be terminated). As prime minister Pitt used patronage wisely, attracting support, rewarding loyalty, and showing men of talent and ambition that there was more to gain from adherence to the ministry than from siding with the opposition. In requesting favours from the king, he often stressed that government business could not be conducted without them, and that, if requests were turned down, public opinion and the parliamentary opposition would conclude that the prime minister no longer enjoyed the king's backing. It was vital for Pitt as a political leader to obtain for his associates the appointments, honours and other benefits they desired, and thereby to demonstrate that the government retained royal confidence. It was also significant that Pitt rarely accepted anything for himself (he had been prime minister for nearly nine years before he became Warden of the Cinque Ports). This was a matter of personal pride and public reputation: Pitt's leadership style required him to leave observers in no doubt of his patriotic virtue and independence from the court. His patronage requests were almost always for colleagues and supporters, and with the king's co-operation he was able to gratify many of them. When he delivered on his promises, he frustrated the opposition and rendered his regime more secure.

George III was never a pushover, however, and when he decided to make a stand it was difficult, sometimes impossible, for Pitt to change his mind. Generally the king was amenable, but for those individuals who had already received (in his opinion) what their talents or services merited, he was reluctant to make further gestures. Pitt could not obtain a dukedom for his demanding cousin Temple. The king twice refused to bestow this honour (in 1784 and 1789), though Temple was created Marquess of Buckingham in 1784.[5] The king also set a limit to the advancement of two of Pitt's close friends: George Pretyman, Pitt's private secretary and former tutor, and the lawyer Richard Pepper Arden. In 1787 Pretyman was appointed Bishop of Lincoln. Pitt also wanted to make him Dean of St Paul's, and there was a quarrel before the king finally agreed. Later, in 1805, when Pitt proposed that Pretyman should be named as the new Archbishop of Canterbury, George III ruled this out. As for Pepper Arden, the king was willing to make him attorney general (March 1784) and master of the rolls (June 1788), but in 1799 would not advance him to the office of lord chief justice. Another candidate was preferred, and Pepper Arden had to wait until May 1801 for the promotion he sought.[6]

Having to accept George III's decision in disputed cases was a cause of much annoyance to Pitt, who did not like others to regard him merely as the king's servant. Pitt resented the fact that the king appeared to be the fount of patronage, and responded angrily when applicants made claims to him on the grounds of attachment to the crown. Pitt wanted to be in charge of the government, and to be *seen* to be in charge. This is why, though he had to include royal favourites Thurlow and Howe in the cabinet in December 1783 (not least because other men of rank had refused to join it), he only brought George III's former confidants Jenkinson and Robinson into office years later. He intended it to be clearly understood that they were joining the administration on *his* terms (Jenkinson, now Lord Hawkesbury, became president of the board of trade in August 1786, and Robinson was appointed surveyor general of woods and forests in December 1787). Despite these tensions between the king and Pitt, George III tended not to make difficulties on patronage, and Pitt was careful not to antagonize the king with unreasonable or excessive applications. It is true that by 1790 the king was expressing concern about the growing number of peerages requested by Pitt. George III pointed out that a larger House of Lords would be more difficult to manage, and that the dignity of the peerage would be undermined unless creations and promotions were made more sparingly. Yet he continued to be guided by Pitt's advice on this matter, making titles and honours available for the prime minister's nominees as well as his own favourites.

George III jealously guarded any appointment that by convention was left to the king's personal discretion, such as the lord chancellorship,[7] and he disliked any suggestion of political bargaining with respect to promotions in the church, law and armed forces. The king's preferences inconvenienced Pitt, who was constantly pressed by influential patrons to advance their own relatives and clients, some of whom had little else to recommend them. In approaching the king, therefore, Pitt often had to emphasize the identity and status of the patron rather than the special qualities of the candidate for preferment. George III might refuse applications on various grounds. Sometimes he had made previous arrangements himself, and was unwilling to change them, or he objected to Pitt's nominee for reasons of character, or insisted that there was a far more suitable candidate available. George III occasionally asked Pitt to consult others, named by the king himself, before recommending anyone for particular posts. The king expected candidates for a bishopric to have certain personal qualities and a high standard of education. As for the armed forces, Pitt was aware of George III's desire to supervise military and naval appointments closely, and before the war did not get involved unless he had to for political reasons. Only when colleagues were disappointed or offended did he venture to offer the king his own suggestions.[8]

In May 1786 there was a typical exchange between Pitt and the king (and one that offers a useful insight into their working relationship) concerning an ecclesiastical vacancy in Worcester. An important government supporter, the second Earl Bathurst, had an interest in the post, and Pitt recommended his nominee to George III. The king responded:

> Mr Pitt has I believe forgot that when Dr Langford at the request of Lord Sydney had the last vacant Stall at Worcester, I waived the application of the Bishop of Worcester for his relation and Chaplain, but assured the Bishop he should have the next in that Church. Mr Pitt, on my mentioning it to him in the winter, said he remembered the gentleman at Cambridge. I think his name is Kilbert. Therefore Lord Bathurst must wait for some other Prebendary.

Pitt could do nothing but accept.

> Mr Pitt recollects your Majesty's having made mention of the Bishop's application, but it escaped his memory that your Majesty gave any directions concerning the next vacancy, or he would have avoided giving your Majesty the trouble of Lord Bathurst's application, and producing the sort of embarrassment which it now occasions.[9]

Pitt knew better than to jeopardize his relationship with the king by seeking to control all aspects of patronage. He chose not to get into arguments needlessly, and mastered the art of graceful retreat. When quarrels arose, Pitt made sure that they did no permanent damage. Often he and the king would try to outmanoeuvre each other, making arrangements before the other could suggest a nominee. Fortunately, for both of them, even serious conflicts were eventually settled. In 1794 there was a dispute concerning George III's favourite Howe (the first Viscount Howe, who had served in Pitt's cabinet as first lord of the admiralty from December 1783 to July 1788, and been created Earl Howe in 1788). On 1 June 1794 Howe won a great naval victory over the French off the Brittany coast. There was a vacancy in the Order of the Garter, and the king promised to reward Howe with this honour, but Pitt wanted it for the Duke of Portland. Significant inducements were needed, Pitt explained, in order to attach the Portland Whigs to the government. When the king refused to gratify Portland, Pitt suggested that Howe could be offered a marquisate instead of the Garter, and persuaded Howe to assure George III that he was willing for Portland to take precedence. The king accepted this arrangement, did not lose face, and Pitt's alliance with Portland and his followers went ahead. In the event Howe refused the marquisate, but in 1797 the king was finally able to offer him the Garter as promised three years earlier.[10]

In addition to patronage matters, Pitt's relationship with George III was complicated by the financial and personal problems of the royal family. The civil list had become a major political issue, with demands raised both in parliament and out of doors for cheaper government and curbs on royal extravagance. Pitt knew that he could win over independent and economy-minded MPs, and public opinion, by working out a settlement. But this was no easy task. The civil list had been established to meet the crown's private and public needs. It was meant to cover expenses incurred by the royal family (which was growing in size) *and* many of the costs of government. By the 1780s it was clear that the civil list was inadequate and that royal debts would continue to rise quickly unless a remedy could be found. George III resented any attempts to interfere with royal finances, however, which hampered Pitt's efforts, and by far the worst spendthrift in the royal family was the Prince of Wales, an ally of the Foxites. Pitt secured parliamentary grants in 1784 and 1786 to pay arrears on the civil list.[11] In return, George III reluctantly agreed to issue statements of royal expenditure (the Commons insisted). The indebtedness of the Prince of Wales remained a cause for concern, though, and he proved completely uncooperative when it was suggested to him that money might be made available if he abandoned the parliamentary opposition. He also refused to accept his father's offer of assistance, because the king required full details of how the debts had been incurred and a binding commitment from the prince that he would live within his means in future. The prince's scandalous lifestyle brought the monarchy increasingly into disrepute, which added to Pitt's desire for a settlement. Through Dundas, who was on good terms with the Prince of Wales (they sometimes got drunk together), Pitt tried to arrange the gradual redemption of the prince's debts and payment to him of a fixed annual sum from the civil list. After much negotiation George III, the Prince of Wales and the Commons accepted the plan, despite yet another complication in the form of the prince's secret marriage (1785) to a Catholic widow, Maria Fitzherbert. This was illegal under the 1701 Act of Settlement (which ensured the Protestant succession) and 1772 Royal Marriages Act (by which members of the royal family could not marry without the sovereign's consent). The financial package did not prompt the Prince of Wales to change his ways or withdraw from opposition politics, and this made the regency crisis all the more serious for Pitt. It highlighted his dependence on George III and created a situation in which a ministry dominated by Foxites threatened to replace his own. The regency crisis also made Pitt even more personally objectionable to the Prince of Wales.[12]

The civil list again required Pitt's attention during the 1790s, as the cost of government rapidly increased and the disparity between the crown's income and the demands upon it grew wider. Parliament had already approved generous grants, and was reluctant to give more, and from 1793 the war necessitated massive government expenditure and heavier taxation, rekindling popular demands for retrenchment and reform. Pitt could not request more money for the royal family without spurring on extra-parliamentary protest, and MPs were sure to demand greater parliamentary controls, which would annoy George III. Matters came to a head in 1794. The financial embarrassment of the Prince of Wales forced him to co-operate with his father. In return for more money he agreed to secure the line of succession by marrying (legitimately) and producing an heir. Pitt had to persuade parliament to approve the necessary grants. Many government supporters disapproved of them, and Pitt's leadership began to be questioned. In the spring of 1795, faced with obstruction in the Commons, he settled for a lower sum than that expected by George III and the Prince of Wales. The angry king, who had demanded that the original plan should be adhered to, now complained that the prince was not sufficiently protected from his creditors. One of the prime minister's young followers, George Canning, noted on 14 May:

> Pitt has got into a scrape, not indeed of his own making – for there was no way of avoiding the business on his part ... There is nothing left but different modifications of which he must adopt the best, or the worst, as the torrent of popular inclination out of doors, and of country gentlemen's fancies within may carry him. All modes that have been or can be proposed in so disgraceful and calamitous a business are bad.

In addition, the prince's marriage (1795) to Caroline of Brunswick soon

ended in an acrimonious separation. There never was a lasting rapprochement between the Prince of Wales and the king, and the prince continued
to despise Pitt.[13]

As the civil list system and financial independence of the crown declined,
parliamentary control over government expenditure and the finances of the
royal family increased. After the problems of 1795, and faced by the pressures
of domestic administration and the war effort, Pitt tried to minimize the
controversy surrounding royal finance. He refrained from applying to parliament for money to cover civil list arrears until such times as further
delay became impossible, and rather than add new charges to the civil list
he obtained special grants in order for the government to meet its obligations. By 1799 these grants covered more government expenditure than did
the civil list. Pitt also used parliamentary grants to provide for the king's
children as they came of age. In June 1800 George III asked for a formal
recognition of the distinction between his personal property and the property
of the crown, so that he could make private provision for members of his
family. The necessary legislation was guided through parliament, but Pitt
insisted that the king should pay tax on his private income. This sacrifice,
thought the prime minister, would strengthen the people's attachment to
George III: they would love him more for taking a share of wartime burdens.
Indeed, one of the general results of Pitt's civil list and associated reforms
was that they helped to raise the reputation of the crown. Despite the
Foxites' anti-court agenda, based on old Rockingham warnings about executive corruption and dangerous royal influence, it became obvious that
George III did not have the financial means to manipulate the political
system as his enemies claimed.[14]

In dealing with the monarch Pitt's ability to get what he wanted was
greatly enhanced when he could demonstrate that he was backed by a united
cabinet. His influence in cabinet rose through the 1780s and he was usually
able to make sure that ministerial colleagues followed his lead. The king's
favourite, Thurlow, proved to be an obstructive force as lord chancellor,
but Pitt often managed to circumvent his scheming and after a long struggle
Thurlow was removed from office in June 1792. Pitt's cabinet became more
Whiggish in profile, and potentially less complaisant towards the crown,
with the inclusion of Portland's group in July 1794. Meanwhile, those
ministers who from time to time had disagreed with Pitt nevertheless
remained loyal (preferring to be recorded in cabinet papers as absent, for
instance, rather than dissentient), which meant that George III could not
use them against Pitt. During the 1790s the war against France prompted
the king to involve himself in many matters relating to national defence,
war strategy and foreign policy. Yet Pitt, Grenville (foreign secretary) and

Dundas (war secretary), the dominant ministerial trio, were able to persuade him to accept most of their decisions. They were better informed than he was and acted with the cabinet's backing. Since there was no obvious alternative government available, Pitt could use ministerial unity and persistence to overcome royal objections. But he had to be tactful, for if he offended or humiliated the king their relationship would collapse. Pitt never denied that George III had the right to dismiss as well as appoint his advisers, although in practice it could only be used in certain circumstances. Pitt's manner, therefore, was polite and formal. When George III blocked something for which Pitt had cabinet approval, he reminded the king of the merits of what he was proposing and sometimes offered to take the matter back to the cabinet so that ministers might reconsider it along with the king's remarks. If the king wanted to consult a third person, Pitt made sure beforehand that the person in question would know what to say (as in October 1796, when Pitt's peace envoy Lord Malmesbury had an audience with George III before leaving for France; the king was not in favour of peace talks at this juncture).

Pitt preferred to put matters to George III in writing rather than personally, because he could not be sure of controlling the conversation. The king would interrupt, often straying from the point, and etiquette dictated that the prime minister could not resume until the king stopped speaking. As the relationship between Pitt and George III became more settled, it contributed enormously to Pitt's political ascendancy and facilitated effective government. That there was never much personal sympathy or affection between monarch and minister did not seem to matter. Like Chatham before him, Pitt tended to treat the king as an institution, not a person, and preferred to use official channels (especially when difficult issues arose) rather than face-to-face contact. They found little to talk about, indeed, apart from public affairs. Pitt had no wife or children, did not share the king's interests in agriculture and the arts, and was rarely in the king's private company. Their relationship remained respectful, formal and reserved.[15]

The vital importance of royal support to Pitt was highlighted by the regency crisis. In November 1788 George III began to show signs of mental deterioration (probably a symptom of porphyria, an inherited disease affecting the body's metabolism). Pitt knew that the king's incapacity, if it proved permanent, would necessitate a regency, which in turn would rob him of essential royal favour. In the hope that George III would recover, Pitt maintained that the regency should be defined by parliament. In contrast, Foxites argued that the Prince of Wales had an inherent right immediately to assume the powers that George III could no longer exercise.

But the precedents were not clear, and there was confusion about whether George III should be regarded as absent, or whether the situation could properly be treated like a royal minority. Excitement grew as newspapers, pamphlets and prints commented on the crisis, and government and opposition issued streams of self-serving propaganda. Town and county meetings were organized, addresses were sent to parliament, and preparations were made in many constituencies in case there was a dissolution.

To Fox the king was constitutionally dead and should be regarded also as physically dead. By all the rules governing property and inheritance George III's heir must succeed, and to interfere with this process would be to threaten the foundations of British law and society. Pitt, on the other hand, regarded the throne as temporarily unoccupied, and argued that it was for parliament to determine who should exercise royal powers, and on what terms. In some respects the battles of 1783 were being fought again. Then the focus had been on the extent of the royal prerogative; now the question concerned who should exercise it. Only the establishment of an unlimited regency could free Fox from the prospect of having to compromise with the men who had triumphed in 1/83. This would also free him from having to rely on a House of Commons which, he maintained, had been improperly elected in March 1784. Thus there was some consistency in Fox's reasoning, even if arguments for unlimited regency were constitutionally dubious and failed to accord with his previous claims about parliamentary sovereignty. But he considered tactics to be relatively unimportant. According to Fox, victory was assured because George III would not recover.

The regency struggle was therefore notable for some curious arguments, with Fox denying that parliament was sovereign and upholding the rights of the crown, and Pitt realizing that his statute of limitations could only be passed into law if by a new device, placing the great seal in commission, royal assent was given despite the incapacity of George III. Fox paraphrased Pitt's opinion as follows: 'when the king of England is in good health, the monarchy is hereditary; but when he is ill, and incapable of exercising the sovereign authority, it is elective'.[16] Fox's apparent departure from his previous position played into Pitt's hands, however, for the prime minister could present Fox (yet again) as a cynical opportunist who was prepared to abandon principles for immediate advantage. Pitt could earn greater respect, meanwhile, as a defender of George III and a champion of parliamentary privilege. Fox's biggest miscalculation was to accept reports that George III's condition would be permanent. He then made the mistake of denying that the Commons could decide on the nature of the regency. This gave the advantage to Pitt, who justified delay on the grounds that all relevant details needed careful consideration. The Foxites never recovered. Ministerial disquiet was almost gone by the end of 1788,[17] and George III's recovery in February 1789 prompted mass celebrations all over the country. Fox's influence declined, opposition leaders blamed each other for their defeat, and the crisis confirmed the unpopularity of the Prince of Wales. Pitt had weathered the storm and his success was confirmed at the general election of 1790. Before the French wars he and his government were never more vulnerable than during the regency crisis. Some in the cabinet had wanted to strike a deal with the opposition, and the prime minister at one stage seems to have thought of returning to the legal profession. The Irish parliament had voted to offer full regency powers to the Prince of Wales (though its address was never presented by the lord lieutenant, Buckingham).[18] That Pitt came through the whole emergency so well, and emerged stronger, was a testament to his nerve, tactical surefootedness and good luck. He continued to increase his power as prime minister because he continued to enjoy George III's co-operation and support.

In addition to a successful working relationship with George III, Pitt's political ascendancy depended upon his relationship with cabinet colleagues and position within the government. Just as the relationship with the king needed time to develop, so too did Pitt's manner of dealing effectively with his senior ministerial colleagues. Initially there were problems. During his early months as premier Pitt had to survive defeats in the Commons, intrigues among leading politicians who feared or hoped that he would not last, and demands for the establishment of a broadly based administration. Despite the general election victory of 1784, doubts about Pitt and his ministry persisted. The cabinet lacked talent and cohesion, and Pitt himself had no previous experience of heading a government (his only ministerial experience was as Shelburne's chancellor of the exchequer, from July 1782 to April 1783). Royal support was of course an essential bulwark, but to remain premier Pitt also had to maintain control over the cabinet and parliament. Without this control he could not hope to govern decisively, so he needed to make the best possible use of executive influence and in time would have to bring in more accomplished associates as ministers. Individual talent mattered a great deal to any government, and in order to be the prime minister he wanted to be, Pitt had to prove himself as debater, administrator, motivator, director and conciliator.

Despite important reverses on Irish trade and parliamentary reform, Pitt's position improved during the 1780s. His administrative ability, command of facts and figures, careful argument and eminently practical approach to public affairs convinced most observers that nobody else could be a better chief minister. George III valued him, MPs respected him, and cabinet colleagues appreciated his talent and reliability. The longer he stayed in office, indeed, the more secure his administration appeared to be, and rising men of ability and ambition were naturally drawn to the government side. The growing security of the government may also have owed something to a decline in faction after the unusual turbulence of 1783 and 1784.[19] Another useful advantage, already mentioned, was that Pitt could reward supporters with patronage, a facility denied to his immediate predecessors by George III.

Honours, offices and titles were essential to Pitt, and he used them to acknowledge service and encourage loyalty. In the process he altered the balance of power in the Lords, facilitating government control of parliament. Despite the objections of those who were anxious about the independence and dignity of the Lords, Pitt promoted nearly a hundred allies and supporters to the upper house during his premiership. In the period between 1783 and 1801 there were only two years in which no new peers were created (1795 and 1800). The Orders of the Garter and Bath were enlarged, and a new one, St Patrick, was established.[20] Though Pitt promoted rich landowners and the heads of prominent political families, as well as distinguished administrators, lawyers, generals and admirals, some titles went to commercial men, and Pitt worked hard to win the City's support – just as his father had done.[21] In this sense the attempt to control parliament was linked with efforts to attract support for the government out of doors. Some City interests did well out of Pitt's economic and financial policies. They needed a favourably disposed government if they were to prosper. Pitt also needed the merchants and bankers. He had no close links with any great noble family, for in terms of wealth, property and lineage neither the Pitts nor the Grenvilles were of the highest rank, and his association with reformers was an alliance of which the king disapproved. To combat opposition Whig magnates Pitt needed approval from both king and City. He may have been relieved, therefore, when his parliamentary reform plan failed in 1785 and when later moves to abolish the slave trade were frustrated, because worthy defeat at least absolved him of further responsibility. Before the French war he did what he could for reformers, which happened to be the minimum necessary to retain their backing, but he did nothing that would greatly antagonize king, City or parliament. Pitt was careful to do what was politically safe as well as honourable.

A secure hold on office was facilitated by Pitt's success in promoting economic recovery and relative political stability after the strains of the American war and the controversies of 1782 to 1784. By the early 1790s Pitt had demonstrated his worth. He had provided strong government and presided over a regime that was less factious and corrupt than its predecessors. Economic conditions were improving. Public finances were under control. Pitt's reputation and ascendancy became significant assets in future political battles, alongside his acknowledged aptitude for administration. Yet still he refrained from building up a large personal following in parliament. Like his father he preferred (and made a virtue of preferring) to speak of patriotism and duty. Instead of forming a party and attending to its organization and discipline, Pitt picked out ambitious and talented individuals, promoted them to positions of responsibility, and instilled in them his own code of administrative pride and competence. He eschewed party ties and remained a distant figure even to close allies. He rarely confided in cabinet colleagues, and would not announce reform intentions until he thought the time was right, which served to increase his influence over the ministry. Such was his prestige and control, indeed, that at his peak little was done by the government without his knowledge or consent. Collective ministerial responsibility began to develop both as an idea and a practice, and this also was due in large measure to the way Pitt viewed the premiership. Responsibility was moulded from above, not determined (as Fox might have preferred) by deference to parliament. Under Pitt the cabinet tended increasingly to be the place where he tested his ideas, not the place where policy was settled. By the 1790s he was framing measures *outside* the cabinet, after consulting Dundas, Grenville and, when necessary, the king.

Despite the quickening evolution of a cabinet system and the office of prime minister, collective appointment and resignation, and collective responsibility for policy, were only in their formative stages. Pitt knew that if he resigned or was forced out because of royal displeasure or parliamentary defeat, the cabinet would not necessarily break up but might carry on under a new leader who was acceptable to George III. Any shared ministerial responsibility for policy, moreover, was limited to the most crucial areas, especially finance and foreign affairs.[22] Pitt also knew that he could not determine cabinet personnel. Thurlow, the king's choice as lord chancellor and a powerful debater in the upper house, was unwilling to co-operate with Pitt on several issues, and temporarily went over to the opposition during the regency crisis. But Pitt could not remove him because he retained royal favour. Only later, when Thurlow repudiated the government's financial policies, could Pitt force him to resign. Under normal circumstances Pitt could not simply oust any minister with whom he had a disagreement. Certain questions were left open, notably parliamentary reform, religious toleration and the slave trade. Pitt could not require all cabinet colleagues to agree with him on these issues. Some departmental autonomy also survived. Although Pitt brought a clearer pattern to government activity, especially with his drive for administrative efficiency and checks on expenditure, too rapid a reorganization would have created controversy, and there were still many aspects of departmental business with which the prime minister could not properly interfere.

Pitt was aware of the possibility of obstruction from court, cabinet and parliament, and developed the skills needed to avoid such difficulties. He thought carefully about policy proposals and often sought the views of others beforehand. If a particular measure seemed unlikely to pass, Pitt would not risk a loss of influence by pressing it pointlessly. This drew forth claims that he was a procrastinator whose policies were muddled and injudicious, but he valued his ascendancy and governing style more highly than outward shows of consistency. Though committed to reforms, and prepared to speak in favour of proposals made by others if he supported their principle, he sometimes voted against them because he considered the timing and details faulty (this was his position on various motions for parliamentary reform, slave trade abolition and toleration for Dissenters in the late 1780s and early 1790s). Pitt did not wish to alienate mainstream conservative opinion in parliament and nation. Revolution and war in Europe also had a profound effect on his political methods. He became more cautious, and made a sharper distinction between necessary reforms and those that were ill advised or dangerous. Pitt's consistency is still questioned, but he was flexible by choice and necessity. He has to be seen first and foremost as a model of pragmatic leadership: hence the limited usefulness of attempts to delineate a permanent intellectual foundation for Pitt's politics.[23]

How did Pitt strengthen the cabinet while also increasing his influence within it? Certainly he was ambitious, self-assured and determined to lead (as many observers noted), but it took constant and sustained exertion before he attained the position he sought. Three essential and related features of Pitt's rise to ascendancy within the government were his formation of a core team of capable assistants, the eventual removal of Thurlow, and his success in ruling out any arrangement by which he would have to share power with anyone else. Each of these has already been mentioned, but it is worth examining them in detail in order better to appreciate Pitt's methods and achievement.

At first Pitt had to work with experienced and well-connected ministers who were not prepared to accept his lead on every issue. In some respects the ministry formed between December 1783 and January 1784 was a joint effort: George III had entrusted its formation not only to Pitt, but also to Thurlow, Gower and Richmond.[24] There were disagreements on key questions, and internal cabinet discord was exacerbated by the ill will of Thurlow.

Senior members of the cabinet were not much help to Pitt. Gower was personally close to Thurlow, while the two secretaries of state, Sydney and Carmarthen, lacked influence. In fact they had not really wanted to take office. Pitt appreciated their adherence and felt obliged to retain them for a while, despite their shortcomings. Sydney proved to be doubly disappointing because, like Thurlow, he was hostile to reform (Pitt tried not to alienate him, though, because his elder brother John had married Sydney's daughter Mary). Even Pitt's pro-reform colleagues Rutland and Richmond were less useful than he had hoped. Rutland joined the cabinet as lord privy seal in December 1783, but left for Ireland in February 1784 to take up the post of lord lieutenant. This made Richmond all the more important to Pitt. Though he was a competent administrator, with considerable military and diplomatic experience, Richmond's advice was not particularly sound and if Pitt was going to strengthen the cabinet and improve his own position within it, he needed to find other willing collaborators. Initial proposals for a ministerial reshuffle came to nothing. Pitt wanted to bring in men he knew he could work with. Preferably, they would also have strong Whig credentials, to combat any talk of improper royal influence, and social standing, to reassure respectable public opinion of the government's character. After long negotiations some minor changes were made. Gower agreed to move from the lord presidency and took the privy seal vacated by Rutland, which made it possible for Pitt to bring in his father's former associate Camden (December 1784). But Carmarthen refused to move from the foreign office to make room for the third Duke of Grafton, a former prime minister (1768–70), and Camden was now too old and ill to be much of an asset. He brought Pitt prestige rather than active assistance.[25]

During the mid-1780s Pitt struggled to impose more control over his ministry. In some Commons debates, however, he was unable successfully to defend measures introduced by cabinet colleagues and about which he had no detailed knowledge. This made the government seem divided and incoherent. Indeed, department chiefs often acted without much reference to the rest of the cabinet, and could even end up competing with each other. Occasionally one minister might instruct his staff members, dependants, and friends who sat in parliament to oppose the measures of another minister. In May 1786 Rutland was informed by his follower Daniel Pulteney of 'differences in the cabinet, which show themselves in the House of Commons' (members of the ordnance department and admiralty board had voted against each other). In cabinet discussions Pitt was not always the dominant force. After a meeting on foreign policy in May 1787, James Harris (later Lord Malmesbury) recorded that Thurlow and Richmond, not Pitt, were the main speakers.[26] It is not surprising that Pitt's capacity to lead the government continued to be questioned in these early years, and most of the ministers were regarded as mediocre at best, which highlighted the need to bring in more talent. Pitt's personal manner may have made matters worse. He seemed detached and diffident in dealing with colleagues, some of whom felt insulted by his quirky aloofness. Nor did disagreement within the ministry on such matters as electoral reform, the Hastings impeachment and abolition of the slave trade make for cordial co-operation.

Pitt saw that he would not be an effective patriotic premier unless he gained the assistance of a close circle of friends and advisers, men who could gather and utilize the expertise and ability without which his government could not easily establish itself in power. In forming this core team of efficient office holders, Pitt knew that there was a price to pay. Members of the cabinet would object to being by-passed, and a few were likely to cause trouble if there was any interference with their own departmental business.

Pitt's most valuable assistant was Dundas. He was trusted by Pitt and often in the prime minister's company (they shared a love of the countryside and a taste for strong drink). Apart from his management of Indian affairs and Scottish patronage, administrative efficiency and importance as a government speaker in the Commons, Dundas served as Pitt's agent in taking care of difficult and unpleasant tasks. Others resented his rise. Late in 1784 Sydney complained about the lack of consultation on Indian appointments, which had all been settled by Dundas, and Rutland was told of 'hints of jealousy respecting Dundas'. In July 1789 Camden opined that Dundas had too much influence over the prime minister. But Pitt defended Dundas and emphasized his capacity for business whenever there was pressure for his removal. In July 1794 Pitt wrote of 'the advantage of Dundas's turn for facilitating business, and of every act of his being as much *mine as his*'. In negotiating the juncture with Portland Whigs at this time, Pitt was determined to make sure that Dundas remained in charge of the war. To this end, certain responsibilities had to be removed from the home office. 'If all the details of the war ... were to be settled by communication with a person both new to me and to others', Pitt affirmed, 'I am sure the business could not go on for a week.' From the very beginning of their political collaboration in 1783 Pitt and Dundas worked well together. Gradually they became close personally, and the prime minister relied on Dundas more and more as Indian policy and the Hastings affair raised the latter's profile. Dundas was good company for Pitt (he lived near to London at Wimbledon). Their constant co-operation during the war made him a fixture of Pitt's political regime and circle of intimates. He was one of Pitt's most essential supports, privately as well as publicly.[27]

Increasingly important to Pitt was his cousin William Wyndham Grenville, brother of the second Earl Temple and youngest son of George Grenville (prime minister from 1763 to 1765). Dundas was an old hand, having previously served North, but Grenville was a relative newcomer (born in the same year as Pitt, he was first elected to parliament in 1782). The family connection assisted his rise, but Grenville's political talents were quickly apparent too. From 1784 he was joint paymaster of the forces, and from 1786 vice-president of the board of trade. He served on the Indian board of control, and as chairman of the Commons committee on finance he helped Pitt to plan the sinking fund. The cousins also worked together on commercial negotiations with France during 1785 and 1786. Like Dundas, Grenville became indispensable (and Pitt was happy to find that, as expected, they both proved to be far more efficient and co-operative than the men they replaced in the cabinet). Grenville successfully tackled difficult jobs, as in 1787 when he served as Pitt's emissary to Holland and France at a time when war seemed likely, and during the regency crisis when he briefly became Speaker of the Commons following the death of the incumbent Charles Wolfran Cornwall. When he went up to the Lords in 1790 as Baron Grenville, he assisted Pitt to combat Thurlow and took over as the government's main spokesman in the upper house. Grenville was also close personally to Pitt (among their common interests were classical literature and economics). Both were hostile to the slave trade, though they disagreed on parliamentary reform and the Hastings affair. Grenville served as home secretary from June 1789 to June 1791. Pitt had wanted to promote him sooner than this, but waited because Grenville's brother, now Marquess of Buckingham, did not want to have to pay for his re-election (MPs had to stand for re-election on accepting ministerial office), and because something had to be done to compensate Sydney. Eventually Sydney gave up the home office in return for a viscountcy, a sinecure, and junior office for his son. In November 1790 Pitt looked forward to the assistance Grenville would provide as home secretary in the House of Lords:

> By the help of this arrangement, I think we shall open the new Parliament with more strength than has belonged to us since the beginning of the government; and it is a very pleasant circumstance in the business that all parts of the government are highly satisfied with the measure, and that those who please themselves with reports ... of divisions among us will find themselves completely disappointed.

Grenville subsequently served as foreign secretary, from 1791 to 1801. Dundas took the home office in 1791, and became secretary of state for war in 1794 (when the home office passed to Portland).[28]

Another useful ally was Charles Jenkinson, though Pitt was wary of too close an association with this renowned intriguer who had been the king's friend and informant since the early 1760s. As an expert on trade and finance, however, Jenkinson helped to formulate policy (including Pitt's Irish and French commercial schemes), and in August 1786 Pitt recognized his services by appointing him president of the board of trade. Jenkinson was also raised to the peerage as Baron Hawkesbury. In view of his patriotic image and suspicion of court influence, the prime minister may have thought twice about making these changes, but he described them as part of the effort 'to put the business of government into a form that will admit of more regularity and despatch than has prevailed in some branches of it'. Furthermore, he was convinced that Hawkesbury merited the elevation: 'he has really fairly earned it and attained it at my hands'. In September 1786 Hawkesbury was awarded a lucrative sinecure when Pitt made him chancellor of the duchy of Lancaster. Yet the two men were not close. Though Pitt valued his expertise, and though Hawkesbury was less involved in political intrigues after joining the cabinet, Pitt did not take him fully into his confidence. He was sure to name his own men as Hawkesbury's deputies at the board of trade, and the stress on Hawkesbury's promotion 'at my hands' reveals Pitt's true interpretation of their relationship. This is not to deny Hawkesbury's influence. He consistently advised against a quick transition to the Adam Smith system of free trade and *laissez faire*. Pitt respected his views, approving of Hawkesbury's navigation bill of 1786 and regulating the food supply during the wartime dearth of 1800 (much to the annoyance of the free trader Grenville). By this time Hawkesbury had been advanced within the peerage. He became Earl of Liverpool in 1796.[29]

Pitt frequently consulted other advisers, men such as the treasury secretaries George Rose (1783–1801) and Charles Long (1791–1801), the financial expert William Eden (Lord Auckland from 1789), who negotiated the Anglo-French commercial treaty in 1786, and the diplomat Harris (Lord Malmesbury from 1788), who was sent by Pitt to talk peace with the French during 1796 and 1797.[30] Among Pitt's most loyal lieutenants were William Huskisson, head of the aliens department from 1793 to 1794, under-secretary at the war office between 1795 and 1801, and joint secretary to the treasury in Pitt's second administration, from 1804 to 1806, and George Canning, who served as under-secretary at the foreign office from 1796 to 1799, commissioner of the Indian board of control from 1799 to 1801, joint paymaster of the forces from 1800 to 1801, and treasurer of the navy from 1804 to 1806.

In time, therefore, Pitt strengthened his position within the government by bringing forward and then relying on a small number of efficient and influential allies, who remained outside the cabinet during the early years of his premiership and gradually expanded their activity to encompass all the vital areas of government. Pitt had the treasury already, while Indian affairs and Scottish patronage were taken over by Dundas. Though he was home secretary (1783–89) and president of the board of control (1784–90), Sydney lost out to Dundas in these areas, and his nominal responsibility for Ireland also became irrelevant as Pitt communicated directly with the lord lieutenant, his friend Rutland. Buckingham took over as lord lieutenant when Rutland died in 1787, and he corresponded regularly with his brother Grenville, so again Sydney was by-passed. On foreign affairs Pitt could marginalize the ineffectual but proud Carmarthen, who succeeded as fifth Duke of Leeds in 1789, by consulting diplomats or entrusting a close confidant, like Grenville, with special missions. As Pitt grew increasingly assertive, senior figures complained about the lack of consultation. In June 1786 Rutland was informed that 'Lord Sydney is little consulted or regarded in his department and ... often rather indignant at the neglect with which he is treated'.[31] There were threats of resignation (some of which were not altogether unwelcome to Pitt). Howe, the first lord of the admiralty, left the cabinet in July 1788 because he objected to Pitt's co-operation with Middleton, the reform-minded comptroller of the navy. Pitt decided that his own brother, the second Earl of Chatham, should replace Howe. He could thereby further extend his personal control over the government, while ensuring that there would be no serious disagreements about the future management of the navy. In 1789 Grenville succeeded Sydney as home secretary. Dundas became home secretary in 1791 when Grenville replaced Leeds at the foreign office. The latter had resigned after making several protests about Pitt's meddling in his areas of responsibility. Meanwhile Richmond objected when Grenville was given a peerage and named leader of the House of Lords in November 1790,[32] and Thurlow added his weight to these complaints. Too much power was being amassed by Pitt's inner circle, it was claimed, and salutary conventions relating to ministerial discretion and authority were being eroded.

Thurlow was a major obstacle to Pitt. He held a special position as George III's favourite and was clever, conscious of his power, and a strong debater. In July 1786 Rutland suggested that any serious breach between Pitt and Thurlow would be fatal to the ministry ('nothing but such an event, or the king's death, or an unsuccessful war, could weaken the existing government and give a triumph to its enemies'). Rutland also thought that George III might sacrifice Pitt for the sake of Thurlow. Like his royal patron, Thurlow did not share Pitt's reforming tendencies, and as a minister he was difficult to deal with, quick to lose his temper yet slow in dealing with business. The king admitted that Thurlow was 'rather famous for loving delay', and in January 1791 Pitt warned Grenville not to leave papers with the lord chancellor, for he would keep them a week and thereby interrupt the flow of business. As the prime minister began to by-pass Thurlow, the latter complained to the king and stirred other ministers into open dissension. Pitt lost patience with Thurlow's conservatism and procrastination, while Thurlow made little effort to disguise his lack of respect for the prime minister. To Thurlow, Pitt was an upstart and hypocrite who, while making much of his patriotic virtue, cynically dispensed patronage and allowed his allies (especially Dundas) to corrupt and manipulate others without restraint.[33]

From 1788 Pitt and Thurlow were openly at odds. Pitt realized that it would not be easy to remove Thurlow, not least because there was no obvious alternative as lord chancellor (except perhaps the first Baron Loughborough, and he was in opposition as part of the Portland Whig connection). With the backing of the king and the legal establishment (including master of the rolls Sir Lloyd Kenyon and solicitor general Sir John Scott), with influence in the Lords, with his legal opinion on legislation and treaties carrying great weight, and his seal needed on patents of appointment, Thurlow became Pitt's most formidable opponent. He led the Lords' opposition to Dolben's slave bill, which Pitt supported. He tried to resist Pitt on patronage matters, especially those on which the lord chancellor could expect to have a say. There was a bitter struggle in June 1788 when Pitt promoted his friend Pepper Arden to succeed Kenyon as master of the rolls and treasury secretary George Rose was named clerk of the parliaments, a House of Lords post. On 4 July William Eden was informed by John Moore, Archbishop of Canterbury:

> Pepper Arden is at last Master of the Rolls. It was delayed foolishly by the Chancellor … The profession abuses him, saying it was unmanly and ungentlemanlike; he is sulky and Pitt no less so; in short, there has been and is much heart-burning. Tomorrow the Chancellor means to make a motion that Rose, the new clerk of the House of Lords, shall not make it a sinecure … another ebullition of ill-humour. But with all these ill-humours he must be borne with, for without him the House of Lords would be a wretched, insupportable place.[34]

During the regency crisis Thurlow negotiated with Fox and the Prince of Wales, hoping to remain in office if there was a change of ministry. In fact opposition leaders decided that Loughborough would be the new lord chancellor and, to Pitt's relief, Thurlow eventually declared himself in favour of the government's regency bill. Thereafter, attempts by George III and others to draw Pitt and Thurlow together were a complete failure, and Pitt prepared for a final reckoning. Grenville went up to the Lords, and talks were opened with amenable members of the opposition (they welcomed Pitt's support for the impeachment of Hastings and his apparent willingness to offer honours, offices and pensions). Pitt was strengthened by the general election victory of June 1790 (the government now had about 340 seats, the opposition 183, with 35 others) and a foreign policy success over Spain.

Thurlow refused to submit to Grenville's leadership in the Lords, continued to complain about lack of consultation, and was quite prepared to obstruct government policy. Pitt warned the king on 20 November 1790 that 'in the present state of the House of Lords, and while the Chancellor's disposition is such as is represented, it can hardly be expected that the public business can long proceed without leading to some disagreeable incident'. On 12 March 1791 Thurlow spoke with the Duke of Leeds, who recorded that 'he was convinced they meant to get rid of him when their minds should be made up respecting his successor'. The Portland Whigs were not yet willing to abandon Fox and join the government, however, and the Ochakov crisis of 1791, which almost resulted in war between Britain and Russia, diverted Pitt's attention and temporarily weakened his position. Fortunately for him, the Foxites' continuing enthusiasm for the French Revolution alarmed the Portland group and opened up divisions within the opposition, prompting Pitt to make further overtures (through Auckland) to Loughborough, Portland and their friends during the spring of 1792.

Then Thurlow made a fatal mistake. He not only opposed anti-slave trade resolutions which had been backed by Pitt, but attacked Pitt's sinking fund arrangements and, as Grenville put it, 'nearly beat us' on the National Debt Bill. 'I think the consequences must be decisive on his situation or ours', Grenville commented. 'Such an extempore and gratuitous attack upon the measures of the administration of which he forms a part,' wrote under-secretary at the foreign office James Bland Burges, ' is undoubtedly very singular.' These financial projects related directly to the treasury, Pitt's department, and he could now justifiably insist (on 15 May 1792) that the king must remove Thurlow. Forced to choose between them, and knowing that he could not lose his chief minister, George III sided with Pitt. But no replacement could be found to take the lord chancellorship, which temporarily had to be put into commission, and the king was displeased to learn of the offers made by Pitt to the Portland Whigs, which he thought excessive. The situation became more difficult for Pitt when Leeds approached the king and offered to take the premiership as nominal head of a united government, in which Pitt would be on an equal footing with opposition Whig leaders. Pitt and George III ruled this out. Pitt had subsequently to reassure the king that there would be no compromise with the opposition while carefully keeping open the possibility of a union with Portland. Radicalism at home and turmoil abroad eventually led the Portland Whigs to abandon the opposition, first as individuals, then as a group. The king reluctantly agreed to appoint Loughborough as lord chancellor in January 1793, and this confirmed Pitt's ascendancy because Thurlow remained a potential threat until his successor was found.[35]

Once Thurlow had been removed and Pitt was more clearly master of the cabinet, there was no question that he would agree to share power in the manner proposed by the Duke of Leeds and leaders of the opposition in the summer of 1792. Indeed, this had been Pitt's position ever since his appointment as premier in December 1783. From the outset his desire was to establish a personal authority over the ministry as quickly as possible. He was unwilling to play a subordinate role or share the lead with anyone. Though there was talk of an arrangement with Fox and Portland in February 1784, and pressure grew for the cabinet to be reconstructed on a broader basis, Pitt's apparent willingness to explore these matters was simply a ploy to buy time. He was not prepared to relinquish the premiership, and in this he had the support of George III. The talks failed, which was what Pitt wanted, but at same time he had appeased some of the non-aligned 'independent' MPs who wanted a more inclusive government. As ascendancy came within his reach, Pitt moved to prevent any serious challenge to his pre-eminence. The idea broached in February 1784, March 1791 and August 1792, while Pitt was in office, and in March 1803, when he was in opposition, that he might agree to share power with his political rivals in a cabinet nominally led by a compromise choice as first lord of the treasury, was a non-starter.

Pitt's determination to lead was not only a matter of personal ambition and preference. It related also to his patriotic image and his notion of the correct constitutional role and authority of the prime minister. In March 1803 he told Dundas (now Viscount Melville) – though this was also meant for wider consumption –

> that there should be an avowed and real minister possessing the chief weight in council and the principal place in the confidence of the king. In that respect there can be no rivalry or division of power. That power must rest in the person generally called the First Minister; and that minister ought, he thinks, to be the person at the head of the finances ... if it should come unfortunately to such a radical difference of opinion that no spirit of conciliation or concession can reconcile, the sentiments of the Minister must be allowed and understood to prevail.[36]

Pitt was in opposition when he made this remark. As well as offering his thoughts on what the office and function of the prime minister should be, he was describing the terms on which he wanted to return to the premiership. But in looking to the future he was also remembering the past, especially the problems he had experienced as leader of the government between 1783 and 1801. Pitt was concerned about the prime minister's relationship not only with the king, but also with the rest of the cabinet. This reflects the difficulties that arose even after the departure of Thurlow and alliance with the Portland Whigs. The alliance was itself a source of tension. Pitt hoped to make it work, but some of Portland's friends had never trusted him and found it difficult now to do so, and many of Pitt's followers complained about all the offices and honours that had been offered to these erstwhile enemies in order to win their adherence. From July 1794, six of the thirteen posts in the reconstructed cabinet were held by men who had opposed Pitt before 1793, and after further changes in 1795 the prime minister was the only survivor from the cabinet formed at the end of 1783.

Although Pitt was still in charge of the government, the Portland Whigs were no ciphers. One of their leaders, William Windham, considered that they now had a *real* share of power. Shortly after the bargain with Pitt had been concluded, Windham wrote: 'the effect of this measure was felt, I think, immediately in the alterations made for the better in the king's speech, and has since had, perhaps, its influence on the counsels of the state in some material articles'. For George Canning, however, the merger was a potential disaster. Though he had faith in Pitt and respected Portland and Windham, Canning thought that the public character of the new members of the cabinet would have remained higher had they agreed to support the government without taking office.

> It may be doubted too whether or no such an accession as the present does in reality confer strength and stability upon an administration, when we recollect that there is not an instance in the history of the country of a ministry composed of two distinct parties, uniting, coalescing (or whatever it may be called) which has not split and fallen within a very short time after its establishment.[37]

The Portland Whigs had their own ideas about war strategy and the administration of Ireland, and there were serious quarrels on these points. With time and effort, however, Pitt was able to weaken the cohesion of the Portland group and integrate its members more successfully into the ministry. Portland himself was reasonable and compliant, which obviously helped. After the merits of Pitt's ideas about the management of the war and government of Ireland were clearly demonstrated, there were fewer disputes with his new allies. In the summer of 1795 Britain, at the Portland Whigs' insistence, supported a landing by French royalists in Quiberon Bay, and the utter failure of this operation enabled Pitt to regain the initiative. Henceforth war strategy (and indeed almost everything else) was decided principally by Pitt, Dundas and Grenville – notwithstanding pressure from Windham, among others, who demanded changes in policy.[38] In Ireland, meanwhile, the Portland Whigs' reforming agenda had caused enormous instability and, again, Pitt was able to step in and regain control. In March 1795 he installed his own choice (his old friend John Jeffreys Pratt, now second Earl Camden) as lord lieutenant of Ireland. After 1795 the Portland Whigs rarely combined together to force Pitt to adopt or change a policy, and the Pitt-Dundas-Grenville triumvirate was firmly in control. The personnel and balance of power within the cabinet had changed considerably between the late 1780s and 1795, and, following further ministerial changes in the late 1790s, the triumvirate seemed all the more dominant. By the summer of 1798 there was a cabinet of twelve, only four of whom had formerly been members of the opposition.[39]

On most important issues Pitt, Dundas and Grenville decided what the government's position should be before the matter came before the cabinet. By their joint efforts they could usually overcome objections, and in this they took advantage of the frequently loose and informal procedures by which business was transacted. No agenda was issued to ministers in advance of cabinet discussions, and no full written record of these discussions was kept to which they could later refer. Windham, secretary at war from 1794 to 1801, protested about this lack of precision in August 1799. He wrote to Grenville, 'I have never known distinctly what the sort of minutes were that were kept of the proceedings of cabinet; or how far those who were present, and have entered no express declaration or dissent, would appear on any sort of record as parties to the measures adopted'. There were certain policies to which Windham did not wish to be considered agreeable. Decision-making was so confused, he complained, that he never knew the appropriate moment to express his opposition to what Pitt had proposed. No doubt this was how Pitt wanted it. If a group of ministers did act together to question or block something, moreover, Pitt, Dundas and Grenville would simply meet again before the next cabinet and decide how to get round the obstruction.

These methods of control could not work, of course, when there was a disagreement within the triumvirate. On these occasions the rest of the cabinet might enjoy more influence, though such opportunities did not arise very often. Clashes over foreign policy between Pitt and Grenville, for example, were settled in such a way that the triumvirate never broke apart. Early in 1795 Grenville opposed Pitt's idea for a new treaty with Prussia, and may have threatened to resign. Eventually he decided to remain in place, but wrote to the king (8 April 1795) to explain his opinion and register a formal protest. The most serious breach between Pitt and Grenville occurred in 1797. In May Grenville objected to Pitt's plan to enter into peace talks with France. Grenville argued that this move would humiliate and weaken Britain. But Pitt took the matter before the cabinet, and there were several stormy meetings in June, with (according to Windham) three ministers backing Grenville and five siding with the prime minister. Pitt connived with the under-secretary at the foreign office, Canning, who kept an eye on Grenville's manoeuvres, and managed to maintain a narrow cabinet majority for a more conciliatory attitude towards the French than that proposed by Grenville. The foreign secretary chose to have his disagreement officially recorded rather than resign at this difficult time for the government, and, as before, he wrote to the king (16 June 1797) to explain his conduct. On 12 July Wilberforce noted that Pitt and Grenville were 'very like breaking friendship'. Pitt was able to persuade a doubtful George III to approve the peace policy, but the resulting negotiations at Lille were discontinued in September after a coup in France. Pitt and Grenville were soon reconciled and able to work closely together as usual.[40]

Pitt recognized the importance of the cabinet, and was content to work through it, but to him it became more of an inconvenience than an effective administrative or policy-making mechanism. Key decisions continued to be made outside the cabinet, not only because this was how Pitt chose to lead, but also because there were limits to his control over cabinet colleagues. If Pitt lacked his own personal contacts with a particular department he could not easily supervise its business – or even inform himself of what was going on there. Portland was quite autonomous in this respect as home secretary, and Grenville often exercised considerable independence too as foreign secretary. Pitt could not simply instruct a colleague to do as he wanted. He could encourage or discourage, if necessary with the assistance of Dundas or Grenville, but a collective decision of the cabinet was needed to force an individual into line. Yet Pitt disliked confrontation. He proved reluctant to remove ineffective ministers (notably Sydney, Carmarthen and Richmond), and allowed those who would not participate in his rearrangements to remain in their posts longer than he wished. Carmarthen refused to leave the foreign office in 1784, Liverpool refused to vacate the duchy of Lancaster in 1796, and Windham turned down the offices of master of the mint and treasurer of the navy at the end of the 1790s. As manager of the cabinet Pitt was generally cautious, a result of his personal reticence and awareness that he could not always impose his will. But this self-restraint also indicates his low opinion of the cabinet and its role. He needed its backing, and he had to respond quickly if threats emerged within it, but he saw the cabinet as a supporting rather than an initiating body, essential but not supreme.[41]

Once he was dominant it was easier for Pitt to get unanimous ministerial support, and this was useful to him in dealing with difficult situations and royal opposition. In time, as Pitt gained confidence, he also had more say in cabinet appointments (a far cry from the situation in late 1783 and early 1784 when he first became premier). Sometimes Dundas and Grenville were also involved in arranging appointments, and the king always had to be consulted, persuaded or reassured, but in practice Pitt's role in making cabinet changes expanded considerably during the 1790s. It was really Pitt who decided how and when to shuffle the pack. He brought in individuals who had special expertise or experience from which the cabinet might benefit; persuaded existing colleagues to move to other departments; obliged newcomers to accept specific posts or take on particularly irksome duties; rewarded loyal allies who had given up other positions or done valuable service elsewhere; and promoted men of talent on whom he knew he could rely. Occasionally Pitt preferred to leave a post vacant so that he could use it in future political bargaining (the privy seal was held in reserve, for example, from March to November 1784, and from September 1796 to February 1798). He also became bolder in interfering with his colleagues' areas of responsibility. As Windham complained to the prime minister in December 1800: 'I have had occasion more than once to remark to you the inconveniences that arise from the irregular and very unceremonious way which the Treasury sometimes has of stepping into different Departments without any previous notice, public or private, to those who are at the head of them.'[42]

Any explanation of Pitt's longevity and ascendancy as prime minister must explore not only his relationship with George III and position within the cabinet, but also his relationship with and influence in parliament. Pitt's strengths as a parliamentarian appeared all the more impressive because, though it could not be ignored, the parliamentary opposition became weaker during the 1780s. In fact the opposition was never a united force. Many former followers of North refused to join Pitt but failed also to merge with the followers of Portland and Fox.[43] Meanwhile, as Pitt's influence grew, Fox's began to decline. After the reverses of 1783 and 1784 Fox and his party considered their self-appointed political function more necessary than ever.[44] George III had shown that he would never willingly accept them in office, and proscription strengthened their arguments about dangerous royal machinations. The scale of their electoral defeat in 1784 was extremely disheartening, as was Pitt's success in establishing himself in power. Fox abandoned active politics for long periods despite his desire to vindicate his principles and past conduct. He became a leader who frequently failed to lead.[45] Close association with the Prince of Wales was also a burden rather than a source of strength to opposition leaders. By the end of the 1780s, divisions within the Foxite circle seriously limited its influence, and Pitt's position seemed more unassailable as a result.

Pitt's ascendancy was partly founded on Fox's humiliation and defeat, which is why all talk of ministerial changes after 1784 prompted Fox to insist that the prime minister must resign before he could involve himself in any new arrangement. Fox also maintained that he would never serve under Pitt and that Pitt's premiership was an affront to the constitution. Apart from personal animosity, therefore, there were public reasons for opposition to Pitt. As Fox explained in February 1786: 'I say that the people of England have a right to control the executive power, by the interference of their representatives ... The right honourable gentleman maintains the contrary. He is the cause of our political enmity.'[46] Stark differences in character and style added to the ongoing rivalry between the two antagonists. Pitt was austere and sometimes melancholic. Fox was as devoted to pleasure as he was to politics. Pitt did not have an endearing manner. He was respected, not loved, while Fox could be enormously charming and had none of Pitt's frosty aloofness. Fox was a party leader. Pitt seemed less concerned to build up a personal following in parliament and had little contact with or interest in his supporters, although he often cultivated influential backbenchers and sought to control business through appointments to parliamentary committees.[47] Fox was self-indulgent, impulsive, amusing, while Pitt's probity and lofty view of his calling meant that he placed himself under much greater pressure. His political judgement improved with experience, but Fox's was often faulty. Both ranked among the finest debaters in the Commons, though it was probably Pitt who made the more lasting impression. If Fox was a dazzling orator, Pitt's speeches were superior in terms of organization, clarity and detail. This was certainly the opinion of Sir Francis Baring, a co-founder of Baring's Bank and director of the East India Company, who had been a supporter of North before siding with Shelburne and Pitt. Baring was MP for various boroughs between 1784 and 1806. He observed Pitt and Fox in their prime.

> He said that in his youth Mr Pitt had listened to *instruction* more than Mr Fox had done ... He said the consequence was that, from early habits of attention and correctness, Mr Pitt always spoke with a regular flow of expression, never requiring to go backward to correct himself but proceeding with an uninterrupted stream of delivery. On the contrary, Mr Fox went *forward and backward*; not

satisfied with his first expression, he would put it another way ... Sir Francis seemed to think that in his oratory Mr Fox occasionally had flashes of genius beyond Mr Pitt, but he said the character of an orator was not to be determined by a single speech but by the effect produced in different debates, in two or three years, and then he granted that Mr Pitt had the ascendancy.[48]

Pitt and Fox evolved different parliamentary styles and tried to influence the Commons in different ways. While Pitt appealed to the mind and relied on force of argument, Fox often appealed to the heart, relying on the force of his own personality.

Pitt saw from the start of his political career that success depended upon mastery of the Commons, the dominant branch of the legislature. His father had risen to power as a result of his influence there, and it was in the Commons that Pitt had to prove himself if he was to win acclaim as the vigorous national leader. After he became prime minister, control of the Commons was necessary for security of tenure. This control depended primarily upon debating ability: natural talent combined with the training he had received in his youth gave Pitt a decided advantage as a parliamentary speaker. The general verdict was that, although he was not as overwhelming as his father had been, Pitt's contributions had more reason and structure to them, and he was better able to explain complicated matters and impress MPs with logic and detail. From such acolytes as Canning, of course, there was warm praise for Pitt's speaking. 'Such a manly impressive speech from Pitt – never was anything like it', Canning wrote after a budget debate in February 1794, and on arriving at the Commons during a debate on army estimates in January 1795 Canning found Pitt 'speaking most brilliantly'. Even Pitt's opponents commended his oratory (Fox, Windham and Grey were highly impressed by Pitt's speech on the slave trade of 2 April 1792). Canning did discern, however, that Pitt was less effective in defending than in advocating measures. When Fox moved for a committee on the state of the nation in March 1795,

> Pitt answered him at length and with less brilliancy and effect, I think, than usual – owing, however, to a very natural and obvious cause, that it was Fox's business to *bring forward* every topic for enquiry, and Pitt's to *keep them back*, and to persuade the House not to enquire at all.[49]

Especially important was Pitt's ability to explain complex financial policies, not only because these were his direct responsibility as first lord of the treasury and chancellor of the exchequer, but also because his obvious financial competence reassured parliament and nation that the government was in safe hands. Pitt spoke mainly from memory, often amazing MPs with his performance. His views were respected, and as he gained in experience and information his speeches carried all the more weight. As Canning wrote of Pitt's budget of February 1795:

> The expenses to be provided for were indeed tremendous, and the provision he has made in a way manly and full and satisfactory, and against which either in the whole or in detail little if any exception can be taken ... Indeed the best part of Pitt's character as Minister, is the fair, bold way in which he meets, without shrinking, the necessities of the times – not under-rating expenditure, that he may have the less income to find – not over-rating income, that he may seem to more easily to find it – but calculating every call at its full extent, and providing even beyond that extent for answering it.

Pitt put in a lot of effort to maintain his influence in debate. He was rarely absent from the Commons. He listened closely to other speakers, organized his own material carefully, and practised – indeed, the more he spoke the better he became, and the more MPs were anxious to hear him. Pitt learned quickly how to undermine opponents by identifying and exploiting weak points in their arguments, and he made the most of his own oratorical weapons – the pleasing voice, fluent delivery, and elegant and lucid language. Another feature of his speaking was less highly regarded. He could be sarcastic and discourteous, and would not take back personal remarks. His duel with opposition MP George Tierney on 27 May 1798 was partly caused by this tendency. In the Commons Tierney had objected to the haste with which Pitt had tried to push through war measures, in this case a bill for expanding naval recruitment, claiming that the lack of proper debate and reflection posed a threat to liberty. An impatient Pitt accused Tierney of seeking to weaken the nation's defences, and refused to withdraw the charge when invited to do so.[50]

The fact that Pitt never inspired much affection outside his circle of close friends can be linked to his personality and techniques of management. Towards his supporters he was Olympian and inattentive, even disdainful. While other political leaders acted as if they knew the importance of good relations with backbenchers and borough patrons – and offered the necessary favours, flattery and personal contact – Pitt seemed not to care about such things. Contemporaries noted that he rarely acknowledged a bow or nod in the Commons, and held few dinners for loyal MPs. There were complaints about his failure to answer letters (in February 1786 Daniel Pulteney informed Rutland that having recently left a letter at Downing Street, he would probably have to wait a year before Pitt made any response). This had wide ramifications, because correspondents were often making requests for themselves or their relatives and clients, and the smooth operation of patronage networks was essential to Pitt's ascendancy in parliament. If he annoyed his main backers, who in turn were unable to satisfy their own underlings, he risked losing influence. During the regency crisis, and at other times, there was talk of defections from the government, and in some cases this was attributable to Pitt's attitude towards his supporters. Even minor figures expected a share of patronage, and were annoyed to find their applications ignored or rejected. The Cheshire MP Sir Robert Cotton, who had been a consistent government supporter, retired from the Commons in 1796, it was said because of ill health. But he also wished to indicate his displeasure with Pitt. He had repeatedly asked for a friend to be appointed as collector of salt duties in Nantwich, but the prime minister had not replied even once, let alone made the desired appointment.

The point about Pitt's failure to hold dinners, however, requires qualification. There were different types of dinner party involving Pitt. Each type had its own guest list. There were formal dinners for MPs who were privy councillors and office holders, held at the beginning of each parliamentary session in advance of the debate on the address. There were dinners attended by members of the government who were due to speak on the most pressing issues of the day. There were informal gatherings too, and these were open to any of Pitt's friends who happened to be free. To somebody like Canning, who was regularly in the prime minister's company, it was noticeable when dinners became less frequent. On 23 June 1795 Canning wrote of the 'bad style – that into which Pitt has fallen this year – of not giving dinners'. No doubt Pitt realized how important these occasions were for building up morale and *esprit de corps*, but the pressure of public affairs during the war pushed them off his list of priorities.[51]

Pitt was inattentive because he had so little time to spare. There was simply too much government business for him to deal with. Reluctant to think of parliament in 'party' terms, moreover, he did not feel the need to cultivate a party. In any case he was temperamentally unsuited to personnel management, and could not negotiate in an easy and open manner with people who were not of his inner circle. In the early part of his premiership he was also conscious of his relative youth (most of his colleagues and allies were older than he was). Pitt's friends often remarked upon his inability to make small talk and his indecision when confronting any difficult or unpleasant matter. Wilberforce thought that his shyness often came across as arrogance and rudeness. There was a suggestion that he had risen too early to high office, without gaining enough experience of life, and that this prevented him from appearing relaxed in his personal dealings. With respect to patronage, of course, the problem was exacerbated because many applications had to be turned down, and Pitt lacked the patience and affability to maintain cordial ties with some of those who were disappointed (the second Earl Camden wrote to Pitt in December 1804: 'you have told me that nothing makes you so bilious as arrangements').

Pitt could not have satisfied all applicants even had he wanted to, for the offices and other rewards at his disposal were not abundant. When Canning asked about a promotion in June 1795, Pitt 'lamented indeed that the number of efficient working offices ... was so small as to make the selection out of very few indeed'. In addition, Pitt was disinclined to meddle with provisions made by department heads for their own adherents. Nor did it help when two of Pitt's allies both asked for the same office, usually to reward their followers, reinforce their reputation and strengthen their power base. In May 1786 the Duke of Rutland found that another patron – the second Baron Mulgrave, a loyal Pittite who had been appointed joint paymaster in 1784, sat on the board of trade and was a commissioner for the Indian board of control – had requested the post of collector of Whitby. Rutland himself wished to dispose of this office, and complained to Pitt: 'Lord Mulgrave's application for the collectorship of Whitby has embarrassed me extremely. I am the last man to press you, except where my essential interests are concerned. My credit and weight in Scarborough must depend on the conviction which must there be entertained, that my influence with the government is insuperable.' Ecclesiastical appointments, meanwhile, were complicated not only by George III's stipulations, but also by special requests made by others (including the Marchioness of Stafford in February 1787, a royal chaplain, the Rev. Rhudde of Suffolk, in June 1791, and Wilberforce in August 1797).

As for party cohesion, here the Foxites led the way. Fox generally maintained close contact with his followers, and his section of the opposition was more united and easier to organize than were supporters of the ministry. Pitt's aversion to party spirit was highlighted by his description of himself as an 'independent Whig', which indicated general adherence to the principles and achievements of the Glorious Revolution rather than membership of a fixed political party. His father had tried to operate outside the great aristocratic connections, on the basis of 'measures not men', and Pitt also wanted to avoid a close association with the Whig magnates and patrons who for so long had dominated political life. He did not want them to dominate *him*. One of the reasons why he took up parliamentary reform was his desire to weaken the grip of aristocratic patrons and their party formations (he thought he could do this by disfranchising rotten boroughs and redistributing seats).

Notwithstanding his anti-party views, in time Pitt became the acknowledged leader of an identifiable group in the Commons. This group was not large (it was estimated in 1788 that he had fifty-two close followers, and in 1802 fifty-seven), and the government's majority in the Commons depended on much more than Pitt's personal following. Even among his regular supporters, indeed, he did not expect absolute obedience. He told Canning that a generally favourable attitude towards the ministry was enough, and he seems to have been quite prepared for junior members of the government (and individuals who had benefited from his patronage, such as Canning's friend the ninth Earl of Abercorn) to vote against the ministerial line on certain issues. Pitt insisted on unanimity only when specific divisions were likely to affect the government's stability or survival. After the regency crisis he moved against those who had departed from this rule, dismissing some, refusing to promote others (among the 'rats' were Sir John Aubrey, MP for Buckinghamshire, Robert Laurie, MP for Dumfriesshire, and Alexander Stewart, MP for Kirkcudbright). Wilberforce remarked upon the nature of the government's 'party' in 1788 on the question of the slave trade. Ministers and their supporters in the Commons were not united on this issue, even though Pitt himself was for abolition.

> It is undeniably the established rule that all official men are to vote with their principal; but notwithstanding the systematic support of a Ministry which has resulted from systematic opposition, the Minister is not considered as entitled to require the votes of the inferior members of Government except on political questions. What shall, and what shall not be a Government question, is not an arbitrary arrangement dependent on the part of the Minister – it turns upon the question, is the credit or stability of the Ministry at stake? In the instance therefore of my motion ... everyone was perfectly at liberty to vote as he saw fit. It was in no sense a party question.[52]

Pitt's respect for his supporters' freedom of opinion meant that he did not seek to enforce loyalty. Instead, he hoped that the merits of the government's position on important questions would be seen without the need for tight discipline. This approach to parliamentary organization may have been forced upon him. The government's following was really a broad coalition (including allies of the crown, reformers, and various groups that had opposed the Fox-North administration) and therefore could not be treated as a united party, whatever Pitt's preferences might have been. Inevitably, with no clear position agreed or enforced on particular issues, government supporters were often unsure of Pitt's views and sought more direction. Sometimes he made his wishes known in advance of a crucial division – notably that on the motion to repeal the Test and Corporation Acts in 1787 – yet these interventions seem to have been quite unusual. In April and May 1785, Daniel Pulteney reported a serious want of clarity with respect to parliamentary reform and the Irish commercial propositions. For government supporters, wrote Pulteney, there was the problem of 'never finding out but with great difficulty what Mr Pitt intends when he first moves any resolution', since he tended to wait and see what opposition leaders would do before making his own position clear.

Lack of communication caused problems when Pitt negotiated the juncture with Portland Whigs in 1794. Agreement had to be reached on appointments and patronage, and for their part Portland and his colleagues bargained collectively. On behalf of the government, however, Pitt negotiated everything by himself, and Canning found that a number of Pitt's followers were annoyed when they discovered how much Pitt had offered to persuade the Portland Whigs to join the government: 'many, very many ... either grumble pretty audibly or at best, shake their heads and wish that it may answer in the end. I know there are persons who yet have nothing, and for whom something must in justice first have been done'. This unease increased when one of the Portland Whigs, the second Earl Fitzwilliam, went to Ireland as lord lieutenant and proceeded to reorganize the administration there rather more rapidly than the prime minister had sanctioned. Some of Pitt's supporters wondered if he really was still in charge of the government, and were not reassured until Fitzwilliam was recalled, measures were passed to combat radical agitation, and the Portland Whigs' war aim of restoring the French monarchy was dropped.[53]

But the changes in Ireland and generosity to the Portland Whigs continued to rankle. A prominent critic was Buckingham, who sought promotions for himself and his family at this time, and lamented that while titles and cabinet posts had gone to Pitt's former enemies, his own loyalty and past services had not been adequately rewarded. He was also sensitive about reforms in Ireland, in case these were taken to imply that his own performance as lord lieutenant there (from 1787 to 1789) had somehow been deficient. Pitt tried to reassure him that no slight was intended, and promised to look into the possibility of an Irish peerage for Buckingham's second son. As for the juncture with the Portland Whigs, however, Pitt insisted that he had only done what was necessary.

Anything that appeared to me to convey an imputation of your system of measures in Ireland, or to injure the fair claims of those who supported you, I felt myself bound decidedly to resist, from a sense of what was due to you, as well as to myself. But, on the other hand, I could not feel that, under the present circumstances, the past conduct of those of whom you and I had so much just reason to complain, ought to be a bar against re-admitting them to a share of the government, provided they were willing to join on fair and honourable grounds, and on the same principles as have been felt sufficient to bury former distinctions of party in this country. In this point seems to consist the only material difference between our sentiments; and even if, upon reflection, you retain your opinion, you will, I trust, admit that you have no reason to be dissatisfied with the motives which influenced mine.[54]

Perhaps Buckingham was a special case, in that he was a relative and notoriously proud and difficult, but his complaints typify the need – one to which Pitt often could not or would not submit – for a political leader to communicate with, and indulge and gratify, his supporters.

According to Pulteney, writing in April 1785, Pitt created a rod for his own back:

> From having no immediate intercourse with the generality of the House of Commons, he is as ignorant of their opinions on particular questions as if he was minister of another country ... His living and conversation with a very small circle and acting only on abstract principles will, I foresee, involve him at some time or other in difficulties, from which no minister of this country can be free without more extensive information.

Pitt's early disappointments as premier were largely the result of mismanagement. The repeal of some of his taxes, abandonment of the Westminster scrutiny and rejection of his parliamentary reform plan all had something to do with the failure to consult backbench opinion and explain clearly his intentions and commitments. On the other hand, it could be argued that consultation and explanation would have made little difference on these particular issues (for instance, there was little enthusiasm for parliamentary reform in parliament and out of doors in 1785). These early defeats temporarily dented Pitt's confidence, and throughout his career it appears that serious reversals prompted him to delay the introduction of further measures even when he knew they would secure parliamentary majorities. As Pulteney noted,

> His whole conduct proves he can only be Minister with an independent House; and the very proofs they give of independency, *i.e.* dissenting from him on points where, according to plain common sense, I think they have been in the right, startles him so much that he is too much frightened for some time to bring questions before them.

Pitt's handling of the Irish commercial propositions, the most important measure of the 1785 session, illustrates this point. His hesitance and willingness to make concessions allowed his opponents to rally, which in turn prompted the Irish parliament to reject the scheme after it had been amended.[55]

Problems created by Pitt's management style gradually became less troublesome. He had the willpower to get through early difficulties, enhanced his authority with important successes, especially his financial reforms, and benefited from the weaknesses of the parliamentary opposition. Pitt developed the strengths and skills he needed to be an effective leader. He brought in men of drive and talent as responsible assistants, and used his debating and patronage capabilities remarkably well. The dispensing of offices, honours and rewards helped to make up for his personal shortcomings as a parliamentary manager, and the fact that an increasing number of former opponents fell in behind the government indicates the growing awareness that Pitt was well worth supporting. As has been mentioned, the opposition's financial expert William Eden, who had helped to defeat Pitt's Irish commercial propositions, was won over with a special commission (he went to France to negotiate the Anglo-French commercial treaty of 1786). Another high profile convert was Malmesbury, who sided with the government in 1793 (having previously supported Fox during the regency crisis).[56]

Pitt used titles and honours far more than his predecessors had done, and among the beneficiaries were borough patrons who controlled seats in the Commons. This increased Pitt's influence in both houses of parliament. Indeed, many peerages went to men who were or had at some time been members of the House of Commons, and this encouraged lasting rather than merely short-term adherence to the government. The coalition with the Portland Whigs in 1794 very much depended on what Pitt could deliver in terms of reward. Although Portland and his friends were moved by concerns about the war with France and radical agitation at home, and saw convincing public grounds for an accommodation with the government, the alliance could not have been arranged without Pitt's generous offer of five places in the cabinet, five peerages and one promotion in the peerage, the Garter for Portland, a pension for Burke, two offices in the royal household, the lord lieutenancy of Middlesex, and the promise of the lord lieutenancy of Ireland. Portland brought sixty-two MPs with him, leaving the Foxites in the Commons as a small and isolated party of about fifty-five MPs.[57] Pitt made a similar bargain late in 1804, though not on the same scale, when he negotiated a union with Henry Addington and his followers, but times had changed and this merger was not as useful as that of 1794.

Careful electoral arrangements were necessary for the development and retention of influence in parliament. Pitt took a keen interest in elections, and worked closely with such advisers as treasury secretaries Rose and Long in order to enhance the government's prospects. The number of seats directly under government control was small. Pitt told Canning in 1792 that there were only six, and in the spring of 1796 there appeared to be only three. But many seats were controlled by patrons who made them available in return for money, favours, contracts or appointments. The main role of government agents was to bring suitable candidates together with amenable patrons. Candidates usually paid their own way, though when necessary secret service money was used to seal electoral bargains. The general election of 1784 was a resounding success, despite the prevalent political instability and lack of time for preparation. Planning for the next election began during the summer of 1788, but was interrupted by the regency crisis. Nevertheless, at the general election of June 1790 the ministry won an overall majority of about 120. The next general election, for which preparations were made during 1795, took place in May 1796. The government won 424 seats, the opposition 95, and there were 29 'independents' and 10 'doubtfuls'. Under Pitt, therefore, the government enjoyed a lasting electoral dominance, winning over patrons and voters by various means and exploiting to the full the shortcomings of the Foxites and wartime loyalty to the established order. Scottish patronage networks headed by Dundas were particularly important. At the 1784 election the government won 24 of the 45 Scottish seats. In 1796 the share rose to 43 seats. Compared with other groups of government supporters, moreover, the Scottish bloc was more disciplined and reliable.[58]

Governments did not lose general elections during the eighteenth century, and only rarely did a prime minister fall because he lost the confidence of the House of Commons. After 1784 Pitt could reasonably expect to get opportunities to increase his influence in parliament, especially if he demonstrated competence and made no glaring mistakes. Though he did not seek to impose a strict party discipline on government MPs, there were other ways to control business and strengthen the ministry's position. One was to have dependable men in key posts. To have a sympathetic Speaker of the Commons, for example, was to have a useful advantage, and two important divisions went against Pitt on the casting vote of Speakers who were not of his choosing. The fortification project of 1786 was defeated on the casting vote of Speaker Cornwall, an ally of North who had been appointed in October 1780, and the 1805 censure motion against Dundas (Viscount Melville) was passed thanks to Charles Abbot, who had been named as Speaker in February 1802 while Pitt was out of office. It was fortunate for Pitt that Cornwall died during the regency crisis, for he was able to secure the appointment of Grenville as Cornwall's successor (January 1789). After the regency crisis Grenville became home secretary. The new Speaker was Henry Addington, an old friend of Pitt and son of the Chatham family doctor. Addington became Speaker on 8 June 1789. He helped the ministry out on many occasions, as in 1796 when a Commons division on Pitt's legacy duty ended in a tie and Addington used his casting vote for the government (Pitt subsequently withdrew the proposal, owing to its unpopularity). In 1798, after Pitt's severe attack on Tierney, Addington would not ask him to retract his remarks. This was one of the reasons why Tierney challenged Pitt to a duel.

Chairmanship of the ways and means committee in the Commons was also a key position, most notably with regard to the fate of Pitt's financial measures. The prime minister took pains to ensure that the chairman should be amenable. After the 1784 election the post went to Thomas Gilbert, MP for Lichfield. Gilbert was an advocate of economical reform, like Pitt, and an associate of Earl Gower, who sat in Pitt's cabinet as lord president (and subsequently lord privy seal). Gilbert had been Gower's land agent, and his seat in the Commons was a Gower seat. In 1791 Gilbert was succeeded by Henry Hobart, MP for Norwich, one of Pitt's most reliable independent supporters. In 1799 the chairmanship passed to Addington's brother-in-law Charles Bragge, MP for Bristol. It is worth noting that Pitt persuaded the Commons to establish regular salaries for both the Speaker and the chairman of the ways and means committee (in 1789 and 1799 respectively), substantially increasing their remuneration and demonstrating the importance he attached to these posts. His desire to obtain these salaries may have been increased by the requests for money and favours he received from the relatives of Gilbert and Hobart, following their deaths, which made much of the sacrifices they had made in the government's service.[59]

Parliamentary management had its social side, but as indicated above this was not Pitt's forte. He attended dinners and social events, but mainly relied on others to organize or attend these networking occasions on his and the government's behalf. Pitt's sister Harriot acted as his hostess in Downing Street after her marriage in 1785 to his friend Edward Elliot, but she died in September 1786. During the later 1780s the main government hostess was Jane, Duchess of Gordon (whose husband, Alexander, fourth Duke of Gordon, had given Pitt useful support during the regency crisis). Pitt also communicated with government supporters at White's Club, though he does not appear to have been there very often, and indeed his socializing trailed off considerably after the outbreak of war in 1793. In any case he preferred familiar faces and settings, and was most comfortable in the company of his small band of friends and assistants. Links with government supporters were maintained by Pitt's chief aides, especially Dundas, who was a friendly and accessible contact. Dundas transacted many of the deals that reinforced the ministry's position in parliament. During the 1790s Addington co-operated as well. A respected and popular Speaker, Addington was on good terms with most MPs and relayed news and gossip to the prime minister. He engaged in confidential negotiations at Pitt's request, and helped to conciliate disappointed applicants for patronage.

One of these applicants was the Devon MP John Rolle. Pitt had promised Rolle a peerage, but by August 1794 Addington was urging Rolle to be patient, for Pitt had first to satisfy the Portland Whigs, and in any case the timing had to be right for Rolle's ennoblement (that is, the government would have to prepare properly for the resulting by-election in Devon). Rolle did not get his peerage until June 1796, when he became Baron Rolle. Addington also helped Pitt to mollify the ambitious Richard Colley Wellesley, second Earl of Mornington in the Irish peerage, who repeatedly requested high office and a British title. Wellesley had to wait until 1797 before he was created Baron Wellesley in the British peerage and appointed governor general of Bengal (he gained an Irish marquisate two years later). Addington often passed on Pitt's compliments to MPs who had done well in debates and in whose careers the premier had decided to take an interest. In early 1795 Addington approached Sylvester Douglas, later Baron Glenbervie, who had made his mark with two recent speeches in the Commons. After the second of these, Douglas recorded, 'many kind things were said to me by the Speaker both with regard to this and my other speech, and I heard from him that Pitt had been struck and pleased with the last of them, having repeated my very words at a dinner two days after'.[60]

While Dundas and Addington dealt mainly with the rank and file, Pitt trained potential leaders. He had a gift for recognizing and bringing forward young men of talent and ambition. For this some social mixing was necessary, and Pitt occasionally identified promising individuals at dinners or on his visits to Oxbridge colleges, but his principal method was to observe and listen in the House of Commons. As political apprentices he enlisted administrators and debaters whose views accorded with his own, and in whom he could cultivate a creed of efficient and patriotic public service. If his habit of leading from the front and personally taking charge of business limited the opportunities for his protégés, and prompted some of them to complain, Pitt made a point of affording them a chance to prove themselves by giving them real responsibility – notably the prestigious tasks of proposing and seconding the address in reply to the king's speech at beginning of each parliamentary session (tasks normally given to more senior figures).[61] Pitt also enabled his 'new men' to make an impression in other ways, by recommending them for promotion, nominating them for committees, entrusting them with government business, and providing them with information and guidance in advance of debates in which they were due to speak.

Most of those drawn into Pitt's select coterie during the 1780s and 1790s went on to have distinguished public careers, which suggests that Pitt's faith in them was not misplaced. Among the leading beneficiaries of Pitt's tutelage, friendship and encouragement were six future prime ministers: Addington (1801–4), Grenville (1806–7), Spencer Perceval (1809–12),[62] Robert Banks Jenkinson (Lord Hawkesbury from June 1796 and second Earl of Liverpool from December 1808, prime minister 1812–27),[63] Canning (1827),[64] and the fourth Earl of Aberdeen (1852–55).[65] Among the other future cabinet ministers who gained invaluable experience and early opportunities from Pitt were Dudley Ryder (later second Baron and first Earl of Harrowby),[66] Viscount Castlereagh,[67] Charles Yorke,[68] Viscount Morpeth,[69] Granville Leveson Gower,[70] Lord Apsley (later the third Earl Bathurst),[71] Nicholas Vansittart,[72] the Earl of Mornington[73] and Charles Bragge.[74]

Most of Pitt's protégés were admitted to his inner circle of friends and political associates, which added to the cohesion of the efficient administrative corps at the heart of Pitt's regime. They were much in his company, speaking frequently to him and each other, and as well as their talent their sense of collective worth and personal devotion to Pitt were important assets for the government. With them Pitt's aloofness and reserve faded away. Canning found him an agreeable host, 'attentive without being troublesome – mixing in the conversation without attempting to lead it – laughing often and easily'. Mutual trust and respect quickly increased, and Pitt often invited his younger allies to meetings of the main government speakers in Downing Street prior to important debates. He also allowed them regular access to him. He gave them time, listened, advised and assisted. In private, Canning recorded, Pitt was 'just as I would have him – open, free, ready to answer questions without reserve, or to say without reserve that they were such questions as he cannot at present answer'. Granville Leveson Gower noted that Pitt conversed 'with the most unreserved confidence upon almost any subject, argued and discussed points with us upon which he had any doubts, and made jokes ... as if he was exactly our own age'. Here was a different Pitt, not socially awkward at all, and there are many accounts of his cheerful demeanour in private, domestic and recreational settings. This more informal and approachable side to Pitt was politically useful: his loyalty and assistance to his chief allies inspired in them a remarkable attachment to him in return. In May 1804, when Pitt offered Malmesbury's son Lord Fitzharris a seat on the treasury board, he also arranged for the government to pay towards the cost of the appointee's re-election expenses in the constituency of Helstone. Malmesbury wrote that such consideration 'fills the measure of Pitt's kindness, who, during the whole of this transaction, has behaved towards Fitzharris and me as he would towards his nearest relations'. In December 1794 Canning discovered that some of Pitt's supporters were complaining 'that my manner with

Pitt in the House of Commons is too familiar'. While they felt it proper to maintain a deferential distance when speaking with the prime minister, 'I, it seems, stand in no awe whatever, but talk to him without reserve or hesitation at all times, and laugh and make jokes – and *once* was seen ... to put my hand upon his shoulder'. Canning insisted that if his detractors imagined Pitt to be offended by such familiarity, they had no idea what he was really like: 'he is in fact a very hearty, *salutation-giving, shake-handy* sort of person'. A few weeks earlier Canning had dined in a select group at the home of Dundas, and found Pitt 'in very good spirits – for even in these desperate times one is allowed to be very merry if one likes'.[75]

Along with this social interaction, reciprocal loyalty and gathering of expertise, so crucial for managing parliament, Pitt and his subordinates engaged in efforts to guide debates, test opinion, and ensure that government business was conducted in the desired manner. There would be meetings before and during the parliamentary session, and regular correspondence (especially to encourage MPs' attendance and support). When the government faced serious difficulty, extra energy was expended on contacting and rallying supporters, a pattern established in the early months of Pitt's premiership. Hence Sydney's report to George III in January 1784, that a cabinet meeting had been delayed 'on account of Mr Pitt's being obliged to consult with several members of the House of Commons on the subject of the India Bill in the earlier part of the day'. In April 1788 Grenville wrote of having engaged in 'a personal canvass' before an important division, and Canning noted in January 1794 that he had received 'the pressing circular letter which has been sent (as I believe is usual) to every Member of Parliament'. Canning also remarked that Pitt liked to select the days on which specific items of business would be dealt with.

There was careful planning behind the government's approach to major debates. Usually Pitt lined up a group of speakers to answer opposition spokesmen in turn. He arranged the running order, clarified the points that needed to be made, and tried to anticipate and deal with any problems. By the mid-1790s there was a select cluster of powerful speakers on the government side. This group regularly met in Downing Street to agree a strategy for debates, and included cabinet ministers who sat in the Commons (especially Pitt and Dundas), the crown's law officers (master of the rolls, attorney general and solicitor general), influential junior ministers (such as Dudley Ryder), and younger supporters of Pitt who had a talent for debate (normally Canning and Robert Banks Jenkinson). One of the Portland Whigs' best speakers, James Adair (MP for Higham Ferrers, 1793 to 1798), often attended these meetings too, as did Pitt's friend Thomas Steele, a former treasury secretary (MP for Chichester, 1780 to 1807) who advised about backbench opinion. When necessary Pitt invited 'experts' on the specific issues at stake, particularly when they related to foreign policy or finance.[76]

Without his diligent junior assistants, Pitt would never have been able to manage parliament. Not all of them were appointed to government office. Some were most useful on the backbenches or in Commons committees. Pitt's mastery of the committee system through his allies and nominees, indeed, was one of the main foundations of his ascendancy in the Commons. He paid close attention to committee affairs. Though rank and file government supporters found him aloof and distant in the Commons chamber, in committee rooms he was busy and watchful. Once Pitt had identified and recruited men of ability, he appointed them to strategic positions on committees and attended committee meetings in order to keep up with developments (and spot more talent).

Sometimes he resorted to questionable methods in order to make sure that important committees would not obstruct the government. One tactic was to propose that their members should be chosen by secret ballot. The outcome of any ballot would not be in doubt if the names of Pitt's nominees were circulated in advance to supporters of the ministry. Pitt made good use of his most reliable adjutants in managing the committees: during the session of 1799–1800, Dudley Ryder and Robert Jenkinson sat on nine and fourteen committees respectively. Pitt's overall control meant that committee recommendations helped to justify measures that he and his cabinet had already decided to implement. Some reports were used to extenuate speedy legislation (emergency measures to suspend constitutional liberties, for example, in 1794 and 1799). They could influence backbenchers, undermine criticism and hamper opponents, as in 1797 when Pitt moved to defend the suspension of cash payments. They could help the government to deflect pressure or postpone action on difficult issues, notably sinecures and salaries. Committee reports also enabled ministers to change course without alienating supporters or creating unwelcome controversy. During the dearth of 1795, Pitt pursued in swift succession both an interventionist and a free trade approach to the situation. If proof were needed of his tactical shrewdness, we need look no further than Pitt's skilful use of committees: obviously policies could proceed more successfully if parliament was made to feel involved.[77]

Although Pitt became the dominant figure in parliament, he never had complete hegemony. For all his talent and influence, and despite his ingenious deployment of colleagues and assistants, he did not have everything his own way. There was tension within the broad government coalition. Defections and enmities were not unknown. Offence was taken at Pitt's aloofness and lack of response to requests for patronage, and there could also be genuine disagreement on policy. In the absence of strong party discipline on the government side, backbench discontent was always a possibility and, on some measures, Pitt's majority declined. He had to be wary of this. Many MPs and peers were proud of their 'independence' and openly avowed their intention to support good proposals and oppose bad ones, no matter where they originated. Pitt's defeats during the mid-1780s were followed by obstruction of the government's naval programme and Indian policy in 1788, and then the regency crisis dramatically polarized parliamentary opinion and placed ministers under an enormous strain. Pitt recovered, but serious trouble arose again early in 1791 at the time of the Ochakov crisis. Pitt hoped to win his dispute with Russia by preparing for war. Support in the Commons dwindled, however, and he had to modify his position. Thurlow's departure from the ministry in 1792 made Pitt stronger, and the cabinet looked more robust after the juncture with the Portland Whigs in July 1794. But the war against revolutionary France brought new pressures   not only in terms of its cost and the domestic disorder that accompanied it, but also because of the impact of the peace movement (with Wilberforce and other MPs at its head). There were controversies relating to the royal family, especially the Prince of Wales. The year 1797 was particularly difficult for Pitt. The war was going badly in Europe, there were invasion scares, a run on the banks (necessitating the suspension of cash payments), naval mutinies, and growing doubts about Pitt's leadership as his energy and health began to falter. Over the following two years he had to fight hard to overcome objections to further financial reform.

Although Pitt's dominance was far from complete, defeats were unusual. His debating power and command of procedure, the mistakes and weaknesses of his opponents, and the ability he developed (drawing on his experience) to predict what the Commons would and would not approve, helped him to avoid or get himself and his ministry out of embarrassing scrapes. When he had no choice, of course, Pitt looked for an honourable way of altering or abandoning his plans. Sometimes he could retrieve the situation with an outstanding speech. On 29 October 1795, as pressure mounted for an end to the war, Pitt triumphantly defended his policy of continuing to fight and negotiating only when circumstances improved. Many MPs who had been complaining about the prime minister were won over, and Canning was one of many observers who paid tribute to Pitt's performance. He deemed 'the impression of it upon the House beyond anything that I ever witnessed'.[78] When eloquent arguments failed to work, Pitt retreated. To some observers he gave way too easily. George III was especially touchy on this score. In March 1797, when MPs questioned Pitt's efforts to protect credit and improve the public finances, the king noted his chief minister's tendency to offer concessions:

> I think Parliament generally enters warmly into all measures brought forward, but of late years, unfortunately, the subsequent steps get a languor that often shews a want of energy, which I fear often arises from too much candour, and that those who are disinclined to any exertion somehow or other are too much attended to, and consequently, that whilst the object is getting through its various stages it is totally different to the original proposition. My nature is quite different. I never assent till I am convinced that what is proposed is right ... then I never allow that to be destroyed by afterthoughts which on all subjects tend to weaken, never to strengthen, the original proposal.

In January 1798 the king complained about alterations that had been made to the bill for assessed taxes. He told Pitt that a worthy measure had thereby been rendered far less useful: 'sometimes, unfortunately, right gives way to expedience. When it does, I am ever hurt; for, as a plain man, I think right and wrong ought never to be blended for any momentary purpose, and try to inculcate that principle as much as possible.' In fact, depending on the issue at stake, a willingness to defer to parliament's wishes may have strengthened Pitt's position by persuading Commons and Lords that the government respected them and deserved their confidence. Defeating the government on particular measures made MPs and peers feel that their views really mattered, and they became more willing to pass Pitt's most ambitious measures in the knowledge that they could stop him as and when they wished. Pitt used this trust to carry far-reaching reforms that would otherwise have been impossible – the introduction of income tax and the legislative union with Ireland. The Commons majority also accepted some remarkable offences against parliamentary authority, particularly the extension of the volunteer movement in 1794 without parliament's sanction, and secret payments to Austria in 1796. Austria's urgent request for £1,200,000 came during the 1796 general election. Pitt went ahead and made the loan. When pressed by opposition MPs in December, he defended this as an extraordinary wartime necessity, promised not to repeat it, and secured an indemnity by 285 to 81 votes.[79]

Pitt's position in parliament was enhanced by his popularity out of doors. As noted, he tried to win over influential sections of respectable public opinion (the City of London, reform associations, property-owners and members of the Established Church), and by claiming to have extra-parliamentary support for particular measures he could increase their appeal within the legislature. Meanwhile, Pitt's performances in and management of the Commons were also likely to impress the public. The prime minister knew that parliament could be used to influence outdoor opinion, and vice-versa. Therefore he was keen to have his budget speeches, and the king's speech at the beginning of each session, widely reported and discussed. This linking of parliamentary and public arenas helped Pitt to shape the course of events in both. Sometimes he called parliament to meet early, in order to prevent the spread of alarm among the people (as in the early stages of the war, or during the subsistence crises of the 1790s).

Foxites realized that Pitt's dominance in parliament affected his reputation in the country, and this was one of the reasons for their secession of 1797. Following the defeat of Charles Grey's motion for parliamentary reform in May 1797, many Foxites abstained from attending parliament. Fox himself stayed away for several years. In part the secession was a confession of failure, for the opposition could make little impression on parliament or out of doors at this time, but it was also a highly principled protest against the government's manipulation of political life. The idea was that Pitt's measures should not be accorded the legitimacy bestowed by parliamentary debate and division. Foxites hoped that parliament would thereby lose its value to Pitt as a place where he could defend his policies and gain opportunities to shape public opinion.[80]

Press reports of parliamentary proceedings helped Pitt because they made plain the force and quality of his speeches, and like previous governments Pitt's was directly involved with the press. During 1784 there were payments to printers, writers, and six metropolitan newspapers (including the *Morning Post*, *Morning Herald* and *London Evening Post*) as part of the ministry's effort to establish itself in power. For a while Lord Mahon acted as go-between, supplying editors with copies of Pitt's speeches. The regency crisis stimulated a more active engagement with the press, for opposition as well as government, and this continued beyond the 1790 general election. By 1792 Pitt's administration was subsidizing seven of the fourteen London daily papers, and individual writers and publishers were also on the payroll (the total expenditure was nearly £5000 a year). When the government established its own papers, the *Sun* and *True Briton*, subsidies to other papers were phased out. The post office was increasingly used to distribute material to friendly newspapers in the provinces. Pitt did not usually handle the press himself, preferring to have others perform the necessary tasks, though he sometimes corrected his own speeches for publication in newspapers or as pamphlets, and advised others who wrote in support of the government. James Bland Burges had Pitt's co-operation late in 1792 when he wrote on events in France. His purpose in writing was to prepare the public mind for the possibility of war.[81]

In examining Pitt's leadership style, one cannot escape the paradox between his managerial stance and his lack of system. On one hand, he was ambitious, determined to lead and inclined to take charge of all key areas of policy. But on the other hand, his manner of dealing with business was frequently haphazard and disorganized. This is not to deny that he was hard working, nor to gainsay his reputation for efficiency and thoroughness. The paradox really arose because Pitt much preferred a personal and informal method of government to a tidy, structured, regular and carefully minuted one.

As a policy maker Pitt engaged in painstaking research in order to get his facts straight before making plans. He would put in a long day, working far into the night, and was often so preoccupied with business that he skipped meals. Normally he liked to relax and have company over dinner, but after a break he went back to work, assisted by the relevant officials. To major policy plans Pitt would devote himself single-mindedly for days or even weeks. His wartime financial measures involved exhaustive preparation and many long discussions with colleagues and advisers (on the income tax he sought the views of, among others, Rose, Auckland, Addington, Liverpool, Grenville and Canning). This concentrated effort helped Pitt to identify problems and contemplate solutions. Consultation was central to his approach. In September 1788 he confessed to Grenville his need for some pointers on the situation in Holland: 'I do not like to trust to my own single opinion, which is nearly all I have to trust to on this subject at present. I should be glad therefore, if possible, to talk it over with you as soon as you can make it convenient.' Pitt often engaged his experts, political friends and (sometimes) junior officials in open discussion, during which he expressed doubts as well as confident expectations.

After making his decision he energetically pursued it, and was able to motivate others too, encouraging them with his enthusiasm and command of detail. Bland Burges wrote of Pitt's 'talents, quickness, temper and application', and John Fordyce, a commissioner for the crown lands, was impressed by the 'extreme quickness of his apprehension' and his 'undivided and unprejudiced attention'. According to Wilberforce (writing in February 1806), Pitt had the qualities necessary for effective leadership:

> a clear and comprehensive view of the most complicated subject in all its relations ... fairness of mind which disposes a man to follow out, and when overtaken to recognize the truth; magnanimity, which made him ready to change his measures when he thought the good of his country required it, though he knew he should be charged with inconsistency on account of the change; willingness to give a fair hearing to all that could be urged against his own opinions ... For personal purity, disinterestedness, integrity, and love of his country, I have never known his equal.

It was unusual for Pitt to embark upon a risky course of action without first testing the ground. One of the reasons why the Ochakov crisis is so notable is because Pitt was not properly prepared.[82]

For all the planning, there was great flexibility and improvisation. The appointment of William Huskisson as head of the aliens department in January 1793 illustrates the way in which Pitt dealt with matters in an informal, ad hoc fashion. After the French Revolution many émigrés came to Britain and Pitt decided that an office should be created for dealing with their claims and interests. As with his solutions to so many other problems, once he had decided on the appropriate action he looked around for a suitable person to whom responsibility could be delegated. Huskisson fitted the bill. He had lived in France, was fluent in the language, and had become a confidant of Lord Gower (eldest surviving son of the second Earl Gower, subsequently Marquess of Stafford, lord privy seal from 1784 to 1794). Gower had been British ambassador in Paris, and Huskisson had served as his private secretary from 1790 to 1792, when they both returned to England. Huskisson frequently met Pitt and Dundas through his association with Gower. With respect to the new aliens department, therefore, Huskisson's availability combined with Pitt's pragmatic fondness for dealing with problems as they arose, with whatever means were available, resulted in a satisfactory outcome.[83]

In working with colleagues and subordinates Pitt preferred direct contact, most often a simple conversation with those who had advice or information (he disliked writing letters).[84] He tended increasingly to deal with business informally and as a social activity. Dundas and Pitt habitually settled affairs of state while taking their morning ride or evening walk in Wimbledon, where Dundas lived. These practices meant that Pitt rarely had any prolonged diversion from public questions, for he mixed business and pleasure. He often entertained guests at his residences, Holwood House and Walmer Castle, but they usually included cabinet colleagues, so the mixing of public responsibilities and personal life went on. Pitt never took a complete rest from his work as prime minister (and eventually this ruined his health). Having arranged to visit Lord Gower in January 1793, for example, he arrived late and was obviously pressed for time. As Huskisson noted, he 'only stayed during dinner, at which the conversation turned entirely upon business'. Huskisson also remarked that Pitt and his colleagues were so busy that they could not attend to requests for favours or assistance. One result of this 'constant hurry and confusion' was 'the rule laid down by all, to treat all applications as importunous without a proper discrimination'.[85]

Pitt's disorderly methods meant that, although he achieved a great deal, much was left undone, and there was growing concern about possible breaches of confidentiality and the uneven pace of executive action. Pitt failed to answer letters or keep his papers in order (even foreign envoys heard of his reputation for losing important items amidst the clutter in his work rooms),[86] and while Grenville, both as home secretary and foreign secretary, improved the collection and assessment of information by arranging for the preparation of useful synopses, Pitt (recorded Charles Abbot) 'will not suffer anybody to arrange his papers and extract the important points for him'. Preferring to take care of business personally rather than in writing, it was not Pitt's practice to keep minutes of meetings. During the Fitzwilliam crisis one of the main problems was the lack of a clear record of what had been discussed and agreed prior to Fitzwilliam's departure for Ireland. If Pitt became enthusiastic about a plan, he pursued it with speed and energy and appears to have thought that personal action was more likely to achieve the desired results. Therefore there was no need for minutes, records or letters – paperwork would just cause delay. The prime minister approached the weightiest of issues in this spirit, including the legislative union with Ireland. He set up an informal, unofficial committee to arrange the union, and did not even confirm its existence to parliament. Pitt also preferred to put off business that he found uninteresting, but if forced to settle it he did so quickly. George III believed that this irregular pattern of procrastination and haste contributed to Pitt's health problems.[87]

Pitt's desire for involvement in all the main areas of government imposed a heavy burden, and the pressure of responsibility was exacerbated by his working habits. The strain began clearly to show in the late 1790s. His consumption of alcohol increased; his optimism drained away when problems defied rapid solution; he also depended more on the praise and companionship of close friends, and this need for approval may occasionally have clouded his judgement. Perhaps these frailties relate to his relative youth and inexperience when he became prime minister, which made him more likely to attend to matters personally and informally, to arrange things verbally without keeping a full record, and to take a large burden of administrative work directly upon his own shoulders. The volume of business in itself limited the time available to get things done, reinforcing Pitt's eagerness to lead from the front. At the same time, his disorganized manner made him all the more reliant on those who *were* methodical and orderly. Without the contributions of Dundas, Rose and Grenville, Pitt would have found it even more difficult to conduct business successfully. He worked hard, but his labour lacked a systematic pattern. Pitt tried to be thorough and to meet major problems with comprehensive solutions. The fate of his Irish commercial propositions, however, demonstrates that his all-embracing schemes were not infallible. For the most part, Pitt's essential pragmatism prompted expedients and, quite often, changes of direction in the face of obstacles. Despite all his planning, therefore, the government could not always follow a consistent course.

As has been suggested, these difficulties were compounded by Pitt's awkwardness outside his intimate circle. He was unable easily to restore relations after serious disagreement on a public question, a serious handicap in view of the fact that his leadership style made personal clashes likely. The Duke of Richmond felt he had reason to complain at the end of 1794 when it became clear that Pitt intended to remove him from the ministry. The truth is that Richmond had to go: his office (master general of the ordnance) carried important wartime responsibilities, yet he had missed cabinet meetings, reacted badly when he could not get his way, and had offended the Portland Whigs with his apparent lack of commitment. Richmond chose to focus instead upon his relationship with Pitt, which had cooled, and he blamed Pitt's awkward manner.

> I am not conscious of ever having been deficient in friendship towards you. If you have anything to complain of, I think I have at least that call upon you to desire you will explain what you have taken amiss. And I am sure you will find it to have arisen from some error or misunderstanding that had misled you. If it is merely the shyness of your disposition, which when there has been any little rub knows not how to bring matters to rights again, it were a pity that such a circumstance should separate you from a real friend.[88]

Taken together, the problems outlined above reveal much about the enigma of Pittite government. It appeared to be confident, sure-footed and careful, but it could also be erratic, unpatterned and disorganized.

1. Willliam Pitt the Younger, portrait by Thomas Gainsborough. (*Bridgeman Art Library*)

4. William Pitt the Elder, first Earl of Chatham, by artist in the studio of William Hoare. (*National Portrait Gallery*)

5. George III, portrait by Sir William Beechey, 1800. (*National Portrait Gallery*)

6. Charles James Fox, portrait by Karl Anton Hickel, *c.* 1793. (*National Portrait Gallery*)

7. Henry Dundas, first Viscount Melville, portrait by unknown artist; exhibited 1810. (*National Portrait Gallery*)

8. William Pitt the Younger, portrait by artist in studio of John Hoppner, 1804–5. (*National Portrait Gallery*)

6

Revolution and War

The French Revolution and subsequent war had a profound effect on Britain's internal politics and external relations. Pitt came to the premiership in 1783 with limited knowledge of foreign affairs, but in the following years he managed to raise Britain's prestige and international influence. By the mid-1790s, after the merger with the Portland Whigs had broadened its basis, the government seemed better able to face the challenging situations created at home and abroad by revolution and war. Pitt, however, erred in believing that the war against France would be brief, and wartime pressures posed serious problems for him and his regime. Popular distress and radical agitation, financial and economic dislocation, cabinet quarrels, difficulties in managing parliament and the king, questions of strategy, recruitment and supply, and unreliable European allies stretched the energies of Pitt and his associates to their very limits.

The French Revolution transformed British politics by introducing new controversies and quickening developments already in progress. By now Pitt's government had attracted wide support domestically, and the king was enjoying a wave of popularity after the regency crisis. The Foxites had made little progress with the trial of Warren Hastings, there was tension between Fox and Burke, and Fox's union with the Portland group was increasingly in doubt.[1] Divergent opposition Whig responses to the French Revolution deepened these divisions, while Pitt, cautious as ever, waited to see how events in France would proceed before openly committing himself to a particular course of action. Revolution in France, and reactions in Britain, stimulated greater political activity out of doors as radicals reinterpreted concepts of reform and 'rights', and focused more stridently on the shortcomings of the representative system. Extra-parliamentary organization and protest took on added significance.

In fact British politics had been unsettled for some time before the outbreak of the French Revolution in 1789. From November 1788 there was widespread celebration to mark the centenary of the Glorious Revolution. Then came the regency crisis, which further increased public excitement. By the following summer, only four months after George III's recovery,

France had experienced the early stages of revolutionary confusion. The Foxites welcomed what they saw as a French version of Britain's Glorious Revolution. Freed from the shackles of monarchical despotism, they assumed, France could now enjoy ordered liberty and progress. George III regarded limitation of the French king's powers as just recompense for his alliance with American rebels between 1778 and 1783. Pitt hoped that reforms in France would increase the benefits of the Anglo-French commercial treaty. He and Grenville also looked forward to safer times in Europe.[2] Pitt's chief concerns were still domestic: to improve administration and balance budgets. He said little about France at this time, believing that the question of how to respond to the French Revolution would be more troublesome for the opposition than for the government.

Pitt had done much to restore Britain's strength and influence since 1783, when the position had been bleak. As the newly appointed premier he had inherited not only the political instability promoted by the downfall of North and loss of America, but all the financial and economic problems caused by the unsuccessful American war. Ireland had demanded and secured a measure of self-government. The French had lived up to their record as traditional enemies by joining the Americans against Britain, threatening the security of British colonies and the home islands. What could the young Pitt offer with the nation's fortunes at such a low point? He was not very knowledgeable about the international scene. Indeed, he spent no time abroad except for six weeks in France during the autumn of 1783, and his reading and learning were based mainly on the classics, not foreign languages or international affairs.[3] But he had the undoubted advantage of a famous name, for his father had been a glorious war leader in the past, and he was not associated with the failures of North. Untainted by defeat in America, Pitt could not be blamed for Britain's loss of prestige. As prime minister Pitt realized that he had to attend to foreign affairs as an urgent priority. The key to a recovery of great power status, he decided, lay in economic improvement and financial reorganization.

Pitt knew that it would take years to restore confidence, increase prosperity, expand trade and enhance the resources of the state, and that until these ends were achieved Britain could not hope to influence events abroad. In readiness for this he carefully studied international affairs, making up for his previous ignorance and preparing himself for the opportunities that would eventually present themselves. The foreign secretary, Lord Carmarthen, noted early on that Pitt paid more attention to the relevant topics than did other members of the cabinet. Pitt and Carmarthen agreed that Britain would not be able to fight another war for some time. It was also clear that no major European power would be interested in an alliance with

Britain, in view of the recent defeat in America and the possibility that Pitt's government would not last. This reinforced Pitt's emphasis on wealth as the basis of international strength, for without a helpful ally the British were reliant on their own efforts and resources. The government's determination to promote trade, develop the navy and consolidate the empire was demonstrated in such measures as the Navigation Act of 1786. Its main author was Charles Jenkinson, Lord Hawkesbury, and it established a register of British shipping, offered protection to British and imperial shipping interests, and helped to create a supply of experienced seafarers for the navy. Pitt also made sure that sufficient funds were available to expand the navy. Between 1783 and 1793, annual expenditure on the construction and repair of vessels rose well above previous peacetime levels (Pitt's careful financial management ensured that the navy benefited from higher government revenue and savings in other areas). On these matters the prime minister worked closely with Sir Charles Middleton, the navy comptroller. Pitt took a detailed interest in improvements, often met with Middleton, and chose not to risk delay or obstruction by referring everything to the navy board.

Imperial trade increased in these years. American goods were excluded from the West Indies in order to boost the economy of Canada, which took over as a supplier. The Canada Act of 1791 also encouraged trade by reorganizing Canada's government and promoting political stability. Pitt recognized the strategic and commercial importance of India as well. The India Act of 1784 and subsequent reforms extended the government's role in Indian affairs, and the French threat receded once Pitt restored British influence over the Dutch and their Indian possessions in 1787. Britain's trade in China and the Pacific expanded during the late 1780s and early 1790s, and Pitt's obsession with trade as a means to international power was underlined by the Nootka Sound dispute with Spain in 1790. To Pitt, Britain's recovery could only be accomplished if the essential foundations of empire, trade and shipping were firmly in place.[4]

Pitt often spoke of these foundations in the Commons. In March 1785, when recommending the plan for new fortifications at Portsmouth and Plymouth, he emphasized 'the two most important interests of this country; the one related to our ability in point of finance ... and the second regarded our marine, a part of our policy, if possible, as essential as that of our Treasury'. As for the empire, Pitt's main concerns were to impose order and cohesion, and to enhance and utilize the empire's resources. A vital requirement was effective administration in the colonies. Britain's imperial system, Pitt remarked in January 1784, rested on stable government at home, and 'all our dependencies cannot continue to exist, unless in our Asiatic

and European politics there be some unity of action'. Aware of the importance of India, Pitt pointed to the need for 'a permanency of system that
gives to the crown of these realms the sway over its Indian, much in the
same manner as over its other dependencies, and insures to it a permanent,
regular, systematic and supreme control over all the political affairs of that
vast country'. Pitt has often been called an architect of empire, although
some commentators contend that his lack of interest in settlement schemes
for Australia denoted a lack of imperial imagination. Another view, that of
Pitt's great-nephew the fifth Earl Stanhope, is that the measures of 1787,
which established the penal colony at Botany Bay, 'laid the foundation of
new colonies, scarcely less important than those which we had recently
lost'. It is obvious that Pitt saw Britain as an imperial power, and that he
appreciated the wider ramifications of his financial, economic, naval and
administrative reforms. Pitt was at least a facilitator, if not a prime mover.
He may not have acted upon a distinctive long-term imperial design, but
his desire to consolidate the empire had lasting impact at home and overseas.

Pitt's policies directly influenced Britain's activities abroad. He promoted
freer trade, a dynamic commercial spirit and the interests of the City of
London; he reformed public finance and established (for the time) a trustworthy method of managing the national debt; he raised and made use of
the political authority of the propertied classes; and he applied all these
resources to the enhancement of national and imperial security. Although
the expansionist tendency of these measures became more obvious after
Pitt's premiership, modern historians have shown that the advantages made
available by late eighteenth-century innovations in credit, shipping and
commerce could be fully realized only by increasing their international
scope. Certainly Britain's global position changed as a result of involvement
in the French wars from 1793. War increased the national debt and prompted
further reorganization of taxation and expenditure. The 'fiscal-military state'
mushroomed. War rearranged the old European frontiers and affected the
balance of power in other continents, providing opportunities for British
expansion, and the gains made between 1793 and 1815 (colonies, bases,
markets, raw materials) made possible the subsequent growth of the empire.
Consolidation of empire, reinforcement of political, social and racial hier-
archies, the greater size and authority of the government, the massive
expansion of trade – all can be traced to the policies pursued by Pitt's
ministry during the 1780s and 1790s.[5]

Efforts to improve Britain's international position were sometimes obstructed by arguments within the government. There may have been general
agreement with Pitt's goals, but disputes about tactics and details often
surfaced. Relations between Pitt and Carmarthen were not close. Another

complicating factor was George III's special interest in foreign policy. George III was Elector of Hanover. Though he disliked Hanover, his powers there were not constitutionally limited as in the United Kingdom, and on the affairs of Hanover his British ministers could offer no advice unless they were asked for it. In fact the king hardly ever chose to consult the cabinet about Hanover (in this he followed the practice of George I and George II). George III's readiness to pursue his own German policy seriously embarrassed Pitt's administration in 1785, when Hanover became a founder-member of the Prussian-led German league that opposed Austria's attempt to exchange its Netherlands provinces for Bavaria. This dispute handicapped Carmarthen, who was trying to establish closer relations with Austria and Russia. When the Russians complained about Hanover's closer association with Prussia, George III insisted that it had nothing to do with them. He plainly informed Pitt in August 1785: 'What I owe in my Electoral capacity to the future stability of the [Holy Roman] Empire has alone actuated my conduct and makes me feel that Russia has no right to interfere'.[6]

Carmarthen was not an especially diligent or gifted foreign secretary at the best of times, and during the mid-1780s Pitt gradually gained more confidence and authority in foreign affairs. Since the proud Carmarthen refused to vacate the foreign office in exchange for another cabinet post, Pitt had to work with him or, as he increasingly did, by-pass him. Sometimes Pitt tried to involve other ministers in particular questions, in the hope that they would push Carmarthen along. But influential figures like Camden and Thurlow were themselves slow in attending to business, and Richmond tended to stay away from cabinet meetings if he thought he could not get his way (even though Pitt specifically asked him to join in discussions of foreign policy). Therefore Pitt assumed responsibility for matters neglected by Carmarthen or on which the foreign secretary could not by himself make a final decision. Perhaps the decisive step in this process was the Anglo-French commercial treaty of 1786. Pitt was directly involved as chief financial minister, and he relied mainly on the assistance of Hawkesbury and Grenville (then Hawkesbury's deputy at the board of trade). Carmarthen was less committed to the treaty, and its terms were settled by Pitt, Grenville and the 'expert' William Eden (Britain's chief negotiator with the French). Other negotiations were opened, too, with Portugal, Spain and Russia, and though nothing came of these, conclusion of the French treaty brought Pitt great acclaim at home and encouraged him to adopt a more proactive approach to the making of foreign policy. Pitt remained cautious about free trade treaties, however, because he was unwilling to jeopardize British naval, imperial, shipping and commercial interests by conceding too much to foreign states. At the same time, the latter were aware that Britain was becoming a stronger economic competitor because of Pitt's reforms, and were therefore less amenable. Between 1783 and 1792 Britain only concluded one commercial treaty, that with France, although eight were negotiated. Pitt's reluctance to make concessions also affected Britain's relations with the United States. Shelburne had wanted commercial agreements as part of the peace settlement after the American war, but Pitt chose not to pursue this idea until the war against revolutionary France increased the value of American friendship (he was also concerned about the security of Canada and hoped to settle outstanding commercial and territorial disputes with the Americans). Despite Hawkesbury's objections, at Pitt's prompting Grenville included elements of freer trade in the Jay Treaty of 1794.[7]

The most important foreign policy test for Pitt's government during the 1780s was the Dutch crisis of 1787. On 20 May 1784 Britain had concluded a treaty of peace and friendship with Holland (the United Provinces) in order to counter French designs and strengthen the Prince of Orange, Holland's head of state. Dutch politics became increasingly volatile as the pro-French 'patriot' party used its ascendancy to bring about an alliance between Holland and France in 1785. Britain's ambassador at The Hague, James Harris (later Lord Malmesbury), urged Pitt's government to intervene. Carmarthen was favourable, and after some initial hesitation Pitt took the initiative. He consulted Harris and convinced waverers in the cabinet, and George III, who wanted no continental entanglements, that Britain should assist the Orange party to withstand French pressure. Pitt dearly wanted to avoid war because it would upset his financial improvements at home, but he was convinced that the French had to be resisted, and in May 1787 the king approved his plan for financial aid to the Orange party.

In June 1787 the 'patriots' arrested the Princess of Orange. Her brother was King Frederick William II of Prussia, and he assembled his forces to avenge this insult. The Orange party also called upon Britain, while the 'patriots' appealed to France. George III was worried by this escalation, but approved British mobilization in support of the Prussians, who undertook to restore the Orange party to power. Pitt sent Grenville to Holland as his personal representative, kept in regular contact with William Eden, who was still in Paris, and united the cabinet behind his policy. After gathering all the information he could about French intentions and the strength of anti-French sentiment in Holland, he decided that France would not go to war. Harris also believed that war was avoidable. Though Eden reported that the French government expected Britain to react, Harris informed Carmarthen (13 July 1787) that the French ambassador in Holland was sure Britain would not intervene. Harris suggested that France could be persuaded to negotiate a settlement without any need for bloodshed.

I remain ... firm in opinion, that unless there be a concerted plan with some other Power, of which I am totally ignorant, France, after having tried the whole effect of menace, will not proceed to extremities, but condescend to settle the degree of influence she is to retain in this Republic by negotiation; for the great object in dispute, as I take it, is not so much how this country is to be governed, but whether France shall, by the exercise of undue influence, get the direction of the Republic wholly into her own hands; or whether it shall be restored to a state of independence, and at liberty either to return to the ancient system, or to form such political connexions as may appear the most suitable to its interests. The attainment of the first point is the end France pursues; that of the second, is the object of England; and on this the whole of the negotiation is to rest.[8]

Pitt realized that there was much to be gained from an aggressive stance. If he could break up the Franco-Dutch alliance and restore closer relations between Britain and Holland, he might rely on the future assistance of the Dutch navy and deny Holland's overseas bases to the French (very important for the security of British India). In August 1787 the British government sent more aid to the Orange party, hired Hessian troops, and offered Prussia a subsidy and naval support. Grenville was sent to Paris for talks, and, once the advancing Prussian army had crushed the 'patriots', the emergency came to an end. 'The business abroad is at length come to a point', Pitt wrote to his mother on 22 September: 'any effort the French can make will come too late; and they will hardly engage in an unpromising contest for a mere point of honour.' This was a remarkable success for Pitt. Although a more experienced minister might have suspected sooner that a crisis was coming, he handled it well, enhancing his personal popularity and demonstrating his competence in foreign affairs. Carmarthen was marginalized. Pitt had communicated directly with officials in Holland, France and Prussia, sent Grenville as his spokesman to The Hague and Paris, and personally interviewed the French envoy to London. He had also retained the backing of George III and cabinet colleagues, not least by choosing when, how and on what questions to consult them. Pitt's triumph in 1787 helped to restore Britain's international prestige after the defeat in America. The veteran Camden considered it an amazing reversal of fortune to emerge from a highly dangerous situation with such credit. The Earl of Mornington wrote on 17 October that Pitt had 'astonished all Europe by the alacrity of the late armament, and his name as a war minister is now as high as that of his father ever was'. In fact, as Pitt admitted, all this was the result of luck as much as judgment. Britain could have done little without the help of Prussia. The Prussians' speedy advance was decisive, and it is not clear what Pitt could have achieved without it.[9]

How could he make effective use of the advantages now offered by this good fortune? It seemed that the best way to build on the Dutch success, discourage French belligerence, and at the same time assist financial and economic recovery at home, was to safeguard European peace with a collective security system. Collective security required general rather than bilateral agreements, however, and great power rivalries presented a huge obstacle. Pitt also knew that formal alliances might oblige Britain to go to war before he was ready, something he was determined to avoid. Nevertheless, fearing that Prussia and France might come together if he declined, he had to accept a Prussian offer of an alliance in the summer of 1788. Following treaties concluded between April and August 1788, Britain was party to a 'triple alliance' with Holland and Prussia. Over the following years Prussia's territorial ambitions alarmed Pitt, and though Britain was not dragged into any war, he, Carmarthen, Grenville and their colleagues remained uneasy about Prussia's tendency to act without consulting the British government. Pitt became even more eager to promote a general peace accord, and made firm proposals to this end during 1790 and 1791, but circumstances quickly became unfavourable as Europe's major powers – including Britain – were preoccupied with their own concerns.[10]

For Pitt the Nootka Sound dispute took precedence in this period. The Spanish claimed sovereignty over America's Pacific coast, and late in 1789 they stopped a British vessel and arrested traders at Nootka Sound, an inlet on the west side of Vancouver Island. News of this reached the cabinet in January 1790. Pitt engaged in detailed research, as was his wont, in order to decide upon a suitable response. Carmarthen's aggressive instincts were checked as the prime minister waited. Information about Spanish mistreatment of traders in the American north west came to light, and it was reported that the entrepreneur who had established the Nootka base and negotiated with local natives had claimed the area for Britain.

Late in April 1790 the cabinet prepared for war, calling upon Spain to compensate the traders who had been detained, and rejecting the Spanish claim to control Pacific navigation and unoccupied territory on America's west coast. Britain's 'triple alliance' partners approved the action, the French government was mollified by Pitt's reassurances (and was in any case distracted by internal problems posed by the French Revolution), and perhaps unexpectedly the United States failed to support Spain. In private, though, Pitt and Grenville expressed misgivings about the course they were pursuing. On 18 May 1790 Pitt confessed to Lord Auckland: 'I can hardly form at present a conjecture of the event of our preparations, as I can hardly conceive either that the Spaniards will ultimately persist, or that they can have gone so far without a determination not to recede.' Grenville had already recorded his opinion (3 May) that although 'the risk and expense

of war' could probably be avoided, 'the object is so important to Spain …
and so much a favourite one with her even beyond its importance, that we
must not be too sanguine in our hopes of succeeding without a contest'.
Eventually, at the end of October, the Spanish government agreed to negotiate. By the resulting convention, Spain compensated the traders and
accepted that British subjects could enter areas beyond Spanish settlement
and fish in the Pacific. Though no distinct borders were established for
Spanish North America, and neither Spain nor Britain would concede
exclusive control over Nootka Sound, these problems did not greatly mar
Pitt's achievement, which was celebrated across the country. George III
offered Pitt the Garter. To the significant diplomatic victory over France in
1787 the prime minister had now added a triumph over Spain.[11]

The Nootka Sound affair represented a high point for Pitt. Auckland told
him after the dispute that 'there never was a business better conducted or
better concluded, and there never was a moment in which our country
held such pre-eminency among nations'. Pitt's regime now presented a
convincing image of confidence and success. Strong in parliament and in
the nation, the premier had also proven himself as supervisor of Britain's
external relations. He was still most interested in domestic affairs, but had
gradually taken charge of foreign policy (helped by personal advisers and
some reliable ambassadors in the European capitals). Pitt did not manage
to reach these heights again. He found it difficult to add to his string of
diplomatic successes, and his personal direction of foreign policy was not
so pronounced after Grenville became foreign secretary in June 1791. The
cousins were close personally and politically, and Pitt shared the making
of foreign policy rather more readily with Grenville than he had with
Carmarthen.[12]

The triumph over Spain came at a price, for it diverted Pitt from his
scheme for a general peace agreement in Europe, which now fell apart. To
Spain's predictable refusal to co-operate was added the Prussians' annoyance
at British attempts to discourage their plans for territorial aggrandizement.
Russia and Austria, meanwhile, were unwilling to talk peace while their
forces were gaining the upper hand in conflicts with the Turks and Belgians
respectively. Pitt persisted, spurred on by the successful outcome of the
Nootka Sound affair. Indeed, one of the negative effects of the affair was
that in leaving Pitt's ministry with too high an opinion of British power it
led to serious foreign policy miscalculations in subsequent years.

While Britain challenged Spain during 1790, an assertive Russia made
advances both in eastern Europe (an area to which Pitt gave insufficient
attention during the Nootka crisis) and on America's Pacific coast (where
spheres of influence remained unsettled even after the British-Spanish

convention).[13] Pitt's collective security arrangement involved re-establishing the European frontiers of 1787, and he believed that this could be implemented if Russia returned the fortress of Ochakov to the Turks. Prussia agreed, hoping to weaken Russian influence in eastern Europe, but mounting pressure from Britain's ally inconvenienced Pitt, and he had to send an ultimatum to Russia earlier than he planned. His intention had been to wait until parliament was in recess. Another problem was the intractability of the Russian empress, Catherine the Great, who, contrary to Pitt's predictions, refused to relinquish Ochakov. On 29 March 1791 Pitt asked the Commons to finance naval operations in an attempt to coerce Russia, but opposition MPs condemned the move and it soon became clear that regular government supporters objected too. Fox made an excellent speech, asserting that an altercation with Russia over Ochakov could be of no possible advantage to Britain. Pitt's performance in debate was uninspiring. He lacked precise information about Ochakov, and could not confirm that other powers would support the 'triple alliance' ultimatum. In cabinet grave doubts were expressed by Richmond and Grenville. Worried that his other measures would be detrimentally affected by the crisis, and recognizing that the Russians would not submit, Pitt backed down. His collective security plan had to be abandoned, and his authority and the reputation of his government were dealt a serious blow.[14]

In assessing the Ochakov crisis it is difficult to find much merit in Pitt's approach. That he should have considered it necessary to stand up to Russia is understandable, but his manner of doing so was open to question. Auckland warned him in January 1791 that Ochakov was itself of little importance – certainly not worth going to war over – and that other ways should be found of checking Russia's ambitions and helping the Turks to defend their territory. As the crisis developed Pitt found his options limited, and he was obliged ignominiously to abandon his original goals. If it was inadvisable to make a stand on Ochakov in the first place, the climb down was equally dangerous. As Grenville observed (16 April) after government policy was attacked in parliament: 'the great fear which I entertain is that the line of concession, which what has happened here compels us to adopt, will too evidently betray our weakness, and that the Empress will rise in her demands instead of being disposed to modify them'. In the end the only course left to Pitt was damage limitation. His anxieties were clearly expressed to Joseph Ewart, British ambassador in Berlin, on 24 May 1791:

> The obvious effect of our persisting would have been to risk the existence of the present Government, and with it the whole of our system both at home and abroad. The personal part of this consideration it would have been our duty to overlook, and I trust we shall all have been ready to do so, if by any risk of our

own we should have contributed to the attainment of a great and important object for this country and its allies; but the consequence must evidently have been the reverse. The overthrow of our system here, at the same time that it hazarded driving the Government at home into a state of absolute confusion, must have shaken the whole of our system abroad.

Various commentators have criticized Pitt's 'lack of nerve', 'miscalculation' and 'failure', yet much was beyond his control and, in contrast to the circumstances surrounding his diplomatic triumphs in earlier years, this time the international situation did not help. Prussia proved unreliable, as did Holland (both of Britain's 'triple alliance' partners decided that nothing could be gained from a confrontation with Russia, and Pitt came to see that the 'triple alliance', by giving Prussia the means to involve Britain in central Europe, was fraught with unwelcome complications). Austria was unwilling to annoy the Russians. Turkey was weak, Denmark aloof, and Sweden resented the lack of British support against Russia in the past. In addition, Catherine the Great was a resourceful and determined adversary. At home the parliamentary opposition took advantage of these problems and the uncertainty within government ranks. The prime minister may have been swayed by cabinet colleagues (Malmesbury later recorded that Grenville 'was the cause of Mr Pitt's giving way'). But it would have been grossly irresponsible for Pitt *not* to challenge Russia at this time. The government's advisers at home and ambassadors abroad had repeatedly argued that if unchecked, Russia's rise would threaten Britain's international position and trade.

There were specific strategic and commercial motives behind Pitt's action, as well as his desire for a collective security agreement in Europe. He wanted to force Russia to recognize British influence, divide Austria from Russia, bring Poland and Turkey under British protection, prevent the Russians from increasing their trade with any power other than Britain, inhibit their expansion southwards towards the Mediterranean, and gain more control over naval supplies and markets in eastern and central Europe. Ochakov was the test. Pitt knew that Prussia and other European powers would draw their own conclusions if he faltered, and that markets in the Baltic region and central and eastern Europe might be lost if Russia came to an understanding with Denmark and Sweden. Ever mindful of the connection between international influence and strength at home, Pitt was also worried that his administration would lose support domestically if he did not take a firm line. In the event he suffered a damaging defeat; he was ill prepared and could not recover as things began to go wrong. In the long run, it has been suggested, the crisis can be viewed as part of a competition for the future leadership of Europe. Pitt learned that his idea of extending British control by using other powers to contain Russia would not work. This affected British involvement in the French wars from 1793. Pitt had failed to organize a coalition against Russia and would need Russian help to organize one against revolutionary France.[15]

Ochakov revived earlier doubts about Pitt's competence in foreign affairs, and, quite apart from the whims and ambitions of foreign powers which frequently frustrated his designs, he still had to contend with disputes and obstruction at home. Although Pitt had persuaded George III to back the government's Dutch policy in 1787, for example, the king could reject ministerial advice when he chose (as in 1788 when he ruled out British intervention in the Baltic after Denmark attacked Sweden). Pitt always had to be wary of the king's fixed ideas about international affairs. He also had to manage the difficult Carmarthen (who succeeded as fifth Duke of Leeds in 1789). The foreign secretary complained ever more insistently about Pitt's meddling and the lack of consultation, and the premier's reliance on an inner circle of advisers. Leeds resigned in April 1791, unable to accept Pitt's decision to adopt a more conciliatory line towards Russia over Ochakov. Leeds had warned against offending Prussia, and resented being overruled (his point about Prussia was sound enough: the Ochakov affair damaged relations with the Prussians, which partly explains why they were of almost no use at all to Pitt during the French wars). The prime minister may have welcomed the opportunity to replace Leeds, but Ochakov had other, less agreeable, political consequences, not only with respect to Pitt's influence in parliament and the nation, but within the cabinet too (most importantly, Pitt had to break off his efforts to oust Thurlow).

Clearly, if a foreign policy success could raise his standing and authority, it was equally true that an embarrassment in foreign affairs could make Pitt vulnerable. There was even talk of his resignation during 1791. Pitt briefly thought of giving up the premiership, but dismissed the idea in case it disturbed the king, whose mental condition remained a cause for concern after the regency crisis. Great as the need was for Pitt to remain on good terms with George III at this time, however, there were definite strains in their relationship in the aftermath of the Ochakov affair. The king disliked the Canada Bill, then being debated in the Commons, and opposed continuing efforts to abolish the slave trade, with which Pitt sympathized. George III was also unhappy about the resignation of Leeds, not least because he linked it with his loss of control over certain areas of patronage, and disapproved of the rivalry between Pitt and Thurlow, for he was still personally close to the lord chancellor. He hated the Empress of Russia and lamented the government's decision to give way to her, and held a grudge against Pitt and other ministers for sanctioning the disagreeable and humiliating medical treatment to which he had been subjected during the regency crisis (in effect, he thought, he had been considered a madman).[16]

By this time the French Revolution had not only dramatically increased international tension, but had also promoted domestic unrest. In Britain it gave rise to animated public debate and the growth of popular political activism. Contention developed as new ideas, claims, vocabularies and aspirations were articulated in books and periodicals and at meetings. The most important contributions to the print controversy included *On the Love of Our Country* (1789) by Richard Price, the radical Dissenter, sinking fund expert and former apologist for the American rebels. Price stressed the similarities between Britain's Glorious Revolution and events in France, advocated religious toleration and parliamentary reform, and upheld the people's right to frame a system of government, choose rulers and dismiss them for misconduct. Edmund Burke's view of British history and events in France was rather different. He rejected Price's claims, and the basic argument in Burke's *Reflections on the Revolution in France* (1790) was that fundamental change could only be safe and useful when it accorded with a nation's traditions. Burke condemned events in France and argued that they had been misunderstood in Britain. While the Glorious Revolution had promoted social stability and political continuity, revolutionaries in France lacked respect for the past and wanted to destroy custom, community and hierarchy. The inevitable results of the French Revolution, Burke thought, would be human degradation, tyranny and war. He therefore contradicted the more positive view of Price and the expanding radical clubs around the country, and was particularly annoyed to find that Fox and members of the pro-reform wing of the parliamentary opposition could not be persuaded to alter their favourable verdicts on the French Revolution. They were convinced that political reorganization in France would assist Whiggism and the reform cause in Britain, and this belief did not seem unjustified during the early years of the French Revolution, when it followed a moderate and constitutional path. But with increasing urgency Burke insisted that Britain should not seek to follow the courses being pursued in France. Foxites ridiculed him, and most of the early published responses to Burke were hostile. Nor was Pitt's government shaken from what Burke regarded as its dangerous complacency (Pitt remained firmly neutral, and Burke was appalled by his apparent lack of insight). Before long, however, Burke's gloomy predictions were upheld by events as the French Revolution became more violent and unstable.[17]

Pitt's initial response to the French Revolution had been one of calm satisfaction, and it was some time before he altered his position. Dining with Beilby Porteous, Bishop of London, in July 1789, his conversation about France was optimistic. If an old enemy was having internal problems, after all, how could Britain fail to benefit? It would be years, Pitt hoped, before France could again threaten British interests. He remarked in the Commons on 9 February 1790: 'The present convulsions of France must sooner or later terminate in general harmony and regular order; and though such a situation might make her more formidable, it might also make her less obnoxious as a neighbour.' Among the premier's associates there was growing concern about the instability of Europe during 1790, and Auckland was among those who advocated timely precautions. Pitt was not to be drawn into hasty over-reaction, however, and non-intervention was also the favoured policy of Grenville, foreign secretary from June 1791. In any case Ochakov forced Pitt to step back from a proactive foreign policy. Pitt told Auckland (2 September 1791) that 'in the singular and uncertain state of Europe, our chief business must be to watch events and keep ourselves quiet'. Britain became less assertive abroad. Pitt's main goals remained prosperity and stability at home. Even the outbreak of war in Europe in 1792 did not greatly alarm him, for he expected Britain to remain uninvolved. He also suspected that the French would soon have to surrender. The European war could be very useful, therefore, in that it would delay France's recovery of great power status and help Pitt to defend what had been achieved in 1787 during the Dutch crisis.[18]

Pitt was concerned about the domestic situation, not events in France, and Burke's estrangement from Fox, and the widening gap between Fox's party and the more conservative Portland group, were developments in which the prime minister and his closest associates took a keen interest.[19] As events in France assumed a more disturbing character, many in parliament and out of doors began to credit Burke as an accurate oracle. In August 1791 Burke publicly urged opposition MPs to desert Fox and rally to the defence of tradition and order.[20] Even admirers of Fox complained that he was too inflexible and had committed himself too early. Burke's conduct, meanwhile, was welcomed by the government, which established tentative links with him during 1791. Though Pitt did not fully accept Burke's prognostications about France, he saw very well that arguments among opposition leaders could be turned to the government's advantage. Still he refrained from long statements of opinion on France, and he shared George III's view that Britain should neither support nor oppose moves to assist the French king (in September 1791 Britain refused to join in a plan proposed by Austria and Prussia for freeing the French royal family). Pitt could not prevent questions of reform from being raised in parliament, or arrest the rise of reform associations in the country, but popular agitation did not yet lead to severe responses from the government. In July 1791 Grenville dismissed reports about revolutionary sentiment among the people and the arrival of French agents intent on causing mayhem. He wrote to Auckland:

> You will have seen that the popular turn is not in favour of the Dissenters and *Democrates*. I have always imagined it to be as the event has shown ... I send you the description I received of certain persons said to be coming over here to fire our ships and dockyards. The measures taken in consequence of this intelligence gave occasion to the alarm, which was not discouraged, as this is one of the cases where security arises out of a general impression of danger. But I strongly believe there was nothing in it. No such persons ever made their appearance anywhere in England where we could trace them.[21]

On the central issue of parliamentary reform, Pitt's stance accorded with that of the majority of MPs during the early stages of the French Revolution. Moderate opinion in the Commons was turning against reform. This became apparent when the Irish orator Henry Flood, MP for Seaford, introduced a proposal in March 1790 (the first substantial plan since Pitt's of 1785) to add a hundred seats to the county representation, extend the franchise to all resident householders paying 50 shillings a year in tax, and reduce by half the representation of decayed boroughs (each would lose one of its two seats). Pitt stated that changes should only be considered if the timing was right and if they addressed obvious abuses. Flood's plan, he argued, failed on both counts. Burke also spoke against it, and Flood's motion was not pressed to a division. The debate indicated a drawing together of conservative elements. Portland's friend William Windham argued that it was unwise to try and repair one's house 'in hurricane season'. Reform must wait for calmer times, he declared, and with France falling prey to visionary schemes it was essential that Britain's legislature should protect rather than tamper with the established order. Windham had never advocated parliamentary reform. He was no ally of Pitt at this time, but had not previously condemned the French Revolution (and had voted for repeal of the Test and Corporation Acts in 1789). Significantly, a prominent opposition Whig had now resisted reform by warning about France.[22]

But parliamentary reform could not be sidelined so easily. Although Flood's effort was not backed by popular pressure, and Wyvill's attempt to revive the county associations failed, in subsequent years there was an impressive revival of reform agitation throughout Britain. Several organizations became particularly influential. The Society for Constitutional Information, originally founded by respectable radicals in 1780, was active again from 1791. For a time it maintained close links with another body, the London Corresponding Society. Made up primarily of workers, shopkeepers, tailors, printers and artisans, the LCS was established in January

1792. Its secretary was Thomas Hardy, a shoemaker, and it encouraged political discussion, communicated with similar bodies in provincial towns, and aspired to 'unlimited membership'. Another group, the Society of the Friends of the People, was formed in April 1792 by opposition MPs, young Whig aristocrats and their wealthy reform-minded adherents. They favoured a more popular representation in the Commons, though they remained an exclusive body, unsympathetic towards the more advanced ideas of other reform associations and eager above all to attract outdoor support for the Foxite party in parliament.[23]

Notwithstanding their differences in terms of social rank, political aspiration, ideology and tactics, reform societies in London and the large provincial towns had in common their commitment to an amendment of the representative system and their tendency to open up political debate and participation, aided, of course, by the burgeoning radical press. Extra-parliamentary politics continued to develop quickly. Delegates from over eighty associations would assemble for a radical convention in Edinburgh in December 1792, a clear sign of the numbers and organization that now lay behind agitation for reform. Dissenters' committees added to the ferment of this period, for they had been pressing for repeal of the Test and Corporation Acts during the late 1780s. Their efforts had been frustrated, and a repeal proposal was heavily defeated in the Commons in March 1790.[24] The campaign against the slave trade also grew in force at this time. In many towns the same individuals who had organized the repeal campaign, or called meetings to protest against the slave trade, were involved in the movement for parliamentary reform.

Pitt was increasingly uncomfortable about this agitation from the spring of 1792. While Fox continued to employ reformist language, the prime minister retreated into a cautious conservatism. Fox's progressive credentials were enhanced by his most notable achievement of this period, the 1792 Libel Act, which gave juries the power to decide on the libel rather than simply the fact of its publication (Fox limited the judge's role and therefore executive power, for judges were appointed by the crown).[25] Pitt welcomed this as a useful measure – Chatham had previously advocated a similar reform – but Fox also favoured religious toleration and abolition of the slave trade, and as has been noted above, on these questions Pitt became more defensive. Fox's lieutenant Charles Grey, a prominent Friend of the People, gave notice of a parliamentary reform motion on 30 April 1792, reminding MPs that Pitt as well as Fox had previously recommended reform. According to Grey, fairer representation would ensure that the real public interest could never be ignored. In reply Pitt attacked the Friends, maintained that reform would threaten the peace and safety of the nation, and stressed that circumstances had changed since he had advocated reform in the 1780s. Burke agreed that it would be unwise to alter the system of government, but Fox sided with Grey, further alienating the Portland Whigs.[26]

Polarization proceeded in parliament and in the nation, where radicals competed with conservatives for political influence and public space. Local conflicts took on a more disquieting aspect as mob violence broke out in Birmingham, Sheffield, Manchester and elsewhere.[27] The government responded to the spread of radical literature and disturbances across the country in May 1792, when a royal proclamation was issued against seditious publications and meetings. Pitt wisely consulted Portland about this in advance, and secured his approval, while Fox denied that there was sedition in Britain and argued that the threat to liberty and order came not from radical societies but from intolerant religious spirit and resistance to reform. Even some anti-radical commentators considered the proclamation counter-productive, but Pitt was determined to divide his parliamentary opponents and did not want the government to lose influence as events unfolded.

In France the revolution was taking a more extreme course than many observers had envisaged, and political argument in Britain had only increased after the publication of Thomas Paine's *Rights of Man*, part one in March 1791, and part two in February 1792. The radical Paine, a former excise officer who had emigrated to America in 1774 and assisted the struggle for American independence, rebuffed Burke's ideas about the authority of tradition. He advocated government by consent and declared that the French Revolution symbolized a genuine advance for human freedom. Whereas Burke had focused on fixed points in history, and assumed that rights then established gained their legitimacy from uninterrupted use, Paine wrote that people were born with inherent natural rights, which were also the basis for civil rights. He claimed that the British system of government had arisen over the people instead of from the people. By contrast, the French had recently established government by consent and recognized the true nature of rights, and now they enjoyed equality, justice and freedom of conscience. Paine went on to make detailed social welfare proposals, describing what democratic governments could and should do, but his idea of wealth redistribution seemed to critics to confirm his desire to destroy property and the established pattern of society. Controversy intensified as many radicals took up Paine's nostrums, for his bold vindication of revolutionary principles rapidly sold tens of thousands of copies in cheap editions.[28]

In the Commons on 17 February 1792 Pitt stated that Britain could reasonably expect to enjoy a prolonged period of peace (he suggested fifteen years). He had decided to cut expenditure on the navy and end the subsidy to Hessian mercenaries.[29] But events over the following weeks and months were hardly reassuring. Many people who had welcomed the French Revolution changed their minds during 1792. This year saw serious economic problems in Britain after a period of prosperity, and domestic unrest added to a sense of impending crisis. In April 1792 the French went to war with Austria, and with Prussia in July. Instability increased within France and the full fury of revolutionary violence was experienced during the September Massacres, when over a thousand priests, aristocrats and royalists were murdered in Paris. The monarchy was abolished, France became a republic, and in November French troops invaded the Low Countries. Revolutionary leaders declared the Scheldt an open river, breaking international agreements, and issued (19 November 1792) the Declaration of Fraternity, a promise to assist any nation that rose to release itself from despotism. The deposed French king, Louis XVI, was executed on 21 January 1793. This outraged George III, and Pitt realized that the forces unleashed in France were out of control. Previously he had been careful not to involve his government in France's internal affairs, but war and regicide changed the situation completely. Pitt prepared for the worst.

The execution of Louis XVI made a swift restoration of European peace unlikely, while France's invasion of the Low Countries was bound to affect Britain's ally Holland, and the opening of the Scheldt contravened treaty rights. Pitt and Grenville agreed that Britain must retaliate if Holland was attacked. They also came to believe that the French were fomenting trouble in Britain; therefore they could not separate events abroad from unrest at home. The wet summer of 1792 had affected food supplies and prices were rising. Trade declined. Radical societies continued to expand, and before the end of 1792 government supporters were demanding action. Ministers hesitated. They had to be sure that foreign and domestic dangers were serious enough to justify intervention, and that public opinion would support it. Indeed, until the autumn of 1792 ministers appear to have doubted that they had sufficient backing to act against popular radicalism. The royal proclamation of 21 May 1792 helped them to increase support for repressive measures. It drew forth a remarkable response: by September addresses in favour of the proclamation had been organized in most British counties and over three hundred towns and cities. The government's firmness also impressed foreigners. In June Auckland reported from The Hague that 'the proclamation, and the debates in consequence, have had the happiest and most creditable effect'. Significantly, at the end of 1792 Paine fled to France and was convicted of sedition in his absence. This indicated the future course of domestic policy as matters deteriorated further.

Meanwhile, Pitt required the French to withdraw the threatening decrees and return to their own frontiers. There were several informal contacts through intermediaries before the government communicated directly with French authorities, because Pitt and Grenville preferred to respond rather than initiate. This hesitation, despite the gathering clouds of war, requires explanation. It seems that Pitt and Grenville still preferred neutrality and hoped to keep Britain out of the European war. They were also negotiating with other powers at this time, and waited to see what these powers would do before finalizing their own plans. Another problem was that, to Britain, the new French regime was illegitimate. It was difficult to deal openly with a government that Pitt and his colleagues could not officially recognize. When Grenville did set out Britain's position in a formal dispatch of 31 December 1792, revolutionary leaders in Paris were defiant. They refused to comply with British requests and demanded that Britain should formally recognize the French republic. On 18 January 1793 William Huskisson concluded that 'after Lord Grenville's letter and the frequent and solemn declarations of the French, with respect to the Scheldt', war could not now be averted. 'There are cabinets held every day', he noted, 'and frequently till very late in the night.'[30]

While some radicals scaled down their activities, hoping thereby to avoid official persecution or the attentions of loyalist ruffians, others persisted, reaffirming their commitment to reform and publicly endorsing events in France. But only a small minority embraced unconstitutional methods, and within reform circles the commitment to violence was never widespread. The majority of radicals looked upon the French Revolution principally as a source of ideas and inspiration, not a process they wished to follow in every detail. What happened in France was important because it seemed to illustrate both the necessity and possibility of extensive reform in Britain, according to British conditions. The talk was mainly of recovering lost rights rather than demanding new ones, and in carrying on the struggle for reform, radicals did not believe that they were acting improperly.

This belief indicates the flexibility of the British constitution. It could be interpreted in both libertarian and conservative ways. Constitutional language and symbol were used by some to galvanize reform campaigns, by others to justify a repressive response. Committed radicals were not very numerous, and for influence they depended heavily on adverse economic conditions. Recession in 1792 assisted recruitment, but even in hard times there was a limit to radicalism's appeal. Groups across the country were never united into a co-ordinated movement with an agreed programme. There was division between reformers of different social backgrounds. Respectable, propertied, professional and educated groups disliked the extreme language, demands for manhood suffrage and plans for national

conventions associated with plebeian leaders. So radicalism remained or-
ganizationally limited and ideologically vulnerable, and there was a crucial
tactical problem. Even Paine refrained from advocating violent insurrection,
and, since most radicals disavowed unconstitutional conduct, they had no
answer to the question of how to reform the political system if parliament
refused to co-operate. In the 1790s, moreover, plebeian radicals were hampered by government repression and the retreat of respectable reformers,
itself a response to official and popular conservative reaction.[31]

Loyalists roused themselves to combat the radical societies. All classes
participated, not just the wealthy and propertied. Unlike their opponents,
loyalists were not impeded by official interference or lack of funds, and
their conservative crusade was well under way by 1793. Extracts from Burke
were issued in many forms and reviewed in provincial newspapers. Print
warfare inspired by Paine and Burke drew forth more loyalist than radical
contributions, and prevalent circumstances enabled conservatives to mis-
represent reformers as French-style revolutionaries. There was effective
organization too. In November 1792 the lawyer John Reeves, an adviser to
the home office, founded the Association for Preserving Liberty and Property
against Republicans and Levellers. Reeves may have consulted the government beforehand about his venture, though opinion is still divided as to
whether or not Pitt and Grenville knew of the Reeves project in advance.
What is certain is that they quickly decided to use it for their own purposes,
and the government gave Reeves plenty of assistance. Based in London,
the Reeves body established or made contact with similar associations in
provincial towns. Soon these numbered over a thousand. They subjected
known reformers to surveillance and intimidation, distributed anti-radical
propaganda, and worked with local authorities to prosecute writers and
publishers of seditious material. Religious services also assumed a more
patriotic tone, with sermons calling on the people to obey their governors.
In 1792 loyalists organized about five hundred addresses in support of crown
and government. Focus was given to anti-radical activity, conservative sentiment was constantly reiterated, and an approved British constitutionalism
was activated so that sound doctrine could be disseminated to the general
public.

Pitt's government welcomed these activities and issued its own propaganda
(material was often leaked to newspapers as part of the effort to encourage
loyalism and prepare the ground for repressive measures). Soon there would
be emergency legislation to suppress disorder and protest, but there was
no panic and the core purpose was always the same: to maintain a balance
between executive power and the liberties of the subject. Agents were
employed to assist in gathering intelligence about radical groups, a task also

entrusted to magistrates, clergymen, port officials and the post office. This was necessary because there was no professional police force or civil service, juries were not totally reliable, and in 1792 the number of troops in Britain was only about 40,000. The voluntary effort of loyalists was therefore crucial, though there was concern that the conservative upsurge might defy guidance from above. Mobs were fickle, and, as Grenville remarked to Auckland (22 July 1791), riots in favour of government were no less objectionable than riots against it. Loyal associations were not established by the government or on the government's initiative, but from the first there was collusion. Associations operated with official goodwill, and their rapid growth demonstrates the strength of popular conservatism in response to perceived crisis.[32]

The association movement became a considerable asset to the government, and Pitt, Dundas and Grenville involved themselves directly in assisting and extending it. The prime minister had often expressed his view that the vast majority of the population wished to preserve the established social and political order. The war prompted him to reiterate this claim ever more stridently. In May 1793 he referred in the Commons to 'the great body of the people of England, animated by the spirit of the purest loyalty, and too much attached to the blessings of the constitution and the present government to wish to hazard them by a change'. He continued:

> I am sensible that ninety-nine out of a hundred of the people of England are warm in those sentiments, are sensible of the security which they enjoy for these blessings from the frame of our excellent constitution, and, so far from wishing to touch it with an innovating hand, are prepared to defend it against every attack.

On 2 February 1801 Pitt rejected Charles Grey's 'curious proposition' that for years the government had been acting contrary to the nation's interests and 'that the minority in this house, in point of fact, speak the sense of the majority of the people'. But Pitt and his colleagues knew that it was not enough to have public goodwill. They had to make this goodwill active, visible, influential and organized. From November 1792 the association movement offered a means to achieve these ends. Pitt immediately appreciated its potential usefulness, communicated directly with Reeves, and decided that the movement must extend over the whole country, with the government offering help and guidance behind the scenes. Dundas promoted associations in Scotland (he held that coercion alone would not end civil commotion). Grenville envisaged a formidable mobilization of the expanding middle ranks in British society, particularly merchants, lawyers, farmers and yeomen. The government needed open and impressive popular backing, yet, as has been suggested, the promotion of an energetic loyalism was risky. No government had attempted it before, and Pitt was determined that the process should help rather than hinder his regime. Associations, he made clear, must uphold the established authorities, not undermine or seek to replace them.[33]

By early 1793, as French excesses led many observers to adopt Burke's apocalyptic view of the French Revolution, MPs expressed concern about the safety of property and institutions at home and deplored the fate of monarchy in France. Pitt wondered how best to respond to these strong currents of backbench opinion. As for the opposition, its disunity became all the more obvious as Fox and his associates obstinately maintained that the French Revolution represented a new birth for liberty. Violence was regrettable, Fox admitted, but evils allegedly committed in France were less significant than the greater good promoted by revolutionary activity. Convinced that the French Revolution would return to a moderate course if Austria and Prussia were defeated in battle, since this would remove the threat of foreign occupation, Fox was horrified by the prospect that Britain might join in the European war on the side of reaction. Portland Whigs were increasingly annoyed by Fox's pronouncements, and complained about his failure to restrain Grey, the Friends of the People, and the radical movement in the nation.

Fox's continuing commitment to parliamentary reform was made clear in May 1793, when a Sheffield reform petition came before the Commons and he argued that it should be received (the Commons voted against this by 108 to 29 votes). Then, on 6 May 1793, Grey moved for a committee to consider reform petitions. Pitt declared that reform debates at this time could only encourage disloyal elements to challenge legitimate authority and the social order. His own proposals in the 1780s had been fairly defeated, he said, and anti-reform arguments had even more force now. Pitt insisted that some British radicals sought to introduce French principles. Parliament must not give the slightest countenance to their designs, he warned, and for his part he was not prepared to endanger the blessings of the constitution by entertaining a vain hope of improving it. He argued that revolutionary aims were being furthered under the cloak of reform petitions, denounced manhood suffrage (dismissing the idea of a right to equal representation as untenable), and called on the Friends of the People to disband. Pitt urged that in time of war, when the nation had to defend itself against a foreign foe, it would be unwise to risk instability at home by reforming the system of government. 'The question is, then, whether you will abide by your constitution, or hazard a change, with all that dreadful train of consequences with which we have seen it attended in a neighbouring kingdom.'

Fox accused Pitt of inconsistency and error, but Grey's proposal for a committee was heavily defeated, by 282 to 41 votes. Fox's support for Grey hastened the rupture in opposition Whig ranks, and Pitt finally cemented his alliance with the Portland Whigs in July 1794. Canning made much of the opposition's weaknesses in the months leading up to the schism. On one occasion Fox gave notice that he would speak against government policies on 17 April 1794, but when the time came the Commons chamber was virtually empty.

> Such a notice as this a year ago from Fox would have filled the House at 4 o'clock. I was therefore not a little surprised on going down at 5 – to find not fifty persons come. This is a melancholy proof for poor Fox of the disrespect into which he is fallen – and it really was quite pitiable to see him sitting almost alone on his Bench, with none of the principal people of his party about him, for even they did not attend in time. It has been evident indeed throughout the Session that Opposition have not drawn well together – and that there must be some little differences of opinion amongst them which unhinge all their plans and operations.[34]

The reconstruction of the cabinet in 1794 enabled Pitt to present himself to parliament and the people as the head of a patriotic coalition that had dispensed with party ties for the sake of national security. By this time official repression had begun in earnest. In parliament only the Foxite rump persisted with resistance and protest. Early in 1793, when bills were introduced to prevent 'traitorous correspondence' and impose restrictions on foreigners, Fox had denounced Pitt for violating liberty and asserted that the government was creating alarm so that inappropriately harsh measures could be pushed through with indecent haste.[35] These were themes repeatedly taken up by Foxites in subsequent years. But in officialdom and in respectable society, repression was considered necessary. In February 1793 the attorney John Frost, a founder of the LCS, was imprisoned for sedition. Scottish judges imposed particularly harsh penalties for political offences. The lawyer Thomas Muir, of the Scottish Friends of the People, and Thomas Palmer, a prominent Unitarian and former fellow of Queens' College, Cambridge, were each sentenced to long periods of transportation (their trials did not follow regular procedure and were almost certainly pre-judged).[36] More reformers were transported after the convention in Edinburgh at the end of 1793.

Nevertheless, arrangements were made for a national convention in 1794. Radical leaders seemed intent on testing the government further, perhaps because of the failure of Grey's reform motion in May 1793. The convention plan was taken by the authorities to represent a direct challenge to parliament.[37] A national body claiming to reflect the people's will more accurately than the House of Commons could not be tolerated, and the proposal to petition for an end to the war made radical preparations even more objectionable. There were arrests and trials, but reports reached the government from many districts warning that radical societies were still growing. Agents were touring the country, it was claimed, to solicit support for sweeping reforms and to assess the likely popular response to a French invasion. The government acted quickly. Leaders of the London radical societies were arrested and their papers seized on 12 May 1794. On 16 May a committee of secrecy reported to the Commons that there had been arming in preparation for the national convention, and that there existed a plan to subvert the constitution. Habeas Corpus was suspended on 18 May.[38]

In recommending suspension of Habeas Corpus, Pitt warned the Commons that radicals, inspired by wild notions of the rights of man, were preparing for insurrection. Some people had been turned away from their attachment to law and order, and the government needed additional powers to deal with this danger. Pitt made no apology for the haste with which measures had to be passed. If a temporary sacrifice of liberty was needed to safeguard the constitution, he argued, this was a price worth paying. In reply Fox questioned the authority of the secret committee and its report, denied that conventions were dangerous or illegal, and pointed out that reform societies had genuine grievances relating to the war and system of government. Fox maintained that laws already existed to deal with the activity allegedly being contemplated, but Pitt was backed by Burke, Windham, Dundas and conservative MPs who wanted a full range of preventive measures. Fox was adamant that the government should not use events in France as an excuse for limiting freedom at home. If the French Revolution had demonstrated anything, he explained, it had shown that only foolish rulers ignored popular opinion and attempted to silence complaints by passing severe laws. The Commons nevertheless approved the suspension of Habeas Corpus by 146 to 28 votes.[39]

Persecution of reformers became more pronounced. In Manchester, Sheffield, Nottingham and other towns the local authorities and their loyalist allies targeted radical groups for political pressure, social ostracism, economic sanction and legal prosecution. London's radical leaders were indicted for treason. Thomas Hardy and John Thelwall of the LCS, and the veteran reformer John Horne Tooke (active since the 1760s), were among the accused. Grey attended Hardy's trial and decided that nobody would be safe if Hardy was found guilty. In the event it was difficult to prove the intent to use force upon which conviction had to rest. A different charge might have succeeded, but of treason the radicals were acquitted late in

1794. It is likely that Pitt and the government desired lengthy trials in order
for dangerous activity to be fully exposed. The acquittals, however, frustrated
this design. Pitt and Richmond had also to suffer the embarrassment of
appearing in court. They were called as former advocates of parliamentary
reform who had made statements similar to those of the defendants.
Fox used the acquittals to bolster his argument that emergency laws were
unnecessary.[40]

Unrest continued as a result of the poor harvest of 1794. Then the summer
of 1795 was wet and cold. Hardship spread and there were growing complaints about food prices and disrupted trade. The mid-1790s saw the most
serious harvest crisis for a generation. Pressure mounted for parliamentary
action. Pitt responded with *laissez faire* arguments drawn from Adam Smith,
though he did propose to extend poverty relief, and there were attempts
to safeguard the supply of bread. The coincidence of war and serious
provision shortages during the 1790s and early 1800s created enormous
trouble for Pitt. Attention had to be given to food supply and social welfare,
though ministerial and parliamentary opinion had been turning against
official regulation for some time. Late in 1795 an opposition proposal for
minimum wage legislation (which would have revived the obsolete power
of local magistrates to fix the wages of agricultural labourers) was defeated
after Pitt criticized it in the Commons. The prime minister held that
excessive intervention would harm the economy and exacerbate rather than
remedy social problems.

> Will it not be wiser for the House to consider the operation of general principles,
> and rely upon the effect of their unconfined exercise? I conceive that to promote
> the free circulation of labour, to remove the obstacles by which industry is
> prohibited from availing herself of its resources, would go far to remedy the evils
> and diminish the necessity of applying for relief to the poor rate. But I should
> wish that an opportunity were given of restoring the original purity of the Poor
> Laws, and of removing those corruptions by which they have been obscured.

In February 1796 Pitt gave notice of his intention to reform the poor
laws, and he introduced his plan on 12 November 1796 (if passed, it was
to come into effect the following July). Pitt's purposes were to improve the
condition of the poor, encourage 'habits of industry and good order', and
thereby lessen the burden on the poor rates. Included in his scheme were
comprehensive relief payments, parish loans to assist paupers to support
themselves (by purchasing a cow, for example), and a combination of public
and voluntary help for the old, sick and infirm. Pitt also provided for land
improvement, the establishment of 'schools of industry' to train children
for useful employment, and the hiring out of teenagers to work with farmers

at harvest time. He circulated his plan widely, inviting detailed comment, and many objections were raised on administrative, financial, legal, moral and social grounds.

The Commons rejected Pitt's measure. Such an ambitious and costly scheme was deemed inappropriate when the nation was already paying heavy taxes to support the war effort, and its complexity raised doubts about its practical implementation. There was broad agreement that the poor laws were in need of reform, but also that assistance should be given without demoralizing the poor or overtaxing ratepayers, and MPs decided that Pitt's proposals were flawed. In fact the provision of poor relief was already being extended, mainly on local initiative. From central government there was little direct involvement in social and economic affairs. This is not to deny that some policies could be changed, either in response to unforeseen pressures or because Pitt and his colleagues decided that they lacked a convincing justification. Therefore *laissez faire* ideas were not the only determinant of policy, though they were often employed by Pitt to explain particular measures. He decided against an excise on iron in 1796 because of a principled aversion to taxes on necessities (as taught by Adam Smith). He also favoured the self-help ideal, seen in such measures as the Friendly Societies Act of 1793. Workers were encouraged to put savings aside and guard against future distress, and this reform, introduced by treasury secretary George Rose and supported by Pitt, was designed to protect the friendly societies' funds.[41]

Could Pitt have done more to tackle the problems of poverty, wages and subsistence? Some historians claim that the prime minister proposed his poor law reform at the wrong time and should have introduced an amended measure when circumstances became more favourable. This was the analysis of some of Pitt's contemporaries (and for a few his plan, far from being too complicated and ambitious, did not go far enough). But it can also be argued that Pitt simply did not have the opportunity to give detailed attention to this matter. There were too many other tasks that had urgently to be performed, especially those relating to the war.[42]

The subsistence crises of 1794 to 1795 and 1799 to 1800 brought famine prices and widespread rioting. To harvest failures at home was added the problem of securing extra supplies from foreign producers in wartime. In most districts emergency committees were established to organize relief. Local authorities competed with each other for grain, which pushed prices up still further. The government tried to secure more imports and to minimize the cost to consumers of imported grain, but stocks were repeatedly exhausted. In Yorkshire the long dearths were punctuated by periods of absolute scarcity, notably during the summer of 1795 and in

September 1800. Distress was particularly acute when industrial recession coincided with food shortages, but only fleetingly did the government respond. In 1795 and 1799 ministers promoted the use of barley and oats in place of wheat, and the Parochial Relief Act of 1800 enabled poor law officials to offer relief in the form of cereal substitutes. In general, however, official action was limited. In 1800, when news reached the home office that magistrates, landowners and farmers in Nottinghamshire were trying to fix food prices in order to combat profiteering, Portland instructed local authorities not to interfere with private property in this manner.[43] Hunger and destitution prompted more demands for government help, but ministers did not revise their convictions or their policies even when dearth, food riots and strikes were at their most disturbing. Pitt was never shaken from his belief that wages and the cost of living ought to remain unregulated, though it is true that his commitment to economic freedom was sorely tested by wartime distress.

In February 1800, when the opposition MP Samuel Whitbread introduced a bill to adjust the wages of labourers in husbandry, Pitt opposed the measure as 'highly improper'.

> It went to introduce legislative interference into that which ought to be allowed invariably to take its natural course. The greater freedom there was allowed in every kind of mercantile transactions, the more for the benefit of all parties. It was likewise always inexpedient to frame a general law to remedy a particular evil ... The distresses of the poor would be best relieved not by any general law, but by parochial aid administered by those who were intimately acquainted with their situation.

Pitt referred to his previous attempt to reform the poor laws. Having been defeated, he said, he probably would not try again. He still considered his plan useful, 'but many objections had been started to it, by those whose opinion he was bound to respect'. Whitbread's bill was rejected on 21 February, and Pitt continued to deny claims that his government should be doing more about hunger and hardship. On 27 November 1800, in resisting calls for a committee on the state of the nation, Pitt declared that the government had done all that could properly be expected of it, and that the people had not been disappointed.

> They see the attention of parliament directed to consideration of the difficulties under which the community labours, and employing every practical remedy to alleviate their distress. I am convinced too that the people are well aware that those do most for their cause, and are most sincerely impressed with their sufferings, who confine themselves most closely to the immediate object of relieving the calamities under which they labour.

The ministry won the division by 157 to 37 votes. Here was yet another example of the ways in which, despite all the pressures of war and the spread of hardship, Pitt's regime managed to cling to a model of limited government while the responsibilities of the state were necessarily increasing. The regime did not collapse, partly because of the efforts that *were* made to mitigate suffering as the war continued.[44]

Inevitably radicals made the most of food shortages, inflation, unemployment and lack of success in the war. Throughout 1794 and 1795 ministers were worried that disaffection might spread to the armed forces, and alarm was also generated by the London crimp-house riots of this period.[45] Inflammatory material continued to circulate, rumours about French invasion plans spread, and government supporters urged Pitt to take further action. He was aware that the failed prosecutions of 1794 had weakened the government's position and that new threats necessitated a robust response.[46] Perhaps he was waiting for an opportunity to do what he had already decided upon, and follow up the suspension of Habeas Corpus with coercive legislation. Yet radical acquittals were only a temporary embarrassment. Trials had deterrent value and forced more reformers into quiescence, and acquittals weakened radical arguments by undermining the allegation that the British system of government was corrupt. Radical claims would logically have been strengthened only if Hardy and the others had been convicted on flimsy evidence. The fact that they walked free could be used to vindicate established institutions.

Nevertheless, Pitt's opinion about the need for additional measures was dramatically reinforced on 29 October 1795, when, with anti-war protest reaching new heights, stones were thrown at the king's coach as it carried him to the state opening of parliament. At the end of 1795 emergency laws were passed to restore order. The Seditious Meetings Act was to operate for three years. Meetings of more than fifty people had to be licensed by local magistrates, and public lectures were also to be regulated. The Treasonable Practices Act, whose preamble referred to the attack on the king's coach, widened the definition of treason by including plans to harm the king, help invaders or coerce parliament. Spoken words came within the scope of this act. Foxites protested that anyone who advocated even the mildest measure of parliamentary reform could now be put on trial, and that the government's real priority was to intimidate critics using national security as a pretext. Foxites had also objected to the opening of subscriptions for defence in March and April 1794. They deemed this illegal, since defence costs were properly parliament's responsibility. Opposition MPs could not reverse the policy, however, and they were left complaining that individuals who decided not to contribute would be vulnerable to official displeasure and popular loyalist retribution. Again the purpose seemed to be to combat anti-government opinion.[47]

In the Commons Pitt justified the introduction of coercive measures in November 1795 by explaining that it was parliament's duty to protect the sovereign, constitution and religion of the people. He recognized the right of individuals to meet and discuss political questions, and their right of petition, but suggested that these rights had been abused. Meetings were a cover for revolutionary plotting. Pitt said he wanted to prevent the abuse of rights while preserving those rights intact, while Fox hoped that this latest offence against liberty would find no favour out of doors. Pitt accused him of questioning parliament's authority and promoting disloyalty.[48]

On 26 November 1795 Pitt wrote to the king of his 'satisfaction' at finding 'the sense of the House completely decided in favour of the vigorous measures which the circumstances require'. But were the 'Two Acts' of 1795 really necessary? There were personal and political choices behind Pitt's move, and he may have been more concerned about the likely consequences of inaction than the level of immediate danger. He had to protect himself and his administration from political failures, and guard against criticism from George III and the Portland Whigs. Domestic threats could be used to strengthen his position and silence complaints about lack of success in the war. Pitt also had to consider what would happen if agitation continued unchecked. There were added complications, such as the possibility of French invasion, and Pitt realized that it would be useful to encourage men of property to assist in defending the established order. For many reasons, therefore, the government had to demonstrate firmness, and with respect to the suspension of Habeas Corpus in 1794 and the 'Two Acts' of 1795, timing was very significant. In 1794 Pitt wanted to improve relations with the Portland Whigs, who abhorred plebeian radicalism, and in 1795 the popularity of the war was fast declining. Pitt thought he had little option but to take a hard line, and he must have been pleased to find that outdoor protest against the 'Two Acts' quickly subsided and that the weight of public opinion was behind the government. Loyal petitions flooded in after the attack on the king's coach, and the number of petitioners who welcomed the 'Two Acts' outnumbered those against by four to one.[49]

After 1795 many radicals either abandoned their campaigns or scrupulously adhered to legal limitations. With their agitation apparently held back, Pitt had fewer domestic distractions and could focus all the more on the war effort (especially the raising of funds to continue the war). Although the danger posed by treason and disorder was exaggerated for effect, however, a smouldering anger continued through 1796 and 1797 and prominent figures were frequently hissed, pelted with mud, or had their coaches stoned and houses attacked. Some extremists did not persist with open protest but decided to go underground. Indeed, repressive legislation changed the nature of radicalism by closing down space for public activity and strengthening the impetus for secret organization and conspiracy. Links have been discovered between underground movements across Britain and Ireland, and between their agents and revolutionary France.[50] These demonstrate the international nature of insurrectionary activity, which suggests that Pitt was right to take this threat seriously, but it does not follow that the revolutionary danger was particularly strong.

The vitality of loyalism indicates that despite war and suffering, there was widespread acceptance of the established order (reinforced by welfare measures, limited though they were, and the coercive powers of the state). Though there were armed uprisings during the late 1790s and early 1800s, these were easily put down and it is clear that insurrectionists never dominated British radicalism. Furthermore, political ideas played little part in the naval mutinies of 1797 at the Nore and Spithead, although several of those involved did have radical connections.[51] But whatever the real level of revolutionary danger, Pitt could not afford to disregard the more violent forms of protest available to discontented groups during the war. He saw how quickly the public mood reacted to harvest failure, falling wages, unemployment and commercial depression, and knew that radical spokesmen could attract more supporters (if only temporarily) by exploiting hardship. It was easy to blame the government for the war, and to blame the war for high prices and disrupted trade. There were serious disorders in 1800 and 1801. Radicals took advantage of discontent to call meetings and placard towns, and the home office received the usual reports of oath taking, drilling and arming. Agitation declined after the summer of 1801, due to exertions by the authorities, lower food prices and peace with France. The ministry did not ignore distress at the turn of the century, and as before Pitt tried to improve food supplies and extend poverty relief. Grenville disliked even limited intervention, preferring a strict *laissez faire* approach, but Pitt hoped that remedial plans would draw in more support for the government. This proved useful when ministers had to deal with disorders prompted by dearth. Relief and restraint were therefore inseparable.[52]

Relief and restraint also continued to be highly controversial. There were embarrassing squabbles between members and supporters of the government on specific policies, reflecting profound disagreements about the principle and nature of state intervention. In an attempt to influence bread prices, for example, the prime minister decided in 1800 to incorporate the London Flour Company. On 5 July, after a difficult debate in the Commons, the master of the mint, Lord Hawkesbury, complained to Pitt:

The situation in which I found myself placed was more distressing than anything I could have conceived, the whole responsibility of the measure being thrown *upon me personally*, abandoned as I was, with three or four exceptions, by every person in office, and opposed by one person connected with Government with a degree of rancour, spleen and vexation, which I should have thought very unwarranted in any person in opposition, upon a question of this nature.[53]

There has been disagreement among scholars about the impact on the reform movement of repressive laws and anti-radical fervour. It has been argued that reformers captured some of the loyalist associations, but also that large sections of the reform movement were turned towards loyalism.[54] Then there is the idea of Pitt's 'reign of terror'. In fact there were only about two hundred prosecutions over a period of ten years. Charges were frequently dropped and trials often resulted in acquittal. Though the definition of treason was extended in 1795, most proceedings were on the lesser charge of seditious libel. It is likely that government repression was less important in subduing radicalism than the force of public opinion, for loyalism imposed enormous pressure to conform. Pitt's emergency laws were harsh, it is true, but they were only temporary and did not alter the constitution, and state tyranny was well beyond the modest resources of the home office. Perhaps the *threat* of a 'reign of terror' was enough. Pitt's aims were really to deter radicals, encourage a loyalist reaction, and prompt propertied men to close ranks in defence of the established order. Once all this was achieved, further legislation and prosecutions were unnecessary.

On the other hand, to those held in prison without trial, or whose health, reputation and livelihoods were harmed despite their acquittal when tried, Pitt's regime was anything but mild. People directly affected by repression would not have agreed that there was no 'reign of terror'. John Holland Rose argues that although some precautions were needed to guard against disorder, the suspension of Habeas Corpus, political trials and 'Two Acts' – the 'nadir of Pitt's political career' – were unjustified. (Holland Rose, it should be noted, was heavily influenced by the liberal values of the early twentieth century, the time in which he wrote.) A more reasonable assessment is that of Clive Emsley, who points out that the government scrupulously adhered to constitutional forms and assumed 'no new or arbitrary power'. Pitt himself was not insensitive to suffering, and Ian Christie has argued that welfare provisions in this period helped to sustain a fundamental political stability which ensured that Britain would not experience revolution. David Eastwood shows that institutions survived the crises of the 1790s primarily because they were able to prove their worth and stimulate active voluntary effort in their defence. A heightened sense of nationalism contributed to these developments, and was manifested in respect for Pitt's regime and in the impressive participatory allegiance to established institutions generally.[55]

A conservative consensus remained intact during the later 1790s, and Pitt continued to represent the values and concerns of his supporters while shaping their ideas and conduct at opportune times. The government ruled out any structural changes to the established order in church and state. When polity and society were endangered from without by a foreign foe, and from within by popular discontent, the willingness to give reformers a hearing quickly declined (though Pitt came to favour a union with Ireland and Catholic emancipation, this was in direct response to wartime emergency). On 26 May 1797, when Grey introduced another reform motion and was backed again by Fox, Pitt maintained that there was no demand for parliamentary reform, no necessity for it, and that this was not the time to grant it. To Pitt's mind parliament enjoyed public confidence, the war and repression had widespread approval, and the electoral system faithfully registered changes in outdoor opinion. As proof he pointed to the re-election in 1796 of MPs who had sanctioned the ministry's prosecution of the war, and the rejection of opposition candidates in London and other populous towns. Pitt commended existing forms of representation, noting that the variety of franchises operated harmoniously together and brought no practical disadvantages. He also repeated his familiar point that reform debates in parliament were best avoided because they tended to encourage disaffected groups out of doors. Grey's motion was defeated by 256 to 91 votes, after which many Foxite MPs seceded from parliament.[56]

In the event secession was incomplete. It symbolized Foxite frustration. The sense that opposition to Pitt was futile had only been heightened by the May 1796 general election, which confirmed the ministry's majority (122 after the 1790 election, it was now about 290).[57] Grey initially viewed secession as an honourable course, but it created rather than solved problems and opposition leaders disagreed about it from the beginning. Some refused to follow Fox's example. Secession was not a party action, and it disappointed reformers out of doors. Though they lacked numbers, at least Foxite MPs had given expression to progressive opinions, and now it seemed that this outlet had been lost. Pitt had also confounded his critics by making genuine proposals for peace during the spring of 1796 and summer of 1797, which weakened Fox's claim that the government sought to perpetuate war for its own sinister reasons.[58]

As popular unrest continued during the late 1790s, mainly the consequence of suffering and privation, Pitt and his colleagues focused attention on the activity of radical societies and workers' combinations. Habeas Corpus was suspended again in 1798, for three years. The Newspaper Publication Act of 1798 subjected publishers to stricter regulations. Combination Acts were passed in 1799 and 1800 to control workers' organizations. The law of conspiracy already covered such unions 'in restraint of trade', but the new acts simplified procedures for arrest and punishment. They were intended as a deterrent (though combinations and strikes did not die out) and Pitt was anxious to control labour unions because he was aware of the ease with which they could be turned to political purposes.[59] In 1799 the London Corresponding Society was suppressed and parliament again sought to stamp out oath-taking and other secret proceedings.[60] Parliamentary resistance to these measures was weak. Some opposition MPs were still observing the secession, but it would have made little difference had they attended. Reports on sedition and disorder from Commons committees convinced the majority within parliament, and respectable opinion without, that new laws were appropriate. Pitt welcomed the reports because they underlined the continuing danger, yet the government and its supporters cared little about substantiating the reports' claims. Sources of information were not revealed. The need for further action against subversion and unrest was simply taken for granted (and no doubt the Irish rebellion of 1798 strengthened this predilection). Pitt had no doubt that 'wise and salutary' measures were required to deal with disturbances in Britain and Ireland and to combat the influence of secret societies. He told the Commons on 19 April 1799 that he wanted to do no more than was necessary to tackle these problems, but that precautions must be equal to the present evils. Seditious societies had to be crushed. Special attention would be given to their leaders, for the prime movers in any plotting were more culpable than those who followed. Notice had also to be taken of lecturers who perverted the minds of the people, and of editors, journalists, booksellers and others who abused press freedoms. The government's precautions were within the spirit of the constitution, Pitt declared, for they were intended to prevent rather than punish.[61]

There were fewer prosecutions for political offences between 1796 and 1800 than between 1792 and 1795. Even while treason and sedition laws were being extended, the number of cases decreased. For most purposes the threat of prosecution was sufficient, and as before legislation was strictly defined in terms of content and duration. Emergency powers could not be used unless certain criteria were met, and since measures were only to operate for a stated number of years, ministers had to justify renewal at the appropriate time. Liberties survived, notably the constitutional right of petitioning. Many types of premises were not covered by restrictions on meetings, moreover, and some forms of association were unaffected. Self-serving as his words may have been, Pitt was not speaking falsely when he argued that his intention was to preserve liberty by ensuring that rights were not abused. He honestly believed that in order to protect the whole constitution, parliament must suspend some of its parts. As a number of historians have pointed out, Pitt only responded to dangers that no government could ignore, and there appears to have been nothing pre-meditated about his repressive measures.[62] This contradicts the Foxite idea that Pitt had ulterior motives and wanted to make use of the extraordinary circumstances of wartime to destroy political opponents.

The war increased the importance to Pitt and his government of popular support. In the crisis atmosphere of the 1790s, Pitt relied ever more on the public approval he had nurtured in the 1780s with his financial and administrative reforms, encouragement of trade, restoration of political stability and raising of Britain's international prestige. In wartime the government faced a range of political and economic problems, which only intensified in the absence of a quick and successful end to the war. Pitt therefore had to stimulate, guide and employ loyal opinion. His experiences during the 1780s had suggested that his regime would be better able to survive if it had popular support, and he saw that this support was absolutely vital in wartime.[63] The established authorities had to enhance their legitimacy and authority by acting – to the greatest possible extent – in an irreproachable manner. They had to be seen to be in the right. Therefore Pitt remained quite willing to listen to reasonable and genuine grievances. But any concession beyond what was clearly necessary was out of the question. Laws had to be obeyed and anyone engaging in illegal activity was to be punished, although, as has been noted, this did not mean that Pitt's regime descended into a 'reign of terror'. Pitt did not have the intention or the means to make such a thing possible. Indeed, the government could hardly be seen to be in the right if it assumed arbitrary powers, and though Pitt opposed sweeping reforms, he also saw that concession was sometimes better than resistance.

The priority was not to rule by terror but to bring the nation behind the government and its war effort. Hence Pitt's approval for a limited extension of civil rights to Catholics in Ireland and England during the early 1790s, and his pragmatic arguments for a temporary abandonment of *laissez faire* economics (despite Grenville, Portland and other associates whose approach was more rigidly doctrinal) in response to wartime suffering. Pitt and his colleagues introduced repressive measures because they believed that there *was* a danger, and with so much at stake they could not separate radical agitation at home from the French Revolution and the war to prevent the spread of revolutionary violence in Europe.

Pitt could not simply assume that parliament and public would see the merits of his position, however, and he had to explain the emergency measures clearly. His basic point was always that a temporary suspension of certain liberties would safeguard all the others. Before the war, in February 1792, he had spoken of a balance between the rights of the people and the responsibilities of government:

> It is this union of liberty with law, which by raising a barrier equally firm against the encroachments of power, and the violence of popular commotion, affords to property its just security, produces the exertion of genius and labour, the extent and solidarity of credit, the circulation and increase of capital; which forms and upholds the national character, and sets in motion all the springs which actuate the great mass of the community through all its various descriptions.

During the war, Pitt developed this notion further by declaring that the French aimed to destroy British liberty and happiness, and that the nation was bound to resist. He explained in November 1797:

> If I could look at this as a dry question of prudence, if I could calculate it upon the mere grounds of interest, I would say, if we love that degree of national power which is necessary for the independence of the country, and its safety; if we regard domestic tranquillity, if we look at individual enjoyment, from the highest to the meanest among us, there is not a man whose stake is so great in the country, that he ought to hesitate a moment in sacrificing any portion of it to oppose the violence of the enemy.[64]

The prime minister needed popular approval for his emergency measures and welcomed the growth of active loyalism, but he was also concerned about violence against reformers. He and the cabinet regretted loyalist excesses at local level, sectarian conflict, 'Church and King' riots, and the harsh sentences meted out by particular judges. Pitt emphasized that restrictions and prosecutions should not cross the boundaries suggested by necessity and propriety. He wanted the government to remain in control. Yet it was difficult to balance liberty and order in the circumstances of the 1790s. Loyalists were demanding action against unrest and subversion, and Pitt realized that he would disappoint government supporters in parliament and out of doors if he appeared to be passive. On the other hand, an excessive response from the government could easily create sympathy for the radicals and play into the hands of their most extreme elements. Pitt's cautious approach, with full publicity, helped the government to retain the initiative. Pitt made use of secret committee reports and stressed that the abridgement of liberties was only partial and temporary. The suspension of Habeas Corpus in May 1794 was directed against nobody but those suspected of treason, and limited to nine months. Parliament had to sanction its renewal. The first suspension lasted until July 1795. The next suspension began in April 1798, and was extended as necessary until March 1801. The 'Two Acts' of 1795 were to last for three years and, again, parliament had to vote on their renewal. Though Pitt considered banning radical societies in 1792, it was not until April 1799 that five named associations were proscribed, and such was his reluctance to interfere with the freedom of the press (shared by George III) that he held off until 1798. Pitt maintained that restrictions were only meant to identify, isolate and frustrate the small but intractable minority who posed a real threat to the established order.[65]

Apart from wartime distress and popular agitation, there were other difficulties that arose as a direct consequence of the war, not least those relating to military recruitment. The strategy and conduct of the war also took time to organize effectively. Dundas was responsible for these matters from 1794, when he was appointed to the new office of secretary of state for war. But he was not relieved of his other ministerial posts (treasurer of the navy and president of the board of control), and there was continual argument in cabinet about particular war measures. Furthermore, the creation of the new secretaryship forced Pitt and Dundas into inconvenient negotiations, for this was the time when the Portland Whigs decided to join the administration. The establishment of a new department complicated the delicate arrangements with Portland's group about honours and offices.[66] Thereafter the war was conducted principally by Pitt and Dundas, in consultation with George III, and the cabinet generally followed their lead.

By 1797 several problems posed by the war had assumed a most dangerous complexion. There was the growing likelihood of a French landing in Ireland, and naval mutinies broke out at Spithead (April) and the Nore (May). Though some concessions on pay and conditions were made, the Nore mutiny was severely put down. Concern about the circulation of subversive handbills among soldiers prompted the Incitement to Mutiny Act, which made such incitement a capital offence, but there was also a pay rise for the army. Another crisis in 1797 concerned the Bank of England, which suspended cash payments in February. For some time Pitt had been uneasy about war expenditure. The nation had to pay for military and naval operations, subsidies to continental allies, and (when there was dearth) foreign grain. By 1797 the finances were in a parlous state and there was a balance of payments deficit. An invasion scare, Pitt informed the king on 25 February 1797, caused 'a demand for cash from London which has produced the greatest difficulties'. Panic was spreading.

> Mr Pitt entertained a hope that its progress could not be so rapid as not to be checked by the first opportunity of public discussion; but from the reports made him yesterday and today from the Bank, he is satisfied that the evil cannot be

suffered to proceed farther without the danger of its producing permanent consequences which could neither be obviated nor easily repaired.

Pitt decided to release the Bank of England from the obligation to honour its notes with gold. There was no alternative, for he had already raised loans and taxes and there was still a pressing need for cash and for more flexibility in the money supply, without which the government could not hope to stimulate business. Though Pitt was intellectually committed to 'sound money', he now promoted flexibility by increasing note issues, also stemming the outward flow of bullion. In justification he cited the nature of the war and demands of a growing economy. Pitt trusted that in time there would arise a self-regulating relationship between business transactions and the volume of notes in circulation. There was no financial collapse, and Pitt and his successors decided against a quick return to cash payments because they did not want to restrain economic activity or risk a loss of confidence in paper money.[67]

In the Commons at this time, backbench MPs became more openly sceptical about Pitt's administration, and some even contemplated an attempt to bring the prime minister down. Under pressure at home, unable to depend on continental allies, and realizing that French victories in Europe cast serious doubt on the policy of continuing to fight, Pitt made further overtures for peace. He may also have thought about resigning, on the assumption that the French would be more willing to make peace with a different leader.[68] But the French did not want peace, and George III, Portland, Burke, Grenville, Dundas and others were certain that peace would only be possible after the revolutionary regime in Paris was exterminated. The king thought that withdrawal from the war would be humiliating. He and Pitt quarrelled about the wisdom of peace talks all through the autumn of 1796 and spring of 1797. On 10 April 1797 George III expressed to Pitt his grave disappointment that the cabinet, albeit reluctantly, had backed the premier's view that Britain should seek a negotiated settlement.

> I shall certainly not with less sorrow acquiesce in the measure, as one thought by the Ministers of necessity, not choice; and Mr Pitt will, I am certain, not be surprised that the opinion which encouraged me to withstand the difficulties of the war is personally not changed; but I am conscious that if that remains a single one, I cannot but acquiesce in a measure that from the bottom of my heart I deplore.

Even Fox found the French attitude disappointing (but as before he blamed European monarchs for interfering in France's internal affairs). Increasingly pessimistic about the war, Pitt hoped that financial reforms would make Britain better able to fight on and secure an acceptable peace.[69]

Pitt believed that success in war depended largely on a nation's economic resources. Even in the early part of the struggle against France, therefore, when he still cherished an expectation of its swift conclusion, ministers expanded the government's credit facilities, fostered agricultural improvements, and increased trade with the United States. Pitt's concern about protecting the public finances and paying for the war led to the suspension of cash payments in 1797. His plans for lowering the national debt, meanwhile, could not work while the war lasted, but he was anxious to limit the growth of debt. There was more taxation. Indirect taxes already pressed hard on the poor, and Pitt focused instead on direct forms. Late in 1797 he trebled existing burdens on windows, houses, servants, carriages and other property, and introduced differential rates so that contributors paid more according to wealth and possessions. In April 1798 Pitt reformed the old land tax, which became a permanent charge to be redeemed at current valuations. In settlement landowners could make one capital payment. They welcomed the change, and it brought the government some ready money (though less than expected).[70]

Reform of the land tax, however, did not mean that Pitt was prepared to decrease future revenue in order to cover immediate needs. The measure was partly designed to reconcile parliament and the propertied elite to income tax, collection of which began in 1799. Incomes below £60 a year were exempt, those between £60 and £200 were taxed at a graduated rate from 5 to 10 per cent, and incomes over £200 a year were to pay 10 per cent. The yield from income tax was less than Pitt predicted. Evasion was a problem. Merchants and manufacturers often understated their earnings, for example, because income from industry and business was far more difficult to determine than that from land. Pitt later proposed that taxpayers should itemize their incomes in detail, but this idea aroused so much controversy that it was dropped. There was strong opposition to Pitt's income tax. Many contemporaries found it too novel and inquisitorial. It was also said to be unreasonably heavy on the wealthy (who already supported a large tax burden). There were claims that it represented an improper enlargement of government power, and that it would damage the economy and stifle investment. Pitt's real purpose might have been to safeguard the financial measures of the 1780s, especially the sinking fund, rather than to raise money for a larger war. Yet income tax came to be accepted as a wartime necessity, and in later years Pitt would be praised for his effort to employ British wealth in this manner. Property owners decided that an extra sacrifice would be worthwhile if it meant that British territory, interests, institutions and values could be protected against the French. Income tax provided 28 per cent of the money raised for the war, while over half of the new revenue raised for war came from higher rates of existing taxes. This was an impressive financial performance by wartime Britain, although the massive increase in government borrowing would prove to be one of the war's unfortunate legacies.[71]

There was considerable and ongoing financial reorganization, therefore, as it became clear that the conflict with France would not be as limited in scope and duration as was first thought. Pitt's preference for taxation over borrowing established a pattern that was followed by his successors. About 42 per cent of the total cost of war between 1793 and 1815 was covered by loans, compared to 81 per cent of the cost of the American war. Pitt advocated economic freedom and tried as far as possible to adhere to *laissez faire* policies, but an important departure from the Adam Smith system was the suspension of cash payments. Despite his commitment to 'sound money', by 1797 Pitt had decided that the needs of war had to prevail, and suspension did have some positive effects. Inflation stimulated industry, and the more adjustable supply of money facilitated economic expansion despite heavy taxation and commercial dislocation. In this manner, it seems, one major transgression of the Adam Smith system made possible all the rest of the government's indulgence in orthodoxy.[72]

Pitt's call upon the financial resources of the British people did not end with the payment of much heavier taxes. There was also a great deal of voluntary giving. Pitt wanted the ruling class to set a good example, and made sure that special contributions made by members of the political and social elite were widely publicized. He then used this to stimulate a mass display of patriotic sacrifice. In time voluntary contributions were made by all classes. Pitt persuaded a reluctant George III to join in, gave over a portion of his own income, and urged cabinet colleagues to do the same. Aware of the continuing popular resentment against sinecures and pensions, and especially the complaint that the wartime growth of government enabled certain officials to profit from increased fee income, Pitt responded by forcing tellers of the exchequer to forego their extra wartime remuneration, and tried to curb financial waste and inefficiency. By such means he hoped to reconcile taxpayers to the increased demands of the later 1790s. Invasion scares and patriotic fervour helped too, and voluntary contributions were lauded as public displays of national pride. Pitt insisted in April 1798 that the war was being fought to defend Britain's freedom, order, property, honour, law, religion and even existence, and mainstream public opinion agreed. Voluntary contributions reached £2,200,000 by February 1799, when subscriptions closed.[73]

But economical reform was not particularly useful in encouraging taxpayers to support extra burdens, since to the government it was no longer a pressing priority. When opportunities arose to cut costs, or promote greater administrative efficiency, of course Pitt acted, but the relentless wartime growth of the 'fiscal-military state' meant that improvements became rare indeed, and Pitt chose not to do more. There are several possible explanations for this reluctance to carry forward economical reforms after 1793: the wish not to offend powerful insiders or encourage the Commons to tamper with the machinery of state; the volume of wartime business, which limited the time and attention that could be given to economical reform; and the fear of change created by the French Revolution. Whatever the reason for Pitt's failure to reorganize administrative structures more substantially, many observers began to wonder if his regime could still be trusted with taxpayers' money.[74]

Instead of initiating or adding his influence to retrenchment efforts during the war, Pitt sometimes obstructed them. Early in 1797 he tried to dodge complaints about heavy taxation, useless places, sinecures, fees and the squandering of public funds by promising a full inquiry. In the Commons on 13 March he opposed a motion for economical reform, deeming it unnecessary in view of the forthcoming inquiry. He declared that although the government would certainly attempt to make savings, rises in expenditure had to be expected during a war. Pitt explained that he was not against the abolition of useless offices or reduction of salaries. But he preferred to stick with the inquiry that had already been approved, rather than complicate matters with a superfluous motion. Salaries, fees, sinecures and the rest were really part of a larger problem, argued Pitt, and a general inquiry was the best way to proceed. Nothing could be done until details had been gathered concerning the specific salaries that were to be reduced, offices that were to be abolished, the impact of previous retrenchments, departments in which abuses were supposed still to exist, and the public benefit of interfering with the operations of government in this manner. Pitt warned against hasty decisions about 'excessive' remuneration. Though some offices did not involve heavy duties, he said, those who held them usually served the nation in other ways and it was perverse to claim that they did not deserve their salaries. Pitt therefore concluded that parliament should not rush into an extensive plan of retrenchment without first collecting and analysing all the facts. He won the division by 169 to 77 votes.[75]

Out of doors, loyalty to the established order outweighed by far the resentment against higher taxes and official abuses. Extra-parliamentary support for the government and war effort helped to sustain Pitt through the anxieties of the late 1790s. He remarked in December 1800 that 'if the mass of the people were disloyal, the measures of parliament ... would be ineffectual'.[76] The flood of conservative propaganda and repetition of pro-government rhetoric and ritual continued. Pitt was a focus and figurehead, but even more remarkable was the way in which the king had become a talisman for ebullient patriotism. George III's image was projected far and wide, and to some extent the monarchy was reinvented. It came to embody accessibility, paternal benevolence, domestic virtues and a responsible custodial role in politics, and these qualities were repeatedly stressed in the conservative propaganda of the 1790s. The government, courts, church and conservative press persistently justified monarchy and the traditional values it embodied. Novels and cartoons also disseminated a range of conservative sentiments, and over two million copies of the *Cheap Repository Tracts* were distributed between 1795 and 1798 to reinforce this mood. Burke's work was still being discussed, and loyalist societies went on printing and distributing their own books and pamphlets. Aspersions were cast on anyone who wanted social and political change. Clergymen preached respect for hierarchy and tradition. The most talented writers of the time contributed to a new periodical, the *Anti-Jacobin Review*, established in November 1797. A leading mover behind this was Pitt's protégé Canning, and Pitt himself contributed articles anonymously, on the war and public finance. Other members of government also wrote for the new review.[77]

All this assisted recruitment for home defence. Volunteer units were formed in most regions, and their uniforms, banners and parades were open displays of patriotism and enhanced the local status of those who participated. Pitt's ministry had originally called for the establishment of armed companies in March 1794, appealing directly to loyalists for funds. The volunteer movement expanded quickly, though it was more important as a means of advertising patriotism and intimidating reformers than as an effective foundation for home defence, and it added to the government's problem of how to control popular loyalism. Ministers could not simply allow it to develop unsupervised. Hence the long discussions about arming the volunteers, and the unease about recruitment from the lower classes. Some volunteers, obviously not as deferential as had been expected, refused to put down food riots during 1795, 1797, 1800 and 1801, and demanded the right to select their own officers. These difficulties prompted a reform of the volunteer system in 1801. Greater reliance on a permanent local militia improved the nation's defences (about half a million men would be involved in home defence by 1804). Yet the militia was conscripted through the ballot system, which created enormous ill feeling. The system was hardly fair when the wealthy and influential could send substitutes in their place, and there was serious rioting against ballots during 1796 and 1797. This followed the government's decision rapidly to expand the militia: subject to military discipline while on service, militia units were easier to control than volunteers. Manpower

needs prompted another recruitment drive for the volunteers in 1798, however, and in April of that year legislation was enacted to create a reserve
force of males aged between sixteen and sixty who were not already enlisted
for service. Volunteer numbers doubled within four months. But the whole
question of home defence remained controversial.

As well as growing concern about the maintenance of discipline and
doubts about the wisdom of arming civilians, there was the traditional
animosity to standing armies and parliament's insistence that its discretion
in these matters had to be respected. Nevertheless, Pitt presided over an
unprecedented level of recruitment and arming. Previous administrations
had been wary of civil defence formations, fearing that they might assist
local supporters of the parliamentary opposition or agitate for reforms, but
Pitt felt confident enough to proceed. Admittedly, he did so only after
research. His associates and officials regularly contacted local interests to
gauge their reliability and the likely response to the creation of armed units.
Though some of his supporters were doubtful, Pitt insisted that popular
loyalism could safely be relied upon. In July 1803 he told the Commons:

> Much has been said of the danger of arming the people ... but there never was
> a time when there could have been any fear of arming the whole people of
> England, and particularly not under the present circumstances. I never, indeed,
> entertained any apprehensions from a patriot army regularly officered ... From
> an army to consist of the round bulk of the people, no man who knows the
> British character could have the least fear – if it even were to include the disaffected;
> for they would bear so small a proportion of the whole, as to be incapable of
> doing mischief, however mischievously disposed.

That the government's defence policies were carried into effect without
much resistance before 1801 is an indication both of overwhelming public
approval and Pitt's strong position in parliament. Sometimes the prime
minister made minor concessions in order to retain support (as when he
abandoned his scheme to raise a cavalry force from those liable to horse
tax). His practice of consulting widely before introducing measures also
helped, and most contemporaries agreed that home defence had to be
improved as peace negotiations failed and the war carried on.[78]

Pitt and his supporters did not find it easy to mobilize British manpower
for war (and it is not easy today to appreciate the sheer scale and intensity
of this mobilization). Just as there were limits to the amount of revenue
raised from taxation and loans, and the quantity of food available for the
population, so there was a limit to the number of men who could be
recruited for army, navy, volunteers and militia. Allocating resources to the
military effort meant diverting them from farming, industry and commerce,

which generated the income needed to fight the war and subsidize continental allies. Furthermore, elite fears about arming people who might conceivably turn their weapons against the established order never entirely disappeared, and the high level of popular participation in national defence could not be achieved without departing from some of Britain's libertarian and voluntary traditions. This resulted in some of the developments outlined above. In addition, Pitt's government was obliged to accommodate different interests. The co-operation of local authorities, in fact, was vital in terms of military recruitment, public order, and persuading local defence units to serve outside their own districts. The government's need for local help, and the increased opportunities for military and political participation (taken up by various national, social and economic groups), eventually made parliamentary reform a more pressing issue. Many people who joined in the wartime mobilization expected greater representation in return for their effort. The shortage of men for the regular army and navy also prompted the enlistment of criminals. When he was home secretary Dundas authorized this on several occasions.[79]

The government's ability to attract support was affected by struggles to define and direct patriotism. Although patriotic appeals in the 1790s stimulated a loyalist upsurge and dynamic anti-radical and anti-French sentiment, patriotism was itself a contested and flexible tool. It could take both conservative and subversive forms. Like the constitution, patriotism could be used to stress liberty as well as order. Its vigorously radical, egalitarian and independent form has been called a 'bottom-up patriotism'. This clashed with the patriotism shaped and approved by the ruling elite.[80]

Among the most difficult tasks relating directly to the conduct of the war was the need (partly in order to sustain morale and commitment at home) to convince parliament and public that this war was a necessary and worthwhile enterprise. During the mid- and late 1790s the war continued to provide a focus for those in Britain who had all manner of political and economic grievances.[81] There was a persistent questioning of British involvement, and demands for peace grew louder as hardship increased at home. Within just a few months of the war's commencement, even commentators inside the government were predicting the worst. Huskisson, head of the aliens department, wrote on 15 April 1793 of business failures, slack trade and financial turmoil, with London and the large commercial towns prey to 'a degree of terror which it is impossible to describe'. Pitt was constantly receiving 'deputations from every class of the mercantile world', but there was no remedy for their 'melancholy cases'. Huskisson concluded: 'If the genius of the Minister assisted, as I hope it will be, by a speedy cessation of hostilities and the protection of Providence, does not avert the impending calamities, this country, prosperous and wealthy as it is, will soon present a dreadful example of commercial and perhaps national distress.'[82]

The initial stimulus for war was not hostility to republicanism or democracy, but a desire to protect British interests abroad. Pitt had also assumed that the war would be short. Within four years it became obvious that he and his associates would have to reassess their approach (though the war was still explained and justified in non-ideological terms). They had been wrong to assume that Britain would not be heavily involved in European theatres. Britain had to take on more than merely a supporting role, and Pitt had to frame a European policy in concert with Britain's allies. These allies had their own territorial and political goals, however, and though they received British subsidies it was difficult to co-ordinate military operations. Early tension and mutual suspicion hardly receded at all. Pitt and Grenville were not initially committed to the restoration of monarchy in France, for example, though this was a principal aim of Britain's European allies. Pitt was willing to assist French royalists if he could thereby promote counter-revolution, but British efforts along these lines were resounding failures and Pitt always thought it would be a disadvantage to tie himself explicitly to the restoration of the French monarchy. This was his position when dealing with Britain's continental allies during the summer of 1793, and on 17 June he told the Commons that aiding French royalists as an operation of war would not bind the government to any specific policy in the future ('There was no intention, if the country had not been attacked, to interfere in the internal affairs of France. But having been attacked, I affirm that there is nothing ... which pledges us not to take advantage of any interference in the internal affairs of France that may be necessary').[83]

Though Pitt was conscious that the revolutionary principles holding sway in France endangered the established order in Britain, he trusted that the war would undermine these principles, and was less interested in the *type* of government that ruled France than in its stability and longevity. A lasting peace would be impossible to achieve, he thought, unless the French leadership was willing to arrive at suitable terms, and strong enough to persuade the French population to accept them. There were several periods of negotiation during the 1790s, and Pitt suspected that the various revolutionary parties assuming power in France either could not or would not deliver a secure peace. Royalist uprisings in France in the early part of the war prompted Pitt and the cabinet to support a restoration of the French monarchy, and there were clear declarations during the autumn of 1793 that the British government would only assist and deal with monarchists. But this commitment was equivocal. Pitt wrote to Grenville on 5 October 1793 that the absolutist Bourbon regime had posed too many problems for

Britain and other powers in the past, and that a restored monarchy ought to be subjected to constitutional limits. It was difficult to decide what form these limits should take, however, and Pitt realized that French preferences, not British, would carry most weight in France should there be a restoration. His pragmatic approach meant that he was prepared to deal with a republican government if it could make a peace settlement hold. While Pitt agreed to give money, weapons and other assistance to French monarchists inside and outside France, therefore, Britain refused to recognize the Count of Provence (brother and heir of the executed Louis XVI) as regent or king of France. Canning summed up the government's position after meeting with Pitt on 26 January 1795 (the prime minister had called his advisers together to formulate a response to Foxite MPs who were pressing the government to make peace). Canning wrote that 'with respect to a treaty with France ... it is not the *form* of the Government there, but its *power* and *will* to afford and maintain *security* to other countries, that we consider as *indispensable*', and 'about monarchy, or republicanism, or revolutionary Committees, or this or that set of men or set of principles, we have no care nor consideration'. Pitt reinforced this publicly in November 1797:

> If by the blessing of providence, our perseverance, and our resources, should enable us to make peace with France upon terms in which we taint not our character, in which we do not abandon the sources of our wealth, the means of our strength, the defence of what we already possess; if we maintain our equal pretensions, and assert that rank which we are entitled to hold among nations – the moment peace can be obtained on such terms, be the form of government in France what it may, peace is desirable, peace is then anxiously to be sought.

As for the reasons why Britain had gone to war in the first place, Pitt gave his opinion in the Commons on 25 April 1793:

> Gentlemen were continually adverting to the causes of their entering into war, and considering what degree of provocation had been given on the part of France – what resentment and outrage committed against ourselves, should or should not induce this country to commence a war against France. But while they were discussing that principle, the circumstance that arose was that France had declared war against this country. He conceived this country was justly entitled to proceed on the war against France, to repel her unjust attacks, and, if possible, to chastise and to punish her, and to obtain indemnification for the past, and security for the future. These were the principles on which they engaged in the war. These were the principles they must look to in carrying it on, and which they must keep in view at its conclusion.

It does not appear that restoring the French monarchy ranked highly (if at all) among Britain's war aims. The general goal was to remove the threat of French military aggression and so provide for the future security of Britain and Europe.[84]

According to Philip Schofield the destruction of French revolutionary ideology was also a dominant aspiration, while T. C. W. Blanning and Eric Evans insist that this had no role in the decision to go to war (Evans thinks that had there been an ideological motive, Britain would have entered the war much sooner). Jennifer Mori points to a combination of ideological and traditional concerns: fear of French principles merged with well-established British diplomatic and strategic interests. The war was neither exclusively ideological, therefore, nor purely conventional. Blanning argues that the key consideration for Pitt was that British security and interests were bound up with the integrity of Holland. This, and the need to uphold Britain's international position, meant that more could be gained by going to war than by remaining neutral. John Holland Rose regards French designs on Holland as the basic cause of the war, and other matters (such as revolutionary ideas, or the execution of Louis XVI) as relatively unimportant, and John Ehrman agrees that Britain's specific obligation to Holland, and desire to prevent French control over the Low Countries, were of paramount importance. In addition, Pitt evidently decided that Britain could not stand aside in the face of France's aggressive expansionism and disregard of international treaties. For Paul Schroeder the war was at root a competition for security. Britain and France were old rivals, and one could only increase its own security by making the other feel *less* secure. French revolutionaries took up the mantra of 'natural frontiers', seeking territorial gains that would buttress their political system and national defences, but this meant security through hegemony in western Europe, which Pitt could not allow. Some of these themes have been taken up by Jeremy Black. He argues that revolutionary ideology, though significant, was not among the main reasons why Britain went to war, and in any case cannot be viewed in isolation. Black thinks that the grounds for conflict already existed, in 'the mutual antipathy of the two peoples and powers'. The specific points in dispute during the later months of 1792 – the Scheldt navigation and integrity of Holland – might have been settled by negotiation had it not been for the miscalculations that brought about 'war by accident, error, misjudgment and illusion': neither Britain nor France had a very accurate idea of each other's strength and intentions. Evidently Pitt, his colleagues and supporters decided that an international setting in which Britain had its due influence, and the re-establishment of social stability at home, were well worth fighting for. As for strategy, Pitt, Dundas and Grenville (and George III) agreed that an independent Holland and Austrian-controlled Belgium offered the most effective barrier to French expansion in Europe. Operations on the continent were organized with this in mind. Britain's main strength, though, was overseas. Outside Europe, British forces attempted to invade French colonies in the East and West Indies, in order to weaken French power and enhance Britain's wealth and security. Again, the cardinal requirement was to make sure that France could not harm Britain in the future (and, as Michael Duffy observes, to bring to a successful conclusion the long series of wars against France). Therefore Pitt's government was eager most of all to destroy French shipping, seize French colonies, and take over French trade.[85]

On these general points there was substantial agreement among ministers, but this did not prevent serious quarrels. Some had their own personal agendas to advance (Dundas[86] wanted to concentrate on the West Indies, for example, and Windham remained sympathetic towards the French monarchists). Some were jealous of their status, and quick to resist interference from anyone else – Pitt included – in what they saw as their own areas of responsibility. There were also honest differences of opinion about Britain's best interests.

The temporary breach between Pitt and Grenville in 1797, when they disagreed on the propriety of peace talks, indicates that even the closest associates within the cabinet could fall out over war-related matters. When the foreign secretary disagreed with him (there had been an earlier argument in 1795 over Pitt's decision to subsidize Prussia), Pitt did what he could to minimize the damage. Indeed, among the premier's most significant wartime difficulties in cabinet were those created by his clashes with Grenville. Fortunately these arguments did not impair the war effort for long. Though Pitt tried hard to negotiate an end to the war in 1797, the failure of peace talks to which Grenville had been opposed removed a source of friction and was quickly turned to the government's advantage. In France pro-war leaders had risen to power within the Directory, the governing body, and they made sure that the peace negotiations failed. As Pitt told Huskisson, this could be used to rally parliament and people, to undermine the Foxite claim that the government wanted to continue the war for its own purposes, to mollify peace campaigners, and generally to fortify British resistance to French ambitions.

> If we can clearly show that the Directory were not to be shaken in their resolution of continuing the war, whatever might be the terms offered for the attainment of peace, some of our various difficulties will receive some diminution. In this case no time will be taken up on idle talk. The alternative of yielding or resisting will be presented indifferently to all, and I trust that the wearing us out by the expense of the war, one of the brightest hopes of the French Government, will, if we are united, be a more tough piece of work than France is at present aware of.

Another source of anxiety for Pitt, especially in the early part of the war, was the Portland Whigs' espousal of co-operation with French monarchists. But this only affected strategy on one important occasion. During 1794, when presenting their terms for joining the ministry, they insisted that restoration of the French monarchy should be a stated war aim. Despite the misgivings of Pitt and Dundas, therefore, in June 1795 Britain supported a landing by French royalists at Quiberon Bay. Pitt was persuaded by the Portland Whigs to send British troops to assist in July, but this offensive came to nothing and British forces had to withdraw. As stated above, Pitt regained the initiative. Although Windham continued to uphold the French monarchists' cause (as in October 1799: 'For God's sake let us at length exert ourselves to support these people'), other Portland Whigs agreed with Pitt that in order satisfactorily to end the war it would be better to negotiate with France's republican government.[87]

Pitt's relationship with George III became more difficult after 1793 as war strategy prompted disputes between king and cabinet. Pitt had previously found it difficult to win the king's approval for an active foreign policy, since George III's inclinations were non-interventionist. During the war, however, ministers were inconvenienced by George III's suggestions and demands. Usually the king wanted a more vigorous approach. His long-standing interest in military matters presented a further complication. Early in the war he sought more support for his favourite son, Prince Frederick, Duke of York, who held a command in Flanders, but the campaign in Flanders proved to be disappointing, and to devote further resources to it would have been to jeopardize operations elsewhere. At the end of 1794, after the juncture with Portland Whigs had strengthened the cabinet and enhanced the premier's position vis-à-vis the crown, Pitt was able to recall the Duke of York, much to George III's annoyance. The situation improved when the king promoted York to field marshal in February 1795, and commander-in-chief of the army (a post more suited to the duke's talents – he proved a competent administrator) in April 1798.

On some matters George III dug his heels in. He objected to a plan for transferring troops to the West Indies in 1795, and the aforementioned link with Hanover was also problematic. By the spring of 1795 the French had occupied Holland and Prussia had made a separate treaty with France. Hoping for peace in Germany, Hanover declared itself neutral in the autumn, but Pitt and Grenville wanted Prussia and Austria to fight on until the time was right to negotiate a general settlement. They were prepared to offer the Prussians territory, at the expense of weaker German states, and to assist Austria to exchange the Netherlands for Bavaria. George III opposed all this, partly because he wanted the interests of the smaller

German states to be properly respected, but at length he had to give way. This was important for Pitt, for strategic decisions were now more clearly the cabinet's affair.

The dominant trio of Pitt, Dundas and Grenville normally worked well together, pressing George III to accept advice they had framed jointly. To the king they proffered identical or complementary arguments, denying him alternatives, and they were also better informed than he was. In addition, they had sufficient tact and influence to force ministerial colleagues into line, and Pitt had an advantage over the king when he could show that he was backed by a united cabinet. Though George III demurred whenever Pitt broached the subject of peace talks, those in the cabinet who at different times might have sided with the king (because, like him, they preferred to continue the war) knew better than to endanger cabinet unity or undermine Pitt in his dealings with the court. On most questions, great or small, George III had little option but to consent to what the cabinet had approved. When Grenville informed him in January 1796 of the plan to co-operate with Austria in making peace overtures to the French, the king responded with one of his characteristic expressions of resentful compliance: 'though I own I cannot feel the utility of it, I do not in the least mean to make any obstinate resistance to the measure proposed'.[88]

Such was Pitt's personal authority that he was involved in all the main aspects of foreign policy and the war effort, and acted for foreign secretary Grenville and war secretary Dundas whenever they were absent. As prime minister he assumed responsibility for the active co-ordination of war measures. He tried to make sure that the different government departments did what was required, chiefly by supervising the departmental heads. If an individual minister seemed unwilling to co-operate, Pitt moved to correct or sidestep the problem.[89] Even before the war Pitt's preferred method was to deal with individuals directly, rather than to manage affairs through the cabinet. The need to get things done quickly during the war accentuated this tendency. Grenville and Dundas agreed with Pitt: to wait for the cabinet to decide every important question was to run the risk of dangerous delay. Though Pitt, Grenville and Dundas had the collective weight to get their prepared plans through the cabinet without much trouble, they normally chose to settle matters themselves without a cabinet discussion. Key decisions were implemented after consultation with the king and those few ministers, officials or 'experts' who had a special contribution to make. Partly for security reasons, only certain facts were given to the whole cabinet. In November 1799 Pitt told Grenville that recent dispatches could be made available to ministers if they wanted to read them, but that there was no need to arrange a cabinet meeting unless there were any objections to what these dispatches contained. Sometimes papers were sent to the king before the cabinet had seen or discussed them. If members of the cabinet insisted on a meeting, Pitt made prior preparations. On 20 March 1800 he wrote to Grenville: 'A cabinet has been summoned tomorrow, at the desire of several of our colleagues, to discuss further our military plans and prospects. It will be desirable that you and Dundas and myself should have some previous conversation.' Grenville warned Pitt on 11 April 1800 of a pressing point of strategy that had to be settled, adding: 'I cannot take upon myself in such a business to guess at the opinions of my colleagues. But before we summon our numerous cabinet, it is much better that those who are to execute should understand each other upon the subject.' Meetings of the full cabinet could potentially help to settle disagreements within the triumvirate, but they never played an important role in Pitt's war management. He had more control without them.[90]

Pitt's leadership style, generally disorganized and spasmodic, caused extra problems in wartime. He tended to follow his own enthusiasms and neglect other topics in which he lacked interest. Fascinated by military planning and eager to attack the enemy wherever possible, his energy and optimism carried others along with him – members of the cabinet, officials, advisers, and even Britain's foremost military and naval commanders (with whom he often communicated personally). In view of Britain's financial and economic power, Pitt thought that the French could soon be exhausted if assailed in several theatres simultaneously. But his critics, who included at various times George III, Grenville, Wilberforce and the experienced Richmond (who had seen action during the Seven Years War, been minister-plenipotentiary at Paris in 1765, served as a secretary of state under Rockingham in 1766, and first became master general of the ordnance in 1782) argued that it would be better to concentrate forces rather than spread them out, that there could be no decisive breakthrough without a more focused attack, and that Pitt was trying to do too much too quickly. It seemed to them that the prime minister always underestimated the obstacles to the ends he had in view, and that with no military experience or proven record as a war leader, his judgments were often rather faulty.[91]

These shortcomings were exacerbated by Pitt's constant devotion to business. He hardly had the time to relax and refresh his energies. The need he felt continuously to attend to business was noted in the early months of the war, and as the war dragged on, so Pitt became all the more jaded. In April 1793 Huskisson, who had been asked by a friend to intercede with Pitt on some urgent matter, was informed by treasury secretary Charles Long that though Pitt might receive a letter and open it, he probably would not read it. Long complained of the weight of affairs. Huskisson recorded:

During the holidays, Pitt, I was informed, could not find time to go to Holwood; consequently the expected opportunity of relaxation had not offered itself ... I asked Long if he had hopes of another, or any idea when it would occur. He plainly told me that he had not; and that as long as parliament was sitting, it was absolutely impossible. I have, says he, more than twenty matters of public business now in sufferance. Whenever he sends for me, I go with my bundle of papers, but am almost to a certainty dismissed before he can examine one.[92]

As Pitt immersed himself in war management, he could not resist the temptation to interfere when he noticed a difficulty, but in trying to speed things up he sometimes added to the confusion. He established no clear procedure for dealing with specific tasks, as was demonstrated by the ill-fated Dunkirk operation of 1793. Pitt promised to arrange naval support for the chief of staff in Flanders, Sir James Murray, but was subsequently distracted by other business. Dundas awaited Murray's instructions while Murray, of course, thought that Pitt was dealing with the matter personally. So nothing was done. Eventually Dundas acted, but the delay proved costly and the operation failed.[93]

Pitt did not make use of the best available military advice. He acknowledged his need for guidance to Windham in September 1794 – 'I distrust extremely any ideas of my own on military subjects' – and yet he liked to make up his own mind and only listened to others when it suited him. Richmond became a bitter critic of this lack of consultation. Pitt was annoyed by Richmond's opposition to campaigns in the West Indies and Flanders during 1793 and 1794, and decided not to include him in future discussion of war matters. As a result, Richmond rarely bothered to attend cabinet meetings from the spring of 1794. In February 1795 the first Marquess and second Earl Cornwallis, a military veteran of the Seven Years War and American war who had distinguished himself as governor general and military commander in India from 1786 to 1793, was appointed master general of the ordnance in Richmond's place, but Pitt found him too cautious and pessimistic. His advice did not accord with Pitt's proactive approach, and by 1798 Cornwallis was also complaining about lack of consultation. Occasionally Pitt sought the views of other military friends, such as the third Baron Mulgrave (who advised about operations on the Meuse in September 1794 and was eventually promoted to the rank of general in 1809, having joined the army in 1775). But the usual practice was for Pitt and Dundas to decide strategy. They either proposed operations themselves, or selected one from the schemes put to them. They appointed the field commanders, with whom they also discussed supplies and other requirements (treasury secretary George Rose sometimes helped Pitt to arrange for the provision of money and food). Pitt reacted impatiently when a chosen commander made difficulties, and Dundas became concerned about his reluctance to listen to senior military figures. Late in 1799, when contemplating offensive efforts in western France, Dundas urged the prime minister not to allow his natural eagerness to get the better of him. It was essential, he stressed, to ensure that plans under consideration had a chance of success before resources were committed.[94]

If Pitt's war leadership was deficient, however, it was also inspirational. At least some of his failings were mitigated by his determination and optimism. By remaining positive, despite reversals, Pitt instilled confidence in others. 'It is certainly a severe check', Pitt told Rose in September 1793 after the retreat from Dunkirk, 'but I trust only a temporary one; and it ought only to have the effect of increasing, if possible, our exertions.' In April 1798, Pitt admitted to Grenville that he was worried about the struggle in the Mediterranean and the intentions of Austria and Prussia, and did not know how best to plan and execute a successful offensive at this time. But he did so in a typically uplifting manner: 'I will not despair ... We must endeavour to overcome all these impossibilities.' Auckland wrote of Pitt in the same month: 'excepting perhaps during the naval mutiny, he has never inclined to despondency, or even to serious discouragement. At present he entertains strong hopes that all will somehow end well.' Wilber-force also noted Pitt's composure in the face of adversity, and if the testimonies of Dundas and Earl Spencer are anything to go by, the premier had no trouble sleeping. 'I envy the rogue,' Dundas would say, for Pitt could sleep soundly 'while I am lying tossing and tumbling in my bed, and cannot sleep a wink for thinking of expeditions and storms and battles by sea and land.' Spencer, when first lord of the admiralty, visited Pitt late one night and woke him to talk over a matter of great urgency. He received his instructions, but shortly after leaving remembered something else, and returned to find that Pitt had already gone back to sleep.[95]

Patriotic faith and devotion were part of Pitt's image as the selfless national leader. His reputation for virtuous public service, so carefully created in the years before the war, survived into the difficult period after 1793, and Pitt tried to live up to this reputation. Though he was prone to depression and indecisiveness at various times, and by the end of the 1790s his health and morale were fading fast, he never gave up the belief that Britain would come through the war undefeated. Others picked up on Pitt's resilience and hope. His Commons speech of 10 November 1797, on the failure of peace talks at Lille, roused MPs into a patriotic chorus. Pitt stressed that the negotiation had been ended not by his government but by the French, and that Britain, having no choice now but to continue the war, possessed all that was needed to press on towards victory. 'Englishmen will not 'hesitate', he declared; 'we know great exertions are wanting, but we are prepared to make them, and at all events determined to stand or fall by the laws, liberties, and religion of our country.'[96]

The government's popularity held up well. Naval victories were especially important in reassuring the nation, prolonging support for the war, and increasing Pitt's security of tenure as prime minister. Britain's strong navy, which Pitt had built up in peacetime, kept alive the prospect of ultimate victory, and there was enthusiastic celebration of naval successes against the Spanish at Cape St Vincent (February 1797), the Dutch at Camperdown (October 1797), and the French at the Battle of the Nile (August 1798). Naval strength impressed Britain's European allies, which was useful to Pitt. It was also essential in the West Indies (as a source of wealth the West Indian possessions became vital to the war effort as a whole, and, contrary to what had been experienced in earlier wars, during the 1790s Britain's overseas trade grew rapidly).

As well as improving the navy, Pitt had made Britain better able to fight a long war with his financial and administrative reforms. He had earned the trust of the propertied classes and restored financial confidence, and after 1793 creditors and taxpayers were persuaded to make huge sums available for the war. This in turn helped Pitt to deflect much criticism of his war policies, as did his political and parliamentary talents. The prime minister had to make use of all these advantages in dealing with the peace movement. During 1795 pressure for peace grew rapidly. The First Coalition (Austria, Prussia, Sardinia, Britain, Holland, Spain, Naples and the Papal States) was breaking up, French armies had made advances against the allies in Europe, British conquests in the West Indies were vulnerable because of native rebellions and fever among the troops,[97] and there was serious unrest at home due to rising prices, hunger and distress. After ruling out peace talks Pitt changed his mind and agreed that it might be possible to reach a settlement. But as talks with the French kept breaking down, Pitt was able to shift responsibility away from himself and his government, and by 1797 all blame for the failure to end the war rested on France.

One of the key moments in this development came on 29 October 1795, when – as mentioned above – Pitt won over many of his detractors and persuaded them to rely on him to do what was necessary to protect the nation. At the opening of a new parliamentary session, Pitt told the Commons that when and if such a move became appropriate, he would explore the possibility of negotiations with the French Directory (which had only recently risen to power). Canning noted that Pitt's 'magnificent' speech 'seemed to take the weight off people's minds and set them shouting with approbation'. The government's position was much stronger as a result.

'Wilberforce and his conscientious followers, the effusion-of-human-blood party, all came back to us, and thus at the end of three years of unsuccessful war, here is Pitt stronger and gaining strength – and Opposition further from their object than ever.' Pitt knew how to respond to criticism in parliament and out of doors. He said what people wanted to hear, stressing that his opinions on war and peace could alter in line with changing needs and opportunities. Pitt had repeatedly to convince people that he had done all he could to bring peace, otherwise he could not reasonably ask them to make more sacrifices as the war continued. He told Chatham in September 1796 that the extension of the war 'does not come unexpectedly; and (if we can satisfy the country that we have done enough towards general peace) it will not, I trust, produce much embarrassment. Our great apparent difficulty is finance, which can only be removed by bringing people to a temper for very unusual exertions.' The failure of peace talks in February 1796 and again at the end of the year helped Pitt to secure parliamentary and public approval for a massive expansion of home defence forces. Furthermore, when the government asked for a 'loyalty loan' of £18,000,000 in December 1796, the amount was raised within just four days. In May 1797 Pitt persuaded parliament to sanction a compensation package for subscribers who suffered losses as a result of their patriotic gesture.[98]

Though the government enjoyed high levels of support during the 1790s, both in parliament and the nation, war weariness, food shortages and economic problems could never be ignored. Indeed, the war went on for so long, and was so costly, that the lack of a decisive breakthrough undermined Pitt's position at court and in the cabinet and jeopardized his relationship with parliament and the people. The questioning of Pitt's strategic decisions has already been noted, but the inadequacies of British strategy were probably less significant than the failings of Britain's continental allies.

Britain's main weapon was the navy, and the focus on maritime operations and colonial conquests was quite in keeping with the pattern established in earlier wars. But in the general conflagration after 1793 military victories in Europe were required as well, and with a small army by continental standards Britain had to find and co-operate with European allies. Pitt also thought that wartime alliances would be useful in settling peace terms after the war (he had not given up on his previous plan for collective security). Although by the summer of 1793 Britain, Austria, Prussia, Holland, Spain and some of the German and Italian states were all at war with France,[99] it was not easy to bind these powers into an effective coalition. British influence was limited (Pitt and Grenville had withdrawn from European affairs after the Ochakov crisis), and the selfish ambitions of the major states hampered co-operation. Austrian, Prussian and Russian designs to partition Poland frustrated Pitt, who argued that the great powers should seek war reparations from France, not plunder neutrals, and Austria's desire to exchange Belgium for Bavaria did not accord with Britain's idea of how to check French influence in the Low Countries. There was also the question of peace terms. Pitt pointed out that excessive demands would never be accepted in France and might put off a counter-revolution there. The British government could not insist that its allies should abandon their own goals, however, and had to compromise in order to promote unity (attempting, for instance, to arrange a bargain on Belgium and Bavaria). In fact the jealousies and disagreements carried on, especially as conquests in the West Indies and the expansion of trade meant that Britain was better able than the continental powers to recoup some of the costs of war. French successes in battle also disrupted allied co-operation.

Pitt strongly favoured the coalition approach, but was constantly worried about how to keep the allies together. He did his best to combine their efforts by offering British support for particular operations, and especially by paying subsidies. Pitt paid out more to European allies than had any previous administration (his successors carried on this policy, and spent even more than Pitt). Pitt used subsidies primarily as a means of persuading allies to carry on fighting when it seemed that they might withdraw. Yet the money did not give him much influence, and, despite the claims of his apologists, it seems perverse to deny that the subsidies were wasted if their purpose was to secure for Pitt a decisive sway over Britain's allies. He could not prevent the partitions of Poland in January 1793 and October 1795. These were strongly condemned in Britain, and an embarrassed Pitt was forced to admit that, though the partitions were disgraceful, Britain could not do without the military assistance of Austria, Prussia and Russia. This military assistance turned out to be less helpful than Pitt and Grenville had supposed. Their refusal to recognize or guarantee new territorial arrangements in eastern Europe made Britain's main allies reluctant to help out in the west, which hastened the fall of Holland. Grenville was ready to give up on the coalition policy, but Pitt chose to persist. The prime minister's mistakes did not help. After agreeing to subsidize Prussia early in 1794, for instance, he was distracted by unrest and sedition at home, and the late payment of the first instalment gave Prussia an excuse to delay military action. Despite his longing for dependable allies, at various times Pitt confessed that Britain's fate would rest on something other than his coalition policy – as Canning put it in November 1794, 'a vigorous prosecution of the war, *with* or *without* Allies'.[100]

Pitt liked to believe that a significant breakthrough was just around the corner, that the French could not carry on for much longer, and that one more offensive would end the war. He often went against sound advice in the hope of salvaging something from a policy that had run into difficulty. This tendency led to his quarrel with Grenville in 1795 over the offer of more money to Prussia. There had long been doubts about Prussia's strength and reliability, and as Malmesbury wrote to Grenville on 20 September 1794: 'The disgraceful failure of every military operation His Prussian Majesty has undertaken since the year 1791 has destroyed the reputation of the Prussian army; and the duplicity and versatility of his Cabinet put an end to all confidence and good faith.' In Brunswick to arrange the marriage of the Prince of Wales, Malmesbury gave another warning against the Prussian government in December: it had 'as many bad qualities ... as can possibly exist at the same time in the same power – weakness, perfidy, insolence, avarice and folly'. But Pitt wanted the Prussians to help liberate Holland. Grenville protested that Britain could not appear to condone Prussia's actions in Poland, and that Prussia was weaker and less committed to the war than either Austria or Russia. Nevertheless, Pitt did not change course until he discovered that Prussia had concluded a separate peace with France in March 1795. His altercation with Grenville occurred mainly because he had more invested in the coalition approach. Pitt shared Grenville's annoyance at Prussia's previous conduct. But Grenville was determined to maintain good relations with Austria, and feared that these would be upset if Britain gave more money to Prussia, whereas Pitt did not want to have to choose between Prussia and Austria. He wanted the coalition to remain intact, which could not happen if Prussia stopped fighting.[101]

Prussia's withdrawal from the First Coalition made Britain more reliant on Austria and Russia (ironically, Carmarthen's goal back in 1784, shared by Pitt, had been a triple alliance of Britain, Austria and Russia). The Russians refused to commit men and resources, however, and their real priority was to further their eastern ambitions, while the victories of Napoleon Bonaparte in Italy prompted Austria to make peace in October 1797.

Pitt had negotiated with the French during 1796, sending Malmesbury to Paris in the autumn, but the talks failed. Now that Austria had stopped fighting Pitt tried again. In 1796 he had suggested that captured colonies might be returned if the French withdrew from Belgium. So urgent was the situation in 1797 (with financial problems and naval mutinies at home, and the lack of strong allies in Europe) that Pitt was willing to leave Belgium out of the deal. Instead, Britain would retain the colonies to counterbalance French gains in Europe. It seems that Pitt was even prepared to bribe individuals who claimed to be able to influence the French leadership. Malmesbury again acted as Britain's chief negotiator, but these talks, beginning in July 1797, broke up after a power struggle within the Directory led to a coup and a change of policy (moderate elements were pushed out in September). There can be no question of Pitt's desire for peace in 1797, but the timing was inopportune in that British power and credit were at a low point. The French were bound to try and impose harsh terms. Not content with security, the arrogant pro-war faction in the Directory wanted maritime dominance and control over Italy and Germany, and conspired with extremists in Britain and Ireland. The 1797 peace effort must therefore be seen as the unilateral venture of a prime minister who had concluded – despite the objections of George III, the foreign secretary and almost half the cabinet – that the war might go on uselessly for years unless Britain gave up certain points in order to reach a settlement with France. As Dundas would write of Pitt in November 1800: 'When in war, his hopes and confidence are sanguine beyond all reason; and when aiming at peace there is no sacrifice which at times he has not been ready to make for the attainment of it.'[102]

The continuation of the war made Pitt think again about a detailed collective security plan. The central requirement was a quadruple alliance to unite Britain, Austria, Russia and Prussia. Instead of trying to restore the pre-1793 situation, the new system would establish stronger buffer states around France, supported by the four main powers, whose interests would be carefully balanced in order to prevent future rivalry. There would be mutual guarantees of rights and frontiers. Though Pitt and Grenville had accepted that European stability required the restoration of the French monarchy, this was not an explicit feature of the plan. On the face of it Pitt and his advisers appear to have come up with a comprehensive solution to the problem faced in 1784 – how to include Britain in an alliance network while guarding against the prospect of being dragged unwillingly into European wars. The scheme was never implemented, of course, because the major powers could not agree to co-operate for long.

Pitt tried to change things, and put together the Second Coalition in December 1798. Britain, Austria, Russia, Naples, Portugal and Turkey agreed to combine against France. With the Directory divided, and France's best commander, Napoleon, off in Egypt, Pitt made £2,500,000 available for subsidies. The Prussians remained aloof, however, feeling secure in northern Germany, and there were arguments over money between Britain and Austria. The Austrians also suspected that Britain had designs on Belgium. Though Austrian and Russian forces were initially successful in Italy, quarrels continued within the coalition. The main military effort was to be a Russian attack in eastern France, subsidized by Pitt and supported by Austria. But the Austrians were more concerned about recovering Belgium, and failed to join in as required, so that the advancing Russian force was defeated in September 1799. Grenville accused the Austrians of treachery. Pitt was only a little more restrained when telling Windham (30 August 1799) of 'the vexatious accounts from Vienna, which give too great a chance of our being disappointed in our best hopes by the blind and perverse selfishness of Austria's counsels'. In August a combined British and Russian landing in Holland failed to trigger a Dutch uprising and ended in retreat. Russia withdrew from the coalition in October after a dispute with Austria, and following a series of defeats at the hands of Napoleon (who had returned from Egypt, overthrown the Directory and made himself dictator of France), the Austrians made peace in February 1801. Turkey had already made peace in January 1800, and the Portuguese were defeated by Napoleon's ally Spain in September 1801. The Second Coalition therefore proved to be a complete disaster, and once again Britain was left alone.[103]

Before and during the operations of 1799 Pitt had been optimistic, and their failure only affected him temporarily, for he regarded Napoleon's seizure of power in France as a sign of the enemy's weakness and instability. Reverses during 1800, however, made him realize that the war was unlikely in the near future to take a turn for the better, and by this time he was increasingly preoccupied with other issues that would lead to his resignation – the legislative union with Ireland and Catholic emancipation.

7

Decline

Pitt resigned on 3 February 1801 and spent just over three years out of office, first as a friend of the Addington government, later as its outspoken foe. Though peace was finally concluded with France in March 1802, it only lasted for fourteen months. Questions of war and peace continued to dominate the politics of this period, and Addington's inability to control parliament led to Pitt's reappointment as prime minister in May 1804. This second Pitt administration was brief and unproductive. In terms of physical and mental energy, and ability to shape opinion and events, Pitt was past his best. The main reasons for his resignation early in 1801 related to failure in the war, the troublesome condition of Ireland, difficulties concerning the respective constitutional positions of monarch and prime minister, Pitt's uneasiness about his personal relationships with leading colleagues and George III, the declining cohesion and effectiveness of his administration, and fatigue after more than seventeen years as chief minister. Some of these obstacles and irritations continued to hamper him during his time out of office. Try as he might, he could not deal with them or govern as he wished and intended after returning as prime minister in the spring of 1804.

Irish problems, unresolved in the 1780s, were exacerbated in the 1790s by new pressures associated with the French Revolution. In particular, radical-ism and nationalism became more pronounced in Ireland. Long-standing economic grievances continued to rankle, and from Pitt's perspective there was still a need to improve relations between the British government and Dublin parliament. Economically under-developed and prey to social and religious division, Ireland had not been pacified by earlier concessions, and the war made it even more important to ensure that Britain and Ireland, with their separate legislatures, followed the same lines of policy (Pitt had seen what could happen when discord arose – as in 1785 over the Irish commercial propositions, and during the regency crisis of 1788–89, when Irish leaders sided with Pitt's opponents). Ireland's Protestant landed elite disliked in-terference from Westminster, however, and mistrusted the crown-appointed Irish executive. Spokesmen such as the barrister Henry Grattan, a friend of Fox, demanded greater independence and more reform, but revolution and war in Europe turned the British establishment against fundamental change, and alarm rose because of the activities of the United Irishmen, a patriotic radical society founded in 1791. The United Irishmen rejected Grattan's constitutionalist approach and adopted separatist revolutionary goals. Meanwhile, Ireland's Catholic masses longed to own the land they tilled and were fiercely indignant about having to support an alien Protestant church. By the mid-1790s there was a growing danger that small but determined revolutionary cells would build up popular support, invite French intervention, and overturn the established order in Ireland.[1]

Pitt was anxious about the violence of Catholic peasants and the radicalism of Ulster's Presbyterians. During the 1790s he attempted to lay the foundations for future security and social peace. Propertied Catholics were encouraged to join associations for national defence. From 1793 Catholics could vote on the same basis as Protestants (which changed the complexion of Irish county electorates). Catholics were also allowed to sit on juries, hold minor civil offices and take up junior commissions in the army, but they were not admitted to parliament. Pitt knew better than to attempt too much too quickly. He had to consider what king, cabinet, parliament and public opinion in Britain would accept. At the same time, experience suggested that a flexible approach was best (in Pitt's view the government could not commit itself against additional concessions).

Further conciliatory moves became likely after the Portland Whigs joined Pitt's administration. Among their priorities was 'justice for Ireland', and they persuaded Pitt that one of their group, Fitzwilliam, should be appointed lord lieutenant. Advised to move cautiously, Fitzwilliam attempted instead to speed up the reforming process. George III was deeply offended, Portland agreed that Fitzwilliam had been hasty, and Pitt forced him to resign only three months after his appointment.

Grattan kept up the pressure for reforms, and sectarian violence increased in the north of Ireland as Catholics clashed with Protestant 'Orangemen'. The United Irishmen committed themselves fully to armed struggle. Coercive measures were implemented as necessary, but Pitt became more and more frustrated. He knew that something had to be done for Ireland, and grew annoyed when policies did not have their desired effect. He resented the Irish question because it took attention away from what he regarded as more important and interesting problems. Nevertheless, when Ireland required his input he was quick to react. In March 1795 Canning heard 'alarming accounts of the ferment raised in Ireland by Lord Fitzwilliam's recall'. It appeared that Fitzwilliam and his abettors in Ireland had defied the prime minister because they did not expect him to interfere. But, as Canning wrote, 'in this case he has acted wisely and spiritedly, and it is to Lord F. and his advisers that the responsibility for what may happen must attach'. After a meeting with Pitt on 21 March, Canning recorded:

> Upon this subject of Ireland Pitt seems stout and in heart even beyond what I should have expected from his firmness. He appears convinced ... that the struggle is whether the *English Govt* or *Ld Fm and Grattan* shall be uppermost in Ireland – in short, that Lord F. had staked his personal interest against the general interest of England in that kingdom. He has no fear about the event.

Although Pitt was obliged to appoint Fitzwilliam and had no choice but to recall him as events took a turn for the worst, some modern historians have slated the premier's handling of the affair (it has even been called 'one of his biggest political misjudgements'). It is true that there were some unfortunate consequences. In vying to regain control over Irish policy, Pitt seemed to be admitting that legislative independence was a sham. He alienated moderate reformers, who regarded Fitzwilliam's dismissal as a betrayal of trust, and pushed many Catholics into the orbit of the United Irishmen.[2]

A French army attempted to land in Bantry Bay in December 1796. In the preceding autumn Pitt had sent Malmesbury to arrange peace talks with the government of France, and the Irish expedition (involving about 15,000 troops, in forty-three vessels) was approved by French leaders as a means of improving their bargaining position. Bad weather prevented the landing, but Irish conspirators continued to negotiate with the French in the hope of co-ordinating their planned insurrection with a French invasion. Pitt and his colleagues decided that only a small invasion force would be necessary to prompt a popular rising, and precautionary measures were introduced. These provoked a violent rebellion in the spring of 1798, fired by anti-land-lord, anti-Protestant and anti-British fervour. Irish rebels were defeated in battle in June 1798. Although a French force arrived in August, it quickly surrendered. (Ireland never mattered much to French politicians and strategists, and military action there indicates their lack of options.) The Irish revolutionary leader Theobald Wolfe Tone, a Belfast lawyer who had returned to Ireland after periods in America and Paris, committed suicide in prison. Other leaders of the uprising were executed.[3]

Although the Irish rebellion was an organizational and military failure, it confirmed Pitt in his opinion that Ireland and Britain should be united under one legislature. Instability in Ireland had encouraged French intervention, and since Ireland was a weak point in Britain's defences it had to be brought into a more concerted war system. Then, as Portland reflected, 'we shall ... have it so much more in our power to give stability and security to the other powers of Europe and to hold that balance which cannot be

safely held by any other hands than our own'. Pitt made a similar remark
(23 January 1799) when considering the likely benefits at home and abroad
of the proposed union with Ireland, using as his reference point the Act
of Union between England and Scotland of 1707,

> under which has grown up and flourished the prosperity of both; under which
> the laws of both have been improved; under which property has been protected;
> under which has been cherished a principle of cordial co-operation, which has
> led to the happiness of Great Britain, and has rendered it the envy, and, I trust,
> will make it the protection of surrounding nations.

George III's message to parliament respecting legislative union stressed
the need to defeat the supposed French design of separating Ireland from
Britain. Britain's security and international position were also on the mind
of Auckland, one of the union's strongest advocates. Auckland wrote on
28 August 1801:

> The more I reflect on the measure of union the more I am convinced of its
> gigantic importance, and of its tendency to double the strength and resources of
> our Empire. It is more than ever desirable that the effect of the union should be
> such as to add to our means and powers; for we can no longer conceal from
> ourselves that the war is likely to end without any settlement of the independence
> of Europe, and with great accessions to the continental domination and resources
> of France.

The union had other recommendations. Here was an opportunity to end
the political and administrative inconveniences created by the Irish parliament's ability to frustrate policy-makers in London. Pitt also believed
that legislative union could provide a framework for improving Anglo-Irish
relations in the future. His premise was simple. Ireland had to be brought
under closer supervision. In addition he decided that Catholics should be
emancipated, for without this there could be no lasting settlement. Union
and emancipation would bring social peace to Ireland, thought Pitt, because
the Protestant minority would no longer feel any compulsion to abuse its
power and could rest easy as part of a United Kingdom in which Catholics
were outnumbered overall.[4]

Pitt had probably seen the need for a workable union, with emancipation,
long before 1798. He would have preferred a gradual, uncontroversial process, with reforms achieved in stages, but security considerations now made
delay impossible. Pitt's ruminations can be placed in a wider perspective.
The idea of an Anglo-Irish union was not new, but eighteenth-century
political leaders had been unwilling to try it, no doubt balking at all the
time, planning and difficult negotiation that would be required. By the end
of the century, however, a tendency towards union could be discerned as

France annexed territory and the United States of America developed into a distinctive federal republic. In an era marked by revolution and war, strategic necessity seemed to demand consolidation and centralization. Pitt responded accordingly. In May and June 1798 he told Camden, the outgoing lord lieutenant of Ireland, that arrangements should be made for a union as soon as the rebellion was crushed. He canvassed the views of senior Irish office-holders. Initially Pitt was optimistic, writing to Grenville on 16 October 1798 that the latest correspondence was 'very encouraging with a view to the great question of the union, in which I do not think we shall have much difficulty; I mean, in proportion to the magnitude of the subject'. News of disturbances in Ireland in January 1799 made Pitt all the more determined to press ahead: 'they can only make it more necessary to open fully and state decidedly our plan'. He decided against legislative union without Catholic emancipation. As he later advised George III (January 1801), emancipation would 'conciliate the higher orders of the Catholics, and by furnishing to a large class of your majesty's Irish subjects a proof of the goodwill of the United Parliament, afford the best chance of giving full effect to the great object of the Union – that of tranquilizing Ireland, and attaching it to this country'.[5]

Legislative union and Catholic emancipation would certainly be opposed, however, and Pitt realized that some exceptional political chicanery was called for to push these measures through. He was ably assisted in Dublin by Marquess Cornwallis, Camden's successor as lord lieutenant, and by the Irish chief secretary, Viscount Castlereagh, and there were long discussions with Grenville, Dundas and Portland, as well as some experienced former Irish officials. The Dublin parliament voted to end its own existence in the spring of 1800 after rejecting union in 1799. Pitt and his assistants overcame resistance by offering titles and jobs, and made improper use of secret service funds in Ireland to pay supporters of the union, finance propaganda and purchase seats in the Irish parliament. They also appealed to the Irish elite's sense of self-interest. Pitt insisted that the Act of Union would strengthen rather than weaken the elite, and bring commercial advantages. Another motive was fear, for the rebellion had indicated to the Protestant ascendancy that its position in Irish society was not invulnerable. Patrons of Irish boroughs that lost seats under the union were compensated (some received about £15,000 per seat in a remarkably generous settlement that cost over £1,250,000 in all). A hundred Irish MPs would sit in the united House of Commons at Westminster (the Irish Commons had numbered three hundred), and thirty-two Irish peers were added to the House of Lords, notwithstanding the charge that these changes would increase the 'influence of the crown'. The Established Churches of England and Ireland were merged. Ireland's textile industry was granted twenty years protection to prepare itself for freer trade, and the Irish contribution to British public expenditure was fixed at just under 12 per cent (which became a huge burden after 1815 because the French wars massively increased the national debt).[6]

The union has to be seen above all as a war measure. The goal was security and Pitt, Grenville and Dundas wanted to settle the Irish problem in a way that assisted the war effort. Since Ireland could not be controlled within existing constitutional arrangements, these arrangements had to be changed. If security concerns determined the actions of the government, however, in parliament and the press legislative union was most commonly discussed with reference to the historically difficult relationship between Britain and Ireland, the shortcomings of Ireland's ruling class, and Catholic demands for equal rights.[7]

There was some suspicion that Pitt employed harsh repression in order to provoke rebellion in Ireland, and then used the rebellion as an excuse to abolish the Irish parliament, his purpose all along. This claim has not found favour with modern historians. It should also be noted that many people did well out of the union, a political manoeuvre for which patronage and bribery were employed on a much greater scale than had been seen before, even in Ireland – where extensive jobbery was the norm. On top of the generous compensation for disfranchised boroughs came numerous official appointments, five English titles for Irish peers, and sixteen new creations and nineteen promotions within the Irish peerage. In some quarters the extent of corrupt influence was exaggerated, to make Ireland's elite look better, perhaps, or to present Pitt and his helpers as wholly responsible for the demise of the Dublin parliament, but the fact remains that many individuals were happy to take what was offered. The union would never have happened had these bargains not been made.

As for Catholic emancipation, which Pitt considered the essential corollary to union, Camden, Cornwallis, Castlereagh and Dundas all favoured it, and even the formerly hostile Grenville came to admit its necessity. The government relied on Catholic goodwill when seeking approval for the union in Ireland. There were careful negotiations to keep Catholic leaders on side, and the Irish administration was pressed to make conciliatory gestures. During 1799 Buckingham, a former lord lieutenant, wrote that 'the Catholics are coming forward very roundly, but the British Government must urge that of Ireland to the Catholic questions, or else nothing will be done, and their support will be lost'. The trick was to retain Catholic support for the union without alarming Ireland's elite, but in any event, Buckingham urged his brother Grenville, the Catholics had to be satisfied: 'You know that they are your sheet anchor (in this project) with the lower ranks of people, and that every care must be taken to knit them both now and for the future with Government'.

Although the promise of emancipation was implied, however, there was no guarantee. Pitt did not want to turn Ireland's Protestants and conservatives against the union, and he knew that British voters and MPs would more easily accept union than emancipation. He regarded the two reforms as inseparable. They were necessities of war, and there appeared to be no other way of ensuring effective administration and good order in Ireland. In addition, emancipation would be a salutary act of justice, useful in extending the moral and political authority of Pitt's regime.

Unfortunately for the prime minister, influential government colleagues disagreed with his analysis. Before long Portland, who as home secretary had special responsibility for Ireland, and particularly the lord chancellor, Loughborough, were arguing strongly against emancipation. George III, moreover, was to prove implacable. The king favoured legislative union but was bound by his coronation oath to defend the Established Church, which he thought would be undermined by emancipation. On 13 June 1798 he had reminded Pitt, yet again, of his opinion on this matter: 'No further indulgences must be granted to the Roman Catholics, as no country can be governed where there is more than one established religion.' Nor did Pitt find much support out of doors. Opponents of emancipation saw no reason, during a war and at a time when the threat of revolution was still taken seriously, to enfranchise a mass of unruly and unpropertied Irish peasants who professed obedience to the pope, a foreigner. So Pitt faced sturdy lines of defence, rooted in the aversion to sweeping constitutional change, a deep respect for the status and privileges of the Established Church, and general concern to retain basic qualifications for civil rights and control access to public offices, corporations and the professions. These tendencies generated strong objections to emancipation, and were reinforced by the widespread anti-Catholicism that had characterized British society for many generations.[8]

The cabinet discussed the Catholic issue during September and October 1800. As Camden recorded, several ministers warned that any plan of emancipation would inevitably arouse royal, ecclesiastical and legal hostility.[9] Pitt refused to be swayed. As he saw it, political necessity compelled him to alter his position on religious toleration. He had previously opposed the weakening of penal laws against non-Anglicans, mainly on pragmatic grounds. Pitt told Canning in May 1794 that nothing was to be gained by pointlessly antagonizing the church and its supporters. He and Dundas had recently briefed the new Irish secretary, Sylvester Douglas (later Baron

Glenbervie), and explained that, although civil equality for Ireland's Catholic majority seemed a straightforward matter of justice and policy, the truth was more complicated. Any change had to come 'by degrees ... as it were insensibly to the Protestants'. The Protestants monopolized political power and their real priority was to maintain this monopoly, but they preferred to resist Catholic claims by posing as protectors of Protestantism and property. After his discussions with Pitt, Douglas summed up the prime minister's position as follows:

> Mr Pitt thinks, truly, that such a monopoly is unjust and cannot be long main-
> tained, but that on the other hand it is natural that those who have it should be
> very unwilling to relinquish it, and that it would be impolitic, and also even in
> some degree unjust to wrest it from them with violence. This doctrine, which
> seems to me sound and moderate, must not be avowed in Ireland.

In the aftermath of the 1798 rebellion Pitt had to be more proactive, but on emancipation he could give no explicit commitment. Indeed, he temporarily dropped it in order to secure Irish Protestant backing for the union. Irish Catholic leaders were led to believe that emancipation would be granted once the union was in place, and fell in behind Pitt's policy. The Act of Union received the royal assent in August 1800. The united parliament of Great Britain and Ireland was to assemble on 22 January 1801, and Pitt expected emancipation to be the first major issue to receive its close attention.[10]

Pitt prepared a comprehensive plan. For Catholics and Protestant Dissenters in Ireland there would be tithe reform, state salaries for their clergymen, and the removal of civil disabilities. In order to appease the church, Pitt and his advisers came up with several palliatives. Office holders would have to take an oath of loyalty to the established order, and improvements within the church would provide better financial support for the poorest Anglican clergy and extend the authority of the church hierarchy. The idea of paying Catholic and Dissenting clergymen in Ireland was accepted because remuneration offered a means of monitoring their activity. Another safeguard was that the oath to be sworn by all office holders, Catholic and Dissenting clergy and schoolteachers would include a firm rejection of the sovereignty of the people. Catholics should no longer be regarded as a political threat, Pitt avowed, but this was not true of radicals and revolutionaries.[11]

Pitt's plan was unlikely to find favour at court. George III had objected to Fitzwilliam's policy as lord lieutenant in 1795, ruled out further measures of Catholic relief in 1798, and declared in January 1799 that he would block the union if it altered the status of Catholics. He had declared to Pitt that such matters were 'beyond the decision of any Cabinet of Ministers', and, though he wanted fair toleration for non-Anglicans, he thought that anything more would be inappropriate. The king specifically ruled out the possibility of paying public salaries to Ireland's Catholic clergy. Pitt informed the cabinet in September 1800 that he would consult with influential figures around the country, and present the necessary advice to the king. But other matters soon diverted his attention, particularly the military campaign in Egypt, dearth and disorder at home, and disputes with Russia and the Baltic powers over British interference with neutral ships. The prime minister was also incapacitated by illness. Therefore he was unable to return to the Catholic question until January 1801, just as the united parliament was about to assemble for the first time.[12]

Some of Pitt's colleagues later opined that he should have done more to prepare the king. But would George III have co-operated, even had Pitt done so? Though the king complained to Grenville and Dundas that he had not been informed of Pitt's intentions or the cabinet's deliberations until it was too late to avoid a crisis, he gave no indication that he would have been willing to alter his own position had circumstances been different. His point was, rather, that 'if more confidence had been placed in me whilst the subject of contention was in contemplation, perhaps persons would not have pledged themselves when they had known the real dictates of my mind'. The breach between Pitt and George III could only have been avoided had Pitt abandoned Catholic emancipation. Malmesbury's criticism – that Pitt 'either from indolence, or from perhaps not paying always a sufficient and due attention to the king's pleasure, neglected to mention *ministerially* to His Majesty, that such a measure was in agitation, till he came at once with it for his approbation' – therefore misses the central point. The *timing* of Pitt's advice on emancipation mattered less than the fact that George III could not accept it. Even so, Pitt subsequently speculated that things might have been different had he clarified matters for the king much sooner. He was bound to recommend Catholic emancipation, he thought, but he ought to have handled the king more carefully. Former treasury secretary George Rose discussed this with Pitt in February 1801.

> The most remarkable thing that fell from him was a suggestion that on revolving in his mind all that had passed, it did not occur to him that he could have acted in any respect otherwise than he had done, or that he had anything to blame himself for, except not having earlier endeavoured to reconcile the king to the measure about the Catholics, or to prevail with his Majesty not to take an active part on the subject.

Pitt may have underestimated George III's determination to resist, allow-ing himself to be misled by the king's surrender on other disputed matters

– the opening of peace negotiations with the French in 1796, 1797 and 1800, for example, and the expedition to Egypt in 1800. But even before Pitt was ready to deal directly with the king, he found that he could not carry the whole of the cabinet with him. His own brother Chatham (lord president of the council) joined Loughborough, Portland, Westmorland (lord privy seal) and Liverpool (president of the board of trade) in opposing Catholic emancipation. Pitt resorted to trickery and subterfuge in order to manipulate cabinet discussions and prevent critics of his policy from explaining and substantiating their objections. He had employed similar tactics when the Egyptian expedition was being planned. Now, on the Catholic question, there was ongoing discussion within the cabinet, during which Pitt avoided taking a vote and held out the prospect of further discussion to deter his opponents from making a formal stand. Pitt obviously realized his weakness. He could not proceed in an open and honest manner because he knew he would be blocked. So he took advantage of the absence of his opponents, called meetings at short notice, and muddied the waters so that nobody was really sure what had been settled. When Loughborough could not attend a cabinet meeting on 25 January 1801, several of those present insisted that he should be heard. Pitt agreed to consult the lord chancellor and convene another meeting the next day, but he subsequently said that what he had actually agreed to do was arrange another meeting *if Loughborough requested it* (this was also Windham's understanding of what had occurred). When no such request was made, Pitt carried matters forward as if he had cabinet approval. This façade could not last. George III already knew that there would be no unanimous cabinet advice to bolster Pitt's emancipation policy. Loughborough and Westmorland had both communicated with the king and reinforced his resolve. Late in January 1801, at the king's request, the Speaker of the Commons, Henry Addington, saw Pitt and urged him to reconsider.[13]

Though Pitt knew from the outset that the court would be hostile to Catholic emancipation, he had hoped to have the backing of a united cabinet. With the cabinet divided it was easier for the king to resist. George III could not in conscience accept emancipation. He may also have come to imagine that Pitt considered himself indispensable, and was not prepared to allow the impression to spread that Pitt ruled, not the king, or that the crown had lost the ability to assert itself at times of crisis. Furthermore, George III was dissatisfied with the ministry's conduct of the war. During the summer of 1800 Pitt, frustrated by the king's criticisms, told Dundas that if these persisted the sovereign would have to be advised 'to find servants whose judgement he can trust more than ours'. This rift added to George III's discontent. For several reasons, therefore, he was determined to stand up to his chief minister on emancipation, although he appreciated that, if Pitt resigned, it would be difficult to find an alternative premier who could both win the war and effectively manage the Commons. Pitt had always tried to avoid a direct clash with George III. In 1785 the king had allowed him to propose parliamentary reform in his individual capacity, rather than as a government measure, and Pitt may have expected the same arrangement on emancipation. Instead, George III stood by his coronation oath and rejected Pitt's view that emancipation would not harm the Established Church and that Catholics no longer posed a threat to the state. The king's annoyance only increased when he reflected that Pitt had brought the matter before the cabinet for discussion without consulting him first.[14]

By the end of January 1801 George III knew that he could rely on Addington to serve as prime minister if Pitt resigned, and that some of the cabinet would stay on under a new premier (therefore Pitt's departure would not open the door to Fox). The king asked Pitt to drop emancipation and remain in office. Pitt decided that this was a resignation matter, and he presented it as such to the cabinet, possibly in an attempt to force ministers into line. Yet he had already discussed matters with Addington in some detail, and seems to have had no qualms about resigning. The loss of royal support was crucial, but Pitt's health and determination were also fading. Exhausted after dealing with finance, administration and war for such a long period, and unable to persuade the king to accept a policy to which he felt committed, Pitt tendered his resignation on 3 February 1801. The appointment of Addington was delayed for several weeks because the king fell ill. Addington resigned as Speaker of the Commons on 10 February, and became prime minister on 17 March.[15]

Among the other ministers to depart were Dundas, Grenville and Windham. They had sided with Pitt on emancipation, and shared his frustration at the lack of a breakthrough in the war. Portland remained in office. Indeed, four of the nine members of Addington's original cabinet, formed during February 1801, had been in Pitt's ministry. Addington also made contact with opponents of Pitt, notably Grey, who refused to take office without Fox. In fact Grey's unreasonable demand that Foxites should have the majority of cabinet places in any new arrangement betrayed his unwillingness to take office at this juncture. It also alienated Tierney, who had earlier argued with Grey about the Foxite secession. Tierney wanted office and was prepared to serve under Addington. Angered by Fox's ineffective leadership, he temporarily broke with the opposition in 1802 and accepted the post of treasurer of the navy (outside the cabinet) in May 1803.[16]

The resignations of Dundas and Grenville probably owed more to the war than to the Catholic question. It was widely thought that Dundas retired in order to quieten the demand for an inquiry into his conduct of the war. Grenville, meanwhile, preferred to resign rather than accept responsibility for peace negotiations with France. He had been unable to construct a strong European coalition; his own strategic proposals had been overruled or (when implemented) unsuccessful; and, though he agreed with Pitt that Britain must make significant concessions in order for peace to be concluded, he had no wish personally to be involved in these compromises. It was with some relief, therefore, that Grenville read Pitt's communication of 1 February 1801: 'I was right in my supposition of the extent of the king's opinions', and as a result, 'our line ... will be very easily settled'. Now Grenville was certain that the government would fall. His elder brother disagreed. Unaware of the full facts, Buckingham wrote to Grenville on 3 February:

> The matter in dispute has always been very sore to the king's feelings; and I knew (as you did) that it would be a very severe struggle; but I really had imagined that he had made up his mind to what was in fact the *avowed* corollary to the Union, as one that was essentially necessary for the attainment of the essential benefits to be derived from it. I was aware a month ago of this difficulty ... But it is indeed matter to me of the most serious alarm to find that the king is (to your belief) firm in his decision to change his Ministers on this dispute ... I am persuaded that he will ultimately give way; particularly too when it is manifest that he could not out of any materials form a new Ministry on such grounds, which you will observe are exactly those on which almost every public man is pledged so deeply; and on which the difficulties would be multiplied tenfold on any such new Minister by the resignation of the king's servants on a ground on which all Ireland will run riot ... The king will concede either from his own sense of the magnitude of the danger of every sort that he runs, or of the little chance of his carrying his point by a new Ministry, or of the little chance of finding any Ministry who would be rash enough to undertake it.

In truth George III had no regrets about Pitt's resignation, though he was grateful that Pitt had not engaged in a long and bitter contest over emancipation. Pitt had shown due deference to the king's scruples, identified Addington as a suitable successor, and promised the new ministry his friendly support. Pitt's return to the premiership in 1804 came after he agreed never again to raise the Catholic question in George III's lifetime. It was and is argued that if Pitt had been genuine about emancipation, he would have provided for it in the Act of Union, and that he posed as a supporter of emancipation only to win backing for the union and was content to relinquish office because this relieved him of responsibility. These claims ignore the fact that Pitt regarded emancipation as just and necessary. He was invariably cautious when promoting controversial measures, hoping to persuade doubters gradually, and his error between 1799 and 1801 was the assumption that others would agree that the time had come for emancipation. Realizing his mistake, he decided that resignation was the honourable step to take. Disagreement about a specific policy, Pitt maintained, should not be allowed to jeopardize sound government, without which there could be no effective direction of the war. This stance explains his deference to the king and expressions of goodwill towards Addington's ministry. He also saw that to press emancipation after 1801 would be to invite more controversy and threaten the king's peace of mind. Had Pitt tried to include emancipation in the Act of Union, the British and Irish parliaments would have rejected the whole project; and had he refused to abandon emancipation after 1801 he would probably have ensured that George III would never again call on him to lead an administration.[17]

Pitt disliked having to make definite pledges, and usually managed to keep his options open, but some of those who purported to know his mind in February 1801 suggested that he would not renounce Catholic emancipation. They offered assurances in an attempt to present Pitt's resignation in the best possible light to disappointed supporters of emancipation. On 12 February William Huskisson told the fifth Earl of Carlisle (a former ally of North and Fox who had defected to Pitt with the Portland Whigs in 1794) that emancipation was still on the agenda. All Pitt wanted was a period of calm, during which the question would not be brought up. Huskisson wrote:

> Had the king's objection rested solely on his sense of the inexpediency of the measure, it would (as on so many other occasions) have been overcome; but ... he is prepared for any extremity rather than yield up the point – and I leave your Lordship and every well-meaning friend to the Catholic claim, and indeed to every honest Catholic himself, to decide whether, in the present state of the country and with this impression on the king's mind, the question ought to be pressed to a decision in Parliament with a certainty of its being defeated in the last stage ... Unless a man can doubt the Minister's firmness, in a case where the preservation of his office, joined to so many important public considerations, called upon him to be firm, or his discernment as to what would be the issue of pressing the question in Parliament, I think he will agree that the line Mr Pitt means to adopt, holding out on the one hand the strongest pledge of his future intentions and calling upon his friends to give the same pledge to the Catholics; but on the other deprecating immediate discussion, is one in which he ought to be supported.

Pitt was uncomfortable about engagements of this kind, and for good

reason. What if circumstances changed and he could not act upon under-
takings he had publicly given? On the evening of 24 February George Rose
urged him not to bind himself to anything. Pitt admitted that he wished
to leave himself room to manoeuvre. The king's latest illness was also
preying on his mind. Rose spoke of duty. Pitt's political opponents, it was
clear, would try to trick him into affirming that he would not return to
office unless the king gave him permission to propose Catholic emancipation. This would give them an enormous advantage. Pitt's duty, insisted
Rose, was to attend to the best interests of the nation. In any case, the
House of Lords would never pass an emancipation bill.

> Surely the higher duty of saving his country was to prevail over his wish to grant
> this indulgence ... He would not absolutely promise not to pledge himself, but
> I am satisfied that he will not ... I entreated him to leave himself at liberty to
> act as the situation of the country should demand; that this was true patriotism,
> and that nothing else could secure to him the confidence of the people or give
> a chance of our being extricated from our present difficulties.

When Pitt did make a commitment, it was in response to the king's
mental relapse (which, so he was told, George III blamed on him and the
emancipation crisis). It is possible that Pitt's promise never again to raise
the Catholic question in the king's lifetime was relayed to George III in
more emphatic terms than Pitt intended. He has been accused of an 'ignoble'
surrender, but it was quite understandable in view of the fact that the Prince
of Wales, Fox and their allies were demanding a regency. Pitt had to do
what he could to speed George III's recovery, and Dundas, Cornwallis and
other associates agreed that the royal conscience should not again be
troubled by the Catholic question.[18]

In contemplating resignation, stalemate in the war certainly influenced
Pitt's decision. Not only was the king complaining about the lack of success,
but ministers had argued about how to conduct the war. Pitt wanted peace,
even if it was only temporary, while Grenville and Windham had repeatedly
pressed for an intensification of the war effort. Dundas could not choose
between peace and a limited war. This eroded their collective energy and
resolution during the emancipation crisis, and reconciled them all to resignation early in 1801. Dundas emphasized ministerial wrangling in his
memorandum on the state of the cabinet of 22 September 1800. There were
too many disagreements relating to the war. Should restoration of the
French monarchy be a priority? Could Britain properly negotiate with the
existing government of France? Was it possible to sway the French regime
at all by force of arms? If peace negotiations were appropriate, should
Britain act alone or only in conjunction with allies? What might be gained,

or lost, by associating Britain's interests with those of Austria? What terms should be sought? Should Britain ask for a settlement, or wait for the French to make the first move? On all of these matters, Dundas remarked, there was continual disputation.

> If this difference of sentiment could be considered as so many abstract theories it would be of no moment to examine them minutely, but they daily enter into every separate discussion which occurs on the subject of either peace or war. It is natural for every man to be partial to his own view of a subject, but neither that partiality nor the sincere personal respect or reciprocal good opinion we may entertain of each other can blind us so far as not to perceive that amidst such jarring opinions the essential interests of the country must daily suffer. It is earnestly hoped that Mr Pitt will take these observations under his serious consideration before it is too late.

The situation was exacerbated by serious divisions on economic policy, especially the management of the corn trade in periods of dearth. In July and October 1800 there were indignant complaints from Hawkesbury and his father, the Earl of Liverpool, after regulatory measures with which they had been entrusted were openly opposed in the Commons and Lords by regular supporters and even members of the government.[19]

It is unlikely that Pitt resigned in order to avoid the disagreeable task of negotiating peace with France, for he had been prepared to talk peace in the past, was not averse to a negotiated settlement, and would in due course welcome Addington's effort to end hostilities. A more significant motive for resignation was his physical and mental exhaustion, which magnified Pitt's doubts as to whether he could tackle all the difficulties now facing the government. But would he have entertained these doubts had George III been more flexible? Pitt explained his decision to resign by pointing to the king's conduct. George III had refused to prevent his name from being used to influence opinions on emancipation. Here were reminders of 1783 and Fox's India Bill, and Pitt offered explicit constitutional grounds for resignation. He left office not simply because he was resisted on Catholic emancipation, but because of the *manner* in which he was resisted. The king was taking advice from others. In his letter to George III of 31 January 1801, Pitt outlined why emancipation was necessary, claimed that the measure was backed by a cabinet majority, and pressed the king to consider the matter carefully, during which time Pitt would refrain from pursuing it in parliament. He expressed his wish to resign if the king continued to object to his proposal. But he was reluctant to leave office when domestic unrest was growing, and when expeditions to Egypt and the Baltic were under way. He therefore offered to remain as premier until difficulties receded or if it became necessary to prevent agitation on the Catholic question while George III was making up his mind. Importantly, Pitt reserved the right to disclose his position publicly at a suitable moment and urged that the king's name should not be used to influence others.

In a reply of 1 February George III, while asking Pitt not to resign, declared his unalterable opposition to Catholic emancipation, and pointed out that since his opinions on emancipation had always been clear, it was impossible to prevent interested persons from being influenced by them. Obviously Pitt found this response unsatisfactory. As Camden noted, 'there were many symptoms at this time, of the king's eager interference with those persons he could influence upon this question'. Irish under-secretary Edward Cooke wrote of

> an unfair game playing against the Cabinet. There seems to be a little Court Windsor party that were always irritating the king, always endeavouring to make him form opinions of his own, to make arrangements and appointments without the advice of his Cabinet, and who used every sinister artifice and low flattery for the purpose. This set must now highly plume themselves upon having fretted his mind at this crisis to take a decision against his Ministers.

After speaking with his friend and leader, Canning told Malmesbury that 'if on this particular occasion a stand was not made, Pitt would retain only a nominal power, while the real one would pass into the hands of those who influenced the king's mind and opinion out of sight'. Pitt was sure that, had he acquiesced, his position as premier would have been virtually ruined and he would have found himself on 'a footing totally different from what he had ever before been'.[20]

The events of early 1801, argues John Ehrman, were really determined by the government's failure to evolve a coherent war strategy, and by Pitt's inability to unite a divided cabinet. Ehrman downplays the importance of Pitt's exhaustion, poor health and declining morale. Was Pitt tired of office? Had he run out of energy and willpower to the extent that he sought release from his duties as premier? Ehrman thinks not. Pitt's main desire was peace with France, and he was loath to desert his post at a time of mounting pressure. The answer was to hand over to a pre-arranged successor who would be better placed to make peace, and Pitt always intended to guide Addington from outside the cabinet. Emancipation, though, was not merely an excuse for resignation. Pitt was eager to preserve accepted constitutional processes, especially the offering of advice to the monarch by the premier. He objected to George III's public outbursts against emancipation, and was affronted by court intrigues and the king's conversations with persons other than the prime minister (including individuals who were not even in the cabinet). While the king insisted that he must stand by his coronation oath, Pitt upheld ministerial competence.

Pitt was not seeking to question royal prerogatives. Rather, he complained that legitimate constitutional practice was being disregarded. This problem was complicated by the deteriorating personal relationships between George III on one side, and Pitt, Grenville and Dundas on the other. The king was quite willing for them to resign. Pitt, meanwhile, could not separate emancipation from his own reputation. Surrender would have had unacceptable consequences, whereas resignation salvaged some prestige. Pitt then agreed never to raise the matter again, in response to George III's mental collapse just after the resignation. He had no wish to disturb the king further, and he knew that this manoeuvre would leave open the possibility of a return to office.[21]

Dundas had clashed several times with George III, especially on the war, and Grenville decided early in 1801 that he could not give way on Catholic emancipation. Plenty of rumours circulated about the part played in the ministry's fall by Pitt's closest colleagues. According to one interpretation, they both wanted to go. Since Pitt would not let them resign they had to bring down the government, and manufactured a crisis by encouraging the prime minister to challenge George III. It was also said that Grenville came under pressure from his own relatives. There had long been friction between the Grenville family and the king, and at court much was made of the fact that the Marquess of Buckingham had married a Catholic and was an outspoken advocate of emancipation. An alternative story was that Pitt had tired of the foreign secretary's obstinacy, and thought that he could only distance himself from Grenville by himself resigning. The gossip recorded by Malmesbury, however, reinforces the idea that Pitt was pushed into resigning – Grenville preferred resignation to compromise, Dundas could not cope with the government's failure in war, and they could only cover their retreat (and make it seem less discreditable) if Pitt resigned too. Yet George III was told that Dundas had not been aware of Pitt's intention to bring matters to a head, and only heard of the premier's resignation *post facto*: 'he protests he did not look on the last conversation on the enabling Catholics to sit in both Houses of Parliament as a final decision'. The king suggested to Addington (13 February 1801) that Pitt was persuaded to propose emancipation, and resign over it, by its main champions – Camden, Castlereagh and Canning – and 'his own good heart now makes him, by exertion in favour of my service, take the line most to his own inclination as well as honour'. Dundas predicted that nobody would believe the Catholic question to be the real reason for the ministry's fall. Certainly there were Foxites who suspected that Pitt would soon return and that his departure was a temporary device by which he could shift the government's problems onto some hapless stooge. A few commentators declared that Pitt had gone mad (as had his father in later life). Others thought that he jumped before being pushed: the cabinet was split on the war, ministerial changes were likely, and, it was said, Pitt knew he would be supplanted. A different scenario was that Pitt wanted to make peace, but saw that he could only do so if he got rid of the pro-war members of the cabinet. His resignation was therefore meant to break the ministry up, and in due course he hoped to return at the head of a reorganized government that would unite behind his peace overtures. Philip Ziegler contends that most of the rumours of early 1801 were wide of the mark because they failed to recognize that the Catholic question *was* the basic cause of Pitt's resignation, as was made clear in Pitt's conversations with Addington. Of course there were other causes too. Ziegler mentions Pitt's poor health, the war abroad and hunger and disorder at home. But the emancipation controversy was vitally important because it opened up an honourable course of action for Pitt at a time when he doubted his ability to deal creditably with all these other matters.[22]

'The story of Pitt's retirement is full of loose ends', writes John Ehrman, 'and motives are seldom unmixed.' The picture changes, depending on which of its parts one chooses to focus. For Piers Mackesy, 'no explanation of Pitt's resignation is complete which ignores his state of mind and health ... The underlying cause of the ministry's collapse was the intolerable pressure of the war upon Pitt.' To Charles Fedorak, the most significant point about the crisis of 1801 is that George III determined the outcome. In stark contrast to Richard Willis, who (like Ziegler) has maintained that emancipation was the principal cause of Pitt's resignation, Fedorak contends that the crisis must be interpreted with reference mainly to the political power of the crown, and that Pitt was not firmly committed to emancipation or constitutionally obliged to resign. Willis recognizes that Pitt and George III were not close personally, and deems this important because the premier's inattention to the king enabled the latter to develop alternative channels of communication with the government, 'and it was more than coincidence that such channels comprised men who were either not in Pitt's immediate circle of advisers or who were hostile to Catholic reform'. Indeed, Fedorak's analysis might be questioned on at least one central point – that of Pitt's position on Catholic emancipation. As suggested above, Pitt unmistakably committed himself to emancipation, and his idea of its necessity cannot be omitted from any worthwhile assessment of the causes behind his resignation. It may not have been the principal cause, as Willis thinks, but it ranked highly in Pitt's calculations. The constitutional context also mattered a great deal, and though it would be going too far to argue that Pitt was constitutionally obliged to resign, in his view there were compelling public as well as personal reasons for doing so. The king's method of frustrating his plans, and Pitt's own sensitivity about propriety and status, made resignation a more eligible option than it would otherwise have been.[23]

Parliament's mood was also significant. Many peers and MPs thought that Pitt should not have taken up emancipation. This did not help Fox and his party, however, since the Commons majority was prepared to back Addington's government while it had royal approval and remained uncontroversial. Addington had been a capable, approachable and highly respected Speaker. The opinion spread that he might make a competent prime minister (to some he was preferable to the aloof and arrogant Pitt). Remarkable neither for his mind nor talents, but trustworthy and efficient, Addington seemed a suitable choice. Though he regarded the war as just, he was concerned about its expense and sympathized with calls for peace. He listened to the complaints of backbenchers. He opposed hazardous innovations, among which he counted parliamentary reform, Catholic emancipation and abolition of the slave trade. He wanted broad consensual government and respected the crown's political influence. Addington's appointment was to a large extent a victory for George III and the royal prerogative. The king had been intent on exercising his right to select ministers and have a say in policy, which lends credence to at least some of Fedorak's conclusions about the events of 1801. Here was a striking reminder that no government could survive unless it had royal confidence. Most politicians knew and (with the obvious exception of the Foxites) accepted this.

Pitt gained a lasting reputation as the upholder of balance in the constitution, a political leader whose suspicion of crown influence co-existed with a readiness to support it in the appropriate sphere, and to Robin Reilly his resignation was above all a matter of principle. If it was an untidy affair, Pitt's own miscalculations were to blame. He had been over-optimistic. His belief was that the king could be persuaded to allow emancipation by reasonable and substantiated arguments, backed by support for emancipation in parliament. But the king was not persuaded, and parliament was not favourable to emancipation.[24]

Notwithstanding the importance of public questions and political principle, and the prominence accorded to them by modern historians, in seeking out the real reasons for Pitt's resignation the impact of his illnesses, exhaustion and declining morale cannot be discounted. During the late 1790s Pitt and his ministry fell more deeply into uncertainty and gloom. It is true that these years were not without some cheering developments: another upsurge in popular loyalism strengthened home defence, the Irish rebellion was crushed, many opposition MPs absented themselves from parliament, and crucial government measures – notably income tax and the Irish union – were implemented as planned. But the failure to overcome France or even make decisive advances in the war overshadowed everything else. Pitt and his colleagues were worn down by the weight of government business and disappointments associated with the war. As the pressure grew they became more tired and pessimistic.

For Pitt himself there was loneliness and stress, and his morale was not sustained by many private sources of happiness. Marriage might have made a difference. Pitt courted Eleanor Eden, daughter of Lord Auckland, during 1796 (she was twenty, he was thirty-seven), but the prime minister eventually decided that his public responsibilities and lack of money disqualified him from taking a wife. He broke off the relationship early in 1797, explaining to Auckland that there were 'decisive and insurmountable' obstacles to the match (though he chose not to be very specific). John Holland Rose claims that Pitt's scrupulous sense of honour prompted him to deny himself the pleasures of marriage, but Robin Reilly discounts his embarrassing financial position (Pitt was never too worried about his personal finances), and suggests that concerns about his health and public duties were marginal. Reilly emphasizes Pitt's 'sexual incapacity or deviation'. In stating that Pitt was not attracted to women, and that he was most comfortable in male company, Reilly bases himself (as other historians have done) on a consid-erable amount of anecdotal evidence. According to some contemporary cartoons, poems and gossip, Pitt was homosexual. But even Reilly has to admit that there is no direct evidence to support this slur (for that is what it was), only 'strong inferences'. John Ehrman doubts that Pitt was homo-sexual. He thinks that lack of money might have been of some importance, though not much, and that Pitt's ill health should not be underestimated. Ehrman also draws attention to Pitt's relationship with Auckland, the pros-pective father-in-law. Auckland had made enemies, was not highly respected in elite circles, and had been pushing for a place in the cabinet. Pitt may have decided against marriage to Eleanor Eden because he was wary of becoming too closely associated with Auckland.

Eleanor Eden was the only woman Pitt came close to marrying, and it is true that when he gave her up there was considerable reflection upon his apparent lack of interest in women, his cold and aloof manner, and his supposed inability to form close attachments. Whatever the personal and public considerations that prompted Pitt's decision, it is clear that the single life made him more dependent on his established bachelor friendships, and unfortunately the advantages of these friendships – relaxation, camaraderie, fulfilment, respite from government business – were fading. Pitt was deeply saddened by the death of Edward Eliot in September 1797. Eliot had been a close friend since Pitt's time at Cambridge, and had married his sister Harriot in 1785. The three of them briefly lived together in Downing Street until Harriot died in 1786. Eliot stayed on and shared Pitt's house for several years (at least until 1794, according to Canning), and thereafter the two men regularly visited each other's residences (Eliot lived at Battersea Rise, Clapham). Eliot's death was a considerable blow to Pitt. Meanwhile, another of his old friends, William Wilberforce, became more distant. Wilberforce had devoted himself to the anti-slave trade campaign after a religious awakening in 1785. Though Pitt sympathized with the end in view, his natural pragmatism jarred with Wilberforce's zeal. From 1795, moreover, Wilberforce pressed for an end to the war, another issue on which he and Pitt could not agree. Though the two remained friends, their relationship was never as close as it had been in the early 1780s. Wilberforce admitted in February 1798 that 'our friendship has starved for want of nutriment'.[25]

Pitt's personal and public connection with Dundas and Grenville, his chief political assistants, had also become more problematic. Dundas longed to free himself from government business and war management. He suggested in 1797 that he might take a peerage and resign, and in 1799 and 1800 he directly asked Pitt to accept his resignation on the grounds of illness and exhaustion. Pitt persuaded him to carry on, but now their relationship was under greater strain than in previous years. As for Grenville, he had married in September 1792 (his wife was Anne Pitt, daughter of the first Baron Camelford and grand-daughter of Thomas Pitt, the first Earl of Chatham's elder brother) and was spending more time at Dropmore Park, Buckinghamshire, which he had purchased as a family home. The mounting pressure of business prompted Grenville to think of retiring from office. In 1794 he told Pitt that he would probably resign when the war came to an end, and by the late 1790s his readiness to quit was quite as strong as that of Dundas.[26]

Another disconcerting development for Pitt was that as the war continued, frustratingly and fruitlessly, Dundas and Grenville began openly to quarrel. This threatened to break up the dominant triumvirate that had directed affairs for so long. War strategy was the main area of dispute. Dundas maintained that Britain's security and long-term interests were best served by overseas operations, while Grenville argued that the only way to defeat France and end the war was to unite with the powers of Europe. As Dundas wrote to Grenville on 25 July 1800:

Most of you being of opinion that we ought not to send any force out of Europe (the reverse of which is my decided opinion), and the king and those in whose councils he confides being of opinion that our force is to go nowhere (which is the plain English of all this), my situation is become too ridiculous to be longer submitted to.

Pitt's own confidence was shaken by the failure to liberate Holland in the autumn of 1799 and by Russia's withdrawal from the war in October 1799. He then wavered between the rival recommendations of Dundas and Grenville, unable to decide between them or provide a new initiative himself. Many plans were debated and dropped. Some were then revived, as in June 1800 when Pitt abandoned one scheme in favour of another, only to reverse his decision when new information arrived. In 1797 Windham and his friend Burke had privately expressed strong misgivings about Pitt's competence as a war leader. By the end of 1800 these doubts were being voiced far and wide, but Dundas and Grenville were also culpable. The two were not fond of each other, differing in temperament as well as policy. There were times when Pitt benefited from this dichotomy, since it gave him the casting vote and the final power of decision, but it was obvious by the end of 1800 that his closest colleagues had moved so far apart that they were hindering rather than helping the government's labours. Disagreements within the cabinet increased, and Pitt was less able to take a firm line as those who shared responsibility for managing the war constantly pressed for their own plans to be adopted. Against the idea of new offensive operations was raised the suggestion that another attempt must be made to negotiate peace. Rather than continue stopping and searching neutral vessels in the Baltic, it was argued, the government ought to conciliate indignant foreign states. The prime minister seemed to lack the strength to curtail these disputes.[27]

Pitt's health and resolve were giving way. From the mid-1790s he rarely hosted dinner parties. He drank more. In physical appearance he displayed obvious signs of tiredness and sickness. He may have suffered a breakdown in the autumn of 1797, a time of extraordinary pressure (and consequently no relaxation) marked by Eliot's death, the failure of peace talks in Lille, and the need for major financial reorganization in order to continue the war. That the stress had not abated by the following spring is indicated by Pitt's allegations against Tierney, and refusal to retract, which led to their duel on Putney Heath on 27 May 1798 (an episode that Pitt, in calmer times, would no doubt have managed to avoid). Pitt told several friends and correspondents in these years, and they could see it for themselves, that he had been exerting himself beyond his strength. He succumbed to several debilitating illnesses, and on at least two occasions (in October 1798 and again in the autumn of 1800) had to retreat to Addington's residence at Woodley in Berkshire for a period of convalescence. As Earl Bathurst informed Marquess Wellesley in May 1800: 'Pitt's health has not been ... as good as we could wish, and any exertion seems always to affect him, which you know used not to be the case.'[28]

Stress and sickness added to longstanding problems associated with Pitt's style of leadership and mode of dealing with the transactions of government – especially his habit of leaving difficult or unpleasant matters to the last minute, and then settling them hastily and haphazardly. He lacked drive and energy, stayed in bed until midday, and no longer demonstrated the same command of facts and figures when dealing with business. He left others to do much of the work. Addington noted his indolence, and Dundas later recalled of this period that Pitt 'never attended to *details*, other persons went through that part, and he took only the results'.[29]

During 1800 Pitt's authority was questioned as never before. Formerly regarded (and able realistically to present himself) as the talented, imposing, conscientious leader of a vigorous administration, this image gradually became less convincing. Pitt was losing control. A number of mistakes and embarrassments crept into government activity. There were problems with Pitt's income tax, which soon had to be modified, and 'by some unaccountable negligence' (as Pitt told Grenville on 7 November 1800) the Seditious Meetings Act was not renewed at the appropriate time. Food shortages prompted intervention in the flour trade, and as noted Pitt backed the plan introduced by Hawkesbury for chartering the London Flour Company as a means of promoting competition. Some junior members of the ministry voted against this measure, however, heightening tensions within the government and presenting a picture of division and disorganization to outside observers.[30]

Pitt tried to respond positively to disappointments in the war, but it was a struggle, and recurrent illness undermined his resilience. Nevertheless, he could occasionally exhibit the familiar signs of active leadership and employ his political skills to influence cabinet and parliament. One outstanding Commons performance from this period was his speech of 3 February 1800. Napoleon had written personally to George III and Emperor Francis II of Austria to propose peace (December 1799), but Pitt and Grenville were unimpressed. Pitt was anxious to keep together the anti-French coalition of European powers and thought that, if he agreed to enter into negotiations with Napoleon, he would wreck the coalition without obtaining a lasting peace. In the Commons he declared that a 'system of revolution' was still dominant in France. Although Britain and the allied powers would eventually defeat it, this was no excuse for complacency and ministers had to consider what might happen if the alliance broke up or if for some reason

Britain's strength was reduced. Therefore, Pitt continued, it was better to go on fighting rather than allow the French to regroup:

> Do we believe that the revolutionary power, with this rest and breathing-time given it to recover from the pressure under which it is now sinking, possessing still the means of calling suddenly and violently into action whatever is the remaining physical force of France, under the guidance of military despotism; do we believe that this power, the terror of which is now beginning to vanish, will not again prove formidable to Europe?

Pitt insisted that Britain had to persist in war if genuine peace was to be achieved. No settlement was possible while Napoleon ruled France.

> I see little hope of permanent security. I see no possibility at this moment of concluding such a peace as would justify that liberal intercourse which is the essence of real amity; no chance of terminating the expenses or the anxieties of war, or of restoring to us any of the advantages of established tranquillity; and as a sincere lover of peace I cannot be content with its nominal attainment; I must be desirous of pursuing that system which promises to attain, in the end, the permanent enjoyment of its solid and substantial blessings for this country, and for Europe. As a sincere lover of peace, I will not sacrifice it by grasping at the shadow, when the reality is not substantially within my reach.

The government won the subsequent division (on the address to the throne, approving of the answer delivered to France) by a majority of 201.[31] In the following autumn, when the idea of fresh peace talks was more agreeable, Pitt considered all options and elected to improve Britain's position by pushing the French out of Egypt. He approved a plan advanced by Dundas, overcoming objections from Grenville, Windham and George III, and swayed the crucial cabinet discussion so that he got his way (only those ministers who backed the Egyptian plan gained a proper hearing). The campaign in Egypt proved successful. French forces evacuated Cairo in June 1801, and finally surrendered in Alexandria at the end of August. This in turn diminished the French threat to India.[32]

A problem to which Pitt had to give extra time and attention before his resignation was the serious harvest failure of 1800 (which followed the deficient crop of 1799), and this provides a further example of the manner in which he stirred himself when the need was greatest. As food reserves dwindled, Pitt told Addington in October 1800 that famine placed an even greater burden on the government than did war management. Pitt favoured an energetic response, despite the free market sentiments of Grenville and Portland, and secured parliamentary approval for cautious remedial measures. Exports of grain ceased, duty on food imports was reduced, and there was a ban on the use of grain in the manufacture of spirits. Poor relief was extended with special allowances. The situation improved slightly, though prices remained high and popular agitation continued. It has been argued that Pitt was willing to depart only slightly from *laissez faire* practice, and that his priorities were political rather than humanitarian. It is true that Pitt was concerned most about the centre of power, not the distressed localities. In the latter there was a strong sense that government should be doing more, which spread through the local networks of mutual obligation and respect in which deference from below met with paternal benevolence from above. Pitt was personally committed to the relief of hardship, but in his public capacity as prime minister he avoided hasty responses. He arranged for parliamentary committees to investigate the distress, and gave time for the necessary political will to develop before official assistance was given. To Pitt's detractors, however, this approach was woefully inadequate: urgent problems were referred to parliament instead of being addressed at once on ministerial authority, and the powers and propaganda of the state were employed to negate the popular will. On the other hand, it could be argued that Pitt was bound by his keen sense of political expediency to conclude that remedial steps (however limited) should only be taken once parliament and the governing classes showed a willingness to co-operate. The question of social welfare, moreover, could not be separated from the question of social discipline. By providing some relief Pitt satisfied those local magistrates and propertied notables who were reluctant to act against protest and disorder until the government did something to help the needy.[33]

As Pitt worked on his Irish scheme, therefore, he was still able to get other measures through cabinet and parliament, and in difficult times he could occasionally take decisive action despite his failing energies. But he did not retain the firm backing of George III. Though the king had always valued Pitt as a barrier against Fox, Pitt had been so successful a parliamentary operator and head of government that Fox and his party now seemed a broken force. As a result, Pitt's influence over George III decreased. By 1800 the king was more frequently objecting to government policies and complaining about ministerial shortcomings. He did nothing to prevent his third son, William, Duke of Clarence, from speaking against government measures (or measures favoured by Pitt) in the Lords. Bathurst wrote in May 1800 that 'the Duke of Clarence is certainly desirous of establishing a sort of princely influence in the House, which I think will in time become troublesome'. Dissatisfied with the conduct of the war and resenting what he regarded as a domineering attitude on the part of Pitt and Grenville, the king may have contemplated a change of ministry during the summer of 1800. According to a later account given by Malmesbury, in August 1800 George III told Windham (who did not welcome or encourage the design) that he intended to appoint him prime minister, with Malmesbury as foreign secretary. No changes occurred, however, and the king's attention was soon diverted by Napoleon's military successes over Austria and the prospect of peace talks between Britain and France.[34]

Nevertheless, it is obvious that when Pitt tried to implement his Irish settlement, the prospects were not auspicious. He demonstrated great resourcefulness and determination, as he had done previously when planning and executing complicated reforms, but his strength and morale were already flagging. He could not carry a united cabinet along with him on Catholic emancipation, a highly controversial proposal that also lacked popular approval, and his intentions directly affected George III's strongest religious and constitutional predilections. Relationships within the government, and between the leading ministers and the court, had deteriorated, and for a variety of personal as well as public reasons – detailed above – Pitt decided that emancipation had to be a resignation matter. In the final analysis he was not too reluctant to hand over to Addington, not least because he hoped and expected to return when circumstances permitted. This makes Malmesbury's comments of February 1801 all the more interesting:

> It looks at times to me as if Pitt was playing a very selfish, and, in the present state of affairs, a very criminal part; that he goes out to show his own strength, and under the certain expectation of being soon called upon again to govern the country, with uncontrolled power. But, besides the culpability of this conduct (which it is perhaps unfair to attribute to a man of his established character), it may be a very erroneous calculation. His followers will leave him in shoals; and it remains to be seen whether they will range themselves under the banner of the new Administration, formed out of the shreds and parings of his; or whether it is not more likely that they will form Opposition; and the next change (and that a very near one) may be, Fox and Opposition taking possession of the Government.[35]

Addington's priorities, peace and retrenchment, were sensible in view of prevailing conditions: subsidies to continental powers and purchases of grain had drained gold reserves, the pound was losing value abroad, the French had excluded British goods from many European markets, and at home there were bread riots. Though in the long run Britain's maritime supremacy brought control of the re-export trade, and inflation promoted by suspension of cash payments stimulated industrial expansion, the situation was alarming early in 1801. Addington's cabinet was widely disparaged for its apparent lack of quality. The tone was set by Dundas, who wrote to Pitt on 7 February 1801:

> I know not to what stage the Speaker's endeavours to form an arrangement have proceeded, but it is impossible for me not to whisper into your ear my

conviction that no arrangement can be formed under him, as its head, that will not crumble to pieces almost as soon as formed. Our friends who, as an act of friendship and attachment to you, agree to remain in office, do it with the utmost chagrin and unwillingness, and among the other considerations which operate upon them, the feeling that they are embarking in an Administration under a head totally incapable to carry it on, and which must of course soon be an object of ridicule, is almost uppermost in all their minds. Add to this, that although they will not certainly enter into faction and oppose him, all the aristocracy of the country at present cordially connected with Government and part of it under you, feel a degradation in the First Minister of the country being selected from a person of the description of Mr Addington, without the smallest pretensions to justify it and destitute of abilities to carry it on.

Addington, a doctor's son who had trained as a lawyer, was the first prime minister drawn from the professional classes. He was not an aristocrat. He was no orator. But he had the king's confidence, and in time recruited talented allies. Castlereagh joined the government in October 1802 as president of the board of control. Addington initially had the goodwill of Pitt, Grenville was willing to back the new government so long as its foreign policy accorded with his own preferences (in time he decided that this was not the case), and Foxites expressed approval for peace with France and cuts in expenditure. By September 1801 Wilberforce felt able to write to Wellesley that despite the doubts and jibes of many, Addington was doing well as premier, though Wilberforce linked this with the manner in which Pitt had undertaken to assist the new ministry.

It was not possible *at last* for Pitt to avoid retiring; and much as you and I have been used on former occasions to admire his magnanimity, the greatness of mind with which he acted on the late trying occasion was such as to surprise as well as to delight me ... It was the fashion at first to say *that it would not do* ... but I always maintained the contrary, and the event has justified my expectations. You would smile at Sheridan's similes – that the state of the old ministry, after Pitt, Dundas and Grenville had left their colleagues, reminded him of what was called knocking out the brains of a committee; and that surely it was a Hibernian way of cleaning ship, to throw the great guns overboard. But Addington has done very respectably in the House, and with support like Pitt's ... nothing is to be apprehended.[36]

Preliminary peace terms were agreed in London in October 1801 and the Treaty of Amiens was concluded in March 1802, but it did not satisfy either Britain or France, and both failed to abide by its terms. Soon Addington's government was accused of making too many concessions to Napoleon. Even some of Fox's friends came to believe that the French were incurably expansionist, a clear departure from their previous position. Sheridan commented that the peace was one that all men were glad of, but nobody proud of, and, though Pitt's associate Canning denounced it, he saw that MPs were tired of war and unconcerned about scrutinizing the peace terms very closely. George III described peace as unavoidable and experimental. He told Hawkesbury (Addington's foreign secretary) that no lasting accommodation would be possible with France 'till it has a settled Government', and desired that 'such a peace establishment will be kept up as may keep this country on a respectable footing, without which our situation would be most deplorable'. Windham also warned of continuing danger to British interests. Before telling the Commons of his 'deep despair' at the 'degrading and injurious' terms, he expressed his worst fears privately to Addington:

> I can have no idea of the measure in question but as the commencement of a career which, by an easy descent, and step by step, but at no very distant period, will conduct the country to a situation where, when it looks at last for its independence, it will find that it is already gone. I have no idea how the effect of this measure is ever to be recovered; chance may do much, but, according to any conception I can form, the country has received its deathblow.

Grenville found the preliminary terms 'inadequate to any reasonable expectation, and of a nature to leave the country, especially if they are followed by any considerable reduction of our force, in a state of extreme insecurity', and he subsequently told the House of Lords that the peace treaty was 'fraught with degradation and national humiliation' and 'the most disgraceful and ruinous measure that could have been adopted'. Dundas wrote of the 'gloomy prospects' that attended peace on such a basis. Since he could not possibly speak well of the treaty, but had no wish to engage in a factious opposition that would weaken the king's ministers, he thought he should stay away from parliament: 'I have told Mr Pitt that my best consolation was ... the prospect of escaping from being a witness of the calamitous consequences which, in my judgement, must result from such an end of the contest.' Malmesbury said that the terms amounted to 'peace in a week, and war in a month'. Pitt, however, adopted a rather more optimistic line. He welcomed Addington's peace, though added that France must rest content with the concessions made and abandon further territorial ambitions.[37]

By the Amiens treaty Britain retained only Trinidad from the Spanish and Ceylon from the Dutch. Malta, the Cape of Good Hope and Egypt were all to be returned (to the Knights of St John, the Dutch and the Ottoman Empire respectively). Britain was left with no base in the Mediterranean except Gibraltar, and, unlike the treaty of 1801 between France and Austria, Amiens did not guarantee any of the existing frontiers within Europe. The title 'King of France', used by English monarchs since the fourteenth century, was relinquished. France agreed to evacuate southern Italy and respect the independence of Portugal and the Ionian Islands. As a whole the bargain favoured the French. Although he gave Addington useful assistance, urging his own followers to support the government's effort to make peace, Pitt subsequently came to agree with those who complained that too much had been given up. Pitt was particularly disappointed by the loss of the Cape. Nevertheless, he had no option but to accept the Treaty of Amiens as a *fait accompli*, and reflected that in the circumstances no better settlement could have been achieved. Pitt had long been convinced that it was worth paying a high price to end the war, because he believed there could be no financial and economic recovery at home without peace. His position was made clear when he approved of the peace preliminaries in the Commons on 3 November 1801.

> In considering the terms that ought to be accepted, it would be necessary to inquire, in the first instance, what would be the expense of continuing the contest, what were the difficulties with which it would be attended, and what hopes could be entertained of its ultimate success? It was undoubtedly the duty of every government, in negotiating a treaty of peace, to obtain the best possible terms; but it was sometimes difficult to know how far particular points might be pressed without running the risk of breaking off the negotiation. For his own part, he had no hesitation to declare, that he would rather close with an enemy upon terms short even of the fair pretensions of the country, provided they were not inconsistent with honour and security, than continue the contest for any particular possession.

Pitt added a note of caution. It was not clear what Napoleon's future plans might entail, and Pitt recommended that, while Addington's government had to deal with France in a sincere and friendly manner, it should in no measure compromise the nation's safety. Though Pitt was for the peace, he did not want to share the blame if it failed: 'He was inclined to hope every thing that was good, but he was bound to act as if he feared otherwise.' Late in 1801, and into the spring of 1802, Canning did all he could to turn Pitt against the peace terms, but Pitt maintained that he could not honourably take any other line than the one he had adopted. Canning was concerned about Pitt's relationship with Windham and Grenville, for they both opposed the peace, and any breach was likely to prolong Addington's tenure as premier and encourage the Foxites. In April 1802 Canning urged Windham to be careful when attacking the peace terms in the Commons. His point was that Pitt should not be obliged to defend Addington or the treaty.

He can take no distinction without seeming to abandon Addington – and that he will not do. He cannot object to any part of the Peace in public without weakening the grounds upon which he contends Peace on the whole to be preferable to war – and *that* he will not do. You may have the advantage of him in argument. But what practical good will that do? Do not help Addington out of the scrape into which he has blundered himself ... To move for papers – to move for taking the treaty into consideration – all this may be done with great and good effect; but a condemnation of the treaty, such as would force Pitt into a defence of it, and identify him with the makers of it, is what is of all things to be avoided. I hope you think so. Whether Pitt will save us, I do not know. But surely he is the only man that *can.*

Pitt's acceptance of the Treaty of Amiens certainly alienated several of his former colleagues, but it was some time before the consequences of this became clear. The treaty itself was ratified in the Commons by 276 to 20 votes and in the Lords by 122 to 16 votes, and was warmly welcomed in the country.[38]

Pitt's resignation and the peace talks, meanwhile, had prompted Fox's return to active politics. Fox had scant respect for Addington, though he was prepared to support his ministry if Pitt could be excluded and the war ended. The events of 1801 and 1802 appeared to offer Fox vindication, and even the fact that the treaty was unsatisfactory played into his hands, for it sustained the claim that Pitt had gone into war for ideological aims that were impossible to achieve. At the same time, Fox became uneasy about Napoleon. His doubts were confirmed when he visited Paris during the Amiens interlude. He was received as a celebrity, and caused controversy at home by consorting with exiled Irish rebel Arthur O'Connor and prominent French politicians. Yet Fox came to regard Napoleon as a danger to liberty, not its guardian, and viewed the large standing army and press restrictions in France as props of autocracy. He hoped that the peace would last. When it collapsed he instinctively blamed Addington's ministry and George III, though Napoleon's conduct would later force him to alter this assumption.[39]

The short peace gave Addington a chance to gather support in parliament and the nation. Expenditure on the army and navy was cut, bringing savings of about £25,000,000 by the end of 1802. Though Pitt's supporters opposed disarmament, most MPs welcomed these economies and Addington's policy had a favourable reception out of doors. He reorganized public accounting and the civil list, and repealed Pitt's income tax while leaving other burdens in place. There was more borrowing, but sinking fund arrangements were altered to provide for the redemption of loans within forty-five years. Peace brought a revival in trade, which further enhanced Addington's reputation. After the general election of July 1802 ministers had a large majority in the

Commons (over 270 by some calculations).[40] Addington also benefited because his rivals were divided. Pitt and Dundas complained about disarmament, while Fox supported it. Fox advocated Catholic relief, as did Grenville, but Grenville disliked the peace of which Fox approved, and Pitt was no longer willing to press Catholic claims. The Foxites were in disarray at this time. Tierney would no longer accept Fox's leadership. Grey expressed reluctance to attend regularly, was disappointed when his elderly father accepted a peerage (June 1801) because this would mean his own premature removal from the Commons to the Lords, and saw more quickly than Fox that Napoleon did not want peace. In addition, Fox was ready to combine with Addington to preserve peace, while Grey argued for a pact with the Grenvillites. Pitt was urged by his adherents to assert himself, but despite growing criticism of Addington late in 1802, he chose not to join in publicly. Addington approached Pitt about closer co-operation in January 1803, and these talks continued into April. Pitt was offered a place in the cabinet. He would not serve under Addington, however, and rejected the idea that he and Addington should have equal status under a figurehead prime minister. Pitt expected a lot in return for his participation, and Addington was annoyed at the nature and extent of his demands. Finally Pitt declared his independence from all fixed parties and made clear his intention to serve only on his own terms: he wanted control over policy and personnel.[41]

Pitt's relationship with Addington had deteriorated since the spring of 1801. The two had been childhood friends (an early connection formed while Addington's father was the Chatham family's doctor). Pitt had also helped Addington to pursue a public career. Addington was first elected to the Commons (for Devizes) in March 1784. He worked hard, mastered Commons procedure, and became Speaker in 1789 with Pitt's backing. Addington was useful to Pitt's administration during the 1790s, and Pitt knew that George III liked and trusted him. Indeed, in the difficult circumstances of 1797 Pitt briefly thought of installing Addington as temporary prime minister, and during the emancipation crisis it was not surprising that both Pitt and the king chose Addington as a replacement premier. But again Pitt saw this as a *temporary* arrangement. Addington, once he declared his willingness to succeed Pitt, did not consider himself at all as a stopgap, and responded angrily during February and March 1801 to suggestions that Pitt might stay on as prime minister after all. When Pitt offered to remain if George III and Addington were agreeable, Addington made it clear that he intended to lead a new government. Having already promised his backing, Pitt could hardly resist.

These developments led him to conclude that he could not return as premier, and keep intact his virtuous and patriotic image, unless he had the consent of Addington as well as George III. He could not go back on his pledge of goodwill to Addington's administration; and he could not be discovered intriguing against it. He wanted to regain power, but the *manner* of his return was all-important, for Pitt did not want to risk a loss of character. Addington, who for so long had been under Pitt's shadow, may have supposed that Pitt would now give up active politics. This seems to have been the king's understanding, judging by his comments after Pitt's resignation (especially his letter to Pitt dated 18 February 1801), and the idea spread that Pitt would indeed retire. His financial advisers suggested that he could make £3000 a year if he went back to practising law, and probably end up as lord chancellor, and on 7 May 1802 the House of Commons formally offered him the grateful thanks of the nation for his 'great and important services' (the relevant motion was passed by 211 to 52 votes). On 28 May 1802 Pitt's forty-third birthday was celebrated at a grand dinner attended by over 800 guests, for which Canning wrote the song 'The Pilot that Weathered the Storm'. By this time Pitt had received many tributes for his past achievements. But whatever the expectation of others, he himself was not looking backwards and he did not retire. Pitt longed again to head the government. His sense of calling, awareness of his own abilities, executive temperament and creed of high-minded public service all survived. This became apparent to Addington, who resented what he regarded as Pitt's disingenuousness. In 1801, acting the virtuous patriot, Pitt promised to back Addington as premier and persuaded former cabinet colleagues to remain in office. In time Pitt chafed under his self-imposed restrictions. He looked for a way to displace Addington without appearing to undermine or plot against him.[42]

The promise to assist Addington was clearly a mistake. True, Pitt had been worried about George III's mental condition and hoped that his promise would ease the king's mind; but, even so, it was not a very astute move for an experienced politician. It amounted to an unconditional offer of support. In October 1802 Pitt discussed the difficulties of his situation with Canning (who subsequently reported the conversation to Malmesbury). At the time of his resignation, Pitt explained, he had been concerned not to disturb the king or damage the national interests. He had not asked any of his colleagues to resign with him, and made sure that operations already under way in Egypt and northern Europe would not be disrupted. He could hardly be accused of leaving office at a time of crisis, merely to evade responsibility, and his main priority had been to leave behind a ministry that the king would support and whose measures would not drastically depart from the pattern of policy he had established over the preceding years.

It was to forward this his favourite purpose that he had pledged himself, but *himself singly*, to advise and support the present Ministry. This pledge he considered as solemnly binding, not redeemable by any lapse of time, nor ever to be cancelled without the *express* consent of Mr Addington. He perhaps had, in the first instance, gone too far and pledged himself too deeply; and his parliamentary conduct during the last session was to be explained by the strict and solemn engagement into which he had entered. He owned that he was often very sorry to feel it incumbent on him to support measures he could not wholly approve.[43]

At first ministers had regularly consulted Pitt about public affairs. Also, as noted above, he urged his friends to support the government's effort to make peace with France. By the spring of 1802, however, Pitt and Addington were rarely in each other's company and Pitt was no longer being asked for his advice. He began to find fault with government policies. He decided that Addington was too weak to stand up to Napoleon, whose taste for aggrandizement (despite the peace treaty) seemed to be increasing rather than diminishing. Soon the French were interfering in Germany and Switzerland, and Napoleon extended his power in Italy by securing the presidency of the Cisalpine Republic. Fearing that he contemplated another invasion of Egypt, Britain refused to evacuate Malta. Tension grew quickly, and at home Addington could not shake off accusations of weakness. In October 1802 he offered the Swiss encouragement and money to counter French designs, but proved unable or unwilling to do more.[44]

Pitt's dissatisfaction with Addington's government did not relate only to foreign policy. He was also angered by the ministry's failure to protect the reputation of the previous administration. Several Foxite MPs took advantage of this to abuse and condemn Pitt's regime. Even worse than this sin of omission was one of commission: Addington's first lord of the admiralty, the Earl of St Vincent (famous for his victory over the Spanish fleet in February 1797), initiated an inquiry into naval affairs, which implied that they had been mismanaged under Pitt. Addington gave further offence by not informing Pitt that he intended to offer Dundas a peerage (Dundas was created Viscount Melville in December 1802). Pitt also objected to Addington's financial plans, particularly the increase in government borrowing. By January 1803, with Pitt's patience rapidly fading, it was clear that the peace of Amiens would not continue for much longer. This was the moment at which Addington, anxious to strengthen the government, approached Pitt.

The negotiations failed because Pitt would only return as prime minister in a reconstructed cabinet. He insisted on too many changes for Addington's liking, and wanted these to be formally requested by both the cabinet and

George III. Pitt's proposals included Addington's elevation to the Lords as a secretary of state; the removal from high office of such Addingtonians as Baron Hobart (secretary for war and the colonies from March 1801 to May 1804); inclusion in the new ministry of Melville, notwithstanding the corruption then being uncovered by St Vincent's naval inquiry (Melville, as Dundas, had been treasurer of the navy between 1784 and 1800); and the inclusion of other former ministers – including Grenville and Windham – who had been openly antagonistic towards Addington's government. Grenville, in fact, was increasingly unwilling to be part of Pitt's future plans. He wanted the freedom to speak his mind on Catholic emancipation and Addington's performance as prime minister, and was pressing for the formation of a broad coalition ministry (including Foxites) rather than merely a revamping of Addington's cabinet under new leadership. Windham, meanwhile, had no wish to join a Pitt-Addington-Grenville administration.[45]

Why had Pitt made so many demands? His intention, it appears, was to win general approval for the recreation of his former regime. Perhaps he genuinely believed that he could make it as strong as before, and that this time there would be no trouble over Catholic emancipation because he had promised not to bring it up again while George III lived. Pitt's terms, however, were completely unacceptable to Addington and his supporters, and it must quickly have become obvious to Pitt that his former government could not be re-established as he wished. After all, there had been serious cabinet divisions in the years immediately preceding his resignation, and former colleagues had since drifted apart ever more emphatically. Some of Pitt's associates had agreed to serve under Addington (with Pitt's blessing) while others had not, and of those who resigned in 1801, Pitt, Dundas and Camden had accepted the peace treaty with France, while Grenville, Windham and Spencer had opposed it. The former ministerial bloc was splintering, and abortive negotiations for a cabinet reshuffle early in 1803 destabilized the situation further. Addington soon turned to Pitt's opponents for support, most notably George Tierney.

Pitt's bargaining position was also affected by the balance of forces in the Commons, which had altered after the 1802 general election, much to Addington's short-term benefit. In addition, Pitt's conduct since his resignation had enabled others to take the initiative. His stance as a patriotic public servant limited his options. He awaited the call of king, parliament and people, and sought to avoid any conduct that could be deemed self-seeking or factious. He had to respond, not initiate, and since his was not the only agenda at stake during the negotiations of early 1803, it is not surprising that they failed. Pitt may have made excessive demands because he did not really wish to take office at this juncture. But Michael Duffy suggests that he must have wanted to return, otherwise he would not have tried to recreate his previous regime. John Holland Rose argues that Pitt's sense of duty made him anxious to serve his nation at a time of growing danger, and that the talks really broke down because of objections raised by those around Addington. John Ehrman points out that Pitt's cardinal requirement was to preserve his own freedom of action. He had to discern the king's wishes and wait and see how Grenville and his followers would proceed, and could not agree to give way on matters relating to his honour or determination to lead. Hence his insistence that some of Addington's colleagues would have to be replaced. The whole negotiation with Addington was further complicated by the awkwardness that had crept into their personal dealings. Pitt had long viewed Addington as his inferior, but Addington was his successor as premier and no longer so easily dominated. Pitt found it hard to adjust, particularly when it came to discussion of ministerial changes. As Ehrman comments, Pitt 'was not used to being treated as a piece on the board to be placed as others decided'. So Pitt did have the chance to take office early in 1803, but not in the manner he wanted. He was experienced enough to know that precipitate action would be fatal; better to stall, gain the time he needed to reunify his political connection, and only then return to power. This strategy must have appealed to Pitt if he considered the government to be in such difficulty at home and abroad that the call for his return was imminent.[46]

With respect to these talks Addington's chief apologist is Philip Ziegler, who emphasizes that the prime minister offered to make way for Pitt *and* allow him to replace senior and loyal Addingtonians. This would have represented a considerable sacrifice on Addington's part, especially at a time when he still had a Commons majority and the backing of George III. Addington was apparently willing to step aside because he thought that some members of the cabinet would rather have Pitt as premier, and was reluctant to carry on as prime minister now that Pitt was hostile. Addington only ended the discussions, reckons Ziegler, when he realized that Pitt would be satisfied with nothing less than abject surrender, and even then he waited for his colleagues to agree that he should resist. Pitt's understanding of what had taken place was rather different, and after the talks broke down he objected to the version of events related to others by Addington. He further clarified his position and his conditions for returning to office in a letter to the prime minister of 15 April 1803. Pitt referred to

> expressions which seem to imply that you considered yourself as authorized to state to your colleagues a specific and positive proposition as made by me, and as containing the outline of a plan of arrangement, which it was for them to

consider whether they ought to recommend to his Majesty to carry into effect ...
I certainly do not consider myself as having made to you *any* proposition on
the subject. Our interview originated as I conceive, in a strong wish expressed
by yourself that I might be induced to return to my former situation in the
king's service. On this point I stated that the only ground on which I could think
myself called upon to give any positive answer to such a proposition, or to say
anything which could in any degree be binding with respect to the details of any
arrangement connected with it, was that of receiving some direct previous inti-
mation of his Majesty's wish to that effect, together with full authority to form,
for his Majesty's consideration, a plan of arrangement, *in any manner* I thought
best for his service, *as well out of those who were in the former as those who are
in the present Government.*

When Addington went to the king on 20 April with copies of the correspondence relating to his negotiations with Pitt, George III angrily refused
to read them. He complained that he had not been consulted about the
overture to Pitt, spoke of 'the crown being put in commission', and clearly
knew nothing of what Addington and Pitt had discussed. George III's
reaction might well have been different had he heard Pitt's version of recent
transactions. It is likely that Addington suppressed some of the correspondence. The prime minister admitted that he did not want others to read of
sentiments 'repugnant to my feelings' and 'to the justice of which I can by
no means assent'. Pitt and his supporters had hoped that the king would
be presented with all the relevant correspondence, that he would read it,
and that he would approach the matter of future cabinet appointments in
a calm and dispassionate way.[47]

Pitt could not fail to see, however, that if he did return to the premiership
he would probably not be able to rely on Grenville. Unlike Pitt, Grenville
had refused to abandon Catholic emancipation. For him this was a matter
of principle and public character. Having grown considerably in influence
and self-assurance, moreover, he attacked Addington's government while
hoping that it would not be replaced by a Pitt administration. Grenville
advocated the formation of a coalition ministry that would include members
of all the main parliamentary groupings, yet Pitt's reluctance actively to
oppose Addington during 1801 and 1802 indicated no readiness to be part
of a new and wider political alliance. Pitt and Grenville had argued before
their resignations in 1801 on war strategy and social policy. Now Grenville
was influenced by a rumour that in 1801, without consulting anybody, Pitt
had offered to forget emancipation in order to stay in office. Nor does Pitt
appear to have discussed with Grenville his promise (made after his resignation) not to raise the Catholic question again while George III lived. Pitt's
pledge was made to ease the king's mind and was not intended as a betrayal

of Grenville, but in due course Foxites would exploit Grenville's resentment about Pitt's behaviour to great effect.[48]

An economic downturn, meanwhile, increased the pressure on Addington's government. During 1802 and the early months of 1803 Napoleon's expansionist policy closed much of Europe to British exports. Problems also arose because of the cancellation of war orders and ex-servicemen's search for employment. As Addington was blamed for the disadvantages of peace, the French prepared for hostilities and a resumption of the war became politically acceptable in Britain. Quarrels over British occupation of Malta and French ambitions in western Europe could not be resolved, and Napoleon's suggestion that Russia should be invited to mediate was rejected. On 17 May 1803 the government declared war on France. Addington envisaged a limited engagement so that Britain would emerge neither defeated nor bankrupt.

Income tax was re-introduced in the form of a sliding scale ranging from 3d. in the pound to 1s. for incomes over £150 a year (incomes under £60 were exempt). Its collection was simplified. Different types of income were classified in revised schedules and most tax was deducted at source, a significant innovation. Addington proved a better administrator of the tax, indeed, than Pitt had been. The army was also stronger in 1803 following improvements effected by commander-in-chief the Duke of York, though there was still a shortage of men. Planning for a defensive war, Addington's government considered the army less important than the militia and volunteers, but there were not enough arms or equipment for these local units. Windham, formerly Pitt's secretary at war, poured scorn on the government's defence measures and argued for a strengthening of the regular army. Though Addington's retrenchment and disarmament had been popular during the peace, he was now accused of leaving Britain too weak to stand up to France. There was a new wave of war patriotism. Another ministry might have been able to focus attention on the external threat and use loyalist fervour for its own political purposes, but Addington and his colleagues were too closely associated with a failed peace and the lack of military preparedness. Pitt began to join in the criticism of the government's inadequacies.[49]

In the Commons at this time there were about seventy anti-war Foxites. Grenville's following, which demanded a vigorous war effort, was of a similar size, while Pitt, who now wanted to conduct the war himself, had about sixty supporters. Addington's ministry had perhaps 230, but many voted with the government only from habit and a change of ministers was unlikely greatly to disturb them. Fox (who had never truly supported the ministry, he said, only its accommodation with France) decided that co-operation

with the Grenvillites was possible. He noted their animosity towards Addington, the king's choice, and suspected that, although they favoured war, they
could be persuaded to accept an honourable peace. There might be agreement
on other points too, especially Catholic emancipation and Irish policy,
and Fox was willing for the present to forego parliamentary reform,
which Grenville opposed. Yet Foxite disunity remained a problem. Fox only
appeared in the Commons when he felt like it, which annoyed some of his
followers (his excuse was that, since his unpopularity exceeded Pitt's popularity, to be always attending and speaking would be to create support for
Pitt). Sheridan was unsure about closer ties with the Grenvillites – though
it was made known to Grenville in November 1803 that Fox 'is determined
to show that his sentiments are not to be looked for in Sheridan's contriv-
ances' – and many MPs reproached Fox for refusing to blame France for
the renewal of war.[50]

Pitt's eagerness to direct the war and restore his system of government
increased palpably during the summer and autumn of 1803, but Addington
and his colleagues seemed determined to remain in place. A disappointed
Pitt saw that there would be no smooth transfer of power (the deadlock
of December 1783, when Pitt moved to replace the Fox-North coalition but
found his opponents clinging to office, appeared to be repeating itself). His
unease grew as arguments over the conduct of the war drove his friends
and former colleagues further apart. Pitt's view was that all political leaders
had a duty to put aside their differences and assist the war effort, and he
preferred not to get involved in parliamentary conflicts. As a virtuous patriot
he had to remain above the fray. Pitt delivered one of his most celebrated
speeches on 23 May 1803. He approved of the war, he explained, because
it was so clearly in the nation's interests to frustrate prodigious French
ambition, but he said nothing for or against Addington's government. This
was a just and necessary war, Pitt claimed, 'one which we could not decline
without surrendering both our security and our honour'. He called for an
immediate mobilization of all the resources of parliament and people:

> The scale of our exertions could not be measured by those of former times, or
> confined within the limits even of the great, and till then, unexampled efforts of
> the last war. He was convinced that some system, far more vigorous and effectual
> than any even then adopted, would be found necessary, both in our finance, and
> in the preparation for national defence ... We had not an option at this moment,
> between the blessings of peace and the dangers of war. We must consider our
> lot as cast, by the decrees of Providence, in a time of peril and trouble – he
> trusted that the temper and courage of the nation would conform itself to the
> duties of that situation – that we should be prepared, collectively and individually,
> to meet it with that resignation and fortitude, and, at the same time, with that

active zeal and exertion, which, in proportion to the magnitude of the crisis, might be expected from a brave and free people; and that we should reflect, even in the hour of trial, what abundant reason we have to be grateful to Providence, for all the distinction we enjoy over most of the countries of Europe and for all the advantages and blessings which national wisdom and virtue have hitherto protected, and which it now depends on perseverance in the same just and honourable sentiments, still to guard and preserve.

Malmesbury wrote that Pitt's speech was followed by 'incessant and loud applause'. It was 'the finest he ever made – never was any speech so cheered … it was strong in support of war, but he was silent as to Ministers; and his silence, either as to blame or praise, was naturally construed into negative censure'. Canning and other Pittites welcomed Pitt's success, for they had been urging him to take the initiative, and they decided to go ahead with a motion of censure against the government's conduct of relations with France. Pitt, however, could not vote with them. He did not want George III to think he was trying to push Addington into resignation; he still hoped to be *invited* to take over. Pitt realized that this line dissatisfied Grenville and wrote to his cousin on 26 May to express his disappointment that – yet again – they could not act together.

When the censure motion came up for debate in the Commons on 3 June, Pitt tried to put it off. Canning rose to say that he was sorry to disagree with his chief, but he considered the motion to be fully justified. Again Addington and the ministers were angry with Pitt. They had wanted him directly to oppose the motion, and they could not have it put off because this would be taken as an admission by them that they had bungled their dealings with the French. Addingtonians, Grenvillites, Foxites and Canning's group all voted against Pitt's proposal, which was rejected by 335 to 58 votes. Pitt then left the chamber and the government defeated the censure motion by 275 to 36 votes. Canning was pleased that the motion had been debated, while Malmesbury questioned Pitt's action, 'certainly not a judicious measure, though *kindly* intended towards Government by Pitt. Its effect is to furnish a plea for *the many* to desert Pitt, and blame him.' George III was happy with the outcome: 'these events prove the real sense of the House of Commons that parliament truly means support to the executive power, not to faction'. Addington, however, regretted that Pitt was rapidly distancing himself from the government. He and Pitt had not been on good terms since March 1803, when the talks about ministerial changes ended without agreement, and Pitt's impressive speech of 23 May (though he was clearly in poor health) made it increasingly likely that Addington would have to make way for Pitt. The breach became wider on 3 June when Pitt refused to help the government defeat the motion of censure. Though Addington easily won the division, opinion in parliament and out of doors continued to turn against the prime minister. In July Pitt criticized the budget. How long would it be before he went into open opposition? [51]

Pitt's assault on the budget reflected his eagerness both to defend his record and to present himself as an alternative premier. He saw an outline of the government's financial plans on 10 June 1803. Addington announced them in the Commons on 13 June. Pitt did not speak, preferring to wait until new income tax arrangements were debated in detail. Addington intended to renew the tax, but at a lower rate (5 per cent) and with a wider application, and he expected it to bring in £4,500,000. On 13 July Pitt defended the income tax he had previously planned and introduced, and complained that Addington's version of the tax would interfere with 'the usual and spontaneous distribution of property'. The disposal of capital should be left free, Pitt declared, so that people could employ it as they wished. He pointed out that Addington's schedule of abatements and exemptions did not include people who received interest from the public funds. Pitt found this unacceptable, for the state's good faith was at stake, and nothing should be done to discourage individuals from lending the government money. Pitt recommended that exemptions and abatements should apply to all types of property. Charles Abbot, the Speaker of the Commons, noted that Pitt assumed 'a tone of great asperity' during the debate, and that his remarks were highly unfavourable towards Addington. The ministry won the subsequent division by 150 votes to 50, but Addington recognized the force of Pitt's remarks and on 14 July he informed the Commons that the income tax would be altered. [52]

Pitt became more active as he sensed a change in the public mood. A new invasion scare in the summer of 1803 helped him to enhance his patriotic image. He called for popular participation in the war effort, pressed Addington's government to revive and arm the volunteer movement, and set an example by raising three battalions as Warden of the Cinque Ports. Popular excitement rose to levels not seen since the loyalist commotion of the mid-1790s. George III arranged for his wife and daughters to take refuge in Worcester in the event of a French landing. From provincial towns came warnings to the home secretary, Charles Yorke, that food supplies and patterns of employment would be disrupted by an invasion. Demands rose for government action.

Once again Pitt was a figurehead for national unity, and friends noticed his renewed energy and optimism. Wilberforce found him 'rampant about setting Europe to rights ... after vindicating our own safety'. The difficulties of the time obliged Pitt to think again about the composition of any new administration that he would be able or willing to lead. Though he saw merit in Grenville's idea of a broad coalition government, including leaders of all the main parliamentary groups, he did not believe it could work. George III would probably refuse to accept Fox, with whom Grenville was prepared to co-operate, and Pitt did not wish to alienate the king. Nor was he willing to share control over policy in a cabinet composed of 'all the talents'. Furthermore, Addington and his followers were making such a mess of the war that Pitt wanted to exclude them. The king still backed Addington, however, and Pitt knew that royal support would be essential for any new administration at a time of such emergency. Pitt decided that he could not openly join with Grenville and Fox in a combined effort to destroy Addington's ministry. But this allowed others to accuse him of dithering. As attacks on the government continued, Pitt could not side with ministers or with their opponents. Still Addington would not resign, much to Pitt's frustration, while the growing political confusion inhibited the war effort. Eventually, it seemed, Pitt would have to turn unequivocally against the ministry.

He probably made up his mind to do so before the end of 1803, but those who spoke to him in January 1804 still noted his reluctance to take drastic action. He knew what he wanted, but was content to react rather than initiate. Pitt's friend George Pretyman, Bishop of Lincoln, wrote on 13 January:

> His opinions and feelings, both upon public and private grounds, are such that it cannot, I think, be long before he fully expresses them; but this probably will not take place till it is called forth by some new occurrence, I mean some objectionable measure or palpable omission on the part of Ministers, and they will soon furnish such an opportunity. In that case Mr Pitt might not confine himself to the point in question, but might take a retrospective view, so far at least as to afford him a ground for declaring his conviction of the incompetency of Ministers, and the danger in which this country is placed by their negligence and want of talents ... Mr Pitt cannot bear the idea of a teasing, harassing opposition; but, as far as I can judge, he is ready to stand forward whenever there shall be an opportunity of exposing the incapacity of Ministers, in any important degree or upon any material point.

Pretyman may have recorded only those parts of Pitt's conversation that he most wanted to hear. Like Canning, he hoped that Pitt would succeed Addington as premier and co-operate with Grenville. But 'after much political talk' with Pitt at this time, Wilberforce found him 'resolved not to hamper himself with engagements, or to go into systematic opposition'.[53]

Early in 1804 George III suffered another relapse. This made all parliamentary leaders unwilling to cause further political disruption. Time was running out for Addington, however, and his Commons majority fell sharply in April 1804 when the followers of Pitt, Grenville and Fox voted together on defence. On 16 April the margin was fifty-eight votes, on 23 April fifty-two, and on 25 April just thirty-seven. Pitt commended the defence policies of the previous administration and accused Addington's of failing sufficiently to build up Britain's military and naval forces. He claimed (on 23 April) that he spoke on behalf of

> those who are disposed to take a grave and radical review of our public affairs; a review of all the resources which government have brought forward; who think that no part of our defence is adequate to what we ought to expect – all those who are convinced by experience, that after twelve months have been given to these gentlemen to exhaust all the resources of their minds, and to amend and improve their plans from the suggestions of others, nothing satisfactory has been accomplished – all those who are convinced upon mature reflection, that from the present ministers, or under them, nothing is likely to originate to give to this country any fair chance of having what is due to its own zeal and its own exertion, at the most important and critical period that ever existed in its history: and I confess I am one of those who look at this subject in that point of view.

As well as difficulties in the Commons, Addington faced the prospect of losing control of the Lords, which he regarded as decisive. On 29 April he told the cabinet that he had decided to resign. George III wanted to rescue the premier with a dissolution of parliament, but it was clear that this would simply increase political instability. Concern mounted about the effect of Addington's resignation on the king. Many commentators predicted a serious mental breakdown and a regency, with power passing to Fox and the Prince of Wales. According to Charles Abbot,

> The king is earnest to do for Mr Addington everything and more that he can desire or may choose to accept, but to belong to any new arrangement, Mr Addington is resolved not to consent . . . Mr Addington said that the king dreaded his closet being forced: there was no want of zeal or honourable attachment or fidelity to the support of his present Ministers, but a want of confidence in the success of the contest, according to the king's view of the state of affairs.

Preferring not to risk further turmoil by clinging to office, aware of opinion in the country and in parliament, and realizing that the war would continue to make unwelcome demands on him if he stayed, Addington gave way to Pitt.[54]

Pitt, of course, had been waiting for this opportunity with a mixture of eagerness and caution, concerned both to maintain his reputation for integrity and patriotism and to place no obstacles in the way of a return to the premiership. Addington was offended by his manoeuvres and initially sought to resist, Grenvillites criticized him for failing to attack ministers more decisively, and Fox and Grey sought an alliance with Grenville through such intermediaries as Fitzwilliam (now reconciled to Fox after a long separation). Fox and Grey hoped to prevent Pitt's return. If they failed they wanted at least to promote the formation of a coalition government in which Pitt would have to share power, and this was also the aim of Grenville and Windham. Genuinely concerned about the condition of Britain's defences, Pitt believed that the struggle against France was even more alarming than before because the danger of invasion was greater. This was an issue, more-over, that he could turn to personal advantage. By the spring of 1804 he was determined to force ministers to resign. They were incompetent, he thought, and there must be a change, but Pitt would not consider joining a new ministry without being at its head. Whatever the likely advantages of coalition government, he upheld the king's free choice in the appointment of men to replace Addington's ministry. So when Grenville visited Walmer to reiterate his wish for an inclusive cabinet, led by Pitt but bringing in at least Grey and the second Earl of Moira (an associate of the Prince of Wales) from opposition, Pitt said that membership of a new administration would have to depend on the king's approval.[55]

When Addington resigned Pitt did talk of forming a government of national unity including his own adherents, Addingtonians (without their chief), Grenville, and even Fox. Pitt was convinced that such an adminis-tration could win public approval at home and put together an anti-French league in Europe. Coalition was also the best way of sidelining the Catholic question. If the cabinet mixed together opponents and supporters of em-ancipation, the former could check the latter. Pitt used these arguments in his dealings with other political leaders. As expected, however, George III would not admit Fox. As well as personal animosity there was still the obvious difficulty about emancipation, and the king considered that the war effort could hardly benefit from the appointment of one who had been so outspoken an advocate of peace. At first Pitt dealt with the king through Lord Eldon, and George Rose reported that Eldon, along with Hawkesbury, strengthened the royal determination not to accept Fox. Pitt explained why it was necessary to approach Fox as well as Grenville, and the king eventually agreed that Grenville and his followers could be admitted, and some Foxites, but not Fox himself. Although Fox accepted this, and said that he would not object if any of his friends chose to work with Pitt, they refused to serve without him. George III had also stipulated that several members of Addington's cabinet ought to be allowed to remain in place. Rose observed that it would be 'a desperate undertaking' if Pitt formed a government that consisted primarily of men who had served under Addington. Pittites had been ridiculing the late administration for many months, and the inclusion in its successor of Addington's colleagues would make Pitt highly vulnerable. The Prince of Wales and his Carlton House interest had been getting stronger, not least because of the king's advanced age and frequent aberrations of mind, and if George III should die, Rose had no doubt that power would pass to Fox, 'and the recent transaction and intercourse with him will have a considerable effect in lessening the prejudices in the public mind against him'.

Pitt may not have been genuine about making an offer to Fox; his intention could have been to drive a wedge between Fox and the Grenvillites. In fact Pitt's return to the premiership drew Foxites and Grenvillites closer together. Fox and Grenville had increasingly been acting in concert, though Fox was hard pressed to convince some of his friends of the wisdom of this collaboration and his reputation suffered (as with the Fox-North union of 1783, his willingness to join a former enemy led many to question his consistency and principles). Grenville had his own reasons for breaking with Pitt, and he refused to join the new administration because with Fox excluded it could not be the broad coalition he wanted. His decision to stay in opposition with Fox was puzzling in some respects, for Fox wanted peace while Grenville's call for coalition government was rooted in the belief that the war must be supported by all the main parliamentary groups. But Grenville was influenced by senior members of his connection, who declared themselves against any principle of exclusion, and Grenville may have thought that abandoning Fox would be dishonourable. On behalf of himself and his party, Grenville wrote to Pitt on 8 May 1804:

> It is unnecessary to dwell on the mischiefs which have already resulted from placing the great offices of Government in weak and incapable hands. We see no hope of any effectual remedy for these mischiefs but by uniting in the public service as large a proportion as possible of the weight, talents, and character to be found in public men of all descriptions, and without any exception. This opinion I have already had occasion to express to you ... and we have for some time past been publicly acting in conformity to it; nor can we, while we remain impressed with this persuasion, concur in defeating an object for which the circumstances of the present moment afford at once so strong an inducement, and so favourable an occasion.[56]

The Duke of Richmond summed up the view of many outside observers when he stressed that the new administration had to be established upon 'the *broadest basis*'. When this did not happen, Richmond blamed Pitt. Having been removed from the cabinet in 1795, Richmond had become increasingly dissatisfied with Pitt's public conduct. To his nephew Charles Lennox, MP for Sussex, on 12 June 1804, Richmond wrote that Pitt would never agree to share power in an inclusive ministry because he was too dictatorial. Pitt saw that he would not be able to dominate the cabinet if it contained all the senior men of influence. He agreed to serve without Fox, knowing that he could thereby determine the composition of the next government. Pitt selfishly went back on a general understanding that it would be a coalition, Richmond alleged, and this was precisely the understanding that had prompted followers of Pitt, Grenville and Fox to vote together and oust Addington. While Grenville took a correct and dignified line, refusing to serve with Pitt unless cabinet posts were made available to Fox and his associates, Pitt insisted that the king's wishes had to be respected. There was nothing to be done, Pitt claimed, if George III refused to appoint Fox. Richmond found this a weak excuse.

> He knows that the king is as averse to him as to Mr Fox, that if the king were allowed to use his prerogative of nominating a minister after his own choice it would be Mr Addington not Mr Pitt, that the king strongly objected to Lord Melville and yet Mr Pitt would not give way to that objection and consequently did force the king in that respect. Mr Pitt cannot therefore pretend that to have stood out for Mr Fox as he did for Lord Melville would have been more an infringement on the king's choice of ministers in one case than in the other.[57]

Richmond had a point, though his premise that Pitt joined in a general understanding about the formation of a coalition ministry was erroneous. Pitt had made no specific or detailed commitments prior to Addington's fall. Besides, it was hardly surprising that Pitt did not hold out for Fox. He cannot have welcomed the prospect of working with his adversary of twenty years' standing, and doubted that Fox's elevation to high office could greatly benefit the public interest in the long run. Pitt also had to think of what might happen if he did demand Fox's inclusion. The king would resist, any prolonged ministerial hiatus would inevitably affect domestic order and the war effort, and George III could always ask someone other than Pitt to take over as premier. Pitt did not wish to stoke up a crisis, and regarded the king's willingness to accept Grenville as a suitable compromise. Fox's admission might become possible or necessary at a later date, but Pitt would cross that bridge when he came to it, and meanwhile he thought of some compensatory gesture (perhaps Fox would undertake a special mission to Russia, for example).

Although Pitt was determined to return to the premiership, he had discovered that life out of office was not without its compensations. He spent long periods at Walmer Castle, and only infrequently attended the House of Commons (re-elected for Cambridge University at the general election of July 1802, he did not take his seat in the new parliament until 20 May 1803). His health was not good, but at least he could rest when necessary, a luxury he had not often allowed himself as prime minister before 1801. Pitt's loss of official status and salary was worrying, however, for his debts had risen and most of his creditors were demanding repayment. He had never given his personal finances much attention. Now he was forced to act, although his concern to preserve his reputation for independence, patriotism and integrity led him to decline the king's offer of financial assistance, and he did not accept the clerkship of the pells, a sinecure worth £3000 a year, when it was offered by Addington (who was subsequently attacked for giving it to his own son, Henry, in July 1802). City merchants and bankers raised £100,000, which Pitt also refused, but he did accept a loan arranged by close friends and supporters, and made money by selling the gifts he had received from corporate bodies and foreign governments. He sold his interest in the reversion of his mother's pension (she died in April 1803) and the parliamentary grant to the earldom of Chatham (his brother had no children). The sale of Holwood House in 1802 raised £15,000, of which £11,000 had to be repaid in mortgages (thereafter, when in London, Pitt lived in rented accommodation). Relative penury does not seem greatly to have bothered him. He was often a guest at friends' residences, and in the summer of 1803 his household at Walmer Castle expanded with the arrival of his niece, Lady Hester Stanhope, who began to act as his housekeeper and hostess, and her brothers (their father, the third Earl Stanhope, was a strict but neglectful parent, and Hester in particular was a favourite of Pitt's mother Lady Chatham; lively and forthright, she had for a time been courted by Pitt's eccentric relative Thomas Pitt, second Baron Camelford). Despite his bouts of illness, and the times when he chose to cut himself off, Pitt enjoyed the less hectic pace of life, welcomed the chance to relax and socialize, and happily pursued his hobby of landscape gardening at Walmer.[58]

Nevertheless, the king's invitation to return in May 1804 was deeply satisfying. It was unfortunate that some of the men Pitt had intended to include in his ministry could not be brought in, though only time would prove how serious a problem this was. The new administration combined Pitt's remaining associates with men who had served in Addington's cabinet. It seemed at the outset to have several advantages: Pitt's prestige, competent men in key departments, no division on Catholic emancipation, and the goodwill of backbench MPs who still respected Pitt and regarded Fox and the Grenvillites as self-seeking schemers. In the cabinet only a minority could be classed as firm Pittites, but they had the more influential offices. Lord Harrowby, who (as Dudley Ryder) had previously been one of Pitt's chief assistants in the Commons, was foreign secretary, and Pitt's old friend Camden secretary for war and the colonies, the two most important posts for running the war with Pitt. On the other hand, Pitt's restricted choice prompted the inclusion of more Addingtonians than he wanted, and there were time-consuming arguments about appointments to junior posts. The Marquess of Buckingham welcomed the confusion, with the king indisposed (some said deranged), great surprise and much complaint as government appointments were announced, and the likelihood that Pitt's administration would be very weak indeed. 'Under all these circumstances,' he wrote to Grenville, 'you will not wonder that our new Ministers should look very blank, and that they have found great difficulties in filling their vacancies ... God knows it is gloomy enough.'[59]

The survivors from Addington's cabinet were Westmorland (lord privy seal), Chatham (master general of the ordnance), Eldon (lord chancellor), Portland (lord president), Castlereagh (president of the board of control) and Hawkesbury (Addington's foreign secretary, now moved to the home office). Unable to include Grenville and his connection, Pitt filled the gaps with the third Baron Mulgrave (chancellor of the duchy of Lancaster) and the third Duke of Montrose (president of the board of trade). Both were Pitt's friends, but as with some of the other ministers, questions could be asked of their influence, ability and experience. Indeed, George Rose noted the lack of strong speakers in the Commons, and wondered whether, in a parliament elected under Addington, the new government would have a secure majority. There were other early problems. Harrowby and Camden, for example, admitted that they did not quite feel up to their new responsibilities. This may have suited Pitt. He intended to direct the war and had to make sure that the ministers most involved in war management were friends he could dominate. But to appoint them to such important positions, despite their own misgivings, was not the best way to convince observers of the cabinet's talent and reliability.

In Pitt's defence, it must be stressed again that his choice was limited. Only five members of his second ministry had served in the first. The most senior of these were Melville, now first lord of the admiralty, who was under increasing pressure from the ongoing naval inquiry, and Portland, who was old and unwell. Pitt's difficulties were made even clearer by his need to turn to the relatively untested Mulgrave and Montrose, and neither Hawkesbury nor Westmorland had been in his original plan for cabinet appointments. Among the leading ministers only Castlereagh sat in the Commons with Pitt. He was a poor speaker and Pitt relied all the more for debating support on the ambitious Canning, who accepted the treasurership of the navy (outside the cabinet) despite his fervent belief that the government should have united Pittites with Grenvillites rather than Addingtonians. For Addington and his followers Canning had been unable to conceal his contempt, and Canning's continuing insults almost led to his early dismissal (June 1804) when Hawkesbury and others protested to Pitt. That Canning's friends Granville Leveson Gower and Viscount Morpeth decided not to join the ministry illustrates Pitt's failure to attract young men of promise to the government's side. This had been one of his main assets as premier before 1801, but illness and irregular attendance in the Commons meant that he had not subsequently been able to cultivate a new crop of talented individuals. In addition, such individuals were cautious about siding with an administration that might not last. Pitt tried to put a brave face on things. On 12 May 1804 he informed Bathurst (who joined the cabinet as master of the mint): 'My arrangements are completed with respect to principal offices ... The seats at Boards, and offices out of the Cabinet, are also very nearly settled. The appearances of difficulty have diminished every day, and I think we shall on the whole start with a very fair prospect.'

Foxites, meanwhile, were confident that Pitt would not have the upper hand for long. Though they lamented his return as prime minister, they knew that the king preferred Addington. They also saw that if George III's affliction continued, a regency – and their own rise to power – would be unstoppable. The Foxite MP for Thetford, Thomas Creevey, wrote on 2 June:

> I think, considering we have certainly been out-jockeyed by the villain Pitt, we are doing famously. Pitt is in a damnable dilemma; his character has received a cursed blow from the appearance of puzzle in his late conduct, from the wretched farce of ... turning out Addington and keeping those who were worse than him; and from his having produced no military plans yet, after all his anathemas against the late ministers for their delay. The country, I now firmly believe, was tired of Pitt and even of the Court, and conceived some new men and councils, and above all a union of all great men, was a necessary experiment for the situation. Pitt has disappointed this wish and expectation, and has shown no necessity that has compelled him so to do. He has all the air of having acted a rapacious, selfish, shabby part; he is surrounded by shabby partisans; in comparison with his own relations, the Grenvilles, he is degraded; he has no novelty to recommend him; his Master (the king) is on the wane, and to a certain extent is evidently hostile to him.

Despite Pitt's optimism, in its early months his second government was not in a strong position. Its standing remained doubtful as a result of some close divisions on the Additional Force Bill, designed to expand the regular army. Foxites, Grenvillites and Addingtonians all voted against it (ministers won the crucial division in the Commons, on 18 June, by 265 to 223 votes – Pitt was fortunate that habitual supporters of government switched quite

quickly from Addington). The militia was to be reduced from 70,000 to
48,000 men, and the 'army of reserve' expanded to 79,000, of whom 13,000
would be transferred to the regular army each year and be replaced by new
recruits. The unpopular ballot system was discontinued. Bounties were
offered to assist recruitment, and local officials were made responsible for
meeting parish quotas. Pitt's new system was condemned by several military
experts, including Richmond, who had argued with Pitt in 1798 on defence
matters relating to the status and authority of the lord lieutenant of Ireland.
Now Richmond spoke against the Additional Force Bill in the House of
Lords, and subsequently wrote a pamphlet, *Thoughts on the National Defence*.
In attacking Pitt's policy some commentators exploited the traditional aversion to a standing army; they affected to believe that he meant his system
to be permanent. Continuing opposition, a failure to comply with the new
regulations and various practical difficulties prompted Pitt to alter the policy
in March 1805.[60]

George III offered Pitt little help, and (as Creevey and many others
suspected) their relationship was not what it had been. In May 1804 George
III turned to Pitt because he had to, not because he wanted to. The king
deeply regretted Addington's resignation, and, though he still respected
Pitt, he was unwilling to do all that Pitt advised in order to strengthen the
new administration. No Foxites could be appointed, for they were not
prepared to serve without their leader, and the king only agreed to accept
Grenville after protracted argument, which proved futile because Grenville
would not co-operate while Fox was excluded. Pitt desperately tried to win
the king's favour. He carefully explained why he had considered it his
public duty to turn against Addington's ministry. He promised not to raise
the Catholic question, and accepted that Fox was *persona non grata*. But
since resigning in 1801 Pitt had rarely communicated with George III, and
the two had not met at all. Although the king had initially expressed a
wish that they should continue to meet, Pitt preferred not to risk his
reputation for independence and did not want to be accused of using
'secret influence'. Now, in the spring of 1804, Pitt was unable to effect a
rapprochement. George III resisted or ignored many of Pitt's patronage
requests, and the evident lack of firm royal support was a serious blow to
the government. There was a ray of hope in that the king's advancing years
and mental unsteadiness might limit his capacity to inconvenience ministers.
This offered little comfort, however, when Pitt reflected that the stability
of his previous administration had depended greatly on royal favour. He
and his associates thought of approaching the Prince of Wales. Talks began
with the prince's allies, and it was suggested that room could be found for
them in the government.

In the autumn of 1804 and again during the early months of 1805 Pitt tried to improve relations between George III and the heir to the throne. Little was achieved by these manoeuvres, and Pitt chose not to take them further in case he unsettled the king's mind. George III continued to make trouble. In February 1805 Bathurst wrote of

> the bad effects which the constant interference of the king in the distribution of patronage must produce to any Government ... All this was to be foreseen. He has, as all kings must have, a natural inclination for it. During Addington's Administration he became accustomed to it, and illness has left him more eager to oblige, and more impatient of resistance. It requires great management to oppose this, and management of this sort is what Pitt's virtues and infirmities peculiarly disqualify him.

Bathurst noted the king's determination to gratify his favourites, including Addingtonians: 'A person very near him lamented to me a few days ago the embarrassments which the king's desire of obliging those he was in the habit of seeing must soon produce.' George III also wanted to punish previous acts of disloyalty (as he saw them). Shortly after Pitt's return to the premiership, the second Baron Amherst was removed from the royal household because he had not assisted Addington's ministry to withstand pressure in the House of Lords. (As well as being Pitt's friend, Amherst was probably conscious of an obligation to Pitt because his uncle, the first Baron Amherst, had been commander-in-chief of the army with a seat in Pitt's cabinet from 1793 to 1795.) Richmond thought that George III's attitude added considerably to Pitt's misfortunes. The premier, he wrote, lacked

> the influence with the king and the power without which no Minister can serve the country as he ought, since not only he could not carry Mr Fox's appointment, but meets with perpetual contradictions and slights in his other recommendations, and even his friend Lord Amherst turned out for voting with him ... So that in fact Mr Pitt is acting as Minister forced upon the king by the votes of Parliament against Mr Addington's measures in which the Grenvilles and Mr Fox and his friends had a considerable share, and remains so without their support and without the confidence or goodwill of the king.

Pitt did his best to keep up appearances. He was worried about the king's health and rued his unwillingness to co-operate on men and measures, but to parliament and nation the prime minister had to present an air of confidence. This was not very convincing. In September 1804, for example, Pitt and his colleagues regularly visited the king at Weymouth, and as Buckingham reported to Grenville: 'Pitt has taken care that his three Secretaries should relieve each other, so that the king never has been unwatched for more than three days.' It was rumoured that Pitt intended to keep George III in seclusion, in order to enhance his own position and prevent anyone else from finding out how sick the king really was. Indeed, the Prince of Wales complained in June 1804 that neither privy council nor parliament had been kept properly informed of the king's condition, and that ministers had assumed an entirely inappropriate authority over the king's treatment.[61]

With George III withholding his full confidence, Fox excluded, Grenville aloof and Addington offended, Pitt's influence at court and in parliament was limited. He found it impossible to form the strong government he wanted. Although his first cabinet in 1783 had also been vulnerable, this time Pitt lacked the youthful energy and determination to change things. Illness affected his ability to lead, to speak effectively in debates, and to get through business. For several years exhaustion and disappointment had been taking their toll. By the late 1790s he bore the physical signs of sickness and fatigue, and when he returned to the Commons after a long absence in May 1803, Thomas Creevey wrote:

> I really think Pitt is done; his face is no longer red, but yellow; his looks are dejected; his countenance I think much changed and fallen, and every now and then he gives a hollow cough. Upon my soul, hating him as I do, I am almost moved to pity to see his fallen greatness.

Pitt's health would only deteriorate further as war worries and the pressure of public affairs increased. He began to drink more heavily. Those around him noted his relative isolation and stoical frame of mind. In July 1804 Wilberforce found Pitt 'not in spirits', and remarked that there was simply not enough time available for him to do all that he wanted. The prime minister would arrange to meet people, but often they would arrive, wait an hour, and even then have to leave without seeing him because he was too busy. Frequently Pitt was downcast. Some of his closest friends were dead; with others he had little contact. Cabinet colleagues and junior office-holders respected him, but in the circumstances of the time their tendency to put him on a pedestal, combined with his own detached and imperious demeanour, made him seem even more remote. As premier, Pitt regularly consulted the most efficient men of business in the government, Hawkesbury and Castlereagh (who took over as war secretary in June 1805), but he never formed with them the dominant triumvirate he had forged with Grenville and Dundas. Grenville was now in opposition, and Pitt and Melville were not as intimate as they had been (according to Wilberforce 'they were scarcely on speaking terms').

When Pitt needed to retreat from public affairs there was Walmer Castle and his young Stanhope relatives, and dinners or other social gatherings.

But on the whole he had no genuine respite from pressure. Paradoxically, this may have made him even more resolute. His pride took over. He bravely struggled against adversity, determined to overcome the government's problems. Hence his defiant response to Grenville's decision not to join the cabinet. As Eldon later wrote: 'I recollect Mr Pitt saying, with some indignation, he would teach that proud man that in the service and with the confidence of the king, he could do without him, though he thought his health such that it might cost him his life.' Pitt's prediction about the price to be paid was most instructive.⁶²

Politics had changed since the 1790s. Pitt could no longer depend on the sense of patriotic duty that had been a force for unity in his previous administration. The new ministers proved unable to work together, and in June 1804 their Commons majority was not much bigger than Addington's before his fall. Pitt refused to resign and insisted that he would continue to serve while he had royal approval. As he told the Commons on 18 June (when speaking of the Additional Force Bill):

> If the present bill should be lost, I shall be sorry for it, because the house and the country will thereby lose a good measure; but the honourable gentlemen opposite will be much mistaken if they think they will be any nearer getting rid of me. It is well known, and has ever been allowed to be one of the first and most established privileges and prerogatives of the crown, that his Majesty has a right to choose and nominate his own ministers.

Many MPs sympathized with this position, though they soon realized that Pitt was not the strong and energetic leader of former days. Opposition pressure was unremitting, while Pittites resented the presence of Addingtonians in the cabinet and the prospect that Addington himself (still a favourite of George III) might in due course be invited to join the ministry.⁶³

Nevertheless, there were some modest successes during 1804. The Additional Force Act facilitated military recruitment (though not as much as Pitt had hoped), arrears in the civil list were covered, more items of public expenditure were transferred from the civil list to the consolidated fund, and Pitt continued his efforts to improve treasury procedures in order to save money and raise efficiency. After Addington's appointment to the cabinet early in 1805 the government's majority was more impressive: opposition motions were defeated by margins of 207 votes on 12 February, 146 on 21 February, and 140 on 6 March. Promising advances were made in the war. Pitt's was a more active and ambitious approach than that of his predecessor, and during June and July 1804 he began to negotiate a coalition with Russia, Austria, Prussia and Sweden. He also decided on a bold strike against Spain, for the Spanish were building up their navy and, by paying subsidies to France, contributing to Napoleon's strength. Spain reacted to British aggression by declaring war in December 1804, by which time Russian envoys were in London to conclude an alliance. Buoyant trade and an increased yield from income tax (re-imposed and improved by Addington in June 1803) helped Pitt by making money available for increased subsidies to Russia and other foreign powers.

At this point Pitt was also hoping to promote collective security for the future. He had been developing this idea since the mid-1780s, discussed a detailed scheme with Grenville in 1798, and now consulted such colleagues as Mulgrave (who succeeded Harrowby as foreign secretary in January 1805) before presenting his proposals to the Russians. Pitt wanted to establish a protective line of buffer states between the great powers: Austria would back Piedmont in Italy, Holland would back Prussia in Belgium, and there would be territorial adjustments to facilitate this, with rival interests carefully balanced to remove the jealousies that had previously caused conflict. France would be confined to the frontiers of 1793.

Pitt was willing to give up most of Britain's conquests in order to create a favourable context for negotiation (retaining only Malta or Minorca and the Cape of Good Hope), and as in his earlier security plans he treated restoration of the French monarchy as desirable but not essential. After the failure of peace talks late in 1797 Pitt had envisaged a future settlement organized around the quadruple alliance of Britain, Austria, Prussia and Russia. The plan of 1805 was also based on this alliance. Smaller states would be drawn in, Pitt hoped, and a system of mutual defence would develop as all participants agreed to recognize each other's rights and repress any attempt to break the peace. The scheme offered much, but whether the great powers would each accept it in its entirety was another matter, and in any case Pitt's vision was less relevant in the short term than the task of wining the war against Napoleon.[64]

Pitt's fundamental problem at home was the fragmentation of the ministerial team and body of support upon which he had formerly relied. One of the few figures of long cabinet experience, apart from Pitt, was Melville, and the prime minister was dismayed by the report submitted in February 1805 by the committee of naval inquiry because it made serious allegations against Melville relating to his period as treasurer of the navy. Pitt knew that Addingtonians aimed to use the report to vindicate their naval policy, and that if he shielded Melville they would turn completely against the government. Melville was vulnerable because he had failed to ensure that officials in his department maintained a strict distinction between public and private money. Pitt's enemies chose to accuse Melville not of negligence, however, but of corruption. Samuel Whitbread, who led the pro-reform wing of opposition MPs, pressed for impeachment, and the necessary motion of censure was carried on 8 April 1805 (on the casting vote of Speaker Abbot, whose sympathies were Addingtonian). Wilberforce had strongly backed the motion, preaching moral rectitude and swaying many votes in the process, but Pitt was ill and had not spoken well. When the Commons division went against his old friend, he slumped into his place on the government front bench, tears trickling down his cheeks. But soon he was fighting to recover the initiative. The record of his previous premiership was at stake, after all, as well as Melville's reputation.

In fact there was some questioning of Pitt's own conduct. It was discovered that in 1796 he had used navy funds to pay an advance to contractors for a public loan. He was forced to admit responsibility for this irregularity, and pleaded national necessity. Parliament passed a bill of indemnity without much fuss. But Melville could not be spared. Though Pitt did not believe that Melville had engaged in corrupt behaviour ('Pitt says he is quite sure that there was no real pocketing of public money in him', wrote Wilberforce), he accepted that his colleague had to leave office. Melville resigned from the government on 9 April and from the privy council in May. Pitt gained time by referring the allegations to a Commons committee. Impeachment proceedings subsequently failed in the Lords, but the loss of Melville weakened Pitt's administration and the prime minister suffered personally as well as politically. Melville was still a valued associate. This was also a matter of parliamentary arithmetic. Melville had been the dominant political manager in Scotland, and controlled a reliable Pittite voting bloc. When Pitt returned as premier in May 1804 he had a Commons majority of about forty. The fact that his followers included thirty-eight Scottish MPs indicates the importance of Melville's patronage networks.

According to Wilberforce, Pitt was greatly annoyed and felt tainted by the Melville scandal. Yet he chose not to abandon his colleague. Though he and Melville were no longer very close, and he had cause to think that Melville had abused his confidence (there had previously been rumours about the misappropriation of public funds, and Melville had assured Pitt that such talk was groundless), he could not regard Melville as a criminal. Pitt's own virtue and sense of loyalty forced him to stand up for Melville. 'In truth,' thought Wilberforce, 'Pitt was chiefly led into supporting Melville by that false principle of honour, which was his great fault – he fancied himself bound in honour to defend one who had so long acted with him.' Windham, now in opposition, welcomed Melville's fall. In Windham's opinion Melville had been a cynical manipulator of patronage who had long winked at corruption and used any underhand means available to increase his influence and shore up Pitt's regime. Now that he was gone it was possible for politics to enter a new and better age.[65]

Outdoor support for Pitt's ministry declined. Respectable opinion took a dim view of corruption in public life, and some Whigs and radicals used the Melville affair to organize public meetings and press for reforms. Anti-corruption campaigners remembered Pitt's much-vaunted creed of probity and hard work during the 1780s. The Melville affair suggested that administrative and financial improvements had not been carried far enough. Pitt might be honest, it was argued, but what about others who exercised power with him? The size and cost of government rose enormously during the war, and this expansion of the 'fiscal-military state' seemed to offer the elite more opportunities for selfish gain. After the Melville affair the critique of 'Old Corruption' gradually revived, and Pitt was reproached for the cautious manner in which he had pursued economical reform. By July 1805 Addingtonians had made plain their intention to take up the issue of purity in government, and as Fox told Windham:

> I find the Addingtonians are quite ready for open war, and I think they should be encouraged. Their public ground, I mean that of Pitt's systematic protection of delinquents and defence of jobs, is certainly good, and from an odd concurrence of circumstances they are stronger than anyone could suppose such men to be.[66]

The Melville affair soured relations between Pittites and Addingtonians, increasing Pitt's fear that agreement on war policy would be impossible. Fox and Grenville took advantage by proposing that parliament should reconsider the Catholic question. Pitt adhered to the position he had taken in 1801. Though he thought that the legislative union made emancipation less risky (especially if proper safeguards were provided for the Established Church), he maintained that circumstances did not favour the change. He did not think that the matter should be brought before parliament, and considered it his duty to resist any such move. Agitation would serve no useful purpose, indeed, for emancipation could not possibly gain parliament's approval. Debates would simply 'revive those dissensions which we wish to extinguish' and 'awaken all that warmth and acrimony of discussion which has heretofore prevailed'. It was also important to consider public opinion, and Pitt argued that government had to do what was most advantageous to the nation as a whole, not take up measures that were desired only by a part.

Motions for the examination of Catholic claims were defeated in the Lords on 13 May 1805 (by 178 to 49 votes), and in the Commons on 14 May (by 336 to 124 votes), but Pitt saw that he could not control business as in the past and that it would be dangerous to take backbench approval for granted.[67] The willingness of Foxites and Grenvillites to act together disturbed him, as did divisions within the cabinet. Arguments, jealousy, threats of resignation, absences through illness, doubts about the war and concern about the king's health made this administration seem constantly to be at sixes and sevens. Pitt had thought of offering a place in the cabinet to the Prince of Wales's friend Moira. Melville told the prime minister in November 1804 that, although enmity between George III and the prince had not mattered much to Pitt's previous administration, if unchecked it would certainly damage the stability and authority of the new one. Some form of reconciliation, on the other hand, would greatly assist the government abroad as well as at home.

> I do not mean to say that we may not, while the king lives, and is in health, keep our majorities in both Houses of Parliament, and by having recourse to extra measures, even add considerably to it, but that is a very superficial way of considering the subject. Unless a large and powerful party of great property and talents acting under the heir apparent as their head can be dissolved, it is in vain to look for a strong Government in any beneficial sense of the expression. There is more than one way in which you can with ease make room for Lord Moira in the Cabinet ... If Lord Moira was speedily placed there, and known to be so with the concurrence of the Prince, the cabal is at an end; and you might at will pick up from the different ingredients in Opposition any parts you pleased.

No agreement was reached, and in any case George III ruled out Moira's inclusion in the cabinet. An approach was also made to Tierney, who had served under Addington, but he would not take office, and ministers disagreed about the propriety of approaching Grenville or Fox. The only other possibility had been to apply to Addington, whose group in the Commons numbered about forty (twice as many as the Carlton House interest of the Prince of Wales). George III was eager to bring in Addington, but Pittites objected and Pitt himself insisted that Addington would have to go to the House of Lords (he wanted no competitor in the Commons). Raised to the peerage as Viscount Sidmouth, Addington joined the cabinet in January 1805, replacing Portland as lord president of the council. His associate the fourth Earl of Buckinghamshire (formerly, as Lord Hobart, secretary for war and the colonies) became chancellor of the duchy of Lancaster. Pitt explained his motives to his brother Chatham on Christmas Day 1804:

> On considering carefully the state of parties, and the nature of the opposition we have to encounter, I have satisfied myself that though we should certainly have strength enough to stand our ground, our majority would not be such as

to meet difficult questions with advantage, or to prevent much possible embarrassment to the public service, as well as uneasiness to the king's mind. Under
this impression I have felt it my duty not to let any recollection of past differences
stand in the way of recruiting, as far as possible, those whose former habits and
opinions render them most likely cordially to concur in supporting the king's
government.

Pitt originally offered only one seat in the cabinet, but had to give two
in order to finalise the deal. Some Addingtonians gained junior posts. Others
were promised that they would be considered as vacancies occurred. The
prime minister appeared to have bargained well, gaining the adherence of
Sidmouth and Buckinghamshire without appointing them to important
executive offices. As indicated above, the government's position in the
Commons improved immediately. But the alliance did not last long. Pittites
in the cabinet had wanted Grenville, not Sidmouth, and the latter added
to the tension by insisting that one of his own followers should replace
Melville as first lord of the admiralty. Sidmouth grew annoyed because Pitt
restricted the patronage available to Addingtonians while demanding their
'unconditional submission'. No effort was made to appease Sidmouth, which
led him to believe that Pitt cared little about keeping him in the
cabinet.[68]

Pitt's standing at court, meanwhile, had become even more precarious
after a serious dispute with George III in the early part of 1805. On the
death (18 January) of John Moore, Archbishop of Canterbury, Pitt nominated his former tutor and secretary George Pretyman, Bishop of Lincoln,
as Moore's successor. The king flatly rejected Pretyman, considering that
he lacked the appropriate qualities, and decided to appoint the respected
Bishop of Norwich, Charles Manners Sutton. Pitt angrily protested. He
wrote to the king on 22 January:

> It is with great reluctance that Mr Pitt at any time reverts to any proposal which
> does not appear to meet your Majesty's wishes, but he considers it on every
> account his duty not to disguise from your Majesty how much his feelings are
> wounded and his hopes of contributing to your Majesty's service impaired by
> your Majesty's apparent disregard of his recommendation ... Your Majesty's
> refusal to comply with his request can hardly be understood by himself, and will
> certainly not be understood by the public in any other light than as a decisive
> mark of your Majesty's not honouring him with that degree of weight and
> confidence which his predecessors have enjoyed, and without which your Majesty
> must be sensible how impossible it is, especially under the present circumstances,
> that he can conduct your Majesty's affairs with advantage.

George III maintained, as he had always done, that the highest positions
in the church must be reserved for the best candidates of good private

character, orthodoxy and learning. Social standing was less important to the king than these other qualities (some bishops appointed by George III were from humble backgrounds), but one thing he insisted on was that there should be no political favouritism. A candidate's loyalty to the ministry of the day, therefore, did not in the king's view merit promotion to high office in the church, and this may explain why he refused Pretyman. The result was a heated quarrel with Pitt, who by some accounts threatened to resign. George III then forestalled the prime minister by going in person to tell Manners Sutton that he would be the next Archbishop of Canterbury. This came at a bad time for Pitt. His regular supporters were complaining about the juncture with Sidmouth and the offices and emolument given to Addingtonians in return for their adhesion, and soon the Melville scandal would greatly increase Pitt's vexation. Pretyman was personally disappointed, of course, but he also predicted further difficulties for the government as a result of Pitt's dispute with George III. He remarked to George Rose on 4 February 1805: 'I entirely agree with you that this defeat may be of serious mischief on public grounds. And, indeed, I know persons of great consequence who will consider Mr Pitt's acquiescence as very uncreditable to him, and who are represented to me as waiting for the result of this struggle.' [69]

Pitt was surprised at the hostility with which his allies and supporters greeted the union with Sidmouth. Camden, Canning and Pretyman expressed strong objections to the move, as did Rose, who denied that it was necessary to increase Pitt's majority in the Commons. Addingtonians would not join Fox, reasoned Rose, and Sidmouth himself was unlikely to be fully committed to Pitt after all that had happened in recent years. Before Pitt's return to office Rose had warned about the outlook in the Commons. But by the time of Pitt's bargain with Sidmouth, Rose had changed his mind.

> Experience has shown the state of the parties more favourable to him than I foretold, because a very considerable number of Mr Addington's friends would not follow him into opposition ... It is under *a strong impression* that Mr Addington could not have carried ten friends with him to Mr Fox that I so deeply regret the intended arrangement, for that he would join any party in opposition to Mr Pitt I have not the slightest doubt, believing, however, that on account of the king he would not have done so *hastily*.

Harrowby argued that although a coalition seemed fine in principle, the form it took in practice was appalling. Too many offices had been given to Sidmouth's associates, and the new arrangements had not led to any improvement in the king's attitude, for he was still resisting Pitt's advice on various matters. If the juncture was to be beneficial, Harrowby thought, it had to be followed by 'some striking mark of Pitt's preponderance'. This had not happened, and rumours inevitably spread about George III's preference for Sidmouth and the possibility that the latter would soon be the effective head of the government. On 25 January 1805 the third Earl of Hardwicke (lord lieutenant of Ireland from 1801 to 1806) wrote to his half-brother Charles Yorke to warn of a cabinet split. Pitt would find himself in a minority within his own administration, Hardwicke observed, for the premier could fully depend only on Melville, Camden, Mulgrave and Montrose.

> I know the impression is that Pitt's weight with the king is diminishing, and that matters are in a very awkward state. What Lord Sidmouth can expect by encouraging such a schism I cannot imagine, for it is evident that if the king is alienated from Pitt, he must be given up to the enemy, I mean the Opposition.

Pitt's deal with Sidmouth also offended important power brokers in the provinces. He lost the support of such borough patrons as the second Marquess of Stafford (son of his former colleague Earl Gower, first Marquess of Stafford) and Viscount Lowther (later first Earl of Lonsdale). Among the MPs who followed their relatives and benefactors in turning against Pitt were J. C. Villiers, MP for Tain Burghs, James Lowther, MP for Westmorland, and John Lowther, MP for Cumberland.[70]

Another influential critic was the Earl of Carlisle. To Huskisson, who had returned to office with Pitt in the spring of 1804 and was now a secretary to the treasury, Carlisle addressed a fervent protest against the proposed alliance. If it went ahead, he complained, the king would listen to Sidmouth rather than the prime minister. Pitt would generally be seen as desperate and weak, and could gain no real benefit in terms of his Commons majority.

> Your friend putting into his fleet this condemned ship, *condemned by himself as unfit for any service,* holds out such an avowal of distress that I should never have looked for from Mr P., as Mr P. was, when I had the great satisfaction of acting, most agreeably to my inclinations, in support of his measures. I know the value of numbers, and what is gained in this moment; but it is entirely a new idea to me to suppose that you would have run so close as to make this addition of such consequence as to justify a resort to it, with all the humiliation with which it is replete. If in the first instance it adds to your side of the House, it cracks the whip to those who only wanted a consistent opportunity to show that old partialities and leanings were still alive, which will diminish the arithmetical calculation of votes so obtained. If Mr P. really can carry no measure in the Closet without its being oiled by such a hand as A.'s, and if he can make no music on the organ unless so cunning, or so favourite, a power blows the bellows, his situation is indeed lamentable, and I much fear, in the view of a Great

Personage, he who does nothing but fill the instrument with wind, will be dearer to him than the other, and held in higher consideration.[71]

Pitt was well aware of these dangers and made sure that he would not have to give the Addingtonians an equal share of power. But the expected advantages of the alliance never materialized, and Pitt soon came to admit that his friends and supporters had good reason to look upon it as a mistake. Pitt's opponents grew in confidence. As Windham wrote of the Pittite-Addingtonian merger:

All seem to think it a degradation in some sort of Mr Pitt ... For my own individual impression, and I suppose for that of others on our side, I like it much; it makes the game clear and neat. The division of parties and politics is made as it ought to be: Mr Pitt and the persons of his creation, pure and unmixed, on one side, and all the rest of the public men on the other. We have all the authors and actors in the Peace of Amiens now come together, so I hope they will continue till the great crash comes, which may make things set off again upon new principles.[72]

During the spring of 1805 Pitt decided that the pact with the Addingtonians was more trouble than it was worth. To replace Melville as first lord of the admiralty he chose the long-serving naval adviser and reformer Sir Charles Middleton, now in his eighties. 'In general politics he cannot be expected to take any share,' Pitt told the king, 'but his strength and vigour of mind seem fully equal to the business of the Department for a time.' Middleton was also raised to the peerage as Baron Barham, because 'it seems necessary that a person holding so high and responsible an office should have a seat in one of the Houses of Parliament, and his becoming a member of the House of Commons seems in this instance to be neither desirable nor practicable.' George III accepted Pitt's view, only stipulating that Barham need not attend cabinet meetings unless the navy was due for discussion. Sidmouth and his friends protested that they had been promised the next vacant office. Pitt explained that Barham's appointment would merely be temporary, but he lost patience with the Addingtonians' patronage demands and harassment of Melville. They became all the more alienated and finally resigned in June (according to Lord Buckinghamshire, 'Pitt left us no alternative but the surrender of our characters or our offices'). Pitt minimized the damage by prolonging their association with the ministry almost until the end of the parliamentary session, so that the immediate impact of their departure would be limited.[73]

Even so, the cabinet urgently required reinforcement after Sidmouth and Buckinghamshire resigned, and this led Pitt to negotiate again with Grenville, Fox and George III. Nothing was settled. The king condemned Grenville and Fox for their factious opposition. Politicians should be co-operating to win the war, he complained, not reviving controversial issues like Catholic emancipation.

To Fox, meanwhile, co-operation with Pitt was impossible: the prime minister was completely untrustworthy, his whole career depended on royal patronage, and he could never be forgiven for the events of 1783 to 1784 and the misgovernment of the 1790s. Senior Foxites and Grenvillites doubted Pitt's willingness thoroughly to reshape the government. Some of them subsequently opined that he had no choice (and that the king would agree to new arrangements). All was confusion. On 12 July 1805 Fox wrote to his friend the eighth Earl of Lauderdale:

> I now think ... that Pitt will not make any proposal to Opposition. I know that nothing ought to be consented to unless he will consider the present Ministry as annihilated in all its parts, and consult about forming a new one. He will not, I think, bring his mind to this, and yet his weakness since the defection of the Doctor [Sidmouth] is extreme.

Fox thought that there were only about 180 regular supporters of the ministry in the Commons, their number kept down by doubts about the king's health. In open opposition there were about 150 MPs, and this number would rise, Fox predicted, as the king declined and Carlton House extended its influence. Pitt's personal following amounted to about sixty MPs and was unlikely to grow in the near future. Sidmouth's group was of a similar size, noted Fox, but would probably expand if Sidmouth could show that he still had George III's favour and the Addingtonians established themselves as the party of anti-corruption.[74]

Therefore disunity, confusion and drift on the government side in parliament looked set to continue, and Pitt's leadership style made matters worse. His tactics were similar to those of the 1780s and 1790s. He did not try to impose a distinct line on his supporters, and the resulting lack of clarity proved more damaging than before, because the second Pitt administration was not as strong or secure as the first. On many questions Pitt offered no direction. He respected his supporters' freedom of opinion and trusted that the merits of the government's position would be seen without the need for party discipline. This method had occasionally broken down even before 1801. After Pitt's return to the premiership in 1804 his failure to communicate directly and regularly with backbenchers added to the government's difficulties. When no clear position was agreed or enforced, Pitt's opponents found it easier to attack him. As the Melville scandal developed in March 1805, Speaker of the Commons Charles Abbot became aware of a general puzzlement caused by Pitt's failure to respond decisively.

Pitt did not make clear how he wanted to proceed. Other members of the cabinet had no idea, and in the Commons there was 'much dissatisfaction' among government supporters, which added to the unease created by Pitt's unexpected union with Sidmouth. The alienation of Stafford, the Lowthers and others, indeed, is to be explained not only with reference to the Addingtonian alliance in particular, but also to Pitt's shortcomings as a leader. Rarely did he seek to conciliate his followers, prepare the ground properly, or clarify his aims and motives for the sake of unity. J. C. Villiers (returned in 1802 for Tain Burghs in the interest of Stafford's wife Lady Sutherland) explained to Pitt early in 1805 that he could no longer support the prime minister, owing to 'personal disregard on your part, and dissent in principle from measures'.[75]

Pitt lacked the time and energy to do more, and in any case the government side in parliament remained a loose collection of interests that probably would not have responded well had the premier tried to lead it as a coherent party. Such routine organizational tasks, moreover, were beneath the virtuous patriotic statesman and did not accord with Pitt's self-image. Nevertheless, as in the 1780s and 1790s, he did have to involve himself in the dispensing of patronage. He tried to make effective use of the available titles, offices, preferment and other favours at the government's disposal, recognizing loyalty, encouraging supporters, and attempting to win over former opponents. His main effort in this area was the juncture with Addingtonians, but it did not last and the government gained no real addition of strength. Even in his heyday Pitt's patronage capabilities, so essential to the longevity and power of his first government, had not been great, though there was sufficient 'pasture', as it was called, to satisfy many of the most influential applicants. But now there was a limit to what George III was able and willing to do for him, he had lost touch with networks of influence in the localities, and the administrative and financial reforms of recent times had removed former patronage options.

There was also a broader problem. Pitt knew that he was in a weaker position than before, and so did everyone else. His authority in the cabinet and parliament, therefore, could be more easily challenged and undermined. This made it more difficult for him to attract support, to supervise the government's activities, and to get his measures passed and implemented. Pitt's troubles increased as a result of his inability to make bargains. Critics insisted that he could not provide vigorous leadership or prosecute the war, and that he would not survive as premier. The king's failing health was important too. Though George III had been reluctant to take him back in May 1804, Pitt was preferable to Fox and Grenville, and before 1801 the king had worked well with Pitt as his chief minister. Now Pitt's allies and opponents alike saw that, if the king died, a prop that had sustained Pitt throughout his career would be removed. The premier's position also seemed shaky as a result of crucial defeats in the Commons, most notably on the censure motion against Melville in April 1805. These problems made a shrewd employment of patronage all the more vital.

Pitt had to resort to threats. He made it clear that patronage would be withheld from those who did not do as they were told. In June 1804 Sir Evan Nepean, the Irish chief secretary, noted Pitt's readiness to dismiss any office-holder who failed actively and openly to support his administration: 'he will not be trifled with by those who hold employments under the crown or are expecting favours from government'. But, however much he tried, Pitt could not get his way as often as he had before 1801. Now, when he made plans to assist the government, those affected felt able to object and oppose. In October 1805 Pitt wanted an Irish borough seat, Cashel, for his supporter Lord Fitzharris. The sitting MP William Wickham (formerly a senior member of the Irish administration) refused to vacate the seat, and in this had the approval of Lord Grenville, who wrote:

> In above twenty years of political life I never knew an instance where a person chosen for a Government seat, or chosen for a private seat in consequence of any Government arrangement made under one Administration, was called upon to resign that seat under any succeeding Administration; much less where such a call was complied with.

Problems of leadership were complicated by the war. Rapid decisions were needed as news arrived of important developments abroad, but it was not always possible speedily to get the cabinet together, consult the king, and agree on an appropriate response. Knowing that delay in these cases would be harmful, Pitt's natural inclination was to take immediate action and inform cabinet colleagues and George III after the event. Yet this was to risk a confrontation that could only reinforce the impression that there was little teamwork or cohesion at the highest levels of policy-making. Reluctant as he was to allow the government to appear disorganized, Pitt continued to take decisions without waiting for the cabinet to meet or for the king's consent to be obtained (as in September 1804, when he issued instructions concerning a naval operation off Ferrol).[76]

Pitt's attempt to strengthen the cabinet after the resignations of Sidmouth and Buckinghamshire faltered when the king refused to accept Grenville as well as Fox. Pitt had been hoping to restore ties with Grenville and his connection, and was anxious to recruit stronger debaters in the Commons. But after a fruitless meeting with George III in September 1805 he lost heart, and was unable to revive the negotiation for fear of upsetting the king. The best he could do was to expand the cabinet. He proposed to bring in Canning, the treasurer of the navy, and Charles Yorke (who had served under Addington but remained well disposed towards Pitt and had shown himself to be a competent minister). This did not really promise to fortify the ministry as required, but at least Canning and Yorke would add debating talent to the government's front bench in the Commons. Nor did Pitt give up entirely on Grenville. After meeting the king Pitt reported to Bathurst on 27 September:

> The resolution seems decidedly taken to risk all chances rather than consent (before the moment of actual necessity) to take any step towards a junction of any sort with the Opposition. The objections seem now to be as deeply rooted against Grenville as even against Fox; which was certainly by no means the case some time ago ... I should not, however, despair of overcoming this sentiment (as far as relates to Grenville and his friends) if the scene opening on the continent should lead (as is perhaps possible) to his taking a different line on foreign politics from the other branch of Opposition; but this is so doubtful a chance that one cannot at all count upon it; and we must therefore prepare to fight the best battle we can with our own strength.

With respect to further changes in cabinet personnel, therefore, Pitt's only option was to wait and see if external events created a better opportunity for negotiating with the king and Grenville.[77]

Despite his ill health, disappointments and lassitude, Pitt continued to work for a major breakthrough in the war, which he believed would make him better able to improve his position as premier and attract support for the government. Pitt's predilection for comprehensive solutions to complex questions was undiminished, and his scheme for collective security (as the basis for a general European peace after the war) was put to the Russians early in 1805. Napoleon had to be defeated before the future of Europe could be settled, however, and Pitt continued his efforts (commenced in the summer of 1804) to persuade Russia to join a formal military coalition. Although the Russians resented Britain's naval pre-eminence and retention of Malta, fortunately for Pitt they and the Austrians were far more worried about French expansion in Italy. In April 1805 Pitt concluded an alliance with Russia, and Austria joined the coalition in August. Sweden also agreed to side with the allies, and with this foursome in place it seemed that Pitt's labours had finally paid off. Lord Malmesbury commented:

> During the whole of the year Pitt was negotiating his great alliance with Russia and Austria ... Never was any measure, so far as human foresight can go, better combined or better negotiated ... Pitt, whom I saw in Downing Street on 26 September, gave me a most minute and clear account of this whole measure, and was very justly sanguine as to its result.

Pitt's commitment to continental operations and an anti-French combination of powers remained the basis of British strategy. But the key was Britain's relationship with Russia, and this continued to be blighted by rivalry and mistrust. Pitt's alliance with the Russians took a great deal of time and effort to arrange precisely because there were reservations on both sides, and the two powers were only pushed together by French aggression. This phase of the conflict against France, the 'War of the Third Coalition' (the second had broken up in 1801), lasted from 1805 until 1807. The initiative did not lie with Pitt. Though he longed for a decisive allied victory in the field, he realized that Britain lacked the military resources to influence Russian and Austrian planners. His main input was money. He paid out large subsidies to the allies, and offered money to several other states too, while Britain's contribution of men and materiel remained modest. Indeed, Pitt's success in enlarging the volunteer movement for home defence may have inhibited the growth of the regular army. Addington's government had tried and failed to create a large pool of reserves to supplement the army, and Pitt's Additional Force Acts of 1804 and 1805 failed greatly to improve the situation. Recruitment drives only produced about half of the expected number of men. In turn, there was more pressure on the militia to provide recruits for active service abroad. Before long the secretary for war, Castlereagh, was pointing to serious under-manning at home and in the colonies. Pitt's policy was flawed because he did not fully appreciate that manpower was limited. He was convinced that some districts, especially in the countryside, had not yet provided their fair share of recruits – in other words, that substantial new recruiting grounds were available. In this he was mistaken.[78]

Hoping to bring Prussia into the coalition, Pitt sent Harrowby to Berlin in October 1805. He also planned to build up British and mercenary forces in northern Germany to co-operate with the allies. Malmesbury spoke to Pitt in November 1805 and was struck by his growing confidence.[79] News of the great British naval victory at Trafalgar on 21 October 1805 further encouraged Pitt. He urged Britain's coalition partners to be bolder, but Austrian forces surrendered at Ulm on 20 October, and Napoleon reached Vienna on 14 November. Pitt's spirits sank. He had trouble sleeping. Anxiously calling on Prussia to join the coalition, he offered more and more money (far more than he planned) only to find that the Prussians wanted Hanover in return for their help. Pitt was not the only prominent politician to believe that a deal should be done with Prussia.[80] Canning, on the other hand, considered the Prussians untrustworthy. He also argued that rather than focus on northern Germany, allied efforts would be better directed against the poorly defended Belgian and Dutch coasts. In any case

Pitt could not possibly agree to cede Hanover (and thought it best not to give George III full details of his overtures to Prussia). As the year came to its close disaster struck. Napoleon defeated a combined Austrian and Russian army at Austerlitz on 2 December, and Austria made peace with France three weeks later. By dashing Pitt's hopes, Malmesbury later recalled, Austerlitz 'accelerated his end'.[81]

The prime minister carried on, hoping that he would be equal to the military and political struggles ahead. Much depended on his good health and personal exertion, but his strength finally ebbed away just as he needed it most. There were serious financial headaches. The costs of war and government were rising, and yet more money was needed for subsidies if Pitt was to sustain an anti-French league in Europe. Fox continued to demand peace, maintaining that Pitt had only to offer reasonable terms and persuade other states to accept Napoleon as ruler of France. Foxites considered peace to be urgently necessary, and argued that lack of success in battle, the huge national debt, disrupted trade and the hardships of the people all pointed inexorably to this conclusion, while weakening Britain's bargaining position. Fox did not believe that such statements threatened his union with Grenville. Both men regarded Addington and Pitt as failures in war, and Fox supposed that Grenville would soon admit the impossibility of defeating Napoleon and conclude that the war could not go on. In fact Grenville still favoured Pitt's coalition policy and the continuation of the war, and hoped that Fox would not say too much about these matters in public, in case the opposition fell apart. Grenville wondered if there was any point in bringing Pitt's ministry down at this time, but his goal remained a broad-based government of national unity, so he tried not to annoy the Pittites while preserving his co-operation with Fox. The calculations of men, however, could be of little avail as tension and uncertainty increased. Party rancour at home and military failures in Europe made for a dire situation early in 1806. Marquess Wellesley was just back from India, where he had served as governor general (1797–1805). On 10 January Lord Auckland wrote to commend his achievements in India, but added an ominous proviso:

> In some other points of view your return to England is not a subject of congratulation. You will find many grievous changes; several of your more intimate friends are by a discordancy of opinion and other circumstances irrevocably separated from each other. We are engaged in a war of boundless expense, some peril, and incalculable duration. Our continental influence and interests are lost and undone, and with this unpromising state of affairs, and under a pressure of other obvious difficulties, this session seems likely to bring forward a conflict of parties beyond what has happened in our times.[82]

Pitt could find no new source of effective support for the British war effort or the continental alliance. At home he lacked strong assistants on whom he could rely. Hawkesbury, Castlereagh, Canning and Perceval (attorney general from 1802 to 1806) were still establishing themselves, and though they would go on to have distinguished public careers, during Pitt's last days they were still men for the future. They could not replace Grenville and Dundas, whose association with Pitt had been so important before 1801 (and who, in different ways, had seriously weakened his second ministry). Pitt was persistently unwell in the later months of 1805, and unable to devote much time and attention to government business. He was lying later in bed, had no regular contact with most of his cabinet colleagues, and met and spoke with officials and advisers much less than before.

During 1805 Pitt's decline had been remarked upon repeatedly by those closest to him. As Pretyman had written to George Rose:

He is too late for anything. Business presses which *must* be done. Whatever can be put off is put off, and by this procrastination, many things, which, though they belong to no particular day, ought to be done soon, are never done at all ... Perhaps he may not feel all the energy which he did twenty years ago; and even conversation upon matters of business and explanation of conduct may grow in some degree fatiguing for him. I really believe it does, and that he finds solitude and entire rest sometimes necessary to him. Look at his colleagues, and you will be satisfied that he must have many things to do, even of detail, in their departments. All this must be felt by a constitution certainly not in its full vigour ... The critical situation of the country, both as to domestic and foreign affairs, may at times affect Mr Pitt's mind in its present state, and his spirits may, now and then at least, suffer a depression which may give a colour to his external behaviour and manner.

Obviously unequal to the needs of the time, Pitt's notions of patriotism and public responsibility were such that he ruled out resignation, and as his health and morale collapsed he still clung to the belief that his nation needed him. Even in his final days he was sure that he could get well and give useful service. In the last letter he ever wrote (to Wellesley, on 12 January 1806), Pitt reported that 'I am recovering rather slowly from a series of stomach complaints, followed by severe attacks of gout, but I believe I am now in the way of real amendment.'[83]

Pitt took some consolation from the victory at Trafalgar, which confirmed British dominance at sea and ended all possibility of a French invasion. But lack of progress on the continent increased his torment. Desperately needing rest and good news, he had neither. The reversal at Austerlitz was confirmed beyond doubt on 3 January 1806. It was a massive blow. 'God's will be done!' wrote Huskisson at this time. 'Mr Pitt's life is fast hastening to a close. Not a ray of hope remains ... This seems to me like the end of all things, what further trials and misery await us God only knows.' Melville shared in this anguish, writing to Wellesley on 21 January: 'I hope Heaven will guard and restore to us our friend ... There is scarcely anything to which a determined fortitude of mind is not equal, but for such a loss to this country and his friends the spirits can devise no species of consolation.'

Tired, emaciated, in great pain and scarcely able to speak, Pitt died on 23 January 1806 at Bowling Green House, Putney Heath. According to his physician Sir Walter Farquhar, Pitt's main ailments were gout and 'old age'. There was some suggestion that Farquhar had never been firm enough with his patient, particularly in urging upon Pitt a change of habits, and Pitt's closest colleagues had long lamented that he did little to improve the state of his own health. As Camden informed Bathurst in October 1802, after another of Pitt's illnesses:

> He has recovered his appetite, and his strength is returning, but I observe no difference in his diet and he drank at least two bottles of port after dinner and supper last night. I am convinced nothing but a long course of strict regimen will give him a chance of tolerably comfortable recovery and I am equally convinced Farquhar will not speak with decision enough to enforce it.

When Pitt died he was only forty-six years old, but had the body of a man twice that age. Modern commentators have suggested various causes of death: bowel cancer, gastrointestinal lesion, renal failure, cirrhosis of the liver. Pressure and overwork exacerbated Pitt's health problems (though Robin Reilly doubts the significance of depression, anxiety and exhaustion – he attributes Pitt's early death to 'advanced disease', not 'over-exertion'). For Pitt there was no release from the strains of government until he died. He refused to retire, and the huge responsibilities under which he placed himself eventually destroyed his resistance to fatal physical malady. Wilberforce remarked on 1 February 1806 that Pitt had identified himself completely with the fate of the nation: 'Poor Pitt, I almost believe died of a broken heart! For it is only due to him to declare that the love of his country burned in him with as ardent a flame as ever warmed the human bosom, and the account from the armies struck a death's blow within.'[84]

The cabinet could not survive without him. Though it included men of ability there was nobody to take Pitt's place as leader, and the combined weight of Foxite, Grenvillite and Addingtonian opposition prompted ministers to resign. At first George III hoped that some of the cabinet would carry on under a new premier, as in 1801. The home secretary, Hawkesbury, had 'a very long and distressing conversation' with the king, who wanted each member of the cabinet to give him (contrary to the usual practice of joint ministerial advice) 'our opinion in writing of what is best to be done. I do not believe there will be any material difference of opinion.' George III had no choice but to invite Grenville to form an administration, and did not insist on Fox's exclusion. Pitt lay in state on 20 and 21 February 1806, and was buried in Westminster Abbey.

There was no rapid change for the better in the war. Though the Prussians joined the coalition in the summer of 1806, defeats at Jena and Auerstadt forced them to make peace. Britain and Russia continued as uneasy allies until July 1807 when, by the Treaty of Tilsit, the Russians sided with Napoleon. Before his death Pitt had decided that Prussian help would not be very useful after all, and the subsequent Prussian annexation of Hanover not only prompted Britain to declare war on Prussia, but also affected Britain's relations with Russia, because the Russians had encouraged Prussia to take Hanover. Pitt's successors were more suspicious of continental alliances than he had been, and less willing to compromise for the sake of an anti-French combination of powers. Ironically, the final victory over Napoleon was only achieved after Castlereagh (foreign secretary from 1812) had put together a coalition in the manner of Pitt. This 'Fourth Coalition', financed by Britain, took shape during 1813 once Castlereagh had arranged alliances with Russia and Prussia. By the end of the year Sweden, Austria, Bavaria, Wurtemburg and Saxony had all joined in.[85]

8

Achievement

William Pitt the Younger dominated public life in late eighteenth-century Britain. His influence lasted well into the nineteenth century, and his goals, motives, principles, policies, image and rhetoric reveal much about the processes of political change that were in operation (and increasingly evident) during this period. Although Pitt is one of the best known and most written about politicians in British history, there are abiding questions about his career and legacy – especially his meteoric rise and slow, agonizing decline, his measures of reform, support base, responses to revolution and war, political errors and personal foibles.

The reasons for Pitt's early rise are to be found in his personal background, training and talents, his famous name, some influential friends and a great deal of good luck. His drive and ambition, and the manner in which he had been prepared for a public career (helped along by the nurturing of his illustrious father), meant that he was ready to employ all available assets when the chance for self-advancement arose. Most of his opportunities came at just the right time. Notwithstanding his personal strengths, however, his elevation to the premiership was far from inevitable. It required a series of unpredictable events that destabilized elite politics and opened the way for an aspiring young man of promise. The key developments included the surrender of British forces at Yorktown in October 1781, the fall of North's government, and Rockingham's unexpected death less than four months after replacing North as prime minister. When the king's choice, Shelburne, failed to establish himself in power, the scene was set for further controversy, and the struggle over Fox's India Bill led to the dismissal of the Fox-North administration late in 1783. By this time Pitt had been recognized as the coming man, impressing those around him with his speeches in the Commons, capacity for hard work, rapport with public opinion and measured commitment to useful reform. Experienced politicians, including George III, decided that he was worth backing as prime minister (and for the king it was important that Pitt respected the crown's political influence and was willing to defend it, in the appropriate spheres, against the designs of Fox and his party). The popular outcry in favour of Pitt and the king influenced the result of the general election of March 1784, and Pitt never looked back.

Increasingly confident and sure-footed, Pitt continued to take advantage of favourable circumstances and made good use of his enhanced profile, well-placed connections and executive patronage. He was also fortunate in that there were no serious rivals for the premiership: Rockingham was gone, North had been discredited, Shelburne was not popular or trusted, and Pitt's chief adversary, Fox, made mistakes. Fox remained unacceptable to the king, and his dissolute character, fixation with limiting royal influence and determination to vindicate past conduct hampered his own career while Pitt's flourished. Before long Pitt's talent, optimism and political prudence gave him the essential foundation upon which he could seek to deal productively with the court, fashion the cabinet he wanted, improve government efficiency, secure a mastery over parliament and gain more support from the public.

On commencing his career Pitt was hardly an outsider. He had the name, rank and pedigree he needed to enter public life, as well as the friendships, ambition and training. It is not very remarkable that he was elected to the Commons at an early age, since this was normal in a time of rotten boroughs and aristocratic influence, but the speed of his appointment as prime minister is unique. The changing political conditions of the time facilitated his rise, and his personal merits and advantages helped him to make the most of his opportunities as they presented themselves.

Pitt was strongly influenced by his father's example and the distinctive principles he associated with the eighteenth-century 'patriot' ideal. His desire to lead was coupled with a desire to be esteemed as a patriotic public servant. Pitt therefore had to make a show of his virtue and independence. He respected the established constitution in church and state, and sought to mitigate glaring institutional and practical deficiencies in the running of the country. He put the nation's interests before sectional, party or selfish preferences. In terms of policy, this entailed pursuing the path of financial rectitude, promoting social and economic progress, strengthening national defence and consolidating the empire, reorganizing government departments and assessing schemes of reform according to their nature, timing and likely consequences. Although Pitt knew that security of tenure as prime minister depended principally on his relationship with the king and influence over the cabinet and parliament, he also appreciated the importance of his wider reputation and image. As a patriot, an 'independent Whig', a cautious but honest reformer and head of the government who would not shrink from the work that had to be done, he managed to convince popular as well as elite audiences that nobody else was better suited to the premiership.

This approach to the exercise of power was already taking shape before Pitt gained the position he coveted. Indeed, his experiences as Shelburne's chancellor of the exchequer, and especially his involvement in administrative reform, were of long-term importance. They led him to believe that public money could be saved if the government made better use of available resources, and that official remuneration should be based as far as possible on service rather than political favouritism. These ideas stayed with him, as did the core assumption on which they were based: that good government was impossible without sound finances (though matters were complicated in the mid-1790s as Pitt realized that an unprecedented amount of revenue was needed to fight the war). Pitt's early attitude towards power and its possibilities was significant in other ways. During the summer of 1783 he set his mind on being premier, but he also set conditions. He wanted to make it clear that he was a new man, in no way responsible for the mistakes and shortcomings of previous governments, and his own man, not a tool of the court. His touchiness on these matters reveals much about his identity and priorities.

A significant statement of intent was made after Pitt met with George III's representative Thurlow on 19 July 1783, during the early stages of the plot against the Fox-North coalition. Pitt reported the discussion on 22 July to Earl Temple:

> Lord Thurlow's object was to insinuate that a change was not so necessary to the king; and to endeavour to make it (if it should take place) rather our act than his; and on that ground to try whether terms might not be imposed that could not otherwise. This is so totally contrary to every idea we both entertain that I thought it necessary to take full care to counteract it. I stated in general that if the king's feelings did not point strongly to a change, it was not what we sought. But that if they did, and we could form a permanent system, consistent with our principles, and on public ground, we should not decline it. I reminded him how much I was personally pledged to parliamentary reform on the principles I had publicly explained, which I should support on every seasonable occasion. I treated as out of the question any idea of measures being taken to extend crown influence, though such means as are fairly in the hands of ministers would undoubtedly have to be exerted. And I said that I wished those with whom I might act, and the king (if he called upon me) to be fully apprized of the grounds on which I should necessarily proceed.[1]

Pitt may have been young, but he was no fool. He saw that if George III and the king's associates induced him to take over as premier, and made him another North, he would have to govern for the king and through the king's influence, a complete abnegation of the role and status he was seeking. Pitt resisted. He gave notice that he would only come in on acceptable terms and that he was willing to wait. Rather than rush in, he wanted to know if the king was ready to call on him. Indeed, throughout his career, Pitt's conduct rested on these essential qualities: he was ambitious but patient, confident in his own abilities, certain that he had something to offer and daring to expect a lot in return.

Once he was premier his position continually became stronger, despite occasional setbacks. Successful policies and shrewd tactical decisions meant that Pitt's regime gained wide acceptance. By the mid-1790s he was celebrated as the provider of effective government. He was trusted for his reliability and his flexible and reasonable approach to public questions. He had dedicated himself to the pursuit of prosperity, order and progress, both at home and in the empire. He had delivered relative political stability. He was expanding trade, repairing the public finances, and had paid back a considerable portion of the national debt. He had helped to increase British influence abroad and improve the administration of India and Canada. He was raising the level of proficiency in government departments, restoring respect for public men, and dealing in a pragmatic and fair-minded fashion with burning domestic issues such as the slave trade, religious toleration and parliamentary reform. But Pitt's achievements were overshadowed by the French war. As circumstances changed during the 1790s, so did possibilities and priorities. Despite the general belief that the war would be short and successful, it dragged on, and Pitt had to turn his attention completely to war-related problems: popular distress, radical agitation, strategy, and the insatiable need for more money to fight the war.

One of the cardinal features of Pitt's regime was the sinking fund, or to be more precise what it *represented*, for financial probity and competence were crucial to the extension of influence. It was a great coup for Pitt to be able to tell the Commons in April 1785 that the government expected a surplus of £1,000,000. That this announcement could be made so soon after the expensive American war suggested that Pitt's early reconstruction efforts were having an effect, and his intention to devote the surplus to the reduction of long-term debt encouraged many contemporaries to have more faith in the state than had previously been the case. The sinking fund was central to Pitt's financial and economic planning. It reassured the nation, and other measures were framed to assist its operation. By 1793 the fund had yielded about £10,250,000 for debt redemption, but its political uses outweighed its direct financial impact, and Pitt did not suspend it during the French war. Later commentators questioned this policy. After all, the sinking fund required an ongoing revenue surplus, for which growing sums from various forms of taxation were needed. The conflict against revolutionary France brought budget deficits, massively increased the cost of government, and meant that tax money had to be applied to the war effort. Maintaining the fund in wartime proved extremely wasteful. The state borrowed large sums at high rates of interest and applied some of this money to pay off debts that bore a lower rate. Perhaps the full implications were not appreciated at the time. Nobody expected the war to last for twenty years, least of all Pitt. For him the sinking fund could not be given up. Without it public credit would collapse. Support for his regime, and the nation's willingness to join in the war effort, would both diminish, with obvious consequences for the arrangement of loans, payment of taxes, enlistment in the volunteers, participation in loyalism, press comment and other indicators of public sentiment. Pitt might lose his mandate. He persisted with the fund and the policies connected with it, therefore, deciding that to change course would be to weaken his own position.

Pitt was rightly applauded for his financial measures before 1793, and when war came Britain had the resources to fight. Despite his natural caution there was boldness in his approach to loans and the national debt, smuggling, the cost of government, tariff reform and taxation, because the situation when Pitt came to power called for firm remedial action. He promoted a revival, although his measures were not particularly novel. He preferred to adapt and improve existing procedures. He took up previous proposals, added something to them and made them his own. In doing so he provided what the state, economy and society needed, and without his energy and vision it is likely that the revival of the 1780s would have been less impressive. Somebody had to confront the problems of defeat, debt and instability left by Pitt's predecessors. It was Pitt who made amends. Within ten years a mood of confidence had replaced one of doubt and decline. This was also important overseas. The reforms for India and Canada helped to enhance the efficiency, cohesion and viability of the empire after the loss of the American colonies.

Pitt's achievements reinforced his stance as a selfless and dependable public servant. His success before the war was not merely a victory of style over substance. There was delivery behind the spin. Pitt took pride in his probity, calling, capacity for hard work and conscientious devotion to public business, and he and his supporters regularly sought approval and recognition for these qualities. Indeed, a good name and high reputation were great assets to Pitt as a politician, and many nineteenth-century observers (whose moral judgments were stimulated by the Victorian cult of character) focused upon this aspect of his career. It could be argued, however, that Pitt simply made a virtue of his own ambitions and methods. From an early age he was determined to enter politics. In time his longing to be prime minister (and then to remain so) consumed him; this was the only way he could be fulfilled. His eagerness to rise, self-discipline, willpower and assessment of his own abilities indicate that he was no less concerned with personal gratification than with public service. He wanted power and respect. He also cared about posterity's view, beyond the immediate needs of the moment. He prized his upright and honourable character enormously, which meant that the image he fashioned had to be carefully magnified by word and deed.

In some respects Pitt's image is unconvincing. Behind the patriotic rhetoric and veneer of integrity, government carried on much as before. The Pitt regime was supposedly less corrupt than its predecessors, and it probably was, but there was still plenty of chicanery, shady deals, clientage and nepotism. The only difference was that corruption became a little less flagrant. Pitt could not avoid the bargains, intrigues and distribution of spoils, for this was how politics worked. That he was a direct beneficiary is clear enough from any fair consideration of how he became prime minister, how he won the pivotal general election of 1784, and how he strengthened his regime thereafter. Nor can we understand the legislative union with Ireland, one of Pitt's most significant reforms, without acknowledging the deviousness and bribery that made it possible.

Pitt's most important colleagues before 1801 were Dundas and Grenville. As members of the administration they both began in low ranking offices, but they soon became the prime minister's special confidants and advisers. From the early 1790s they formed with Pitt the dominant directing triumvirate at the head of affairs. Personally as well as publicly, Pitt relied heavily on Dundas, his senior by seventeen years, and Grenville, his cousin, with whom he shared an interest in classical scholarship and political economy (he and Grenville had both been born in 1759). Dundas was already an experienced operator before Pitt's appointment as premier. He proved to be a strong debater with a talent for administration and personal relations, a skilled manager of expanding patronage networks, and somebody to whom Pitt could delegate difficult or unpleasant tasks. In 1783 Dundas sided with Pitt because he saw him as the obvious choice as premier – acceptable to the king, respected in parliament and out of doors, untainted by previous failures, and a young man of uncommon abilities who seemed to offer the nation its best hope for a stable and prosperous future. For Dundas there was also the prospect that in assisting Pitt he would be boosting his own career. He and Pitt became close friends, and for many years Dundas was an essential prop of Pitt's regime. Their relationship became strained in the late 1790s as the pressures of war and government increased, but Pitt was anxious to bring Dundas back with him when he returned as premier in 1804, and deeply regretted the scandal that ended their political collaboration.

Grenville's career was closely linked with (and dependent upon) Pitt's from its early stages, and Pitt's rise hastened his own. The family connection and some shared ideas on policy helped them to work well together, and among the greatest strengths of the Pitt-Dundas-Grenville triumvirate were the trust and respect that developed between its members. Grenville was also an accomplished debater and administrator, though like Pitt he was proud and touchy, which exacerbated the quarrels that developed between them over war measures during the 1790s. After Pitt's resignation in 1801 the cousins drifted apart. Grenville's agenda was now shaped by his continuing attachment to the Catholic cause, his dissatisfaction with Addington's ministry and preference for all-out war against Napoleon, and his call for a broad inclusive cabinet that would include the Foxites. He lost patience with Pitt's temporizing and found that he could no longer endorse Pitt's priorities. The former grounds for co-operation between Pitt and Grenville had apparently passed away.

From the mid-1780s Pitt put together a loyal corps of younger assistants. Several were admitted to his circle of close friends, and some went on to hold cabinet rank. There can be no doubt of the indispensability of Dundas and Grenville to Pitt's regime, but the same might be said of his more junior colleagues. He encouraged them, nurtured their talent and entrusted them with important responsibilities. They responded well. For Pitt they developed remarkable affection and respect. They were grateful for the time and attention he gave them and the opportunities they were afforded to make their mark. George Canning, William Huskisson, Dudley Ryder and Robert Banks Jenkinson were among the vanguard. Pitt relied on them increasingly as speakers, administrators, sources of information and men on whom he could try out his policy proposals. Gradually their influence grew, and without their dutiful co-operation Pitt would not have been able to get things done. Having been naturally drawn to the government side (in order to make a career for themselves), they adopted the Pittite creed of high-minded public service. For the rest of their lives they regarded Pitt as their political master and personal mentor.

The support of his closest colleagues and junior assistants brought Pitt considerable advantages as premier, but his record also rests on his own talents and leadership style. Pitt was one of the most gifted orators in parliamentary history, and few politicians of his generation could match his debating power or approach the standards he set for well-informed and well-organized speeches. Clarity, detail and eloquence were his trademarks, and some of his set-piece performances passed into legend. He was also admired as an administrator. He put in the time and effort required to master facts. In collecting information, soliciting advice, framing policies and implementing his decisions he was noted for his thoroughness. He devoted himself to government business. Indeed, he was obliged to do so by his sense of identity and calling. But for all his dedication Pitt's leadership lacked system and order. Ever the pragmatist, and averse to paperwork and letter writing, he liked to deal with business informally and in person. He had no master plan or fixed programme for government. The questions he took up were primarily those in which he *chose* to take an interest, and he formulated most of his measures according to the prevalent circumstances. If obstructed, he often altered or abandoned specific policies (he was normally content to respond to events rather than seek to carry them in a preferred direction). He was never a deeply committed or dogmatic reformer, but saw both sides of an issue, and in teasing out the answer to a problem he could appear indecisive.

As premier Pitt was reluctant to cause trouble unnecessarily, or weaken his authority, by pressing ahead with controversial measures, especially when the outcome was in doubt. This suggests that he had a clear notion of what was practical and possible, a definite source of strength, but it also allowed opponents to rob him of the initiative or accuse him of procrastination and inconsistency. In his prime, long before his energy and enthusiasm were exhausted, he moved about from issue to issue, involving himself in many aspects of government. His attention span was limited; if he encountered difficulty on one question, he turned to another. If something untoward happened, or the government was pressed to act, Pitt responded. As he saw it, the prime minister had to identify, clarify and solve problems. But to view public affairs in this fashion was unrealistic, especially in the crisis-ridden 1790s. Pitt's disappointments inevitably increased.

Pitt's leadership style was shaped by his personality. Effective leadership consists of (among other things) strong direction, energy in pursuing this direction, and sensitivity to the needs of one's followers.[2] Before his decline in the later 1790s Pitt repeatedly showed that he had the direction and energy, but what of the sensitivity? To many who met him he seemed cold and distant. His supporters in parliament respected him, but few of them came to know or like him personally, and other political leaders considered him aloof if not arrogant (George III much preferred dealing with Addington). Pitt's close friends were few in number, for he did not find it easy to develop relationships or relax in unfamiliar surroundings. With his intimates, it is true, he was cheerful, amusing and generous. There are accounts of him playing with children, relating humorous stories, conversing unreservedly and making merry with food and wine.[3] It is not surprising that those colleagues who shared in these private times developed a warm attachment to him personally as well as politically. His ability to inspire them, and their eagerness to reward his trust in them, greatly assisted the government. But in this relationship the vast majority of government supporters had no involvement. To them Pitt was inattentive and brusque. His failure to answer letters symbolized the lack of sympathy and communication.

Pitt expected loyalty from others, but never thought much about how he could earn it. He probably assumed that his own dedication and self-sacrifice would be recognized, and that MPs and others would conclude that he deserved their support (whether or not he asked for it) because of what he was doing for the nation. This approach worked for a time, but the stresses of the 1790s brought a change. Pitt's character traits became even more starkly obvious. In order to be seen as a patriotic premier Pitt had trained himself to be calm and self-possessed, which intensified his natural reserve. Such training helped him to overcome reverses and reinforced his confident belief that he could handle difficult situations. Before the late 1790s he rarely lost his temper, though he did remember offences and was slow to forgive. Ironically, as he declined Pitt relied more and more on his own exertions, in his eagerness to transact business and fight the French, while his energy and optimism were fading.

Of Pitt's political talents there is no question. He made the most of his skills, connections and opportunities, and his mastery in debate, and in this there was a form of genius. In some of his ideas and policies he was not particularly original, but he used the contributions of others very well indeed, absorbing and acting upon them as appropriate, and it is doubtful that any other politician of the day could or would have done so to greater effect. His domineering attitude and haughty demeanour irked a number of contemporaries, but were not necessarily out of place at a time when the nation needed confident leadership. Pitt wanted to govern, and in justifying himself he used the language of service. As he often reiterated, he had no function other than to serve, and for most of his career his conduct persuaded influential people that he could be trusted to serve with honour and distinction.

The French Revolution and subsequent war brought dramatic changes in British politics, and certainly influenced Pitt, but he did not greatly alter his basic outlook on public affairs. There was no sharp discontinuity. Pitt did not discard reform for reaction. Improving ventures did not cease, and Pitt was neither as unequivocal a reformer before the war nor as inveterate a reactionary during the 1790s as was claimed in some quarters. But the war did mean that his moderate reformist approach had to be focused on particular areas, and was not so wide-ranging. After 1793 circumstances ruled out rapid or general change. Pitt was obliged to attend principally to problems relating to management of the war – finance, strategy, manpower, security – and the question of how to maintain domestic order in a period of emergency. Major reforms could still be introduced: income tax and the union with Ireland were both made possible and necessary by the war. To those who had higher hopes of Pitt as a reformer, however, it seemed that he was no longer their standard-bearer.

Some modern historians have been kinder in their verdicts.[4] It should also be noted that many contemporary and subsequent commentators based their assessment of Pitt's progressive credentials upon a reading of his position on parliamentary reform, yet this was only one of many issues to which Pitt gave his time and attention. In turning against parliamentary reform, moreover, Pitt adhered to a consistent line of argument. Unless the timing of any proposal was apt, its necessity clear, its details generally acceptable and the likely consequences beneficial, he felt himself bound to object and oppose. Quite simply, the conditions of the 1790s were not like those in which he had made a case for parliamentary reform in the 1780s.

On the other hand, Pitt's claim that parliamentary reform would be an inconvenient distraction, a dangerous experiment and an encouragement to extremists in wartime, can be questioned. There is no obvious reason why a mild redistribution of seats or a slight change to voting qualifications should have caused trouble in the 1790s. Indeed, a more responsive attitude on the part of the ministry and legislature would have been welcomed out of doors and a moderate reform might have satisfied a majority of extra-parliamentary campaigners. Instead of resorting to repression, the government might have strengthened its position and drawn more people behind the war effort by making a gesture to appease reform opinion. Some of the violence and polarization of the 1790s would thereby have been avoided. The postwar disorders of 1815 to 1821 and 'reform crisis' of 1828 to 1832 might also have been prevented, or at least mitigated, by an earlier, measured concession. Even if we accept that the wartime repression was expedient, it does not follow that it should have precluded moderate parliamentary reform. Pitt could have constructed a broader consensus and stifled agitation by exploring both avenues, not selecting one and ruling out the other.

One of Pitt's main responsibilities in wartime was to raise the money without which Britain could not fight on. The war necessitated massive expenditure, and Pitt's success in managing the public finances and tapping into various sources of wealth meant that Britain was able to sustain its war effort. His economic and financial policies during the 1780s were an important foundation in this respect; the war could only be carried on because adequate resources were available. Nevertheless, the sums involved were, to many, mind-boggling. In 1793 Pitt borrowed about £4,000,000, extended credit by issuing £5,000,000 in exchequer bills, and set aside over £800,000 for subsidies to foreign allies. In April 1794 he agreed to pay Prussia about £1,200,000. His budget of February 1795 reflected serious financial difficulty; he had to increase taxation and raise a loan of £18,000,000 on very unfavourable terms (and there was also concern about the deficient harvest and a possible downturn in trade). In 1796 Pitt borrowed more, raised the assessed taxes, increased the duties on horses and tobacco and imposed a new tax on collateral successions. He also agreed to assist Austria with a loan of £1,200,000. The need for money continued rapidly to rise. A 'loyalty loan' was announced (its levy was £18,000,000 at 5 per cent interest), and the budget of 1797 included a further £2,000,000 of taxation. Assessed taxes were increased again (by 10 per cent), and duties on tea, sugar and spirits also rose. By November 1797 Pitt was facing a deficit of £22,000,000. He borrowed £3,000,000 from the Bank of England, raised £12,000,000 by a new loan, and introduced the 'triple assessment', which he estimated would bring in £7,000,000 (those liable to the assessed taxes were to pay more, according to a graduated scale). Early in 1798 Pitt called for voluntary contributions on top of the previous sums. Then he proceeded to reform the land tax and introduce income tax. In 1798 he borrowed another £3,000,000, and £15,000,000 in 1799. The budget of February 1800 included a loan of £18,500,000 (and at this time Pitt needed £2,500,000 for subsidies). His plan for 1801, which was introduced shortly before his resignation, included loans amounting to £28,000,000 and additional taxation to the tune of £1,800,000. After returning as premier Pitt calculated that, even without the interest on public debts, the cost of carrying on the war and government for 1805 would be £44,000,000. His budget of February 1805 included a loan of £20,000,000, plus higher postage and other duties to cover the interest, and a 25 per cent increase in income tax.

Pitt's financial accomplishments have long been praised, but his wartime initiatives would have been unavailing had not the money already been available, and there was nothing particularly shrewd or inventive about asking taxpayers and creditors for more money when more money was needed. The real key to his success in raising revenue was that his previous measures had restored the public finances, promoted trade, built up confidence and made possible the growth of British wealth. The urgency of the situation in the 1790s helped too, for the French threat, patriotic appeals and the fact that Pitt was still trusted as a steward of public money meant that most people who could afford to pay more did so.

The needs of war also obliged him to promote and oversee political realignment, most obviously his ministry's juncture with the Portland Whigs. The French Revolution and British involvement in the revolutionary war

from February 1793 encouraged Pitt and his colleagues to think of recon-
structing the administration (so that it would incontestably be a government
of national unity) while further destabilizing the parliamentary opposition.
On the culpability of French leaders and the necessity for war to resist their
designs there was agreement among cabinet ministers, most peers and MPs,
George III and the Portland Whigs (as well as respectable public opinion).
Pitt exaggerated the danger of sedition at home and French power in Europe
in order permanently to divide the parliamentary opposition, and Fox's
relationship with the Portland group rapidly cooled. Portland accepted the
view of his friends, that if the war was going to be vigorously conducted,
and radicalism undermined, conservative Whigs would have to work with
Pitt. After 1794 members of the remodelled cabinet were bound together
by a common view of national priorities. Though there were some disagreements, ministers were determined to gain victory over the French and
safeguard the established order at home.

In terms of political control and influence over people and events, the
customary distinction between Pitt the peacetime premier and Pitt the war
leader is not out of place. But of course the circumstances, pressures and
opportunities of peacetime were not the same as those of war, and just as
Pitt probably achieved more than anyone else could have done in facilitating
the national revival of the 1780s, so his performance in contending with
mounting problems after 1793 was better than his critics might have been
willing to admit. Fatigue, disappointment and ill health prevented Pitt from
applying himself to public business from the later 1790s with the same
energy and effectiveness he had evinced in preceding years. But this is not
to suggest that he was a complete failure in war. Before his decline he
continued to provide strong leadership, superintend policy, manage parliament, guide outdoor opinion and keep the government and its supporters
focused on the primary objectives of the war effort and domestic administration. His resilience and inspirational role were especially important (not
for nothing were his war speeches republished during the Second World
War).

By 1793 Pitt had been premier for nine years. His achievements outnumbered his reverses. He was in a strong position, dominant in cabinet and
parliament, influencing all the critical areas of policy, and respected and
valued by the king, ministerial colleagues, parliament and nation. He entered
the war against France with confidence. Pitt remains the longest serving
wartime prime minister in British history, a clear sign of his political talent
and ascendancy. Yet this fact also reflects his failure to bring the war to a
swift and successful conclusion. Obviously there was a great deal that was
beyond his control. His own errors and shortcomings, however, must also

be acknowledged. Pitt misjudged the nature, cost and duration of the war (although he was not alone in this), and secured no overall victory because of basic mistakes. Much of this is unsurprising, perhaps, in view of his inexperience; he had not been a war leader before. But he might have handled certain matters more wisely.

Britain was not fully prepared for war in 1793, and as the French Revolution took an unexpectedly violent path after 1789 Pitt must have realized that war was becoming more likely, and should have responded accordingly. Once Britain went to war, it took too long for him to appreciate that the major powers (Austria, Prussia and Russia) did not share his strategic concern for northern Europe and the approaches to the English Channel, and that he would not be able to persuade them to take the military action that most suited British interests. As the months passed, moreover, he refused to abandon his notion that the war would be short. This upset the government's financial and military planning. Pitt was slow to react to changing events abroad, and underestimated France's martial capabilities. He was indecisive at crucial times, especially when offered contradictory advice. Most obviously, he found it difficult to choose between the colonial operations advocated by Dundas and the continental commitment favoured by Grenville. Another criticism relates to financial management. At the time and afterwards it was said that Pitt should not have wasted so much money on subsidies. Britain received little help in return, and yet he persisted with the policy. He also saddled the nation with a huge debt, partly because he would not suspend the sinking fund, which posed a serious problem for postwar governments. On the other hand, he may have been right to believe that there was no other way to sustain the war effort, and the heavy reliance on loans was reasonable in view of the possibility that too many tax rises would have retarded commercial progress and added to anti-war feeling in the nation (Pitt's defenders argued that these loans utilized capital that could not have been employed in trade anyway).

Inevitably Pitt's war leadership has been compared with that of his father, who was largely responsible for British successes during the Seven Years War. The comparison is not altogether fair. Pitt the Elder did not have to contend with Napoleon, and had a powerful ally in Frederick the Great's Prussia. The Younger Pitt ceaselessly searched for, financed and encouraged continental allies, but they were neither dependable nor very useful. The prospects for a war leader after 1793 differed markedly from those between 1756 and 1763.

Whatever his wartime shortcomings, it cannot be denied that Pitt the Younger was an inspirational leader who mobilized loyalist opinion and managed to find the sums that financed the war. Although the money he offered to Britain's allies made little difference to their selfish priorities in his lifetime, the coalition policy worked in the end and the eventual victory over Napoleon was a joint effort. Investing in coalitions seemed worthwhile, indeed, for Britain had a small army and could not make an equal contribution to the conflict on land. Paying allies to take the leading role on the Continent made sense, and Britain could help the allied cause by destroying French power at sea, attacking French commerce and capturing French colonies. These maritime operations had a lasting impact. By conquering West Indian islands and policing the trade of neutrals, Pitt's regime weakened France while increasing British wealth and resources. The Royal Navy expanded quickly between 1792 and 1800, as did the value of British exports, imports and re-exports, and control over India was extended. Here was the basis for British economic dominance and great power status in the nineteenth century. Britain's main commercial and imperial rivals were not able quickly to catch up. Flawed as Pitt's war leadership may have been in certain respects, it is not clear how the war could have been better managed. French armies proved to be stronger than expected, and in Napoleon the British faced an unusually gifted (and lucky) adversary. It has been remarked that the worst years of the war were 1797 and 1805, but Britain was not defeated, and in both years Pitt was in power.[5]

Pitt's failings as a war leader should not be exaggerated. Nor should his successes before 1793, for there was no unbroken line of achievement in peacetime. Some of his measures were defeated or had to be withdrawn, and there were continuing difficulties. Ministerial supporters never formed a united party, for example, and were not bound together by a shared commitment to particular policies. Misgivings about Pitt persisted, initially because of his relative youth and inexperience, and later as government measures were opposed and the premier's perceived mistakes led to a questioning of his authority. Pitt's manner did not help. As noted, outside his private circle he was frosty and aloof, which fed resentment. MPs and peers who were offended by his failure to inform and conciliate them were unlikely to support him for long. In the main, however, these problems were more pronounced during the war than before 1793. Pitt's political judgments were mostly sound in the 1780s: he knew when to retreat and how to exploit his opponents' mistakes, made excellent use of his opportunities, and dealt adeptly with cabinet colleagues and the king. The domestic and foreign policies pursued during the 1780s certainly made a difference. By 1793 government, society, economy and empire were all in a better condition thanks to Pitt.

Pitt lasted as premier because he formed and maintained the appropriate relationships with George III, the cabinet, parliament and public opinion.

Effective co-operation with the king was essential to Pitt. They shared broadly the same views on policy, and the king was reassured by Pitt's clear attachment to the established order and willingness to allow the crown its rightful influence along the lines suggested by constitutional convention. George III had little understanding of or interest in Pitt's fiscal and commercial measures, but was pleased that they fostered stability, prosperity and confidence. There was some friction on foreign policy, but nothing that led to a serious rupture, and on constitutional questions Pitt trod carefully. Although he pressed for parliamentary reform in 1785, he agreed that his bill should not be a government measure and gracefully accepted its defeat. He opposed repeal of the Test and Corporation Acts in 1787, 1789 and 1790, and turned against parliamentary reform. Pitt persuaded George III to approve a modest extension of rights to Catholics between 1791 and 1793, but accepted the king's wish in 1795 that Catholic emancipation in Ireland must be ruled out. Circumstances changed, and in 1801 the pragmatic Pitt, at odds on emancipation with his more dogmatic sovereign, decided to resign. Various personal and political considerations led him to step down, but the fact that George III was taking advice from others was crucial.

This apparently principled stance was, in truth, rather hypocritical. Pitt, who had been involved in and benefited from behind-the-scenes intrigue with the court in 1783, was the victim of a similar machination in 1801. In 1783 he was appointed prime minister as part of the plot against the Fox-North coalition. At that time he had been willing for the king's name to be used by opponents of the ministry, but in 1801 he condemned the use of the king's name against Catholic emancipation and asked George III to prevent it. He knew how important it was, for he had needed it in 1783. This represents a blatant case of double standards. Pitt had few qualms about involving himself in the scheming that brought down the Fox-North government, but he complained when others used the same methods against him in 1801.

Before the emancipation crisis Pitt and George III had managed to avoid any serious breach, and, though they were never close, their formal relationship facilitated effective government. As his father had done, Pitt treated the king as an institution, not a person, and preferred to use official channels in dealing with him. He tended to communicate in writing rather than in person (especially if difficult issues came up for discussion). Pitt and the king respected each other, but there was little affection between them and they had few common interests outside politics. Pitt's interaction with George III remained businesslike. During the regency crisis he did not contact those who were attending the king to ask about his condition, but used the formal channels (that is, the king's doctors and Queen Charlotte). Though North and Addington became the king's friends as well as his chief ministers, to Pitt the official bond was the only one that mattered. It was broken in 1801 partly because there was no personal link to sustain it. That Pitt chose to conduct affairs in this manner was a consequence of his own social awkwardness, but he also considered it necessary. If he was to govern as he wished, there had to be a purely formal contact, not a personal one. The patriot ideal prohibited friendship between premier and monarch. Friendship would complicate the official working relationship, and Pitt knew that he could not be a success (in his own terms) as politician and prime minister without the proper decorum and reserve in his dealings with George III. Fox and his party, meanwhile, viewed the relationship in their own way, and considered Pitt the king's willing accomplice in the burgeoning executive's assault on parliamentary independence and popular liberty.

As Pitt's energy and influence declined he was less able to stand up to the king, but he was also concerned about the king's mental condition, and on occasion chose not to antagonize George III by demanding his own way. His promise in 1801, that he would not again propose Catholic emancipation while the king lived, indicates this desire to assuage rather than challenge. In 1804 he accepted the king's veto on Fox because he did not wish to be held responsible for pushing the king into a relapse and causing another ministerial crisis. In any case the exclusion of Fox probably accorded with Pitt's preferences at that time. In September 1805, when Pitt tried to persuade George III that room must be found in the government for opposition leaders, he again decided not to endanger the king's peace of mind by pressing the matter.

Pitt's longevity as prime minister also depended on his pre-eminence in the cabinet. After his appointment late in 1783 it took some time for him to extend his control. Other ministers were older and more experienced than Pitt, and resisted interference with their own departmental business. But his talents and determination soon made him the active chief of the ministry, and he was usually able to circumvent difficult colleagues by conniving with Dundas, Grenville or one of his junior assistants. The personnel and balance of power within the cabinet changed considerably between 1788 and 1795. Thurlow's fall in 1792 was decisive and made Pitt's dominance much clearer, although coalition with the Portland Whigs in 1794 was not without risk. Pitt had to give them six places in the cabinet of thirteen. But the Fitzwilliam crisis of 1795 undermined their cohesion and Pitt managed to integrate them into his ministry more effectively. They rarely combined together to force him to adopt or change a policy, and most important matters were settled by Pitt in conjunction with Dundas and Grenville. Pitt made several cabinet changes after 1795 and by the summer of 1798 only four members of the cabinet of twelve were former members of the opposition.

Even at the height of his powers, however, Pitt's control over the cabinet was not complete. If he lacked his own contacts with a department, he could not easily supervise its business. Nor could the premier simply instruct a cabinet colleague to follow orders; a collective decision of the cabinet was needed. Pitt preferred to avoid confrontation, and the possibility of obstruction in cabinet reinforced his predilection for consultation and decision-making *outside* it. Nevertheless, colleagues could still make difficulties. Several refused to vacate their offices when Pitt asked them to participate in ministerial reshuffles, and he became all the more inconvenienced during the later 1790s when open quarrels over war policy broke out between Dundas and Grenville. In his dealings with the cabinet Pitt was habitually cautious and reticent. He was aware of the limits upon his influence, though in time developed the means to nullify this problem. He tended increasingly to use the cabinet as a sounding board, or a mechanism for gaining formal approval for measures he wanted to implement, not as a supreme policy making body. He seems not to have held a very high opinion of the cabinet and its role. He needed its support and responded quickly when threats emerged within it, but all the key decisions were taken by the triumvirate, which then persuaded cabinet colleagues (and when necessary the king) to accept what had been settled.

That Pitt remained prime minister for so long was due in large measure to his success in managing parliament. Many parliamentarians recognized his merits as premier. They were dazzled by some of his speeches and amazed by his aptitude for business. They welcomed his efforts to attend to the needs of the nation. Patronage was important too, and through Dundas and others Pitt made use of the favours, titles, honours and offices at the government's disposal to maintain and extend his parliamentary dominance. He also recruited and employed men of real talent, some of whom were brought into the government. They strengthened Pitt's regime as administrators, debaters and gatherers and assessors of information. Most MPs and peers were willing to rest easy while the government demonstrated competence, and consequently Pitt was less likely to lose divisions or be embarrassed by unexpectedly tough debates. A number of his leading supporters did not join the government but remained on the backbenches: as speakers, canvassers and opinion-formers they were able to render sterling service. Crucially, Pitt used his supporters to control Commons committees, without which he would not have been able to direct parliamentary proceedings as he wished. With careful planning, a quietly efficient application of government influence and the astute deployment of subordinates, Pitt's parliamentary position became stronger. At a time when party discipline was still developing and executive patronage rapidly declining, he needed to find other ways of supervising parliament. He did so, in so far as he was able, by making himself a master of tactics, detail, personnel, structures and procedure. His temperament and leadership style led him to eschew party methods. He was more the pragmatist than an ideological politician, conscious that the government's following was a loose coalition that could not be led as a homogeneous unit, unable to establish close personal bonds with men outside his intimate circle, and concerned to perpetuate his reputation as the disinterested patriotic minister. Pitt's long domination of parliament combined manipulative intervention in a few vital areas with a more relaxed, hands-off approach in others. This combination was adequate before the pressures of war, ministerial wrangling and Pitt's declining energy altered parliament's mood in the later 1790s.

One of the most important bulwarks of Pitt's ascendancy in parliament was the government's commanding electoral position. Most eighteenth-century ministries did well at the polls. In the unreformed system general elections were called by governments at the times they chose and with the purpose of confirming them in office. Voter choice, party contests and national issues did not feature very prominently until well after the Great Reform Act of 1832, although in some places politics were more meaningful and there was unusual excitement at particular pre-reform elections, notably that of 1784. The government's electoral successes from 1784 and the opposition split of 1794 strengthened Pitt, removing as they did potential sources of trouble in parliament. In view of this, one might wonder why there were so many political crises during the war. The answer may be that Pitt's ascendancy was less secure than many observers thought. As one modern commentator has written:

> The monotonous series of failures that the policies of Pitt experienced after 1793 cannot be blamed on the activities of the opposition as can the defeat of his reform measures in 1785 and of his Russian policy in 1791. The only explanations possible are: first, that Pitt lacked ability; second, that the odds against him were too great; and third, that he was unable to maintain solidarity on matters of policy with his ministry and the king. Doubtless all three contributed in some measure to the failures and disappointments of these years.[6]

Another essential support to Pitt was his rapport with public opinion. For most of his career influential sections of outdoor opinion regarded him as the best available prime minister and the one most likely to provide the things they wanted, whether moderate reforms, freer trade, sound finances, social peace, prestige abroad, ministerial stability or more competent and responsive government. Pitt's pose as a patriotic leader who would serve the people rather than the court or a party, and whose virtue and independence kept him above the grubby politics of corrupt influence and factional manoeuvre, convinced plenty of people that he was worthy of their backing. Support in the nation remained important to him. It reinforced his self-understanding and provided a form of legitimacy. Popularity was a platform for political ascendancy, and the standing Pitt gained during the 1780s became a considerable asset in the difficult 1790s. Despite all the problems created by the struggle with France, he could still seek to influence opinion, appealing for and receiving approval for the measures that were passed to assist the war effort and ensure domestic security. His attempts to build up and retain popular support also limited the options of his opponents; from the mid-1780s to the later 1790s they found it difficult to gain a purchase over the public mind.

It was a notable wartime achievement (and one for which Pitt was partly responsible) that the government enjoyed prolonged popular backing. The mobilization of patriotic effort and opinion sustained Pitt and his colleagues, and the wartime experience reveals much about the emerging links between elite politics and extra-parliamentary developments. Pitt's regime could not have lasted without the popular ebullience. He needed it, but he also helped to *make* public opinion important by invoking, shaping and paying so much attention to it. As his rapport with the public evolved, he took advantage of the obvious lack of a strong rival or suitable alternative as premier. He reminded contemporaries of the situation before 1784, the American war, the failures, instability and uncertainty to which the nation did not want to return. Furthermore, there was the potent example of Pitt's father, the true patriot, a non-party figure who made a show of his high regard for extra-parliamentary opinion. Pitt could present his famous father as a legitimate national leader, and himself as the natural successor. By such means he enjoyed wider support than could have been gained had he tied himself to a party or viewed political activity (as opposed to the practical exercise of power) as an exclusively aristocratic affair. When the French war came, Pitt was able to use the popularity he gained in the 1780s to boost his reputation as an earnest and conscientious public servant. He persuaded men of property and influence that he could be trusted in an emergency. Portland Whigs left the opposition and joined him in 1794, adding to this impression.

Throughout the war there were waves of vigorous loyalism that bolstered Pitt's position. He set an example of virtue and reliability, called forth a popular response in return, and, as he hoped and expected, large numbers of people organized addresses and petitions, attended meetings, offered financial gifts, formed loyal associations and participated in paramilitary formations. He had few misgivings about these direct appeals to the public. He wanted to stir opinion, arm the volunteers and rely on the wholesome spirit of the people. But he also had to keep abreast of changing sentiment out of doors. Obviously the war made possible, and urgently necessary, a more proactive direction of public opinion. The French menace could not fail to assist a government that was secure in parliament and led by a prime minister whose pedigree and overt patriotism made him seem more concerned about national duty than personal or party goals. Unfortunately for Pitt, matters eventually went awry. The war went on for so long, at such enormous expense and with no substantial breakthrough, that his position at court and in the cabinet and his relationship with parliament and people were seriously impaired.

By 1804 Pitt's best days were behind him. The circumstances he faced on his return as prime minister was far less favourable than those he had previously experienced in public life. His ability to contend with difficulties (that is, his physical and mental resources and political influence) had been eroded during the later 1790s and his period out of office after March 1801. During the 1780s Pitt had youth, energy and optimism on his side, as well as firm support from George III, a positive reputation out of doors, and a growing band of talented and determined assistants. His parliamentary opponents were discredited and divided. These assets enabled Pitt to rise to ascendancy, and he continued to maintain a strong position into the late 1790s. But decline, drift and division embarrassed him and his colleagues as the war dragged on, and during 1804, when he tried to construct and strengthen his second government, he lacked the advantages he had formerly turned to such good account. He was dying; after resuming the premiership he lasted for only twenty months. In terms of authority and achievements, there is no comparison between Pitt's brief second ministry and the first. Between 1804 and 1806 members of the cabinet were less capable and united than before, the opposition more formidable, the king less helpful, the war even more worrying, public opinion more alarmed and less easily placated, and Pitt was almost a broken force.

During the late 1790s retreats and mistakes had crept into Pitt's conduct. He was unable to deal with matters with his former assurance and dispatch. It was difficult for him to adapt once he was forced to accept that the war, despite his predictions, would not be short. His performance as premier was also affected by his constant (and, again, forlorn) hope that the war could be ended with one more offensive campaign or one more peace overture. The breach with the king on Catholic emancipation in 1801 was another shock from which it was difficult to recover, and Pitt admitted that he should have done more to prepare the ground before moving on this highly sensitive matter. Obstacles and difficulties led to greater procrastination than before, and pushed Pitt into vagueness and even misrepresentation. This was true of the Fitzwilliam crisis of 1795, but even more so in 1804 and 1805 when Pitt sought to enlarge his support base. He could not come to an understanding with George III, Grenville, Fox, Moira, Addington or any other prominent politician, and as a result his second ministry never established itself. A master of political tactics would not have made so unconditional an offer of support to Addington in 1801, notwithstanding the need at that moment to ease the king's mind. The problems Pitt faced thereafter were directly related to the delicate situation in which he had placed himself and the angry reactions he elicited on all sides as he tried to extricate himself from the mess. He was losing his touch, and his acceptance of the king's veto on particular men and measures, despite his conception of the nation's best interests, strengthened the idea that he was in irreversible decline.

The traits highlighted above are varied and sometimes contradictory, but Pitt's was such a long and eventful career that the lack of a straightforward pattern should come as no surprise. In the public imagination, official portraits, reminiscences of colleagues and cartoons by both his supporters and opponents, Pitt was youthful, thin and serious, a heavy drinker, an austere workaholic, a confident leader who achieved great things but continued to be beset by shyness, doubts and reverses. Hostile representations, especially from the Foxites and their successors, treat Pitt as a cold, scheming elitist, an authoritarian, an enemy of liberty who corrupted others beneath a veneer of probity, fairness and selflessness. In more flattering portrayals Pitt is an agreeable and attractive figure, restrained, controlled, clever and disciplined, patriotic and devoted. These latter characteristics, of course, are among those for which Pitt most wished to be remembered, but we must not allow him to set our interpretive agenda.

We can take account of the image fashioned by Pitt and imparted by his admirers after his death, but there is much more to his career and legacy than this approved version. To some extent Pitt *was* an upright patriotic public servant who put the nation's needs above his own, but to stress (as some commentators have done) his decision not to marry and his continual indebtedness as illustrations of self-sacrifice is to stretch the point unreasonably. Pitt's bachelorhood and self-denying habits typify the absence of a clear division between public and private in his mindset. In fact, it is difficult to believe that Pitt really had a private life. He may have had hobbies (notably planting and landscaping, chess, classical literature, riding and shooting), but these were hardly consuming passions. His decision not to marry had the same roots as his choice to work long hours and devote himself to government affairs: he *preferred* work. He had nothing else in his life that captivated him because he was incapable of forming the relationships and attachments that might have brought an alternative means of personal satisfaction. His life was given over to politics; this was what he wanted. Power fascinated him, politics made him, and most contemporaries derived their perceptions of him wholly from his actions as a politician. Uncomfortable and uncommunicative outside his small circle of friends, Pitt made a virtue of his preoccupation with affairs of state. But what else was there for him but public life, his arena of acclaim?

As for his debts, supposedly amassed because he was so busy attending to the nation's needs that he neglected his own, again questions might be asked. Pitt never seems to have been greatly concerned about his indebtedness, nor about whether or when he could pay his creditors back. He self-righteously declined many offers of financial help in order to sustain his reputation for independence and probity, and unlike the majority of well-placed public men of the age he refused to seek profit from office and influence. His attitude was either laudable or unnecessarily rigid, depending on one's viewpoint. To some contemporaries debt was no less an impropriety than the scramble for pensions and sinecures. Though Pitt made it his mission to restore the nation's finances, from 1780 he borrowed on a large scale for his own purposes. In time he received ample remuneration for his official functions, but he continued to live beyond his means and mismanaged his personal affairs to the extent that he was cheated by servants and tradesmen. Holwood House, purchased by Pitt in August 1785, was a significant drain on his resources, not only because of the mortgage he arranged, but also because of the improvements he made to the property. By the mid-1790s his debts had risen to about £30,000. In 1801 he owed £45,000, even though his salaries now amounted to £10,500 a year. Pitt's own father had been extravagant and died with debts unpaid, as did many eighteenth-century aristocrats, but Pitt's embarrassments were remarkable because they were so out of line with his public priorities, and even his friends could not understand why he became so heavily indebted.

After Pitt's death it was suggested that parliament should pay his debts. Wilberforce found this a regrettable affair, and argued that the debts should be settled privately. If they were made a public question, he thought, Pitt's reputation would suffer. Two days after Pitt's death Wilberforce wrote:

> I have heard, not without surprise, that his debts are considerable. A sum was named as large as £40 or 50,000. This must have been roguery, for he really has

not for many years lived at a rate of more than £5 or 6000 per annum. I do not say this lightly ... Now an idea was proposed of the nation's paying them; but I own, considering the time and circumstances in which he died, and the situation of the country, the burdens which must be laid on, and the sacrifices which must be borne, I should fear that ... however, through the mutual connivance of parties (Grenville related to Pitt; Fox, Windham etc. connected with Grenville) it might be carried in the House of Commons ... it might be grudgingly paid by the people at large, and create a feeling very injurious to his memory. Then it would be truly said, the precedent might be a very dangerous one, and might lead to sad party practices. But again – to whom are the debts due? If to tradesmen, they ought to be paid, but might not debts to other people, rich connections etc. be suspected; and the very idea of the people's paying these is monstrous. I must say, however, that considering the number of affluent men connected with Pitt, some of whom have got great and lucrative places from him, I cannot doubt but that, with perfect privacy and delicacy, a subscription might be made, adequate to the purpose.

Despite Wilberforce's lobbying, on 3 February 1806 parliament agreed to provide £40,000 to cover Pitt's debts, though it took another fifteen years before his complicated personal liabilities were finally settled.[7] Indebtedness could be taken (both at the time and afterwards) as a serious character flaw. For a prime minister who was so concerned about saving public money and regularly spoke of rectitude, responsibility and solvency, it is curious that Pitt remained indifferent to his own financial predicament and wilfully neglected his obligations.

Whatever his private defects, Pitt's public record remains impressive. He held high office for longer than any other political leader of his generation, and is still the second longest-serving premier in British history (his tenure of just under nineteen years is only surpassed by that of Walpole, who was chief minister from 1721 to 1742). He was also the youngest man ever to be appointed prime minister, and the fastest to rise to the premiership (less than three years after he was first elected to parliament). Before his decline he served with great distinction as chancellor of the exchequer, first lord of the treasury and leader of the House of Commons.[8] He presided over a swift recovery after the American war, consolidating the empire, expanding trade and correcting the finances, restoring British prestige abroad and providing political stability at home. True, the developing economy was basically strong anyway, and Pitt relied heavily on the ideas and methods of others. But he added vital contributions himself.

Pitt combined pragmatism with aspiration, caution with improvisation. As a politician he possessed outstanding gifts. As an administrator and technocrat he led the way in making the British state more efficient. He was incontestably a reformer, but not one who wanted major structural change. Rather, he reformed in order to improve and preserve. He had conservative goals. For him it was important to reinforce not weaken the established order, and to promote the prosperity and confidence that would reconcile others to the continuation of that order. In his war strategy Pitt undoubtedly fell short. In long run, however, he helped to bring about the final victory over France and guarantee Britain's postwar status as a world power. Pitt proved that Britain had the political and financial capacity to win the war. He arranged loans and raised taxes to produce the necessary funds, he organized coalitions with European states to combat the French and paid special attention to the West Indies, an economically important theatre in which the Royal Navy could be used to greatest effect. Pitt made sure that Britain could go on fighting. He found out what was politically and financially possible, an invaluable lesson for his successors.

Another side to Pitt's legacy was the lasting impact he had through his protégés. He trained future statesmen, consciously making himself an exemplar, giving some of them their first appointments, assisting, encouraging and instilling in them his code of professionalism, efficiency and devotion to duty. Huskisson was one of those who fell under Pitt's spell, and continued to judge himself by the standards his leader had set. Even as Pitt lay dying in January 1806, and despite Huskisson's despair at this 'melancholy situation', he knew he had to attend to his public responsibilities: 'Wretched as I am, the state of things is such that the business in parliament must go on, and there I must attend.'[9] This was a testament to Pitt's training and example.

Pitt remained a highly respected figure among parliamentarians, and his stature at Westminster was matched by his reputation in some sections of outdoor opinion, as was demonstrated by the formation of Pitt Clubs across the country during the 1810s and 1820s. It is clear, however, that Pitt's legacy was contested ground. Political leaders and extra-parliamentary organizations looked at his career selectively, extracting only what suited their own purposes and glossing over the rest.

It is also clear that Pitt left many unsolved problems. According to some commentators, he did little for Ireland. The defeat of his commercial propositions in 1785 was a heavy disappointment, and the following years showed that political, social and economic troubles in Ireland could not easily be mitigated. This increased Pitt's frustration, and he much preferred to attend to (for him) more interesting issues. Irish critics claimed that his attitude was not very helpful or constructive. But Pitt's outlook was circumscribed by political realities: it is not clear what else he could have done, and at least he *tried* to evolve a coherent Irish policy. The French

Revolution and war made this all the more difficult. Pitt's approach was sensible because it was flexible. He made concessions to Catholics during the early 1790s, but was careful not to commit himself to further gestures of this kind. To disorder his government responded with repression. Pitt's legislative union achieved its main purposes, and the emancipation crisis indicates that he would have done more for Ireland had he been able.

There were other important issues that had not been settled by the time of Pitt's death, and the result was prolonged political instability after 1806, with several changes of government. A semblance of order was only restored after 1812. Obviously Pitt left a gaping void. There was no clear successor as premier from among his close followers, and conflicts over policy matters and management of the war went on. Nor had Pitt been able to move beyond the narrow perspective shaped by executive routine. Firmly committed to aristocratic rule, Pitt's was a view from the top down, and he may have paid insufficient attention to what was happening out of doors – the economic expansion and social problems associated with the industrial revolution, the growth of the prosperous middle classes, the pressure for a more open and responsive state, the advent of participatory popular politics. He only partially understood and accommodated these forces for change.

Many members and supporters of the Tory administrations of the first half of the nineteenth century pointed to Pitt as their model and inspiration, yet there was disagreement about what Pitt really stood for. Rancorous splits occurred within Toryism, especially over Catholic emancipation, free trade and other reform questions. The divisive struggles over the Test and Corporation Acts, Catholic emancipation and parliamentary reform between 1828 and 1832, and over Irish policy and repeal of the Corn Laws in 1845 and 1846, prompt the suggestion that Pitt could and should have done more to settle these matters when he had the chance. Instead they became more serious and caused damaging crises after his death. Ongoing party battles meant that Pitt's principles and policies continued to feature in political controversy.

For some historians it is tempting to see Pitt as the founder of the nineteenth-century Tory party,[10] the originator of a 'liberal Toryism' that emerged in the 1820s (and came to fruition in the Peelism of 1841 to 1846), and the first recognizably modern prime minister, with his desire for greater professionalism and expertise in government and his focus upon shrewd financial management as the key to political stability, social peace and economic progress. But these things were not necessarily foreseen or intended. Pitt should be seen as a man of his times. His career was more of a culmination than a starting point; he was an eighteenth-century, not a nineteenth-century, politician. Pitt looked back to his father rather than forward to the Victorian era with its own peculiar needs and opportunities. Pitt's preferences, goals and methods are best understood in this context. He hoped to be the devoted and vigorous national leader that he believed his father had been. Of course circumstances had changed since his father's day. Pitt therefore had to strike out in new directions while respecting the lessons of the past. Yet even when he did so, his purposes were essentially conservative. His design was to protect the established order, which meant preserving those achievements of the past that were still apparent and worth reinforcing, and − as time passed − safeguarding the benefits of his own previous policies. By such means he thought he could enhance Britain's influence and security, prolong the mandate for elite rule, and render administrative mechanisms more effective.

In addition to building up a personal ascendancy as premier, Pitt wanted to gain the respect of subsequent generations. The drive to achieve lasting greatness was part of his patriotic calling, but any verdict on his deeds and personal qualities very much depends on the values of the observer's own time and place. What is 'greatness'? Opinions will differ. Perhaps its basic requirement is success in overcoming problems, and if so we cannot ignore Pitt's decline, however impressed we might be by what he achieved at his peak. We should not allow Pitt's self-presentation to determine how we rate him. He was an accomplished statesman but also an image-maker, and we must acknowledge his failings along with his merits. Each generation decides what it most admires in public figures past and present. Significantly, Pitt achieved enough, in difficult circumstances, for his fame to live on. There has been no eclipse. But it is worth remembering that in his own day, and afterwards, Pitt was attacked as well as applauded, hated as well as adored.

Notes

Notes to Introduction

1. *Parliamentary Debates*, first series, VI (London, 1806), 41–73.
2. *History*, 83 (1998).
3. E. g. John Derry's *Politics in the Age of Fox, Pitt and Liverpool* (Basingstoke, 1990) and my own *The Age of Unease* (Stroud, 2000).

Notes to Chapter 1: Beginnings

1. *Dictionary of National Biography*, ed. S. Lee, vol. 15 (London, 1909), pp. 1233–72; D. Englefield, J. Seaton and I. White, *British Prime Ministers* (London, 1995), pp. 45–51, 75–82. See also the family tree in N. Tolstoy, *The Half-Mad Lord: Thomas Pitt, Second Baron Camelford* (London, 1978), p. 3. The first Baron Camelford was William Pitt the Elder's nephew.
2. Thomas Pitt was MP for Okehampton, 1727–54, and Old Sarum, 1754–55 and 1761. Corbet was MP for Montgomery, 1728–41, and Ludlow, 1741–48. Needham served as MP for Old Sarum, 1734–41.
3. He was MP for Old Sarum from 1735 to 1747, Seaford from 1747 to 1754, Aldborough from 1754 to 1756, Okehampton from 1756 to 1757, and Bath from 1757 to 1766. Two useful studies of Pitt the Elder are J. Black, *Pitt the Elder* (Cambridge, 1992), and M. Peters, *The Elder Pitt* (Harlow, 1998).
4. Throughout his life the Elder Pitt was restless and temperamental, and in his later years his mind was unstable. There was a history of mental illness in his mother's family. A strain of eccentricity seems also to have surfaced in some descendants of 'Diamond' Pitt. In fact Ann, the Elder Pitt's favourite sister, died in an asylum. His granddaughter Lady Hester Stanhope and great-nephew the second Baron Camelford were also known for their unconventional behaviour.
5. Richard Grenville was MP for Wendover, 1715–22, and Buckingham, 1722–27.
6. As well as the sources listed above, see E. J. Evans, *William Pitt the Younger* (London, 1999), p. 3; J. Gregory and J. Stevenson, *Britain in the Eighteenth Century, 1688–1820* (Harlow, 2000), pp. 53–55. On the Grenville family in politics, see J. J. Sack, *The Grenvillites, 1801–29: Party Politics and Factionalism in the Age of Pitt and Liverpool* (Urbana, Illinois, 1979), chs 1–2.
7. Mahon was MP for Chipping Wycombe, 1780–86.
8. He was first lord of the admiralty 1788–94, lord privy seal 1794–96, lord

president of the council 1796–1801, and master general of the ordnance 1801–6 and 1807–10.

9. Edward Eliot was MP for St Germains, 1780–84, and Liskeard, 1784–97, and a lord of the treasury from 1782 to 1793.

10. Englefield, Seaton and White, *Prime Ministers*, p. 75.

11. Family letters from about 1765 to 1773 constantly refer to Pitt the Younger's illnesses. Between the ages of six and fourteen he suffered from colds, swellings, loss of weight, bad coughs and debility.

12. P. H. Stanhope, *Life of the Right Honourable William Pitt* (4 vols, London, 1861–62), vol. 1, p. 4, and ch. 1 generally on Pitt's early life. See also Evans, *Pitt the Younger*, p. 3; J. Ehrman, *The Younger Pitt* (3 vols, London, 1969, 1983, 1996), vol. 1, ch. 1; J. Holland Rose, *William Pitt and National Revival* (London, 1911), chs 1–3; R. Reilly, *Pitt the Younger, 1759–1806* (London, 1978), ch. 1.

13. Stanhope, *Life of Pitt*, vol. 1, p. 7.

14. Pitt the Elder had studied at Trinity College, Oxford, from 1726 to 1728, though left without taking a degree (ill health forced him to travel abroad). He had been thinking of Oxford for his son, but took Wilson's advice and sent him to Pembroke Hall instead. Pitt the Younger was only fourteen. It was a little early to enrol him at university, but Wilson and his father both saw him as exceptional.

15. Stanhope, *Life of Pitt*, vol. 1, p. 27. Fox had been a junior member of North's government from 1770 to 1774, but broke with the prime minister (and George III) because of what he regarded as North's weak leadership and reluctance to offer the Fox family more patronage. L. G. Mitchell, *Charles James Fox* (Oxford, 1992), pp. 18–24.

16. Stanhope, *Life of Pitt*, vol. 1, pp. 21–22.

17. Stanhope, *Life of Pitt*, vol. 1, pp. 41, 63.

18. *Selections from the Letters and Correspondence of Sir James Bland Burges*, ed. J. Hutton (London, 1885), pp. 60–61.

19. Englefield, Seaton and White, *Prime Ministers*, p. 81; Evans, *Pitt the Younger*, p. 4.

20. Englefield, Seaton and White, *Prime Ministers*, pp. 76, 80; Evans, *Pitt the Younger*, p. 3.

21. J. Brooke, *King George III* (London, 1972), pp. 217–18; I. R. Christie, 'Economical Reform and "the Influence of the Crown", 1780', *Historical Journal*, 12 (1956), pp. 144–54, and idem, *Myth and Reality in Late Eighteenth-Century British Politics* (London, 1970), pp. 27–54; L. B. Namier, 'King George III: A Study of Personality', in idem, *Personalities and Powers* (London, 1955), pp. 39–58; R. Pares, *George III and the Politicians* (Oxford, 1953).

22. M. Duffy, *The Younger Pitt* (Harlow, 2000), p. 3.

23. Stanhope, *Life of Pitt*, vol. 1, pp. 29–30, 36–38.

24. Stanhope, *Life of Pitt*, vol. 1, pp. 30–31.

25. Stanhope, *Life of Pitt*, vol. 1, p. 47; Duffy, *Younger Pitt*, pp. 1–4; Evans, *Pitt the Younger*, pp. 4–5; Englefield, Seaton and White, *Prime Ministers*, pp. 48–49, 76; Gregory and Stevenson, *Britain in the Eighteenth Century*, pp. 84, 86, 91;

L. B. Namier and J. Brooke, *The House of Commons, 1754–90* (3 vols, London, 1964), vol. 1, pp. 219–21, 404–6.

26. Stanhope, *Life of Pitt*, vol. 1, pp. 46–47; Ehrman, *Pitt*, vol. 1, p. 26.

27. Ehrman, *Pitt*, vol. 1, pp. 52, 55; Englefield, Seaton and White, *Prime Ministers*, pp. 77–78; Stanhope, *Life of Pitt*, vol. 1, pp. 54–58; R. I. and S. Wilberforce, *The Life of William Wilberforce* (5 vols, London, 1838), vol. 1, p. 22; *Parliamentary Debates*, XXI (London, 1814), 1261–66; *Speeches of the Right Honourable William Pitt in the House of Commons*, ed. W. S. Hathaway (4 vols, London, 1806), vol. 1, pp. 1–7.

Notes to Chapter 2: Inheritance

1. Most of this chapter is based on material in Gregory and Stevenson, *Britain in the Eighteenth Century*; Englefield, Seaton and White, *Prime Ministers*, pp. 45–51; *The Eighteenth Century*, ed. P. Langford (Oxford, 2002); F. O'Gorman, *The Long Eighteenth Century* (London, 1997), chs 2–7; G. Williams and J. Ramsden, *Ruling Britannia: A Political History of Britain, 1688–1988* (London, 1995), chs 1–6.

2. K. Wilson, *The Sense of the People: Politics, Culture and Imperialism, 1715–85* (Cambridge, 1995).

3. The vast majority of seats were in England. Scotland had 45, Wales 24, and England 489 seats. England had 40 counties returning 2 members each, 196 boroughs returning 2 members each, 2 boroughs returning 4 members each, 5 boroughs returning 1 member each, and the two universities, Oxford and Cambridge, returning 2 members each. Wales had 12 counties and 12 boroughs, each returning 1 member. Scotland had 27 counties returning 1 member each, 3 combined counties returning 1 member each, one burgh (Edinburgh) returning 1 member, and 14 groups of burghs returning 1 member each. In 1801, Ireland lost its separate legislature and the House of Commons in the United Kingdom parliament at Westminster was expanded to accommodate 100 Irish MPs (64 from counties, 35 from boroughs, and 1 from Trinity College, Dublin).

4. At a by-election he was returned for Old Sarum, a notoriously rotten borough in which the Pitts had for some time cultivated a family interest. The Old Sarum constituency consisted of a hill in Wiltshire and had an electorate of seven.

5. The leader of this faction was Sir Richard Temple, Viscount Cobham, a former supporter of Walpole who went into opposition in 1733. He was joined by three of his nephews: Richard Temple-Grenville (later first Earl Temple), George Grenville, and George Lyttelton (later Baron Lyttelton). Hester Grenville, whom Pitt the Elder later married, was one of his nieces.

6. Pitt's active support for government measures did not appease the king, but Pelham and Newcastle were most appreciative. At the general election of 1747 Pitt was returned for Seaford, where government influence was decisive, and in 1754 he was elected for Aldborough, one of Newcastle's boroughs.

7. Newcastle resigned because Pitt refused to serve under him. Pitt vacated Aldborough on accepting office and was now MP for Okehampton.

Notes to Chapter 3: Arrival

1. *Parliamentary Debates*, XXII (London, 1814), 486–89; *Speeches of Pitt*, vol. 1, pp. 16–20; Stanhope, *Life of Pitt*, vol. 1, pp. 60–62.
2. *Parliamentary Debates*, XXII, 363, 731–35; *Speeches of Pitt*, vol. 1, pp. 20–25; Stanhope, *Life of Pitt*, vol. 1, pp. 65–66.
3. Englefield, Seaton and White, *Prime Ministers*, pp. 62, 78; Duffy, *Younger Pitt*, pp. 4–5; *English Historical Documents, 1714–83*, ed. D. B. Horne and M. Ransome (London, 1957), pp. 122–23.
4. Stanhope, *Life of Pitt*, vol. 1, pp. 70–72; Duffy, *Younger Pitt*, p. 6; Evans, *Pitt the Younger*, p. 6; Reilly, *Pitt the Younger*, p. 66; *Parliamentary Debates*, XXII, 1149.
5. Ehrman, *Pitt*, vol. 1, pp. 80–81; Duffy, *Younger Pitt*, pp. 5–6; Englefield, Seaton and White, *Prime Ministers*, pp. 67, 78; Evans, *Pitt the Younger*, pp. 4–5.
6. *Parliamentary Debates*, XVI (London, 1813), 747–55.
7. *Parliamentary Debates*, XXII, 1416–38, XXIII (London, 1814), 48–51, 101–9; Duffy, *Younger Pitt*, pp. 6–7; Englefield, Seaton and White, *Prime Ministers*, p. 78; Evans, *Pitt the Younger*, pp. 5, 11; Reilly, *Pitt the Younger*, pp. 66–68; A. G. Olson, *The Radical Duke: Career and Correspondence of Charles Lennox, Third Duke of Richmond* (Oxford, 1961), ch. 4.
8. Duffy, *Younger Pitt*, pp. 7–9; Reilly, *Pitt the Younger*, ch. 6; Mitchell, *Fox*, pp. 46–56.
9. Englefield, Seaton and White, *Prime Ministers*, p. 76.
10. Duffy, *Younger Pitt*, pp. 9–10; Reilly, *Pitt the Younger*, p. 74; Englefield, Seaton and White, *Prime Ministers*, pp. 67, 78; Evans, *Pitt the Younger*, pp. 6–7; J. S. Watson, *The Reign of George III* (Oxford, 1960), p. 579; *The Correspondence of King George III*, ed. J. Fortescue (6 vols, London, 1967), vol. 6, pp. 97, 236–37; E. Fitzmaurice, *The Life of William, Earl of Shelburne* (3 vols, London, 1875), vol. 3, p. 342; Duke of Buckingham and Chandos, *Memoirs of the Court and Cabinets of George III* (4 vols, London, 1853–5), vol. 1, pp. 148–49; Mitchell, *Fox*, pp. 57–59.
11. *Speeches of Pitt*, vol. 1, pp. 50–64; *Parliamentary Debates*, XXIII, 543–55; *Diaries and Correspondence of James Harris, the first Earl of Malmesbury*, ed. Earl of Malmesbury (4 vols, London, 1844), vol. 2, p. 35; Duffy, *Younger Pitt*, pp. 10–11; Englefield, Seaton and White, *Prime Ministers*, p. 78.
12. Stanhope, *Life of Pitt*, vol. 1, appendix pp. i–iii; Buckingham and Chandos, *Memoirs*, vol. 1, pp. 206–10; Fortescue, *Correspondence of George III*, vol. 6, pp. 311–12; Ehrman, *Pitt*, vol. 1, pp. 103–4; Duffy, *Younger Pitt*, pp. 12–13; Reilly, *Pitt the Younger*, pp. 84–85; Evans, *Pitt the Younger*, pp. 7–8; Rose, *National Revival*, pp. 124–28; M. Fry, *The Dundas Despotism* (Edinburgh, 1992), pp. 90–95.
13. *The Political Memoranda of Francis, Fifth Duke of Leeds*, ed. O. Browning

(London, 1884), pp. 82–89; *Parliamentary Debates*, XXIII, 827–75, 945–59; *Speeches of Pitt*, vol. 1, pp. 43–52, 72–88; *Speeches of the Right Honourable C. J. Fox in the House of Commons*, ed. J. Wright (6 vols, London, 1815), vol. 2, pp. 171–74; Evans, *Pitt the Younger*, pp. 11–12; Duffy, *Younger Pitt*, pp. 13–14; Gregory and Stevenson, *Britain in the Eighteenth Century*, p. 112; Stanhope, *Life of Pitt*, vol. 1, pp. 118–22; Rose, *National Revival*, pp. 130–32.

14. The definitive treaties of peace with the United States, France and Spain were eventually signed in Paris and Versailles on 3 September 1783.

15. Mitchell, *Fox*, pp. 59–64; Reilly, *Pitt the Younger*, pp. 89–95.

16. *Diaries and Correspondence of the Right Honourable George Rose*, ed. L. V. Harcourt (2 vols, London, 1860), vol. 1, p. 45.

17. *Speeches of Pitt*, vol. 1, pp. 89–98; Mitchell, *Fox*, pp. 64–65.

18. Stanhope, *Life of Pitt*, vol. 1, p. 155; Rose, *National Revival*, pp. 148–49, 152–53; J. Cannon, *The Fox-North Coalition* (Cambridge, 1969), pp. 128–31; P. Kelly, 'The Pitt-Temple Administration, 19–22 December 1783', *Historical Journal*, 17 (1974), pp. 157–61; Duffy, *Younger Pitt*, pp. 15–17; Buckingham and Chandos, *Memoirs*, vol. 1, pp. 283–91.

19. Gower had been a member of several governments from 1755 to 1757 and 1767 to 1779.

20. *Parliamentary Debates*, XXIV (London, 1815), 196–237; *Speeches of Pitt*, vol. 1, pp. 98–100; Stanhope, *Life of Pitt*, vol. 1, pp. 151–53; *English Historical Documents, 1783–1832*, ed. A. Aspinall and E. A. Smith (London, 1959), pp. 252, 284–86; Englefield, Seaton and White, *Prime Ministers*, p. 78; Duffy, *Younger Pitt*, pp. 17–18; Evans, *Pitt the Younger*, pp. 8–9; Rose, *National Revival*, pp. 142–51; Gregory and Stevenson, *Britain in the Eighteenth Century*, pp. 52–57; Mitchell, *Fox*, pp. 65–70; Olson, *Radical Duke*, ch. 5.

21. Horn and Ransome, *English Historical Documents*, pp. 125–27; Fortescue, *Correspondence of George III*, vol. 6, pp. 473–77; *The Later Correspondence of George III*, ed. A. Aspinall (5 vols, Cambridge, 1966), vol. 1, pp. 3–7.

22. P. Kelly, 'British Politics, 1783–4: The Emergence and Triumph of the Younger Pitt's Administration', *Bulletin of the Institute of Historical Research*, 54 (1981), pp. 67–68; Duffy, *Younger Pitt*, pp. 18–19; Englefield, Seaton and White, *Prime Ministers*, p. 78; Mitchell, *Fox*, chs 3–4.

23. Temple may have resigned entirely of his own volition. A proud and difficult man, he wanted a promotion in the peerage in return for his services, and expected Pitt to defer to his advice on appointments and other matters. His resignation was, at least in part, a hasty response to disappointment on these points. Buckingham and Chandos, *Memoirs*, vol. 1, pp. 291–93.

24. Hutton, *Burges*, pp. 66–68; Harcourt, *Rose*, vol. 1, p. 50; Duffy, *Younger Pitt*, pp. 19–20; Wilberforce, *Life*, vol. 1, ch. 3; Kelly, 'Pitt-Temple Administration', pp. 157–61; P. J. Jupp, 'Earl Temple's Resignation and the Question of a Dissolution in December 1793', *Historical Journal*, 15 (1972), pp. 309–13; E. A. Smith, 'Earl Temple's Resignation, 22 December 1783', *Historical Journal*, 6 (1963), pp. 91–97; Browning, *Leeds*, pp. 90–102.

25. Ehrman, *Pitt*, vol. 1, pp. 129–33; Duffy, *Younger Pitt*, pp. 21–22.

26. *Speeches of Pitt*, vol. 1, pp. 101–6; *Parliamentary Debates*, XXIV, 268–99, 347–52, 360–80; 392–412; Aspinall and Smith, *English Historical Documents*, pp. 140–41; Mitchell, *Fox*, pp. 68–70.

27. Pitt's father had made similar gestures. It has already been noted, for example, that as paymaster of the forces from 1746, the Elder Pitt accepted only his official salary. He conspicuously eschewed the perks that normally came with this post, such as appropriating interest payments on the large sums under his control, or taking the commission foreign governments usually paid on receipt of their subsidies.

28. Englefield, Seaton and White, *Prime Ministers*, p. 78.

29. E.g. Wilberforce, *Life*, vol. 1, pp. 388–89; Aspinall and Smith, *English Historical Documents*, pp. 307–8.

30. *Parliamentary Debates*, XXIV, 450–72, 481–84; *Speeches of Pitt*, vol. 1, pp. 139–43.

31. *Parliamentary Debates*, XXIV, 733–44, 774–75; *Memorials and Correspondence of C. J. Fox*, ed. Lord J. Russell (4 vols, London, 1853–57), vol. 4, pp. 276–79; Duffy, *Younger Pitt*, pp. 24–27; Rose, *National Revival*, ch. 7; Reilly, *Pitt the Younger*, ch. 9.

32. Englefield, Seaton and White, *Prime Ministers*, p. 77; Duffy, *Younger Pitt*, pp. 27–28; Gregory and Stevenson, *Britain in the Eighteenth Century*, p. 108; Mitchell, *Fox*, pp. 70–71.

33. W. T. Laprade, 'William Pitt and Westminster Elections', *American Historical Review*, 18 (1913), pp. 253–74, and idem, 'Public Opinion and the General Election of 1784', *English Historical Review*, 31 (1916), pp. 224–37; C. E. Fryer, 'The General Election of 1784', *History*, 9 (1925), pp. 221–23; M. D. George, 'Fox's Martyrs: the General Election of 1784', *Transactions of the Royal Historical Society*, 4th series, 21 (1939), pp. 133–68; P. Kelly, 'Radicalism and Public Opinion in the General Election of 1784', *Bulletin of the Institute of Historical Research*, 45 (1972), pp. 73–88, and idem, 'British Politics, 1783–4', pp. 62–78; Wilberforce, *Life*, vol. 1, pp. 55–64; Fry, *Dundas*, pp. 99–104; Evans, *Pitt the Younger*, p. 14. For conflicting interpretations of the electoral system and its importance, see L. B. Namier, *The Structure of Politics at the Accession of George III* (London, 1963); J. C. D. Clark, *English Society, 1688–1832* (Cambridge, 1985); J. A. Phillips, *Electoral Behaviour in Unreformed England* (Princeton, 1982); F. O'Gorman, *Voters, Patrons and Parties: The Unreformed Electoral System of Hanoverian England* (Oxford, 1989); A. D. Harvey, *Britain in the Early Nineteenth Century* (London, 1978), ch. 2.

34. Englefield, Seaton and White, *Prime Ministers*, p. 76; Namier and Brooke, *Commons*, vol. 1, pp. 220–21; R. G. Thorne, *The House of Commons, 1790–1820* (5 vols, London, 1986), vol. 2, p. 33. After his appointment as first lord of the treasury, Pitt had been re-elected (unopposed) as MP for Appleby on 3 January 1784.

35. *Speeches of Pitt*, vol. 1, pp. 161–65; *Parliamentary Debates*, XXIV, 829–43.

Notes to Chapter 4: Reform

1. *The Manuscripts of the Duke of Rutland, Preserved at Belvoir Castle*, Historical Manuscripts Commission, no. 24 (4 vols, London, 1894), vol. 3, p. 126; Fry, *Dundas*, pp. 111–18.

2. *Rutland Manuscripts*, vol. 3, p. 125; Ehrman, *Pitt*, vol. 1, pp. 119–21, 189–95, 443–66, vol. 2, p. 32; Stanhope, *Life of Pitt*, vol. 1, pp. 179–94, 224, 227–29, 295–305, 327–30, 353–58, 359–62, vol. 2, pp. 86–87, 318–20; *Speeches of Pitt*, vol. 1, pp. 319–33, 361–70, vol. 2, pp. 1–14; Reilly, *Pitt the Younger*, pp. 107–8, ch. 13; Duffy, *Younger Pitt*, pp. 53, 79, 138; Evans, *Pitt the Younger*, pp. 19–20; Rose, *National Revival*, ch. 10; P. J. Jupp, *Lord Grenville, 1759–1834* (Oxford, 1985), pp. 48–52; Mitchell, *Fox*, pp. 76–80; Gregory and Stevenson, *Britain in the Eighteenth Century*, p. 60; *Parliamentary Debates*, XXIV (London, 1815), 1034–1215, 1290–1316, XXV (London, 1815), 1202–44, 1266–93, 1338–48, XXVII (London, 1816), 65–153, 177–263; Fry, *Dundas*, pp. 118–29; Buckingham and Chandos, *Memoirs*, vol. 1, pp. 356, 361; *Historical and Posthumous Memoirs of Sir Nathaniel William Wraxall*, ed. H. B. Wheatley (5 vols, London, 1884), vol. 5, pp. 76–77; Englefield, Seaton and White, *Prime Ministers*, pp. 78–79; Aspinall and Smith, *English Historical Documents*, pp. 825–31.

3. Stanhope, *Life of Pitt*, vol. 1, pp. 207–11, 213–14, 224–25, 253–54, 288–89; Ehrman, *Pitt*, vol. 1, pp. 217–23; *Speeches of Pitt*, vol. 1, pp. 165–79, 210–22, 280–99; *Parliamentary Debates*, XXIV, 843–940, XXV, 1–146, 375–91, 1096–1157; P. Kelly, 'Pitt versus Fox: The Westminster Scrutiny, 1784–85', *Studies in Burke and His Time*, 15 (1972–73), pp. 155–62; Duffy, *Younger Pitt*, pp. 142–43; Reilly, *Pitt the Younger*, pp. 106–7; Aspinall, *Later Correspondence of George III*, vol. 1, pp. 116–18; Englefield, Seaton and White, *Prime Ministers*, p. 78; Watson, *Reign of George III*, pp. 275–76.

4. Duffy, *Younger Pitt*, pp. 80–81; Stanhope, *Life of Pitt*, vol. 1, p. 233; *Correspondence between the Right Honourable William Pitt and Charles, Duke of Rutland*, ed. Lord Stanhope (London, 1890), p. 49; Hutton, *Burges*, p. 68; H. Roseveare, *The Treasury, 1660–1870: The Foundations of Control* (London, 1973), pp. 149–53; J. E. D. Binney, *British Finance and Administration, 1774–94* (Oxford, 1958), pp. 110–13, 262–82; Ehrman, *Pitt*, vol. 1, pp. 239–81; Jupp, *Grenville*, pp. 57–58.

5. Stanhope, *Life of Pitt*, vol. 1, pp. 289–94, 330; Duffy, *Younger Pitt*, pp. 82–83; Binney, *British Finance*, pp. 109–16; *Speeches of Pitt*, vol. 1, pp. 299–319, vol. 2, p. 44; Ehrman, *Pitt*, vol. 1, pp. 260–73; Rose, *National Revival*, ch. 8; Reilly, *Pitt the Younger*, pp. 108–13; Evans, *Pitt the Younger*, pp. 20–21; *Parliamentary Debates*, XXV, 1294–1323, 1362–69, 1416–32, XXVI (London, 1816), 17–36, 733–37, 752–62, 894–913.

6. *Speeches of Fox*, vol. 3, pp. 155–66.

7. *Speeches of Pitt*, vol. 2, pp. 24–49; *Parliamentary Debates*, XXIX (London, 1817), 816–49; Duffy, *Younger Pitt*, pp. 81–82; P. Harling, *The Waning of Old Corruption: The Politics of Economical Reform in Britain, 1779–1846* (Oxford, 1996), pp. 42–55; Stanhope, *Life of Pitt*, vol. 2, pp. 139–41; Evans, *Pitt the Younger*,

pp. 18–19, 20–21. There is a detailed account of Pitt's financial and administrative reforms in Ehrman, *Pitt*, vol. 1, chs 10–11. For a statistical record of
public revenue and expenditure after 1783, see Aspinall and Smith, *English
Historical Documents*, pp. 576–77.

8. Philip Harling rejects the view of William Rubinstein that corruption persisted
'in actual fact as well as in radical rhetoric'. W. D. Rubinstein, 'The End of
"Old Corruption" in Britain, 1780–1860', *Past and Present*, 101 (1983), pp. 55–86;
P. Harling, 'Rethinking "Old Corruption"', *Past and Present*, 147 (1995), pp. 127–
58.

9. See Harling, *Waning of Old Corruption*, chs 2–3.

10. J. Innes, 'Politics and Morals: The Reformation of Manners Movement in Later
Eighteenth-Century England', in *The Transformation of Political Culture*, ed.
E. Hellmuth (Oxford, 1990), pp. 57–118.

11. J. R. Breihan, 'William Pitt and the Commission on Fees, 1785–1801', *Historical
Journal*, 27 (1984), pp. 59–81. See also Evans, *Pitt the Younger*, pp. 21–22, and
on the long-term changes wrought by economical reform, N. Chester, *The
English Administrative System, 1780–1870* (Oxford, 1981), pp. 12–30, 58–66, 123–
68.

12. *Parliamentary Debates*, XXV, 298–311.

13. W. R. Ward, 'The Administration of the Window and Assessed Taxes, 1698–
1798', *English Historical Review*, 67 (1952), pp. 522–42.

14. J. Brewer, *The Sinews of Power: War, Money and the English State, 1688–1783*
(London, 1989), chs 5,8, and conclusion.

15. E.g. P. J. Jupp, 'The Landed Elite and Political Authority in Britain, 1760–1850',
Journal of British Studies, 29 (1990), pp. 53–79; P. Harling and P. Mandler,
'From "Fiscal-Military" State to Laissez-Faire State, 1760–1850', *Journal of British
Studies*, 32 (1993), pp. 44–70.

16. *Parliamentary Debates*, XXV, 311–67, 409–14; *Speeches of Pitt*, vol. 1, pp. 194–209;
Duffy, *Younger Pitt*, pp. 79–80; Evans, *Pitt the Younger*, pp. 63–65; Jupp, *Grenville*, pp. 52–55; Englefield, Seaton and White, *Prime Ministers*, p. 78.

17. *Speeches of Fox*, vol. 3, pp. 54–61.

18. Ehrman, *Pitt*, vol. 1, pp. 197–216; Reilly, *Pitt the Younger*, ch. 11; *Speeches of
Pitt*, vol. 1, pp. 245–80; *Parliamentary Debates*, XXV, 575–778, 820–85, 934–85;
J. Kelly, *Prelude to Union: Anglo-Irish Politics in the 1780s* (Cork, 1992);
D. R. Schweitzer, 'The Failure of William Pitt's Irish Trade Propositions, 1785',
Parliamentary History, 3 (1984), pp. 129–45; Rose, *National Revival*, ch. 11; *The
Journal and Correspondence of William, Lord Auckland*, ed. G. Hogge (4 vols,
London, 1861–62), vol. 1, pp. 78–85; R. B. McDowwall, *Ireland in the Age of
Imperialism and Revolution, 1760–1801* (Oxford, 1979), ch. 8.

19. Stanhope, *Life of Pitt*, vol. 1, pp. 264–75, 286.

20. *Speeches of Pitt*, vol. 1, pp. 237–54; *Speeches of Fox*, vol. 3, pp. 263–82; Englefield,
Seaton and White, *Prime Ministers*, p. 78; *Parliamentary Debates*, XXVI (Lon-
don, 1816), 233–55, 268–73, 342–61, 378–514, 534–96; Mitchell, *Fox*, pp. 57, 122;
Aspinall and Smith, *English Historical Documents*, pp. 557–59; Hogge, *Auckland*,

vol. 1, chs 5–6; Stanhope, *Life of Pitt*, vol. 1, pp. 287, 315–17; Ehrman, *Pitt*, vol. 1, ch. 16; Reilly, *Pitt the Younger*, pp. 114–16; Evans, *Pitt the Younger*, pp. 28–29.

21. Stanhope, *Life of Pitt*, vol. 1, p. 287; Ehrman, *Pitt*, vol. 1, pp. 485–86; Duffy, *Younger Pitt*, p. 170; Hogge, *Auckland*, vol. 1, pp. 86–90.

22. Watson, *Reign of George III*, p. 291; N. Gash, 'After Waterloo: British Society and the Legacy of the Napoleonic Wars', *Transactions of the Royal Historical Society*, 5th series, 28 (1978), pp. 145–57; Ehrman, *Pitt*, vol. 1, pp. 268–69; A. Briggs, *The Age of Improvement, 1783–1867* (London, 1979), pp. 121–22; Aspinall and Smith, *English Historical Documents*, p. 578.

23. *Speeches of Pitt*, vol. 1, pp. 81–88; Ehrman, *Pitt*, vol. 1, pp. 58, 66, 70–71; Chester, *Administrative System*, pp. 1–11, 31–41, 67–68; G. E. Aylmer, 'From Office-Holding to Civil Service: The Genesis of Modern Bureaucracy', *Transactions of the Royal Historical Society*, 5th series, 30 (1980), pp. 91–108; J. Torrance, 'Social Class and Bureaucratic Innovation: The Commissioners for Examining the Public Accounts, 1780–87', *Past and Present*, 78 (1978), pp. 56–81; W. R. Ward, 'Some Eighteenth-Century Civil Servants: The English Revenue Commissioners, 1754–98', *English Historical Review*, 70 (1955), pp. 25–54.

24. D. G. Barnes, *George III and William Pitt, 1783–1806* (New York, 1965), p. 127; Aspinall, *Later Correspondence of George III*, vol. 1, pp. 138–41; Aspinall and Smith, *English Historical Documents*, pp. 286–87.

25. Aspinall and Smith, *English Historical Documents*, p. 312; Fry, *Dundas*, p. 145. Dundas was not personally committed to parliamentary reform, and for the government it was an open question, so he was free to vote against Pitt if he chose.

26. *Speeches of Pitt*, vol. 1, pp. 222–39; Ehrman, *Pitt*, vol. 1, pp. 223–28; Stanhope, *Life of Pitt*, vol. 1, pp. 256–59; *Parliamentary Debates*, XXV, 432–78; Rose, *National Revival*, pp. 196–206; Reilly, *Pitt the Younger*, pp. 130–31.

27. *Parliamentary Debates*, XXV, 455–62; *Speeches of Fox*, vol. 3, pp. 145–52; Aspinall and Smith, *English Historical Documents*, p. 306; Evans, *Pitt the Younger*, pp. 14–16; Mitchell, *Fox*, pp. 252–61.

28. *Parliamentary Debates*, XXV, 475–78; Aspinall and Smith, *English Historical Documents*, p. 287; Englefield, Seaton and White, *Prime Ministers*, p. 78; Phillips, *Electoral Behaviour in Unreformed England*; O'Gorman, *Voters, Patrons and Parties*; P. Kelly, 'Constituents' Instructions to Members of Parliament in the Eighteenth Century', in *Party and Management in Parliament, 1660–1784*, ed. C. Jones (Leicester, 1984), pp. 169–89.

29. G. M. Ditchfield, 'The House of Lords and Parliamentary Reform in the 1780s', *Bulletin of the Institute of Historical Research*, 54 (1981), pp. 207–25; C. Hay, 'John Sawbridge and Popular Politics in Late Eighteenth-Century Britain', *Historian*, 52 (1990), pp. 551–61; C. Wyvill, *Political Papers* (6 vols, York, 1794–1804), vol. 4, pp. 32–33. For context see J. Cannon, *Parliamentary Reform, 1640–1832* (Cambridge, 1972), ch. 4.

30. *Parliamentary Debates*, XXV, 392–409, 913–20, XXVI, 1–5, 178–86; *The Manuscripts of Lord Kenyon*, Historical Manuscripts Commission, no. 35 (London,

1894), p. 525; Stanhope, *Life of Pitt*, vol. 1, pp. 294–95; Ehrman, *Pitt*, vol. 1, p. 228.

31. Duffy, *Younger Pitt*, pp. 135–36; *Parliamentary Debates*, XXVIII (London, 1816), 469, XXXI (London, 1818), 532; *Speeches of Pitt*, vol. 1, pp. 77, 225, 232–37, vol. 2, pp. 89–92, 143–56, vol. 3, pp. 127–40. Wyvill turned against Pitt in the 1790s, but the prominent Whig hostess Lady Holland remarked that Pitt gained as much popularity by resisting parliamentary reform in 1797 as he had by advocating it earlier in his career. *The Journal of Elizabeth, Lady Holland, 1791–1811*, ed. Lord Ilchester (2 vols, London, 1908), vol. 1, p. 102.

32. Pitt took the lead in Commons debates on the measure, because Grenville was elevated to the Lords in November 1790, but Grenville was its main author. Jupp, *Grenville*, pp. 93–97.

33. *Parliamentary Debates*, XXVIII, 1271, 1376–79, XXIX, 104–13, 359–430, 655–60; Ehrman, *Pitt*, vol. 1, pp. 360–71; Duffy, *Younger Pitt*, pp. 93, 168; Englefield, Seaton and White, *Prime Ministers*, p. 79; Briggs, *Age of Improvement*, p. 126; Stanhope, *Life of Pitt*, vol. 2, pp. 89–96; *Speeches of Fox*, vol. 4, pp. 200–28; Mitchell, *Fox*, p. 115; Aspinall and Smith, *English Historical Documents*, pp. 815–23.

34. Wilberforce, *Life*, vol. 1, p. 95, vol. 3, p. 245.

35. *Parliamentary Debates*, XXIV, 113–19, XXVIII, 1262–69, 1364–76; Stanhope, *Life of Pitt*, vol. 2, pp. 100–1; Ehrman, *Pitt*, vol. 2, pp. 81–84.

36. *Parliamentary Debates*, XVII (London, 1813), 440–41.

37. Despite Pitt's sympathy for mild Catholic relief in 1791, he would have preferred not to have the matter brought up in the wake of the Dissenters' campaign for repeal of the Test and Corporation Acts. He wrote to Grenville in January 1791: 'I wish there did not exist the occasion for the application of the Catholics. It certainly never can be agitated without a possibility of its being improperly confounded with the question of the Dissenters. This, however, is no good reason against the Catholics.' *The Manuscripts of J. B. Fortescue Preserved at Dropmore*, Historical Manuscripts Commission, no. 30 (10 vols, London, 1894), vol. 2, p. 13. Grenville's approach to these questions was purely tactical during the 1790s. He did not treat toleration as a matter of principle. See Jupp, *Grenville*, pp. 270, 273.

38. *Parliamentary Debates*, XXVI, 780–832, XXVIII, 1–41, 387–452; Stanhope, *Life of Pitt*, vol. 1, pp. 336–38, vol. 2, pp. 33–34; *Speeches of Fox*, vol. 3, pp. 310–17, vol. 4, pp. 1–10, 55–76, 114–54, 418–29, vol. 6, pp. 586–615; Mitchell, *Fox*, pp. 242–47; Gregory and Stevenson, *Britain in the Eighteenth Century*, p. 254; Kelly, 'Radicalism and Public Opinion', pp. 76–80, 82–83; Stanhope, *Correspondence between Pitt and Rutland*, pp. 13, 175–77; Aspinall, *Later Correspondence of George III*, vol. 2, p. 539 n. 3; Ehrman, *Pitt*, vol. 2, pp. 57–73, 84–85, 221–22, 424–25, vol. 3, pp. 177–78, 827–28; Duffy, *Younger Pitt*, pp. 134–35; G. M. Ditchfield, 'The Parliamentary Struggle over the Repeal of the Test and Corporation Acts', *English Historical Review*, 89 (1974), pp. 551–77; *Committees for the Repeal of the Test and Corporation Acts*, ed. T. W. Davis (London, 1978), pp. 1–61; *The*

Letter Journal of George Canning, 1793–95, ed. P. J. Jupp (London, 1991), pp. 97–100; W. Hinde, *George Canning* (London, 1973), p. 38; Aspinall and Smith, *English Historical Documents*, pp. 668–71.

39. *Speeches of Pitt*, vol. 1, pp. 425–36.

40. Aspinall and Smith, *English Historical Documents*, pp. 793–802; *Parliamentary Debates*, XXVII, 396–97, 495–506, XXVIII, 41–101, XXIX, 250–359; Stanhope, *Life of Pitt*, vol. 1, pp. 366–70, vol. 2, pp. 34–35, 87–88, 142–46; *Speeches of Pitt*, vol. 2, pp. 14–23; Reilly, *Pitt the Younger*, pp. 195–201; D. Turley, *The Culture of English Anti-Slavery* (London, 1991); B. Fladeland, *Abolitionists and Working Class Problems in the Age of Industrialization* (London, 1984); M. J. Turner, 'The Limits of Abolition: Government, Saints and the "African Question", 1780–1820', *English Historical Review*, 112 (1997), pp. 319–57; J. D. Bass, 'An Efficient Humanitarianism: the British Slave Trade Debates, 1791–92', *Quarterly Journal of Speech*, 75 (1989), pp. 152–65; S. Drescher, 'People and Parliament: The Rhetoric of the British Slave Trade', *Journal of Interdisciplinary History*, 20 (1990), pp. 561–80, and idem, *Capitalism and Anti-Slavery* (1986), pp. 67–88; J. R. Oldfield, *Popular Politics and British Anti-Slavery* (Manchester, 1995), pp. 1–62.

41. *Speeches of Pitt*, vol. 2, pp. 50–83; *Parliamentary Debates*, XXIX, 1055–1158.

42. Wilberforce, *Life*, vol. 1, ch. 9; Ehrman, *Pitt*, vol. 1, p. 400; Stanhope, *Life of Pitt*, vol. 2, p. 143; *Speeches of Pitt*, vol. 2, pp. 84–87; Fry, *Dundas*, pp. 199–201. Dundas held that the government should not risk alienating the wealthy and influential West Indian interest, so vital to Britain's imperial future. He hoped that a bargain could be made: abolition would be gradual, and those affected financially would be given generous assistance to help them adjust.

43. *Parliamentary Debates*, XXXI (London, 1818), 1341–43; Duffy, *Younger Pitt*, p. 143; Englefield, Seaton and White, *Prime Ministers*, p. 79; Ehrman, *Pitt*, vol. 1, pp. 387–402. As with the Test and Corporation Acts, on the slave trade Fox's claim to consistency is stronger than that of Pitt. Mitchell, *Fox*, pp. 247–50.

44. *Speeches of Pitt*, vol. 1, pp. 50–64; Stanhope, *Life of Pitt*, vol. 1, pp. 99–101; *Parliamentary Debates*, XXIII (London, 1814), 543–55.

45. *Speeches of Pitt*, vol. 1, pp. 225–26, 237–38.

46. Gregory and Stevenson, *Britain in the Eighteenth Century*, pp. 84, 90; Duffy, *Younger Pitt*, pp. 142–43; Stanhope, *Life of Pitt*, vol. 2, pp. 52–53; Mitchell, *Fox*, p. 257.

47. Duffy, *Younger Pitt*, p. 144; Malmesbury, *Diaries*, vol. 2, p. 464; *Speeches of Pitt*, vol. 2, pp. 327, 334–35; Wheatley, *Wraxall*, vol. 3, pp. 214, 253–54, 337; Kelly, 'Radicalism and Public Opinion', p. 84; Cannon, *Fox-North Coalition*, pp. 185–90; Buckingham and Chandos, *Memoirs*, vol. 2, pp. 17, 41; J. Derry, *The Regency Crisis and the Whigs* (Cambridge, 1963), pp. 127–32; L. Colley, 'The Apotheosis of George III: Loyalty, Royalty and the British Nation, 1760–1820', *Past and Present*, 102 (1984), p. 122.

48. Stanhope, *Life of Pitt*, vol. 2, pp. 16–17, 85–86, 160–62, and appendix p. xiii; Ehrman, *Pitt*, vol. 1, pp. 595–603, vol. 2, pp. 189–90; Englefield, Seaton and

White, *Prime Ministers*, pp. 78–79, 81; Duffy, *Younger Pitt*, pp. 24, 132–33; *Speeches of Pitt*, vol. 1, p. 238; Wheatley, *Wraxall*, vol. 3, p. 277, vol. 5, p. 54.

49. Harling, *Waning of Old Corruption*, pp. 82–88; Fry, *Dundas*, p. 104.

50. Pitt's opponents often cited his youth against him, and sometimes members of the government were described collectively as 'boys'. During a Commons debate of June 1784, on the Westminster scrutiny, Burke declared that he would not be swayed by 'the ill treatment of a parcel of boys'. Opposition leaders resented Pitt's recent electoral victory and the apparent persecution of Fox. But Dundas refused to make allowances and protested that Burke's remarks were abusive and unparliamentary. Burke apologized, assured the Commons of his high regard, and explained that he had only meant to refer to the ministers, 'who, he conceived, were insulting him with their triumph; a triumph which grey hairs ought to be allowed the privilege of expressing displeasure at, when it was founded on the rash exultation of mere boys'. *Parliamentary Debates*, XXIV (London, 1815), 939–40.

51. Ehrman, *Pitt*, vol. 1, p. 591; H. Barker, *Newspapers, Politics and Public Opinion in Late Eighteenth-Century England* (Oxford, 1998); J. Brewer, *The Common People and Politics, 1750–90* (Cambridge, 1986). Michael Duffy suggests that Pitt became the most caricatured prime minister of the eighteenth century, and the one of whom the public had the clearest image. In similar fashion Eric Evans refers to Pitt's 'distinctive profile, the joy of so many cartoonists'. Duffy, *Younger Pitt*, p. 133; Evans, *Pitt the Younger*, p. 3.

52. *Speeches of Pitt*, vol. 3, pp. 248–49; *Parliamentary Debates*, XXXIII (London, 1818), 1270; Duffy, *Younger Pitt*, p. 134; Stanhope, *Life of Pitt*, vol. 2, pp. 76–77.

53. Pitt and his friend Lord Euston served together as MPs for Cambridge University for over twenty years. After heading the poll in 1784, Pitt was re-elected at the June 1790 general election, a by-election of 18 December 1792 (following his appointment as Warden of the Cinque Ports), the May 1796 and June 1802 general elections, and a by-election of 17 May 1804 (following his reappointment as first lord of the treasury). Englefield, Seaton and White, *Prime Ministers*, pp. 76–77.

54. Duffy, *Younger Pitt*, pp. 50–53; Stanhope, *Life of Pitt*, vol. 1, pp. 294–95, 370–73; Ehrman, *Pitt*, vol. 1, pp. 394–95; *Parliamentary Debates*, XXVII (London, 1816), 573–99, 638–52. On Richmond's declining influence see Olson, *Radical Duke*, ch. 6.

55. Wilberforce, *Life*, vol. 2, pp. 246, 270, vol. 3, pp. 206–7, 219.

56. *Speeches of Pitt*, vol. 1, pp. 72–75, vol. 2, pp. 89–90; *Parliamentary Debates*, XXVIII, 468–70, XXIX, 400, 1302–12, XXX, 606; Duffy, *Younger Pitt*, p. 84; Evans, *Pitt the Younger*, p. 54.

57. See Duffy, *Younger Pitt*, pp. 86–87, 92.

58. In May 1787 Charles Grey called for an inquiry into post office affairs, and (so one observer informed the second Earl Cornwallis, who later joined Pitt's government) 'made use of stronger language than ever was heard in the House of Commons, and was not approved by either party'. Pitt was 'firm, and

without losing temper treated his violence and threats with contempt'. The prime minister rejected Grey's allegation that 'he was inclined to wink at abuses in the post office, or any other public establishment'. Stanhope, *Life of Pitt*, vol. 1, p. 326; *Speeches of Pitt*, vol. 1, pp. 370–72; E. A. Smith, *Lord Grey* (Stroud, 1996), pp. 19–20; Reilly, *Pitt the Younger*, p. 111.

59. Duffy, *Younger Pitt*, pp. 86–87; *Letters and Papers of Charles Middleton, Lord Barham*, ed. J. K. Laughton (3 vols, London, 1906–11), vol. 2, pp. 190, 317–50, vol. 3, p. 56; Ehrman, *Pitt*, vol. 1, pp. 293–98, 313–17; Harling, *Waning of Old Corruption*, pp. 62–63; Breihan, 'Pitt and the Commission on Fees', pp. 59–81.

60. Stanhope, *Life of Pitt*, vol. 2, pp. 140–41; Duffy, *Younger Pitt*, p. 93; *Parliamentary Debates*, XXIX (London, 1817), 816–38; *Speeches of Pitt*, vol. 2, pp. 34–38; Binney, *British Finance*, pp. 76–83; Breihan, 'Pitt and the Commission on Fees', pp. 72–74.

61. Ehrman, *Pitt*, vol. 2, pp. 85–88, 650.

62. Ehrman, *Pitt*, vol. 2, pp. 513–14; Gregory and Stevenson, *Britain in the Eighteenth Century*, p. 141.

63. *Parliamentary Debates*, XXXIII (London, 1818), 59–62; Duffy, *Younger Pitt*, pp. 93–94; Harling, *Waning of Old Corruption*, pp. 63–80, ch. 4; Breihan, 'Pitt and the Commission on Fees', pp. 77, 79–80; Ehrman, *Pitt*, vol. 3, pp. 14–16.

64. *Parliamentary Debates*, XXVIII, 469; Stanhope, *Life of Pitt*, vol. 3, p. 40.

65. Fry, *Dundas*, pp. 187–88.

Notes to Chapter 5: Leadership

1. Duffy, *Younger Pitt*, p. 32.

2. C. Hibbert, *George III: A Personal History* (London, 1998), pp. 246, 310, 313–14; Duffy, *Younger Pitt*, pp. 31–33; Evans, *Pitt the Younger*, pp. 38–40; Ehrman, *Pitt*, vol. 1, pp. 187, 636. On the relationship between Pitt and George III, see also the correspondence in Stanhope, *Life of Pitt*, appendices, and Aspinall, *Later Correspondence of George III*. On the development of Fox's anti-court politics, see Mitchell, *Fox*, chs 2–4.

3. Ehrman, *Pitt*, vol. 1, pp. 225–26; Duffy, *Younger Pitt*, pp. 33–34; Aspinall, *Later Correspondence of George III*, vol. 1, pp. 138–42; Stanhope, *Life of Pitt*, vol. 1, appendix, pp. xv–xvi; Aspinall and Smith, *English Historical Documents*, pp. 286–87, 312; *Parliamentary Debates*, XXV (London, 1815), 432–78.

4. Duffy, *Younger Pitt*, pp. 34–35.

5. Stanhope, *Life of Pitt*, vol. 1, pp. 234–35, vol. 2, pp. 40–42; Sack, *Grenvillites*, p. 5. The family did not get its dukedom until after George III's death. Richard Temple Grenville, third Earl Temple and second Marquess of Buckingham, became Duke of Buckingham and Chandos in 1822.

6. Stanhope, *Life of Pitt*, vol. 1, pp. 166, 322–23, 378, vol. 3, pp. 322, vol. 4, pp. 133, 233–34, 252–53; Ehrman, *Pitt*, vol. 3, pp. 749–52; Duffy, *Younger Pitt*, pp. 39–40; Gregory and Stevenson, *Britain in the Eighteenth Century*, p. 240; Hibbert, *George III*, pp. 375–76; Aspinall and Smith, *English Historical Documents*, pp. 177–78.

7. Nevertheless, he agreed to make Lord Loughborough chancellor in January 1793 as part of Pitt's plan to forge an alliance with the conservative Portland Whigs, whom Pitt had long been hoping to detach from Fox and the opposition.

8. Duffy, *Younger Pitt*, pp. 41–42; Ehrman, *Pitt*, vol. 1, pp. 84, 115, 232–35, 287–88, 319, 324, 576 n. 5, 578–79, 624–27, vol. 3, p. 319 n. 5; Stanhope, *Correspondence between Pitt and Rutland*, p. 13; Aspinall, *Later Correspondence of George III*, vol. 1, pp. 146–47, 186, 360, 369–70, 394–95, 408–10, vol. 2, pp. 622–23, vol. 3, pp. 162–63, 196–97; Stanhope, *Life of Pitt*, vol. 4, pp. 408–9; Hibbert, *George III*, pp. 28, 192, 311, 375–76; Brooke, *George III*, pp. 311–12.

9. Aspinall, *Later Correspondence of George III*, vol. 1, pp. 224–26.

10. Stanhope, *Life of Pitt*, vol. 2, pp. 240–43; Ehrman, *Pitt*, vol. 2, pp. 349, 414; Duffy, *Younger Pitt*, p. 42; Brooke, *George III*, p. 312; Aspinall, *Later Correspondence of George III*, vol. 2, p. 224.

11. *Parliamentary Debates*, XXIV (London, 1815), 1238–43, XXV, 1348–62.

12. Stanhope, *Life of Pitt*, vol. 1, pp. 331–36, 383–403, appendix pp. xvi–xvii, vol. 2, pp. 1–31; Hibbert, *George III*, pp. 237–303; Ehrman, *Pitt*, vol. 1, pp. 304–7, 319, 636, 644–66; Brooke, *George III*, chs 7–9; Duffy, *Younger Pitt*, pp. 42–44; Fry, *Dundas*, p. 158; Mitchell, *Fox*, pp. 80–91; Aspinall and Smith, *English Historical Documents*, pp. 302–3; Aspinall, *Later Correspondence of George III*, vol. 1, pp. 233–35, 237, 238–39, 295; *Correspondence of George, Prince of Wales, 1770–1812*, ed. A. Aspinall (8 vols, London, 1963), vol. 1, pp. 189–201, 284–315, 352–500; E. A. Smith, *George IV* (London, 1999), pp. 23–24, 26–58.

13. *Parliamentary Debates*, XXXI (London, 1818), 1464–96; Stanhope, *Life of Pitt*, vol. 2, pp. 315–16, 367, vol. 4, pp. 12–13; Ehrman, *Pitt*, vol. 2, p. 441; Duffy, *Younger Pitt*, p. 44; Jupp, *Journal of Canning*, pp. 247–48, 251–52; Aspinall, *Later Correspondence of George III*, vol. 2, pp. 345–46, 349–52, 460, and idem, *Correspondence of George Prince of Wales*, vol. 3, p. 65; Hibbert, *George III*, pp. 322–34; Smith, *George IV*, pp. 70–95.

14. *Parliamentary Debates*, XXXV (London, 1819), 386–89; Hibbert, *George III*, pp. 78, 210, 250, 252–53; Watson, *Reign of George III*, pp. 232, 247–49, 286; E. A. Reitan, 'The Civil List in Eighteenth-Century British Politics: Parliamentary Supremacy versus the Independence of the Crown', *Historical Journal*, 9 (1966), pp. 318–37; P. Hall, *Royal Fortune: Tax, Money and the Monarchy* (London, 1992), pp. 6–9; D. Cannadine, *History in Our Time* (London, 2000), ch. 2; Harling, *Waning of Old Corruption*, pp. 20, 117–18, 214–15; Duffy, *Younger Pitt*, p. 45.

15. Barnes, *George III and Pitt*, pp. 267, 490; Ehrman, *Pitt*, vol. 3, p. 522; Duffy, *Younger Pitt*, pp. 37–38, 45–46; Hibbert, *George III*, pp. 246, 310.

16. *Speeches of Fox*, vol. 3, p. 423.

17. Buckingham and Chandos, *Memoirs*, vol. 2, pp. 80–81. Ironically, even as the ministers began to feel more secure, Fox persisted in assuming that a change of government was just a few weeks away. Aspinall, *Correspondence of George Prince of Wales*, vol. 1, pp. 383–84.

18. *Parliamentary Debates*, XXVII (London, 1816), 653–1309; Stanhope, *Life of Pitt*, vol. 1, pp. 383–403, vol. 2, pp. 1–31; Ehrman, *Pitt*, vol. 1, ch. 20; Reilly, *Pitt the Younger*, ch. 14; Duffy, *Younger Pitt*, pp. 39, 43–44; Evans, *Pitt the Younger*, p. 55; Hogge, *Auckland*, vol. 2, chs 16–17; Hibbert, *George III*, chs 32–35; Brooke, *George III*, ch. 8; Smith, *George IV*, pp. 48–59; J. Derry, *Charles James Fox* (London, 1972), pp. 260–78; L. G. Mitchell, *Charles James Fox and the Disintegration of the Whig Party, 1782–94* (Oxford, 1971), ch. 4, and idem, *Fox*, pp. 80–89; Harcourt, *Rose*, vol. 1, p. 90; Buckingham and Chandos, *Memoirs*, vol. 2, pp. 146, 156; Aspinall and Smith, *English Historical Documents*, p. 261.

19. P. Kelly, 'British Parliamentary Politics, 1784–86', *Historical Journal*, 17 (1974), pp. 733–53.

20. Aspinall and Smith, *English Historical Documents*, pp. 204–5; Ehrman, *Pitt*, vol. 1, p. 626 n. 1.

21. Political allegiance continued to be important in determining promotion to the Lords, but distinguished public service was beginning to replace land as the main qualification for titles. See M. W. McCahill, 'Peerage Creations and the Changing Character of the British Nobility, 1750–1850', *English Historical Review*, 96 (1981), pp. 259–84.

22. Collective responsibility evolved steadily under Pitt, but was far more obvious in later decades. G. W. Cox, 'The Development of Collective Responsibility in the United Kingdom', *Parliamentary History*, 13 (1994), pp. 32–47. On the earlier situation see Brewer, *Party Ideology*, pp. 112–36.

23. J. Mori, 'The Political Theory of William Pitt the Younger', *History*, 83 (1998), pp. 234–48.

24. Duffy, *Younger Pitt*, p. 49.

25. Browning, *Leeds*, pp. 104–6; Aspinall, *Later Correspondence of George III*, vol. 1, p. 112; Ehrman, *Pitt*, vol. 1, p. 634; Stanhope, *Life of Pitt*, vol. 1, p. 235; Duffy, *Younger Pitt*, p. 51; Gregory and Stevenson, *Britain in the Eighteenth Century*, pp. 59–60, 68–69. On Pitt's relationship with Richmond, see Olson, *Radical Duke*, ch. 6.

26. *Rutland Manuscripts*, vol. 3, p. 301; Duffy, *Younger Pitt*, p. 52; Malmesbury, *Diaries*, vol. 2, pp. 261–64.

27. Fry, *Dundas*, chs 4–6; Stanhope, *Life of Pitt*, vol. 1, p. 228; *Rutland Manuscripts*, vol. 3, p. 152; Wilberforce, *Life*, vol. 1, p. 233; Aspinall, *Later Correspondence of George III*, vol. 1, p. 530 n. 1; *Fortescue Manuscripts*, vol. 2, p. 595, Duffy, *Younger Pitt*, p. 53–54; Ehrman, *Pitt*, vol. 1, p. 584; Aspinall and Smith, *English Historical Documents*, pp. 206–7.

28. Ehrman, *Pitt*, vol. 1, p. 310; Duffy, *Younger Pitt*, pp. 55–56; Stanhope, *Life of Pitt*, vol. 1, pp. 166, 306, vol. 2, pp. 20, 35–36, 73–74, 121–22; Fry, *Dundas*, pp. 157–58, 187–88. On Grenville's rise, and for his years at the home and foreign offices, see especially Jupp, *Grenville*, pp. 16–100, 119–287; Sack, *Grenvillites*, pp. 13–16.

29. Gregory and Stevenson, *Britain in the Eighteenth Century*, pp. 60, 75–76;

Stanhope, *Life of Pitt*, vol. 1, p. 306; Ehrman, *Pitt*, vol. 3, p. 14; Duffy, *Younger Pitt*, pp. 54–55.

30. Eden was created Baron Auckland in the Irish peerage in 1789 and in the British peerage in 1793. He constantly demanded high office after the Anglo-French treaty of 1786, and was British ambassador to Spain, 1787–89, and Holland, 1789–93. Pitt made him joint postmaster general in 1798, but after 1801 their relationship broke down and Auckland was omitted from the second Pitt administration formed in 1804. Thereafter Auckland was a follower of Grenville (who had decided not to join Pitt in office in 1804). Harris was created Baron Malmesbury in 1788, and Viscount Fitzharris and Earl of Malmesbury in 1800. He had served as British ambassador to Prussia and Russia under North. His friendship with Fox led to his appointment as ambassador to Holland in 1783, and in 1784 Pitt confirmed this appointment because he recognized Harris's diplomatic skills. Pitt made no conditions about future political allegiance, and during the regency crisis Harris backed Fox. He left the opposition in 1793, however, and became one of Pitt's key foreign policy advisers (negotiating an alliance with Prussia in 1794 and the marriage of the Prince of Wales to Caroline of Brunswick in 1795).

31. *Rutland Manuscripts*, vol. 3, p. 309; Jupp, *Grenville*, p. 72.

32. Stanhope, *Life of Pitt*, vol. 2, pp. 75–80; Olsen, *Radical Duke*, pp. 90–91, 214–19; Jupp, *Grenville*, pp. 99–100; Reilly, *Pitt the Younger*, pp. 201–2.

33. Duffy, *Younger Pitt*, pp. 49–50; *Rutland Manuscripts*, vol. 3, p. 321; Wilberforce, *Life*, vol. 1, p. 233; Wheatley, *Wraxall*, vol. 3, p. 201; G. M. Ditchfield, 'Lord Thurlow', in *Lords of Parliament*, ed. R. W. Davis (Stanford, 1995), pp. 64–78; *The Diary of Joseph Farington*, ed. K. Garlick, A. Macintyre and K. Cave (16 vols, London, 1978–84), vol. 3, p. 712; Stanhope, *Life of Pitt*, vol. 1, appendix p. xvii; *Fortescue Manuscripts*, vol. 2, p. 12.

34. Hogge, *Auckland*, vol. 2, p. 217. See also H. Twiss, *The Public and Private Life of Lord Chancellor Eldon* (3 vols, London, 1844), vol. 1, p. 188, and Grenville to Buckingham, 23 June 1788, in Buckingham and Chandos, *Memoirs*, vol. 1, pp. 398–99.

35. Mitchell, *Fox*, pp. 86, 108–35; C. Emsley, *British Society and the French Wars, 1793–1815* (London, 1979), pp. 23–25; Stanhope, *Life of Pitt*, vol. 2, pp. 77, 148–51, 158–59, 183; Aspinall, *Later Correspondence of George III*, vol. 1, pp. 449–50, 501–2, 595, 617–20, 646–47, vol. 2, p. 410; *Parliamentary Debates*, XXIX (London, 1817), 1349–55; Ehrman, *Pitt*, vol. 2, pp. 174–77, 187, 189–90; Duffy, *Younger Pitt*, pp. 57–61; Hogge, *Auckland*, vol. 2, pp. 406–7; Browning, *Leeds*, pp. 148–49, 156–57, 175–97; Twiss, *Eldon*, vol. 1, pp. 212–13; Buckingham and Chandos, *Memoirs*, vol. 2, p. 207; Wilberforce, *Life*, vol. 1, pp. 233–34, 286, 385; Ditchfield, 'Lord Thurlow', pp. 74–75; Malmesbury, *Diaries*, vol. 2, pp. 452–73; F. O'Gorman, *The Whig Party and the French Revolution* (London, 1967), ch. 3; Aspinall, *Correspondence of George Prince of Wales*, vol. 1, ch. 9; Aspinall and Smith, *English Historical Documents*, pp. 135–36, 152.

36. Aspinall and Smith, *English Historical Documents*, p. 125; Stanhope, *Life of Pitt*,

vol. 4, pp. 22–25; Ehrman, *Pitt*, vol. 3, pp. 583–85; Duffy, *Younger Pitt*, p. 49; G. Pellew, *The Life and Correspondence of Henry Addington, First Viscount Sidmouth* (3 vols, London, 1847), vol. 2, pp. 114–16; Fry, *Dundas*, pp. 254–55.

37. O'Gorman, *Whig Party*, p. 209; *The Diary of William Windham, 1784–1810*, ed. H. Baring (London, 1866), p. 301; Jupp, *Journal of Canning*, pp. 137–38.

38. Windham, for example, persisted in his efforts to persuade Pitt that the French royalists deserved Britain's fullest support. See J. Holland Rose, *Pitt and Napoleon: Essays and Letters* (London, 1912), pp. 278, 287–88, and pp. 37–59 on the Quiberon disaster.

39. Stanhope, *Life of Pitt*, vol. 2, pp. 242–55, 281–94, 299–308, 333–49, appendix pp. xxii–xiv; Ehrman, *Pitt*, vol. 2, pp. 409–40; Duffy, *Younger Pitt*, pp. 61–66; Pellew, *Sidmouth*, vol. 1, pp. 121–22; Buckingham and Chandos, *Memoirs*, vol. 2, pp. 312–37; D. Wilkinson, 'The Fitzwilliam Episode, 1795: A Reinterpretation of the Role of the Duke of Portland', *Irish Historical Studies*, 29 (1995), pp. 315–39; Aspinall, *Later Correspondence of George III*, vol. 2, pp. 262–63, 278–80, 298–99; Gregory and Stevenson, *Britain in the Eighteenth Century*, pp. 59–60, 76–77; Englefield, Seaton and White, *Prime Ministers*, p. 77.

40. Ehrman, *Pitt*, vol. 2, pp. 548–56, vol. 3, pp. 50–66; Rose, *Pitt and Napoleon*, pp. 242, 260–61; *Fortescue Manuscripts*, vol. 3, pp. 25–31, 50, 329–31, vol. 5, pp. 305–7, 487, vol. 6, pp. 151, 170, 235; Duffy, *Younger Pitt*, pp. 67–69, and idem, 'Pitt, Grenville and the Control of British Foreign Policy in the 1790s', in *Knights Errant and True Englishmen*, ed. J. Black (Edinburgh, 1989), pp. 159–62, 164–68; Aspinall, *Later Correspondence of George III*, vol. 2, pp. 330–31; Wilberforce, *Life*, vol. 2, p. 223; Baring, *Windham*, pp. 365–68, 369, 372, 376–77; Malmesbury, *Diaries*, vol. 3, pp. 355, 553–54, 555–56; Stanhope, *Life of Pitt*, vol. 3, pp. 51–61; Reilly, *Pitt the Younger*, pp. 274–77; Jupp, *Grenville*, pp. 180–82, 198–208; Hinde, *Canning*, ch. 3.

41. Ehrman, *Pitt*, vol. 3, pp. 451–57; Duffy, *Younger Pitt*, pp. 69–70. See also A. Aspinall, 'The Cabinet Council, 1783–1835', *Proceedings of the British Academy*, 38 (1952), pp. 145–252; R. E. Willis, 'Cabinet Politics and Executive Policy-Making Procedures, 1794–1801', *Albion*, 7 (1975), pp. 1–23. On Grenville's growing independence as foreign secretary, and the likelihood that Pitt made his own man, Canning, Grenville's under-secretary (early in 1796) as a counter-measure, see Jupp, *Grenville*, pp. 187–88.

42. W. Windham, *The Windham Papers. The Life and Correspondence of the Right Honourable William Windham, 1750–1810* (2 vols, London, 1913), vol. 2, pp. 162–65.

43. I. R. Christie, 'The Anatomy of the Opposition in the Parliament of 1784', *Parliamentary History*, 9 (1990), pp. 50–77.

44. E.g. Burke's representation to the king (14 June 1784), reprinted in *The Works of the Right Honourable Edmund Burke* (3 vols, London, 1792), vol. 2, pp. 619–55.

45. Evans, *Pitt the Younger*, pp. 35–38; Mitchell, *Fox*, p. 91. Burke complained that Fox retained the status and privileges of leadership while neglecting its duties; Fox argued that Pitt's shortcomings would quickly become apparent in the absence of systematic resistance.

46. *Speeches of Fox*, vol. 3, p. 201. This hostility did not greatly decrease after Pitt's death in 1806, for 'Pitt had given point to Foxite politics by personalizing everything they detested ... For over twenty years, Fox had found it impossible to like Pitt or to credit him with one sentiment that was sincere.' Mitchell, *Fox*, pp. 220–21.

47. On this see M. Duffy, 'The Younger Pitt and the House of Commons', *History*, 83 (1998), pp. 217–24.

48. Garlick, Macintyre and Cave, *Farington*, vol. 7, p. 2795. Some contemporaries held a different view. In the memoirs of Sir Philip Francis, who became a Foxite MP in 1784 after making his fortune in India, there are scathing attacks on Pitt, Dundas and George III, and even on Fox (Francis thought that Fox should have responded more favourably to his requests for advancement). Yet Francis had great admiration for Fox's debating skills. Often capable of 'magnificent exertions', Fox made little impression when forced to open a subject himself, but possessed 'wonderful faculties for debate' and a special talent for reply and contradiction. Though most effective when provoked or excited, Fox 'never sought an advantage by cavil or quibble; or like Pitt, by resorting and swinging round to the audience'. A. D. Harvey, *English Literature and the Great War with France* (London, 1981), pp. 68–79.

49. Jupp, *Journal of Canning*, pp. 63, 192, 227; Stanhope, *Life of Pitt*, vol. 2, p. 143; Wilberforce, *Life*, vol. 1, pp. 38, 345–56.

50. Englefield, Seaton and White, *Prime Ministers*, pp. 79–80; Duffy, *Younger Pitt*, p. 99–102; Pares, *George III and the Politicians*, p. 57; *Parliamentary Debates*, XXIII (London, 1818), 1460–62; Stanhope, *Life of Pitt*, vol. 1, pp. 3, 8–9, vol. 3, pp. 129–34; Wilberforce, *Life*, vol. 2, pp. 280–86; Wheatley, *Wraxall*, vol. 2, pp. 137–38, vol. 3, p. 428; *Private Correspondence of Granville Leveson Gower, Earl Granville, 1781–1821*, ed. Countess Granville (2 vols, London, 1916), vol. 1, pp. 5–6, 177, 183; Jupp, *Journal of Canning*, p. 211; Garlick, Macintyre and Cave, *Farington*, vol. 2, p. 486, vol. 6, pp. 2405–6, vol. 7, p. 2795, vol. 8, p. 2921; *Diary and Correspondence of Charles Abbot, Lord Colchester*, ed. Lord Colchester (3 vols, London, 1861), vol. 1, p. 22–23; Ehrman, *Pitt*, vol. 3, pp. 126–29; Thorne, *House of Commons*, vol. 5, p. 384; Reilly, *Pitt the Younger*, pp. 279–81; Evans, *Pitt the Younger*, p. 81.

51. Duffy, *Younger Pitt*, pp. 102–3; Wheatley, *Wraxall*, vol. 5, p. 217; Garlick, Macintyre and Cave, *Farington*, vol. 2, p. 401, vol. 6, p. 2362; *Rutland Manuscripts*, vol. 3, pp. 220–21, 280; Buckingham and Chandos, *Memoirs*, vol. 1, pp. 361–62, 394; Thorne, *House of Commons*, vol. 3, p. 509; Jupp, *Journal of Canning*, pp. 10, 46, 173–74, 159, 194, 201–2, 254–55, 278.

52. Ehrman, *Pitt*, vol. 1, pp. 58, 323–26, 609–21, vol. 2, pp. 53–57, 622–24; Duffy, *Younger Pitt*, pp. 103–5; Evans, *Pitt the Younger*, pp. 34–35; Garlick, Macintyre and Cave, *Farington*, vol. 2, p. 540; Stanhope, *Life of Pitt*, vol. 4, p. 239; *Parliamentary Debates*, XXX, 606; *Rutland Manuscripts*, vol. 3, p. 298; Aspinall and Smith, *English Historical Documents*, pp. 208–10, 253, 280, 649, 653–54; Thorne, *House of Commons*, vol. 1, pp. 110, 172; D. Marshall, *The Rise of George*

Canning (London, 1938), p. 36; Jupp, *Journal of Canning*, pp. 197, 226 n. 449, 229–30, 248, 274, 278; Wilberforce, *Life*, vol. 1, p. 165; Namier and Brooke, *Commons*, vol. 2, pp. 33–34, vol. 3, pp. 24, 479–80.

53. *Rutland Manuscripts*, vol. 3, pp. 202, 209, 379; Ehrman, *Pitt*, vol. 2, pp. 402–40; Stanhope, *Life of Pitt*, vol. 2, pp. 299–308; Duffy, *Younger Pitt*, pp. 106–7; Jupp, *Journal of Canning*, pp. 137–38; Hinde, *Canning*, pp. 35–36; Hogge, *Auckland*, vol. 3, pp. 220; Rose, *Pitt and Napoleon*, pp. 20–36, 236–37, 250; E. A. Smith, *Whig Principles and Party Politics* (Manchester, 1975), pp. 175–218; *Fortescue Manuscripts*, vol. 3, pp. 13–15, 35–39; Aspinall and Smith, *English Historical Documents*, pp. 158–59.

54. *Fortescue Manuscripts*, vol. 2, pp. 653–54.

55. Duffy, *Younger Pitt*, pp. 107–8; Ehrman, *Pitt*, vol. 1, chs 8–9; Stanhope, *Life of Pitt*, vol. 1, pp. 257–75; *Rutland Manuscripts*, vol. 3, p. 203; Kelly, 'British Party Politics', pp. 733–53.

56. Hogge, *Auckland*, vol. 1, pp. 78–90; Malmesbury, *Diaries*, vol. 2, pp. 11–18.

57. Stanhope, *Life of Pitt*, vol. 2, pp. 242–45, 281; Ehrman, *Pitt*, vol. 2, p. 414; Duffy, *Younger Pitt*, pp. 108–9; D. Wilkinson, 'The Pitt-Portland Coalition of 1794 and the Origins of the "Tory" Party', *History*, 83 (1998), pp. 252–54; Mitchell, *Fox and the Whig Party*, p. 247, and idem, *Fox*, pp. 126–34.

58. Ehrman, *Pitt*, vol. 1, pp. 146–53, 616–18, vol. 2, pp. 56–58, 72, 622–24; Duffy, *Younger Pitt*, pp. 110–12, Namier and Brooke, *Commons*, vol. 1, pp. 87–96; Thorne, *House of Commons*, vol. 1, pp. 110–26, 141–50; Gregory and Stevenson, *Britain in the Eighteenth Century*, p. 108; Fry, *Dundas*, pp. 100–4, 149–51, 201–4; D. J. Brown, 'The Government of Scotland under Henry Dundas and William Pitt', *History*, 83 (1998), pp. 265–79; Marshall, *Rise of Canning*, p. 34; Hinde, *Canning*, pp. 25–28; *The Diaries of Sylvester Douglas, Lord Glenbervie*, ed. F. L. Bickley (2 vols, London, 1928), vol. 1, pp. 67–68; Aspinall and Smith, *English Historical Documents*, pp. 273–76.

59. *Parliamentary Debates*, XXXII (London, 1818), 1041, XXXIII (London, 1818), 1462; Ehrman, *Pitt*, vol. 1, pp. 519, 658–59, vol. 3, pp. 477–79; Thorne, *House of Commons*, vol. 3, pp. 242–48, vol. 4, pp. 22–23, 207; Duffy, *Younger Pitt*, pp. 112–13; Gregory and Stevenson, *Britain in the Eighteenth Century*, p. 81; Jupp, *Grenville*, pp. 78–83; P. D. G. Thomas, *The House of Commons in the Eighteenth Century* (Oxford, 1971), pp. 72, 188, 286–87, 291; Wheatley, *Wraxall*, vol. 3, p. 256; Pellew, *Sidmouth*, vol. 1, pp. 203–5; Englefield, Seaton and White, *Prime Ministers*, p. 79; Namier and Brooke, *Commons*, vol. 1, p. 537, vol. 2, pp. 11–12, 255–56, 499–501, 548–50, 627–28. There is a detailed account of Pitt's parliamentary methods in Ehrman, *Pitt*, vol. 1, chs 7, 19, vol. 3, ch. 14.

60. Duffy, *Younger Pitt*, pp. 113–14; Englefield, Seaton and White, *Prime Ministers*, p. 76; Ehrman, *Pitt*, vol. 1, pp. 583–84; Buckingham and Chandos, *Memoirs*, vol. 2, p. 14; *Fortescue Manuscripts*, vol. 1, p. 342; *Correspondence of Charles, First Marquess Cornwallis*, ed. C. D. Ross (3 vols, London, 1859), vol. 1, p. 446; Garlick, Macintyre and Cave, *Farington*, vol. 3, p. 794, vol. 4, p. 1162, vol. 6, p. 2362; Jupp, *Journal of Canning*, p. 29; Wheatley, *Wraxall*, vol. 4, pp. 13–14;

Browning, *Leeds*, p. 178; Pellew, *Sidmouth*, vol. 1, pp. 122–23, 189; Thorne, *House of Commons*, vol. 5, pp. 35–36, 509–11; Bickley, *Glenbervie*, vol. 1, pp. 52–53.

61. Ehrman, *Pitt*, vol. 3, pp. 37–39; Garlick, Macintyre and Cave, *Farington*, vol. 3, p. 696; Jupp, *Journal of Canning*, pp. 269–71; Bickley, *Glenbervie*, vol. 1, p. 150; Duffy, *Younger Pitt*, p. 115.

62. Perceval, whose family held the earldom of Egmont, was first elected to the Commons in 1796 (for Northampton). From 1801 he served as solicitor general and then attorney general under both Pitt and Addington, and was subsequently chancellor of the exchequer, leader of the Commons and chancellor of the duchy of Lancaster, 1807–12.

63. The eldest son of Charles Jenkinson, he became MP for Rye in 1790 and from early 1792, when he came to Pitt's attention after an accomplished speech in the Commons, was regularly employed as a government speaker. He sat on the Indian board of control, 1793–99, and board of trade during 1799, served as master of the mint, 1799–1801, and was Addington's foreign secretary, 1801–4. Hawkesbury was then home secretary and leader of the House of Lords in Pitt's second administration, 1804–6, home secretary again, 1807–9, and secretary for war, 1809–12. He succeeded Pitt as Warden of the Cinque Ports in 1806.

64. Canning became MP for Newport in 1794. After holding several junior offices between 1796 and 1801, he was treasurer of the navy in Pitt's second administration, and subsequently foreign secretary, 1807–9 and 1822–27, president of the board of control, 1816–21, and leader of the Commons, 1822–27.

65. George Gordon, to whom Pitt became legal guardian and political mentor following the death of his parents in the early 1790s, succeeded to his grandfather's earldom in 1801 at the age of seventeen. In 1813 and 1814 he served as Britain's ambassador extraordinary in Europe, with special responsibility for negotiations with Austria, and he was chancellor of the duchy of Lancaster, secretary for war, and twice foreign secretary before taking the premiership.

66. Ryder was the eldest son of the first Baron Harrowby. He was returned as MP for Tiverton in 1784. Pitt asked him to move the address in November 1787, and forced a reluctant Carmarthen to accept him as under-secretary at the foreign office in 1789. Ryder then served as comptroller of the household and a member of the Indian board of control, 1790–91, and vice president of the board of trade, 1790–1801, joint paymaster general, 1791–1800, and treasurer of the navy, 1800–1. Ryder was Pitt's second at the duel with Tierney in 1798. He chaired the committees on food shortages in 1795–96 and 1800–1, making sure that government policy secured the required majorities. Ryder succeeded to his father's title in June 1803, and was created Earl of Harrowby in July 1809. He served as foreign secretary, 1804–5, chancellor of the duchy of Lancaster, 1805–6, president of the board of control in 1809, minister without portfolio, 1809–12, and lord president, 1812–27.

67. Robert Stewart, Viscount Castlereagh, was the son of the first Marquess of Londonderry. He joined the Irish administration in 1797, and was chief secretary

for Ireland, 1798–1801. He then served as president of the board of control, 1802–6, secretary for war, 1805–6 and 1807–9, and foreign secretary and leader of the Commons, 1812–22. He succeeded to his father's title in 1821.

68. Yorke served as secretary at war, 1801–3, home secretary, 1803–4, and first lord of the admiralty, 1810–12. He never held cabinet rank under Pitt. Though arrangements were made in 1805 for him to join Pitt's second government, with a seat in the cabinet, the promotion did not take place before Pitt's death, and there was then a complete change of ministers.

69. George Howard, Viscount Morpeth, was the eldest son of the fifth Earl of Carlisle. He emerged as a government supporter after entering the Commons in 1795, and Pitt valued him as a speaker. He failed to live up to his early promise, however, and – though a close friend of Canning – began to drift towards the opposition Whigs (marrying a daughter of the fifth Duke of Devonshire in 1801). When Pitt became prime minister in 1804 he offered Morpeth a place on the Indian board of control, which Morpeth declined. When the Whigs held office in 1806–7 Morpeth joined their administration. He succeeded to the earldom of Carlisle in 1825, and served as commissioner for woods and forests in 1827, lord privy seal, 1827–28 and in 1834, and minister without portfolio, 1830–34.

70. Another friend of Canning, and the second surviving son of the Marquess of Stafford (previously Earl Gower, a member of Pitt's cabinet from 1783 to 1794), Leveson Gower became MP for Lichfield in 1795 and was chosen by Pitt to accompany Malmesbury on the peace mission to France in 1796. He served as British envoy to Prussia in 1798, and was a lord of the treasury, 1800–1. Though his claims for higher office went unsatisfied, he joined Pitt and Canning in opposition between 1801 and 1804 and was subsequently Pitt's ambassador to Russia, 1804–6. Pitt's death seemed to put a peerage beyond his reach and he moved closer to Fox before being reconciled with Canning. After briefly serving as secretary at war in 1809, Leveson Gower established himself as one of the senior British diplomats of the age, and was three times ambassador to France. He was created Viscount Granville in 1815, and Earl Granville in 1833.

71. Henry Bathurst, Lord Apsley, was the eldest son of the second Earl Bathurst, and succeeded to the earldom in 1794. First elected as MP for Cirencester in 1783, he was a lord of the admiralty, 1783–89, lord of the treasury, 1789–91, teller of the exchequer, 1790–1834, commissioner of the board of control, 1793–1802, and clerk of the crown in chancery, 1801–34. A close friend of Pitt, he was brought into the cabinet as master of the mint, 1804–6, and was subsequently president of the board of trade and master of the mint, 1807–12, president of the board of trade, 1807–12, foreign secretary in 1809, secretary for war, 1812–27, and lord president, 1828–30.

72. Vansittart entered the Commons in 1796 and made his mark as a pamphleteer and speaker for Pitt's administration. Pitt appointed him to various committees and sought his advice on financial policies. Vansittart became a close friend

of Addington, and after the latter had replaced Pitt as premier in 1801 Vansittart was appointed British envoy to Denmark. He was also a secretary to the treasury, 1801–4. After resigning with Addington in 1804, Pitt brought him back as Irish chief secretary, but in the subsequent battle between Pittities and Addingtonians Vansittart sided against Pitt and went into opposition. He was again secretary to the treasury, 1806–7, and then chancellor of the exchequer, 1812–23, and chancellor of the duchy of Lancaster, 1823–28. Vansittart was created Baron Bexley in 1823.

73. Richard Colley Wellesley had inherited the (Irish) Mornington title in 1781. He was a lord of the treasury, 1786–97, and a commissioner of the Indian board of control, 1793–97. In 1797, now Baron Wellesley in the British peerage, he went to India as governor general, returning home in 1805. He was created Marquess Wellesley in the Irish peerage in 1799. Wellesley longed for a dukedom, but his vanity and limited political ability told against him. He served as foreign secretary, 1809–12, and was lord lieutenant of Ireland, 1821–28.

74. A close friend (and from 1788 brother-in-law) of Addington, Bragge entered the Commons in 1790 and became an important supporter of Pitt's ministry in several committees. He came to be known as an expert on parliamentary procedure, and was widely regarded as a potential Speaker of the Commons. Bragge never held cabinet office under Pitt, and from 1801 he was a firm ally of Addington. He served as treasurer of the navy, 1801–3, and secretary at war, 1803–4. He also sat on the treasury board during 1803. When Pitt made his alliance with the Addingtonians early in 1805, efforts were made to find a suitable office for Bragge, known as Bragge Bathurst from 1804 following an inheritance, but the alliance fell apart before anything was arranged. Bragge Bathurst was subsequently master of the mint, 1806–7, chancellor of the duchy of Lancaster, 1812–23, and president of the board of control, 1821–22.

75. Ehrman, *Pitt*, vol. 3, pp. 92–97 (and on Pitt's recreation generally see vol. 1, ch. 18, vol. 3, chs 3, 16); Duffy, *Younger Pitt*, pp. 115–16; Wilberforce, *Life*, vol. 1, p. 18; Jupp, *Journal of Canning*, pp. 28–30, 45, 48, 81–82, 92, 149–50, 154, 168–69, 192, 200–1, 225, 278; Granville, *Correspondence*, vol. 1, pp. 123, 170, 226–27; Wyvill, *Political Papers*, vol. 4, pp. 88–89; Malmesbury, *Diaries*, vol. 4, pp. 313–14; Reilly, *Pitt the Younger*, pp. 55–56, 83–84, 250.

76. Duffy, *Younger Pitt*, pp. 117–18; Jupp, *Journal of Canning*, pp. 42, 46, 50, 173, 194, 200–1, 254–55; Colchester, *Diary*, vol. 1, pp. 123, 162, 187; *Rutland Manuscripts*, vol. 3, p. 276; Granville, *Correspondence*, vol. 1, p. 289; Buckingham and Chandos, *Memoirs*, vol. 1, p. 377; *Kenyon Manuscripts*, pp. 519, 521; *The Autobiography and Political Correspondence of Augustus Henry, third Earl of Grafton*, ed. W. R. Anson (London, 1898), pp. 398–99; Ross, *Cornwallis*, vol. 1, p. 374; Aspinall, *Later Correspondence of George III*, vol. 1, p. 23; Twiss, *Eldon*, vol. 1, p. 314; Wilberforce, *Life*, vol. 1, p. 285.

77. Ehrman, *Pitt*, vol. 2, p. 395, vol. 3, pp. 9–10, 16, 293, 304–5; Hogge, *Auckland*, vol. 3, pp. 349–50; Thorne, *House of Commons*, vol. 4, pp. 300–3, vol. 5, pp. 76–77; Duffy, *Younger Pitt*, pp. 119–21; Colchester, *Diary*, vol. 1, pp. 91–92; R. Wells,

Wretched Faces: Famine in Wartime England, 1793–1801 (Gloucester, 1988), pp. 184–95, 243, 245–47.

78. *Parliamentary Debates*, XXXII (London, 1818), 182–87; Aspinall, *Later Correspondence of George III*, vol. 2, pp. 415–16 n. 5; Hinde, *Canning*, p. 42; Wilberforce, *Life*, vol. 2, pp. 112–13; Colchester, *Diary*, vol. 1, pp. 3–4.

79. Ehrman, *Pitt*, vol. 2, pp. 401–2, 484, 486–88, 520, 607–9; Duffy, *Younger Pitt*, pp. 125–26; Aspinall, *Later Correspondence of George III*, vol. 2, p. 548; Stanhope, *Life of Pitt*, vol. 3, appendix pp. x–xi.

80. Stanhope, *Life of Pitt*, vol. 3, pp. 40–41, 75; Ehrman, *Pitt*, vol. 3, pp. 41–42; Lord Holland, *Memoirs of the Whig Party during My Time* (2 vols, London, 1852), vol. 1, p. 92; Duffy, *Younger Pitt*, p. 140; Derry, *Fox*, pp. 372–75; D. Powell, *Charles James Fox: Man of the People* (London, 1989), pp. 239–41; Mitchell, *Fox*, ch. 7.

81. Duffy, *Younger Pitt*, pp. 140–41; Ehrman, *Pitt*, vol. 2, pp. 212–13 n. 6; A. Aspinall, *Politics and the Press, 1780–1850* (London, 1949), pp. 6, 66–83, 163–66, 421, 444; H. Barker, *Newspapers, Politics and English Society, 1695–1855* (Harlow, 2000), chs 4, 8, and idem, *Newspapers, Politics and Public Opinion*; Aspinall, *Later Correspondence of George III*, vol. 1, p. 118; Evans, *Pitt the Younger*, p. 35; Colchester, *Diary*, vol. 1, p. 75.

82. Ehrman, *Pitt*, vol. 1, pp. 325–26, 578–79, vol. 2, p. 19, vol. 3, pp. 46–50, 99–106, 844–45; Duffy, *Younger Pitt*, pp. 74–78; Wheatley, *Wraxall*, vol. 4, pp. 427–28, vol. 5, p. 83; Browning, *Leeds*, p. 160; Garlick, Macintyre and Cave, *Farington*, vol. 3, p. 730, vol. 9, p. 3458; Granville, *Correspondence*, vol. 1, pp. 5–6, 172, 456; Stanhope, *Life of Pitt*, vol. 1, pp. 249–50, vol. 4, p. 40; *Kenyon Manuscripts*, p. 518; *Fortescue Manuscripts*, vol. 1, pp. 356–57, vol. 3, pp. 382–84; Wyvill, *Political Papers*, vol. 4, p. 23; Colchester, *Diary*, vol. 1, p. 44; Jupp, *Journal of Canning*, pp. 43–45, 64, 92, 154–56; Wilberforce, *Life*, vol. 1, p. 265, vol. 2, p. 86, vol. 3, pp. 249–50; Hogge, *Auckland*, vol. 3, pp. 114, 331.

83. *The Huskisson Papers*, ed. L. Melville (London, 1931), pp. 3, 6, 16, 18–19.

84. Noting Pitt's preference for dealing with matters verbally rather than in writing, the opposition leader Sheridan once quipped that the prime minister's brain only worked when his tongue was moving. Thorne, *House of Commons*, vol. 4, p. 815.

85. Melville, *Huskisson Papers*, pp. 18–19.

86. E.g. Russian ambassador Count Simon Vorontsov, writing to Grenville in July 1800. See *Fortescue Manuscripts*, vol. 6, p. 259.

87. Duffy, *Younger Pitt*, p. 88; R. R. Nelson, *The Home Office, 1782–1801* (Durham, NC, 1969), p. 59; Colchester, *Diary*, vol. 1, p. 45; Bickley, *Glenbervie*, vol. 1, pp. 149, 337; Rose, *Pitt and Napoleon*, p. 35; Ehrman, *Pitt*, vol. 3, p. 105. On Fitwilliam in Ireland, see also Jupp, *Grenville*, pp. 263–64, 282, and the correspondence between Grenville, Portland and Fitzwilliam in *Fortescue Manuscripts*, vol. 3, pp. 13, 14–15, 35–38.

88. Ehrman, *Pitt*, vol. 1, pp. 195, 585, vol. 2, p. 461, vol. 3, pp. 80–82, 92–97; Duffy, *Younger Pitt*, pp. 89–91; Fry, *Dundas*, pp. 132–33; Pellew, *Sidmouth*, vol. 1, p. 152;

Bickley, *Glenbervie*, vol. 1, pp. 34, 152; Garlick, Macintyre and Cave, *Farington*, vol. 2, p. 486; *Report on the Manuscripts of Earl Bathurst, Preserved at Cirencester Park*, Historical Manuscripts Commission, no. 76 (London, 1923), pp. 706–12; Olson, *Radical Duke*, pp. 91–101, 223.

Notes to Chapter 6: Revolution and War

1. Mitchell, *Fox*, pp. 76–91, 108–35.
2. Ehrman, *Pitt*, vol. 2, p. 47; Evans, *Pitt the Younger*, p. 44; Jupp, *Grenville*, pp. 136–51.
3. In France Pitt was accompanied by his friends Edward Eliot and William Wilberforce. Among the celebrities he met was the American ambassador Benjamin Franklin, and he was also presented to the French king and queen Louis XVI and Marie Antoinette. Stanhope, *Life of Pitt*, vol. 1, pp. 129–35; Wilberforce, *Life*, vol. 1, pp. 34–44; Englefield, Seaton and White, *Prime Ministers*, pp. 78, 80; Duffy, *Younger Pitt*, pp. 166–67; Ehrman, *Pitt*, vol. 1, pp. 111–12; Rose, *National Revival*, pp. 137–41; Reilly, *Pitt the Younger*, pp. 85–88.
4. Duffy, *Younger Pitt*, pp. 167–68; Browning, *Leeds*, p. 101; Ehrman, *Pitt*, vol. 1, pp. 313–14, chs 12–14; P. Webb, 'The Rebuilding and Repair of the Fleet, 1783–93', *Bulletin of the Institute of Historical Research*, 50 (1977), pp. 194–209; Aspinall and Smith, *English Historical Documents*, pp. 815–23, 825–31.
5. *Parliamentary Debates*, XXV (London, 1815), 389; *Speeches of Pitt*, vol. 1, pp. 126–28; Rose, *National Revival*, pp. 442–43; Stanhope, *Life of Pitt*, vol. 1, p. 338; Aspinall and Smith, *English Historical Documents*, pp. 781–87; P. J. Cain and A. G. Hopkins, *British Imperialism. Innovation and Expansion, 1688–1914* (London, 1993), pp. 32, 55, 70, 76, 78–79, 87, 97, 142, 279, 319, 322, 399, 466–68; C. A. Bayly, *Imperial Meridian. The British Empire and the World, 1780–1820* (London, 1989), pp. 9, 11, 100, 104, 131, 139, 152, 162, 195, 214–15, 242–43, 246–48, 250.
6. Ehrman, *Pitt*, vol. 1, pp. 467–77; Rose, *National Revival*, pp. 311–13; Reilly, *Pitt the Younger*, pp. 170–71; J. Black, *British Foreign Policy in an Age of Revolutions, 1783–93* (Cambridge, 1994), pp. 88–93; Evans, *Pitt the Younger*, p. 26; Duffy, *Younger Pitt*, pp. 35, 169; J. Mori, *William Pitt and the French Revolution* (Edinburgh, 1997), pp. 54–55; T. C. W. Blanning, '"That Horrid Electorate" or "Ma Patrie Germanique"? George III, Hanover, and the Furstenbund of 1785', *Historical Journal*, 20 (1977), pp. 311–44; Aspinall, *Later Correspondence of George III*, vol. 1, pp. 177–78; Browning, *Leeds*, pp. 106–16.
7. Ehrman, *Pitt*, vol. 1, ch. 16, vol. 2, pp. 510–16; Mori, *Pitt and the French Revolution*, pp. 55–56; Duffy, *Younger Pitt*, p. 170; Olson, *Radical Duke*, pp. 77–78, 91–92; Cain and Hopkins, *Imperialism*, p. 97; Aspinall and Smith, *English Historical Documents*, pp. 557–59; *Parliamentary Debates*, XXXII (London, 1818), 216–35; *Fortescue Manuscripts*, vol. 2, pp. 578, 607–8, 629, vol. 3, pp. 34, 38–39, 68–70, 76, 87, 136–37, 517, 528–30, 533–36; Jupp, *Grenville*, pp. 55–56, 162–63.
8. Malmesbury, *Diaries*, vol. 2, p. 295.

9. Gregory and Stevenson, *Britain in the Eighteenth Century*, p. 139; Duffy, *Younger Pitt*, pp. 35, 170–73; Stanhope, *Life of Pitt*, vol. 1, pp. 339–47 and appendix p. xxi; Evans, *Pitt the Younger*, p. 27; Reilly, *Pitt the Younger*, pp. 171–77; Aspinall, *Later Correspondence of George III*, vol. 1, pp. 295–97, 321, 324–25; *Parliamentary Debates*, XXVI (London, 1816), 1224–54, 1264–69; Rose, *National Revival*, pp. 349–90; Black, *Foreign Policy*, pp. 130–55; Ehrman, *Pitt*, vol. 1, pp. 520–38; Ross, *Cornwallis*, vol. 1, pp. 334–36; T. C. W. Blanning, *The French Revolutionary Wars, 1787–1802* (London, 1996), pp. 24–26; Malmesbury, *Diaries*, vol. 2, pp. 220–370; *Fortescue Manuscripts*, vol. 1, pp. 278–79, 281–85; P. W. Schroeder, *The Transformation of European Politics, 1763–1848* (Oxford, 1994), pp. 39–41; Mori, *Pitt and the French Revolution*, pp. 56–59; R. W. Seton Watson, *Britain in Europe, 1789–1914: A Survey of Foreign Policy* (Cambridge, 1945), pp. 9–10; Jupp, *Grenville*, pp. 63–70; Browning, *Leeds*, pp. 117–19.
10. *Parliamentary Debates*, XXVII (London, 1816), 553–57, 1329–32; Stanhope, *Life of Pitt*, vol. 1, pp. 380–81; Malmesbury, *Diaries*, vol. 2, pp. 370, 383, 384–95; Englefield, Seaton and White, *Prime Ministers*, p. 79; Duffy, *Younger Pitt*, pp. 174–75; Rose, *National Revival*, chs 21–23, 26–27; Ehrman, *Pitt*, vol. 1, pp. 538–53, vol. 2, ch. 1; Schroeder, *European Politics*, ch. 2; Black, *Foreign Policy*, pp. 167–68, 173–224, 257–328; Mori, *Pitt and the French Revolution*, pp. 59–66.
11. Stanhope, *Life of Pitt*, vol. 2, pp. 49–50, 54–63, 85–86, and appendix p. xiii; *Parliamentary Debates*, XXVIII (London, 1816), 764–82, 784–85, 794–813, 815–24, 891, 914–18; *Fortescue Manuscripts*, vol. 1, pp. 579–80, 606, 611; Aspinall, *Later Correspondence of George III*, vol. 1, pp. 494, 495, 497, 498–500, 508–9; Ehrman, *Pitt*, vol. 1, pp. 553–71; Englefield, Seaton and White, *Prime Ministers*, p. 79; Mori, *Pitt and the French Revolution*, pp. 87–90; Rose, *National Revival*, pp. 562–88; Reilly, *Pitt the Younger*, pp. 179–81; Duffy, *Younger Pitt*, pp. 175–76; Evans, *Pitt the Younger*, pp. 29–30; Black, *Foreign Policy*, pp. 233–56.
12. Stanhope, *Life of Pitt*, vol. 2, p. 63; Evans, *Pitt the Younger*, p. 32; Ehrman, *Pitt*, vol. 1, p. 571.
13. Black, *Foreign Policy*, pp. 255–56.
14. Stanhope, *Life of Pitt*, vol. 2, pp. 101–21; Ehrman, *Pitt*, vol. 2, ch. 1; *Parliamentary Debates*, XXIX (London, 1817), 31–96, 164–218, 434–49, 617–36, 684–703, 849–1001; Mori, *Pitt and the French Revolution*, pp. 95–98; *The Foundations of British Foreign Policy: From Pitt to Salisbury*, ed. H. M. V. Temperley and L. M. Penson (Cambridge, 1938), p. 1; Browning, *Leeds*, pp. 148–74; Aspinall, *Later Correspondence of George III*, vol. 1, p. 523; Duffy, *Younger Pitt*, pp. 176–78; Rose, *National Revival*, pp. 589–632; Black, *Foreign Policy*, pp. 285–328; Schroeder, *European Politics*, pp. 79–83; Jupp, *Grenville*, pp. 119–29; Olson, *Radical Duke*, pp. 77, 91; Reilly, *Pitt the Younger*, pp. 181–84; Evans, *Pitt the Younger*, pp. 30–31.
15. *Fortescue Manuscripts*, vol. 2, pp. 22–23, 25–26, 31, 38–39, 44–54, 64, 65–66, 76–77, 79, 87, 88, 91–92, 110–11, 121–22; Stanhope, *Life of Pitt*, vol. 2, pp. 115–18; Rose, *National Revival*, p. 631; Malmesbury, *Diaries*, vol. 2, p. 406; Black, *Foreign Policy*, pp. 290, 309–10; Schroeder, *European Politics*, pp. 79–80, 81.

16. Stanhope, *Life of Pitt*, vol. 2, appendix pp. iii–iv; Ehrman, *Pitt*, vol. 2, pp. 30–32; Black, *Foreign Policy*, pp. 179–84, 310–11, 314; Browning, *Leeds*, pp. 148–74; Aspinall and Smith, *English Historical Documents*, pp. 135–36; Evans, *Pitt the Younger*, pp. 30–31, 33; Duffy, *Younger Pitt*, pp. 57, 173.

17. R. Price, 'A Discourse on the Love of our Country', in *Richard Price. Political Writings*, ed. D. O. Thomas (Cambridge, 1991), pp. 176–96; E. Burke, *Reflections on the Revolution in France*, ed. L. G. Mitchell (Oxford, 1993); *Edmund Burke on Government, Politics and Society*, ed. B. W. Hill (London, 1975), pp. 279–359; Reilly, *Pitt the Younger*, ch. 16; Mitchell, *Fox*, pp. 108–14; S. Ayling, *Fox* (London, 1991), pp. 169–73; Derry, *Fox*, pp. 302–5; H. T. Dickinson, 'The Eighteenth-Century Debate on the Glorious Revolution', *History*, 61 (1976), pp. 28–45; 'A Letter from Mr Burke to a Member of the National Assembly; in Answer to Some Objections to his Book on French Affairs' (1791), *Works of Burke*, vol. 3, pp. 323–73.

18. Blanning, *French Revolutionary Wars*, pp. 42–43; *Parliamentary Debates*, XXVIII (London, 1816), 351; Stanhope, *Life of Pitt*, vol. 2, pp. 48, 154, 162–74; *Fortescue Manuscripts*, vol. 1, p. 606; Duffy, *Younger Pitt*, pp. 178–79; Mori, *Pitt and the French Revolution*, p. 99; Rose, *National Revival*, p. 629; Ehrman, *Pitt*, vol. 2, pp. 42–52, 88.

19. Mitchell, *Fox and the Whig Party*, chs 5–6, and idem, *Fox*, p. 115; Ehrman, *Pitt*, vol. 2, pp. 77–81; Reilly, *Pitt the Younger*, chs 16, 18; Malmesbury, *Diaries*, vol. 2, pp. 418–34, 435–40; *Speeches of Fox*, vol. 4, pp. 32–55, 200–28; *Works of Burke*, vol. 3, pp. 1–18; Stanhope, *Life of Pitt*, vol. 2, pp. 91–97, 158–59, 183, 242–52; B. W. Hill, 'Fox and Burke: The Whig Party and the Question of Principles, 1784–89', *English Historical Review*, 89 (1974), pp. 1–24; J. Brewer, 'Rockingham, Burke, and Whig Political Argument', *Historical Journal*, 18 (1975), pp. 188–201; J. Holland Rose, *William Pitt and the Great War* (London, 1912), pp. 35–39.

20. E. Burke, *An Appeal from the New to the Old Whigs, in Consequence of Some Late Discussions in Parliament, Relative to the 'Reflections on the French Revolution'* (London, 1791); Mitchell, *Fox*, pp. 114–19.

21. *Fortescue Manuscripts*, vol. 2, p. 136.

22. *Parliamentary Debates*, XXVIII (London, 1816), 452–79; Ehrman, *Pitt*, vol. 2, pp. 75–77; Stanhope, *Life of Pitt*, vol. 2, p. 51; Rose, *Great War*, pp. 11–12.

23. *British Working-Class Movements. Select Documents, 1789–1875*, ed. G. D. H. Cole and A. W. Filson (London, 1951), pp. 43–53; *Selections from the Papers of the London Corresponding Society, 1792–99*, ed. M. Thale (Cambridge, 1983), pp. 5–10; I. Hampsher-Monk, 'Civic Humanism and Parliamentary Reform: The Case of the Society of the Friends of the People', *Journal of British Studies*, 18 (1979), pp. 70–89; Aspinall and Smith, *English Historical Documents*, pp. 216–23.

24. It was lost by 294 to 105 votes. *Parliamentary Debates*, XXVIII, 387–452.

25. W. C. Costin and J. S. Watson, *The Law and Working of the Constitution* (2 vols, London, 1964), vol. 2, pp. 6–7; *Parliamentary Debates*, XXIX (London, 1817), 551–602, 726–42, 1036–47, 1293–1300, 1361–71, 1404–31, 1534–38; Stanhope, *Life of Pitt*, vol. 2, pp. 147–48; Ehrman, *Pitt*, vol. 2, p. 81; Rose, *Great War*,

p. 33; Ayling, *Fox*, p. 177; Derry, *Fox*, pp. 315–16; Mitchell, *Fox*, p. 118; Aspinall and Smith, *English Historical Documents*, pp. 287, 363–64.

26. *Parliamentary Debates*, XXIX, 1300–41; *Speeches of Fox*, vol. 4, pp. 407–12; *Speeches of Pitt*, vol. 2, pp. 87–93; Stanhope, *Life of Pitt*, vol. 2, pp. 151–52; Smith, *Grey*, pp. 43–44; Mitchell, *Fox*, pp. 120–22.

27. J. Stevenson, *Popular Disturbances in England, 1700–1832* (London, 1992), chs 7–8, and idem, *Artisans and Democrats: Sheffield in the French Revolution, 1789–97* (Sheffield, 1989), pp. 47–56; R. B. Rose, 'The Priestley Riots of 1791', *Past and Present*, 18 (1960), pp. 68–88; E. Robinson, 'New Light on the Priestley Riots', *Historical Journal*, 3 (1960), pp. 73–75; Aspinall and Smith, *English Historical Documents*, pp. 313–15; M. J. Turner, *Reform and Respectability: The Making of a Middle-Class Liberalism in Early Nineteenth-Century Manchester* (Manchester, 1995), pp. 38–42; Cole and Filson, *Working-Class Movements*, pp. 60–64; D. Malone, *The Public Life of Thomas Cooper, 1783–1839* (New Haven, 1926), pp. 19–32; F. Knight, *The Strange Case of Thomas Walker: Ten Years in the Life of a Manchester Radical* (London, 1957), ch. 4.

28. *Parliamentary Debates*, XXIX, 1476–1534; Stanhope, *Life of Pitt*, vol. 2, pp. 154–56; Ehrman, *Pitt*, vol. 2, chs 4–6; Mitchell, *Fox*, pp. 117–26; Aspinall, *Later Correspondence of George III*, vol. 1, pp. 596–97; Malmesbury, *Diaries*, vol. 2, p. 424; T. Paine, *The Rights of Man*, ed. H. Collins (London, 1971), pp. 61–131; M. Philp, *Paine* (Oxford, 1989), ch. 3; H. T. Dickinson, *Liberty and Property: Political Ideology in Eighteenth-Century Britain* (London, 1977), pp. 195–269.

29. *Speeches of Pitt*, vol. 2, p. 36; *Parliamentary Debates*, XXIX, 816–37.

30. Duffy, *Younger Pitt*, pp. 178–81; Buckingham and Chandos, *Memoirs*, vol. 2, pp. 209, 222–24; Wilberforce, *Life*, vol. 2, pp. 12–13; Malmesbury, *Diaries*, vol. 2, pp. 413, 440–41; *Fortescue Manuscripts*, vol. 2, pp. 171–72, 177–78, 277, 307–78; Ehrman, *Pitt*, vol. 2, pp. 206–58; R. R. Dozier, *For King, Constitution and Country: The English Loyalists and the French Revolution* (Lexington, 1983), ch. 1; Jupp, *Grenville*, pp. 136–51; Blanning, *French Revolutionary Wars*, pp. 92–93; Temperley and Penson, *Foundations of British Foreign Policy*, pp. 3–8; Black, *Foreign Policy*, ch. 9; Schroeder, *European Politics*, pp. 113–18; Mori, *Pitt and the French Revolution*, chs 2–4; Rose, *Great War*, pp. 69–117; Seton Watson, *Britain in Europe*, pp. 11–13; Melville, *Huskisson Papers*, p. 19.

31. On the nature of radicalism see J. Epstein, *Radical Expression: Political Language, Ritual and Symbol in England, 1790–1850* (New York, 1994), pp. 3–28; J. Belchem, *Popular Radicalism in Nineteenth-Century Britain* (Basingstoke, 1996), p. 1; J. Stevenson, 'Popular Radicalism and Popular Protest', in *Britain and the French Revolution, 1789–1815*, ed. H. T. Dickinson (Basingstoke, 1989), pp. 72–73; J. Vernon, *Politics and the People: A Study in English Political Culture* (Cambridge, 1993), ch. 8; Dickinson, *Liberty and Property*, part 3, and idem, *The Politics of the People in Eighteenth Century England* (Basingstoke, 1995), chs 5, 7; D. Wahrman, *Imagining the Middle Class: The Political Representation of Class in Britain, 1780–1840* (Cambridge, 1995), chs 1–4, and idem, 'Public Opinion, Violence and the Limits of Constitutional Politics', in *Re-Reading*

the *Constitution: New Narratives in the Political History of England's Long Nineteenth Century*, ed. J. Vernon (Cambridge, 1996), pp. 83–122; D. Herzog, *Poisoning the Minds of the Lower Orders* (Princeton, NJ, 1998); O. Smith, *The Politics of Language, 1791–1819* (Oxford, 1984), chs 1–2; E. P. Thompson, *The Making of the English Working Class* (London, 1991), ch. 5; Harvey, *Britain in the Early Nineteenth Century*, part 2, chs 3, 5–6; Evans, *Pitt the Younger*, pp. 55–61; E. Royle, *Revolutionary Britannia? Reflections on the Threat of Revolution in Britain, 1789–1848* (Manchester, 2000), pp. 1–66.

32. Ehrman, *Pitt*, vol. 2, pp. 229–33; Stanhope, *Life of Pitt*, vol. 2, p. 178; G. Claeys, 'The French Revolution Debate and British Political Thought', *History of Political Thought*, 11 (1990), pp. 59–80; J. R. Dinwiddy, 'Interpretations of Anti-Jacobinism', in *The French Revolution and British Popular Politics*, ed. M. Philp (Cambridge, 1991), pp. 38–49; M. Duffy, 'William Pitt and the Origins of the Loyalist Association Movement of 1792', *Historical Journal*, 39 (1996), pp. 943–62; E. C. Black, *The Association: British Extra-Parliamentary Political Organization, 1769–93* (Cambridge, MA, 1963), ch. 7; Jupp, *Grenville*, pp. 142–43; C. B. Cone, *The English Jacobins* (New York, 1968), pp. 145–46; A. Mitchell, 'The Association Movement of 1792–93', *Historical Journal*, 4 (1961), pp. 56–77; C. Emsley, 'The London "Insurrection" of December 1792: Fact, Fiction, or Fantasy?', *Journal of British Studies*, 17 (1978), pp. 66–86, and idem, *British Society*, pp. 16–18; Harvey, *Britain in the Early Ninetenth Century*, pp. 106–14; J. Mori, 'Responses to Revolution: The November Crisis of 1792', *Historical Research*, 69 (1996), pp. 284–305; F. O'Gorman, 'Pitt and the "Tory" Reaction to the French Revolution', in Dickinson, *Britain and the French Revolution*, p. 21; *Fortescue Manuscripts*, vol. 2, p. 136.

33. *Speeches of Pitt*, vol. 2, p. 150, vol. 4, pp. 135–37; *Parliamentary Debates*, XXX (London, 1817), 896, XXXV (London, 1819), 908; Duffy, *Younger Pitt*, pp. 152–53; Buckingham and Chandos, *Memoirs*, vol. 2, pp. 229–30; Dozier, *King, Constitution and Country*, pp. 61–62; H. T. Dickinson, 'Popular Conservatism and Militant Loyalism, 1789–1815', in Dickinson, *Britain and the French Revolution*, pp. 115–16; Fry, *Dundas*, pp. 155–56, 173–76.

34. Stevenson, *Artisans and Democrats*, pp. 61–62; *Speeches of Fox*, vol. 5, pp. 97–117; *Speeches of Pitt*, vol. 2, pp. 143–56; *Parliamentary Debates*, XXX (London, 1817), 775–86, 787–925; Ehrman, *Pitt*, vol. 2, pp. 387–88; Mitchell, *Fox*, pp. 126–35; Ayling, *Fox*, p. 182; Smith, *Grey*, pp. 47–51; Aspinall and Smith, *English Historical Documents*, pp. 246–49, 885–86; Jupp, *Journal of Canning*, p. 84; Evans, *Pitt the Younger*, pp. 40–43; Emsley, *British Society*, pp. 23–25.

35. *Speeches of Fox*, vol. 5, pp. 66–83; Ehrman, *Pitt*, vol. 2, pp. 388–89; Stanhope, *Life of Pitt*, vol. 2, pp. 187–90; *Parliamentary Debates*, XXX, 156–70, 174–238, 581–647, 725–39; Malmesbury, *Diaries*, vol. 2, pp. 442–69; Ayling, *Fox*, pp. 179–84.

36. Briggs, *Age of Improvement*, p. 176; Thompson, *Working Class*, pp. 135–36; Cole and Filson, *Working-Class Movements*, pp. 66–67; Aspinall and Smith, *English Historical Documents*, pp. 315–16; Ehrman, *Pitt*, vol. 2, pp. 389–90; Stanhope,

Life of Pitt, vol. 2, pp. 209–18; Rose, *Great War*, ch. 7; *Parliamentary Debates*, XXX (London, 1817), 1298–1310, 1449–61, 1486–1576, XXXI (London, 1818), 263–87; A. Goodwin, *The Friends of Liberty: The English Democratic Movement in the Age of the French Revolution* (London, 1979), p. 288.

37. Cole and Filson, *Working-Class Movements*, pp. 54–56; T. M. Parssinen, 'Association, Convention and Anti-Parliament in British Radical Politics, 1771–1848', *English Historical Review*, 88 (1973), pp. 504–33.

38. Costin and Watson, *Constitution*, vol. 2, pp. 7–8; Cole and Filson, *Working-Class Movements*, pp. 67–69; M. Elliott, 'French Subversion in Britain in the French Revolution', in *Britain and Revolutionary France: Conflict, Subversion and Propaganda*, ed. C. Jones (Exeter, 1983), pp. 40–52.

39. *Speeches of Pitt*, vol. 2, pp. 192–211; *Speeches of Fox*, vol. 5, pp. 270–92; *Parliamentary Debates*, XXXI, 470–605; Ehrman, *Pitt*, vol. 2, pp. 395–96; Stanhope, *Life of Pitt*, vol. 2, pp. 223–32; Aspinall and Smith, *English Historical Documents*, pp. 316–19; Aspinall, *Later Correspondence of George III*, vol. 2, pp. 206, 207, 208–9; Rose, *Great War*, pp. 191–94; Mitchell, *Fox*, p. 133; Jupp, *Journal of Canning*, pp. 102–4.

40. Turner, *Reform and Respectability*, pp. 42–45; T. Walker, *A Review of Some of the Political Events which have Occurred in Manchester during the Last Five Years* (London, 1794); Malone, *Thomas Cooper*, pp. 35–71; Knight, *Thomas Walker*, chs 5–15; Stevenson, *Artisans and Democrats*, pp. 22–27, 63–71; J. Beckett, 'Responses to War: Nottingham and the French Revolutionary and Napoleonic Wars, 1793–1815', *Midland History*, 22 (1997), pp. 71–73; Cole and Filson, *Working-Class Movements*, pp. 69–72; A. Wharam, *The Treason Trials, 1794* (Leicester, 1992); Ehrman, *Pitt*, vol. 2, pp. 396–98; Stanhope, *Life of Pitt*, vol. 2, pp. 265–74; Mori, *Pitt and the French Revolution*, chs 6, 8; Mitchell, *Fox*, pp. 153–54; Jupp, *Journal of Canning*, pp. 148–49; Olson, *Radical Duke*, pp. 93–94.

41. Speeches of Pitt, vol. 2, pp. 365–73; Aspinall and Smith, *English Historical Documents*, pp. 414–18, 765–67; *Parliamentary Debates*, XXXII (London, 1818), 700–15, 1405–6; Ehrman, *Pitt*, vol. 2, pp. 392, 447–52, 471–76; Stanhope, *Life of Pitt*, vol. 2, pp. 356–58, 395–97; Emsley, *British Society*, pp. 41–46; Harvey, *Britain in the Early Nineteenth Century*, pp. 312–15; Duffy, *Younger Pitt*, pp. 146–47; J. R. Poynter, *Society and Pauperism: English Ideas on Poor Relief, 1795–1834* (London, 1969), pp. 62–76; Rose, *Pitt and Napoleon*, pp. 79–92.

42. Rose, *Pitt and Napoleon*, p. 92; Ehrman, *Pitt*, vol. 2, pp. 474–75; Emsley, *British Society*, ch. 3.

43. R. Wells, *Dearth and Distress in Yorkshire, 1793–1802* (York, 1977), and idem, *Riot and Political Disaffection in Nottinghamshire in the Age of Revolutions, 1776–1803* (Nottingham, 1984), pp. 9–20, 26–36; Stevenson, *Popular Disturbances*, ch. 5; Ehrman, *Pitt*, vol. 2, ch. 12, vol. 3, ch. 10; Stanhope, *Life of Pitt*, vol. 2, pp. 356–58, vol. 3, pp. 247–53; Rose, *Great War*, ch. 13.

44. *Parliamentary Debates*, XXXIV (London, 1819), 1462–30, XXXV (London, 1819), 601–50; *Speeches of Pitt*, vol. 4, p. 110; Aspinall and Smith, *English Historical Documents*, pp. 418–19; Ehrman, *Pitt*, vol. 3, p. 316.

45. Crimps traded in recruits for army, navy and merchant marine, earning a living from the money offered for military enlistment and the advanced wages of sailors. They were unpopular figures, widely regarded as knaves and kidnappers. Stevenson, *Popular Disturbances*, pp. 208–12.

46. Ehrman, *Pitt*, vol. 2, pp. 398–400; Rose, *Great War*, pp. 192–94.

47. Ehrman, *Pitt*, vol. 2, pp. 401, 454–60, 486–87; Stanhope, *Life of Pitt*, vol. 2, pp. 352–54, 358–64; Rose, *Great War*, pp. 282–86; Aspinall, *Later Correspondence of George III*, vol. 2, pp. 414–15, 416, 417, 418, 419–20, 422, 424–28, 430–31; *Parliamentary Debates*, XXXI, 83–136, 206–36, XXXII (London, 1818), 142–207, 242–556; *Speeches of Pitt*, vol. 2, pp. 179–92; J. Barrell, *Imagining the King's Death: Figurative Treason, Fantasies of Regicide, 1793–96* (Oxford, 2000); Costin and Watson, *Constitution*, vol. 2, pp. 10–16; Aspinall and Smith, *English Historical Documents*, pp. 319–22; Ayling, *Fox*, pp. 193–94; Derry, *Fox*, chs 7–8; Mitchell, *Fox*, pp. 139–41.

48. *Speeches of Pitt*, vol. 2, pp. 324–42, 355–65; *Speeches of Fox*, vol. 6, pp. 1–9; Ehrman, *Pitt*, vol. 2, pp. 454–60. The veteran reformer Major John Cartwright, who had first risen to prominence in the 1770s, warmly congratulated Fox for his opposition to 'bills intended for riveting our chains, and silencing for ever the voice of complaint'. *The Life and Correspondence of Major Cartwright*, ed. F. D. Cartwright (2 vols, London, 1826), vol. 1, pp. 231–32.

49. Aspinall, *Later Correspondence of George III*, vol. 2, pp. 422, 431; O'Gorman, 'Pitt and "Tory" Reaction', p. 33; Duffy, *Younger Pitt*, pp. 153–54; Garlick, Macintyre and Cave, *Farington*, vol. 2, pp. 403–6; Wilberforce, *Life*, vol. 2, pp. 113–33; Ehrman, *Pitt*, vol. 2, pp. 459–60; Stanhope, *Life of Pitt*, vol. 2, pp. 361–62; *Fortescue Manuscripts*, vol. 3, pp. 144, 145–46, 147–48.

50. Evans, *Pitt the Younger*, p. 61; M. Elliott, *Partners in Revolution: The United Irishmen and France* (London, 1982), part 1; R. Wells, *Insurrection: The British Experience, 1795–1803* (Gloucester, 1983), pp. 1–27, 44–63, 253–65. See also J. R. Dinwiddy, 'Conceptions of Revolution in the English Radicalism of the 1790s', in Hellmuth, *Political Culture*, pp. 535–60; Thompson, *Working Class*, pp. 515–42; R. Wells, 'English Society and Revolutionary Politics in the 1790s: The Case for Insurrection', in Philp, *British Popular Politics*, pp. 188–226.

51. Wells, *Insurrection*, ch. 5.

52. Stanhope, *Life of Pitt*, vol. 3, pp. 23–39, 41–48, 247–53; Ehrman, *Pitt*, vol. 2, pp. 17–31, ch. 10; Rose, *Great War*, chs 13–14; Aspinall, *Later Correspondence of George III*, vol. 2, pp. 564–65, 270–72, vol. 3, pp. 437–38; *Speeches of Pitt*, vol. 3, pp. 141–53, vol. 4, pp. 96–134; *Parliamentary Debates*, XXXIII (London, 1818), 474–516, 639–44, 796–820, XXXV (London, 1819), 454–63, 495–539, 601–50, 777–854; Aspinall and Smith, *English Historical Documents*, pp. 419–31, 477–80; Jupp, *Grenville*, pp. 47–48, 253, 281–82.

53. Aspinall and Smith, *English Historical Documents*, p. 104.

54. D. E. Ginter, 'The Loyalist Association Movement of 1792–93 and British Public Opinion', *Historical Journal*, 9 (1966), pp. 179–90; Dozier, *King, Constitution and Country*, pp. 192–93.

55. J. Derry, *Politics in the Age of Fox, Pitt and Liverpool* (Basingstoke, 1990) pp. 97–98; O'Gorman, 'Pitt and "Tory" Reaction', p. 33; E. J. Evans, *The Forging of the Modern State, 1783–1870* (London, 1996), p. 77, and idem, *Pitt the Younger*, pp. 57–59; C. Emsley, 'An Aspect of Pitt's "Terror": Prosecutions for Sedition during the 1790s', *Social History*, 6 (1981), pp. 155–84, and idem, 'Repression, "Terror" and the Rule of Law in England during the Decade of the French Revolution', *English Historical Review*, 100 (1985), pp. 801–25; Ehrman, *Pitt*, vol. 2, pp. 445–50, 474; Rose, *Great War*, pp. 193–94, 286; I. R. Christie, *Stress and Stability in Late Eighteenth-Century Britain* (Oxford, 1984), chs 3–4, and idem, 'Conservatism and Stability in British Society', in Philp, *British Popular Politics*, pp. 169–87; D. Eastwood, 'Patriotism and the English State in the 1790s', in Philp, pp. 146–68; Belchem, *Popular Radicalism*, p. 20; R. Hole, *Pulpits, Politics and Public Order in England, 1760–1832* (Cambridge, 1989), chs 7–11.

56. *Speeches of Fox*, vol. 6, pp. 339–70; *Speeches of Pitt*, vol. 3, pp. 127–40; *Parliamentary Debates*, XXXIII (London, 1818), 644–735; Ehrman, *Pitt*, vol. 3, pp. 42–43, 307; Stanhope, *Life of Pitt*, vol. 3, pp. 40–41; Rose, *Great War*, p. 316; Mitchell, *Fox*, ch. 7; Ayling, *Fox*, pp. 197, 199; Derry, *Fox*, p. 373; Smith, *Grey*, pp. 66–67.

57. The 1796 results were, roughly, 424 for the government, 95 for the opposition, with 29 'independents' and 10 'doubtful'. Englefield, Seaton and White, *Prime Ministers*, p. 77; Gregory and Stevenson, *Britain in the Eighteenth Century*, p. 108.

58. Mitchell, *Fox*, ch. 7; Smith, *Grey*, p. 67; Williams and Ramsden, *Ruling Britannia*, p. 150.

59. *Parliamentary Debates*, XXXIII, 1415–21, 1421–33, 1482–87; Costin and Watson, *Constitution*, vol. 2, pp. 17–20; Cole and Filson, *Working-Class Movements*, pp. 89–93; Stevenson, *Popular Disturbances*, pp. 189–93; J. Moher, 'From Suppression to Containment: Roots of Trade Union Law to 1825', in *British Trade Unionism, 1750–1850: The Formative Years*, ed. J. Rule (London, 1988), pp. 74–97; Ehrman, *Pitt*, vol. 3, pp. 297–303; *Speeches of Pitt*, vol. 3, pp. 278–82; Aspinall, *Later Correspondence of George III*, vol. 3, pp. 48–49; Stanhope, *Life of Pitt*, vol. 3, pp. 126, 167, 182; Aspinall and Smith, *English Historical Documents*, pp. 746–52.

60. *Parliamentary Debates*, XXXIV (London, 1819), 984–98; Ehrman, *Pitt*, vol. 3, pp. 303–7; Stanhope, *Life of Pitt*, vol. 3, pp. 181–82. On the LCS and the government's intelligence-gathering networks, see Thale, *London Corresponding Society*, p. 426; Wells, *Insurrection*, ch. 2; C. Emsley, 'The Home Office and its Sources of Information and Investigation, 1791–1801', *English Historical Review*, 94 (1979), pp. 532–61.

61. *Speeches of Pitt*, vol. 3, pp. 403–12; *Parliamentary Debates*, XXXIV, 984–88.

62. Ehrman, *Pitt*, vol. 2, pp. 398–400, vol. 3, pp. 309–16; Mori, *Pitt and the French Revolution*, ch. 8; Stanhope, *Life of Pitt*, vol. 2, p. 188.

63. Duffy, *Younger Pitt*, p. 145; Stanhope, *Correspondence between Pitt and Rutland*, pp. 174–75.

64. *Speeches of Pitt*, vol. 2, p. 46, vol. 3, pp. 173–74.

65. Stanhope, *Life of Pitt*, vol. 2, pp. 187–90, vol. 3, p. 182; *Speeches of Pitt*, vol. 2, pp. 192–211, 335, vol. 3, pp. 403–12; Emsley, 'Repression, Terror and the Rule of Law', pp. 802–3, 813, 819, 822–23, and idem, 'Pitt's Terror', pp. 155–84; A. Booth, 'Popular Loyalism and Public Violence in the North West of England, 1790–1800', *Social History*, 8 (1983), pp. 295–313; Duffy, *Younger Pitt*, pp. 148–50; Aspinall, *Later Correspondence of George III*, vol. 1, pp. 551–52, vol. 2, p. 485; Goodwin, *Friends of Liberty*, p. 182; Wilberforce, *Life*, vol. 2, pp. 297, 327; Buckingham and Chandos, *Memoirs*, vol. 2, pp. 224–31; Mori, 'Responses to Revolution', pp. 284–305; Dozier, *King, Constitution and Country*, p. 169.

66. Ehrman, *Pitt*, vol. 2, pp. 408–14; Stanhope, *Life of Pitt*, vol. 2, pp. 252–55; Aspinall and Smith, *English Historical Documents*, pp. 123–24; Rose, *Great War*, pp. 191–92, 270–72; *Fortescue Manuscripts*, vol. 2, pp. 595–96; Aspinall, *Later Correspondence of George III*, vol. 2, pp. 222–24; Fry, *Dundas*, pp. 187–88.

67. Ehrman, *Pitt*, vol. 3, ch. 1; *Speeches of Pitt*, vol. 3, pp. 59–74, 141–53; Cole and Filson, *Working-Class Movements*, pp. 72–74; Harvey, *Britain in the Early Nineteenth Century*, pp. 320–22; Emsley, *British Society*, pp. 57–58; Rose, *Great War*, pp. 308–20; *Parliamentary Debates*, XXXII, 1517–68, XXXIII, 31–59, 324–94, 474–516, 639–44, 796–820; Aspinall, *Later Correspondence of George III*, vol. 2, pp. 541–42, 545–46, 564–65, 570–72; Stanhope, *Life of Pitt*, vol. 3, pp. 15–39, 41–48; Aspinall and Smith, *English Historical Documents*, pp. 587–90, 877–80.

68. Aspinall and Smith, *English Historical Documents*, pp. 306–7; Ehrman, *Pitt*, vol. 3, pp. 46–50; Stanhope, *Life of Pitt*, vol. 3, pp. 51–62.

69. Ehrman, *Pitt*, vol. 3, pp. 53–54; Stanhope, *Life of Pitt*, vol. 3, p. 52 and appendix pp. ii, iv, vi; Aspinall, *Later Correspondence of George III*, vol. 2, pp. 559–61; *Fortescue Manuscripts*, vol. 3, pp. 310–11; Aspinall and Smith, *English Historical Documents*, p. 136; Barnes, *George III and Pitt*, pp. 285–90; Rose, *Pitt and Napoleon*, pp. 238–39, 242; Jupp, *Grenville*, pp. 198–208; Mitchell, *Fox*, pp. 158–65.

70. *Parliamentary Debates*, XXXIII, 1066–89, 1100–41, 1146–1303, 1360–76, 1434–54, 1481–82; *Speeches of Pitt*, vol. 3, pp. 204–16, 219–54, 259–73; Stanhope, *Life of Pitt*, vol. 3, pp. 76–78, 93–95; Ehrman, *Pitt*, vol. 3, pp. 99–109; Rose, *Great War*, pp. 331–33; Aspinall, *Later Correspondence of George III*, vol. 3, pp. 3–4, 51–52.

71. *Parliamentary Debates*, XXXIV (London, 1819), 1–26, 73–109, 131–48, 179–208; *Speeches of Pitt*, vol. 3, pp. 300–47; Aspinall and Smith, *English Historical Documents*, pp. 582–87; Aspinall, *Later Correspondence of George III*, vol. 3, p. 162; R. Cooper, 'William Pitt, Taxation and the Needs of War', *Journal of British Studies*, 22 (1982), pp. 94–103; Rose, *Great War*, pp. 329, 370; Stanhope, *Life of Pitt*, vol. 3, pp. 162–67; Ehrman, *Pitt*, vol. 3, pp. 260–68, 270–71; Evans, *Pitt the Younger*, pp. 50–51. Patrick O' Brien has pointed out that Britain's eventual victory over France owed more to revenue than to naval or military successes, and that the revenue grew mainly because of Pitt's financial measures. O'Brien, 'Public Finance in the Wars with France, 1793–1815', in Dickinson, *Britain and the French Revolution*, pp. 165–87.

72. Harvey, *Britain in the Early Nineteenth Century*, pp. 313, 320–22.

73. Stanhope, *Life of Pitt*, vol. 3, pp. 92–93, 167–68 and appendix p. xi; Ehrman, *Pitt*, vol. 3, pp. 107–8; Duffy, *Younger Pitt*, pp. 157–58; Aspinall, *Later Correspondence of George III*, vol. 3, pp. 12–13; Hogge, *Auckland*, vol. 3, pp. 385–86; *Speeches of Pitt*, vol. 3, p. 275; Aspinall and Smith, *English Historical Documents*, p. 276.

74. Harling, *Waning of Old Corruption*, pp. 72–73, 79.

75. *Speeches of Pitt*, vol. 3, pp. 74–84; *Parliamentary Debates*, XXXIII, 77–107.

76. *Parliamentary Debates*, XXXV (London, 1819), 726. Pitt was recommending the further suspension of Habeas Corpus.

77. J. J. Sack, *From Jacobite to Conservative: Reaction and Orthodoxy in Britain, 1760–1832* (Cambridge, 1993), pp. 113, 131, 134; L. Colley, *Britons: Forging the Nation* (London, 1992), ch. 5, and idem, 'The Apotheosis of George III: Loyalty, Royalty and the British Nation, 1760–1820', *Past and Present*, 102 (1984), pp. 94–129; M. Morris, *The British Monarchy and the French Revolution* (New Haven, 1998); E. Vincent, '"The Real Grounds of the Present War": John Bowles and the French Revolutionary Wars, 1792–1802', *History*, 78 (1993), pp. 393–420; R. Hole, 'British Counter-Revolutionary Popular Propaganda in the 1790s', in Jones, *Britain and Revolutionary France*, pp. 53–69, and idem, 'English Sermons and Tracts as Media of Debate on the French Revolution, 1789 99', in Philp, *British Popular Politics*, pp. 18–37; Englefield, Seaton and White, *Prime Ministers*, pp. 112–13; Duffy, *Younger Pitt*, p. 157; Ehrman, *Pitt*, vol. 3, pp. 109–12; Stanhope, *Life of Pitt*, vol. 3, pp. 84–89; Evans, *Pitt the Younger*, pp. 58–61; Hinde, *Canning*, pp. 58–65.

78. *Parliamentary Debates*, XXX, 270–88, XXXI, 86–87, 93, 95, 215–20; XXXII, 1209–13, 1230–32, XXXIII, 1357–59, XXXVI (London, 1820), 1642–44; J. R. Western, 'The Volunteer Movement as an Anti-Revolutionary Force', *English Historical Review*, 71 (1956), pp. 603–14, and idem, *The English Militia in the Eighteenth Century* (London, 1965), pp. 219–26; J. E. Cookson, *The British Armed Nation, 1793–1815* (Oxford, 1997), and idem, 'Political Arithmetic and War in Britain, 1793–1815', *Historical Journal*, 32 (1989), pp. 868, 872; Dozier, *King, Constitution and Country*, pp. 138–55; Buckingham and Chandos, *Memoirs*, vol. 2, pp. 255–56; Duffy, *Younger Pitt*, pp. 155, 158–59; *Speeches of Pitt*, vol. 4, pp. 240–48; Ehrman, *Pitt*, vol. 2, pp. 401–2, 484–88, vol. 3, pp. 122–26; Aspinall and Smith, *English Historical Documents*, pp. 872–73; Rose, *Great War*, pp. 188–89, 278–80, 337.

79. Aspinall and Smith, *English Historical Documents*, pp. 859, 874.

80. See especially Cookson, *British Armed Nation*; Colley, *Britons*, chs 2, 5, 7; *A Union of Multiple Identities: The British Isles, 1750–1850*, ed. L. Brockliss and D. Eastwood (Manchester, 1997), pp. 1–8; E. J. Evans, 'Englishness and Britishness: National Identities, 1790–1870', in *Uniting the Kingdom? The Making of British History*, ed. A. Grant and K. Stringer (London, 1995), pp. 223–43.

81. J. E. Cookson, *The Friends of Peace: Anti-War Liberalism in England, 1793–1815* (Cambridge, 1982).

82. Melville, *Huskisson Papers*, pp. 20–21; Emsley, *British Society*, pp. 28–40.

83. J. Mori, 'The British Government and the Bourbon Restoration: The Occupation of Toulon, 1793', *Historical Journal,* 40 (1997), pp. 699–719; Jupp, *Grenville,* pp. 152–54, 163–64, 187; Evans, *Pitt the Younger,* p. 47; Rose, *Great War,* p. 117; Ehrman, *Pitt,* vol. 2, ch. 9; *Speeches of Pitt,* vol. 2, p. 161; *Parliamentary Debates,* XXX, 1016.

84. Duffy, *Younger Pitt,* pp. 181–82, 199 n. 41; *Parliamentary Debates,* XXX, 715, XXXIII, 1000–1; P. Kelly, 'Strategy and Counter-Revolution: The Journal of Sir Gilbert Elliot, 1–22 September 1793', *English Historical Review,* 98 (1983), pp. 340, 346; *Speeches of Pitt,* vol. 2, pp. 161, 174–75, 218, 263–71; *Fortescue Manuscripts,* vol. 2, pp. 438–39; Jupp, *Journal of Canning,* pp. 194–95; Englefield, Seaton and White, *Prime Ministers,* p. 79.

85. P. Schofield, 'British Politicians and French Arms: The Ideological War of 1793–95', *History,* 78 (1992), pp. 183–201; Blanning, *French Revolutionary Wars,* p. 93; Evans, *Pitt the Younger,* pp. 44–46; Mori, *Pitt and the French Revolution,* pp. 143–44, 150–56; Rose, *Great War,* p. 117; Ehrman, *Pitt,* vol. 2, ch. 7; Schroeder, *European Politics,* pp. 115–16; Black, *Foreign Policy,* pp. 459–71; M. Duffy, *Soldiers, Sugar and Seapower: British Expeditions to the West Indies and the War against Revolutionary France* (Oxford, 1987), ch. 1, and idem, *Younger Pitt,* p. 181; P. Mackesy, 'Strategic Problems of the British War Effort', in Dickinson, *Britain and the French Revolution,* pp. 147–64.

86. Though it is difficult to be sure how much credit to give to retrospective explanations, Wilberforce's remarks of December 1828 are worthy of note: 'I am myself persuaded that the war with France, which lasted so many years and occasioned such an immense expense of blood and treasure, would never have taken place but from Mr Dundas's influence with Mr Pitt, and his persuasion that we should be able with ease and promptitude, at a small expense of money or men, to take the French West India islands, and to keep them when peace should be restored: in truth, but for Mr Dundas's persuasion that the war would soon be over.' Wilberforce, *Life,* vol. 2, p. 391.

87. Ehrman, *Pitt,* vol. 2, pp. 548–56, vol. 3, pp. 50–66; Stanhope, *Life of Pitt,* vol. 3, pp. 51–62; Aspinall, *Later Correspondence of George III,* vol. 2, pp. 330–31, 594; *Speeches of Pitt,* vol. 3, pp. 153–74; Duffy, *Younger Pitt,* pp. 67–69; *Fortescue Manuscripts,* vol. 3, pp. 25–31, 310–11, 329–31; *Parliamentary Debates,* XXXIII, 996–1015; Melville, *Huskisson Papers,* pp. 30–31; Rose, *Pitt and Napoleon,* pp. 278, 287–88.

88. Hibbert, *George III,* ch. 38; Duffy, *Younger Pitt,* pp. 36–38; Aspinall, *Later Correspondence of George III,* vol. 2, pp. 455, 498, 506–7, 559–60; Rose, *Pitt and Napoleon,* pp. 238–39, 242; Stanhope, *Life of Pitt,* vol. 2, appendix pp. xxx–xxxii, vol. 3, appendix pp. iv–vi; *Fortescue Manuscripts,* vol. 3, pp. 143, 169–70, 173–74, 186, 227–30, 239–42, 256, 284, 310, 330–31, vol. 5, p. 306; Ehrman, *Pitt,* vol. 3, pp. 34–35.

89. In 1793, for example, Richmond objected to the projected West Indian expedition, and Spencer made difficulties in 1795 over the appointment of a naval commander for West Indian operations, and in 1798 over the deployment of the fleet.

90. Duffy, *Younger Pitt*, p. 184; Aspinall, *Later Correspondence of George III*, vol. 2, p. 537; Stanhope, *Life of Pitt*, vol. 3, appendix p. viii; *Fortescue Manuscripts*, vol. 6, p. 36; Ehrman, *Pitt*, vol. 3, pp. 451–57; Aspinall and Smith, *English Historical Documents*, pp. 94, 137–38.

91. Ehrman, *Pitt*, vol. 2, pp. 266–69; Duffy, *Younger Pitt*, pp. 185–86; *Fortescue Manuscripts*, vol. 2, pp. 592–93, vol. 5, pp. 224–25; Stanhope, *Life of Pitt*, vol. 3, p. 391; Olson, *Radical Duke*, pp. 91–101; Wilberforce, *Life*, vol. 2, pp. 10–11, 71; P. Mackesy, *Statesmen at War: The Strategy of Overthrow, 1798–99* (London, 1974), p. 5; Mori, *Pitt and the French Revolution*, p. 279.

92. Melville, *Huskisson Papers*, p. 20.

93. The siege of Dunkirk, an important base for French privateers, was intended to reconcile British public opinion to military intervention on the continent. But strategic blunders allowed the French to reinforce the town and British forces had to withdraw. Blanning, *French Revolutionary Wars*, pp. 109–10; Duffy, *Younger Pitt*, p. 186; Ehrman, *Pitt*, vol. 2, p. 265; Stanhope, *Life of Pitt*, vol. 2, pp. 202, 205.

94. *Windham Papers*, vol. 1, pp. 246–47; Kelly, 'Strategy and Counter-Revolution', pp. 341–42; Aspinall and Smith, *English Historical Documents*, pp. 95–96; Harcourt, *Rose*, vol. 1, pp. 127, 128–29; Ross, *Cornwallis*, vol. 2, p. 336, vol. 3, p. 174; Ehrman, *Pitt*, vol. 2, pp. 316–17, 374, 428; Stanhope, *Life of Pitt*, vol. 2, p. 298; Duffy, *Younger Pitt*, p. 187; Olson, *Radical Duke*, ch. 6.

95. Harcourt, *Rose*, vol. 1, p. 128; *Fortescue Manuscripts*, vol. 4, p. 152; Lord Wellesley, *The Wellesley Papers: The Life and Correspondence of Richard Colley Wellesley, Marquess Wellesley* (2 vols, London, 1914), vol. 1, p. 55; Fry, *Dundas*, p. 158; Stanhope, *Life of Pitt*, vol. 3, p. 39; Wilberforce, *Life*, vol. 2, p. 71.

96. Duffy, *Younger Pitt*, pp. 188–89; Stanhope, *Life of Pitt*, vol. 4, pp. 346–47; *Parliamentary Debates*, XXXIII, 996–1015; *Speeches of Pitt*, vol. 3, pp. 153–74; Ehrman, *Pitt*, vol. 3, p. 109.

97. Offensive efforts in the West Indies, though quite in keeping with Britain's traditional 'blue water' focus, were costly. About 70 per cent of British personnel sent to the West Indies after 1793 died, mainly of disease, and French power in this theatre was not destroyed. Evans, *Pitt the Younger*, pp. 49–50.

98. Englefield, Seaton and White, *Prime Ministers*, p. 79; Melville, *Huskisson Papers*, p. 38; Ehrman, *Pitt*, vol. 2, pp. 599–602, 639–40; Duffy, *Younger Pitt*, p. 125; Rose, *Great War*, pp. 305–6; Aspinall, *Later Correspondence of George III*, vol. 2, pp. 415–16 n. 5; Hinde, *Canning*, p. 42; Stanhope, *Life of Pitt*, vol. 3, pp. 81–82, 388–89; *Parliamentary Debates*, XXXIII, 783–87; Wilberforce, *Life*, vol. 2, pp. 112–13.

99. This fact, and the knowledge that the French government was experiencing financial problems and serious unrest at home, convinced Pitt and Dundas even more powerfully that the war would be over very quickly. See Baring, *Windham*, p. 386 (in which Windham remembered Pitt's statement that the war 'could not last more than a year'), and Wilberforce, *Life*, vol. 2, pp. 10–11, 391.

100. Aspinall and Smith, *English Historical Documents*, pp. 580–81; *Parliamentary Debates*, XXX, 718, XXXII, 1128; Duffy, *Younger Pitt*, p. 192; Schroeder, *European Politics*, pp. 122–24, 144–50; Evans, *Pitt the Younger*, pp. 46–49; Rose, *Great War*, pp. 208, 269–70; Watson, *Reign of George III*, pp. 366–71; Ehrman, *Pitt*, vol. 2, pp. 340–41, 366, 540–41; Jupp, *Grenville*, pp. 156–57, 166–67, 173, and idem, *Journal of Canning*, p. 149.

101. Rose, *Great War*, p. 195, ch. 8; Malmesbury, *Diaries*, vol. 3, pp. 216, 219, 241–42; *Fortescue Manuscripts*, vol. 3, pp. 25–31; Evans, *Pitt the Younger*, p. 49; Duffy, *Younger Pitt*, p. 192; Aspinall and Smith, *English Historical Documents*, pp. 109–10; Watson, *Reign of George III*, pp. 366–71; Ehrman, *Pitt*, vol. 2, pp. 548–56; Jupp, *Grenville*, pp. 152–84. On the early part of the war see also Mori, *Pitt and the French Revolution*, chs 5, 7; Schroeder, *European Politics*, ch. 3; M. Duffy, 'British Diplomacy and the French Wars, 1789–1815', in Dickinson, *Britain and the French Revolution*, pp. 147–64.

102. Browning, *Leeds*, pp. 101, 106–8; C. Breunig, *The Age of Revolution and Reaction* (New York, 1977), pp. 52–53; Watson, *Reign of George III*, pp. 371–74; Rose, *Great War*, pp. 321–28; Seton Watson, *Britain in Europe*, pp. 14–15; Stanhope, *Life of Pitt*, vol. 3, pp. 60–61; *Parliamentary Debates*, XXXIII, 903–62, 979–1025; *Fortescue Manuscripts*, vol. 3, pp. 369, 370–71, 372–73, 374, 376, 377–80, 381–82; Malmesbury, *Diaries*, vol. 3, pp. 250–354, 355–575; Ehrman, *Pitt*, vol. 3, pp. 50–65, 68; Reilly, *Pitt the Younger*, pp. 274–77.

103. Duffy, *Younger Pitt*, p. 194; *Fortescue Manuscripts*, vol. 5, pp. 243, 500; Rose, *Great War*, pp. 379, 388; Seton Watson, *Britain in Europe*, pp. 15–17; Stanhope, *Life of Pitt*, vol. 3, chs 28–29; Evans, *Pitt the Younger*, p. 49; Watson, *Reign of George III*, pp. 376–82, 386–87; Breunig, *Revolution and Reaction*, pp. 53–60; Ehrman, *Pitt*, vol. 3, ch. 12; Jupp, *Grenville*, pp. 209–61; Schroeder, *European Politics*, ch. 4; P. Mackesy, *War without Victory: The Downfall of Pitt, 1799–1802* (Oxford, 1984), chs 1–5.

Notes to Chapter 7: Decline

1. N. J. Curtin, 'The Transformation of the Society of United Irishmen into a Mass-Based Revolutionary Organization, 1794–96', *Irish Historical Studies*, 24 (1985), pp. 463–92; J. Smyth, *The Men of No Property: Irish Radicals and Popular Politics in the Late Eighteenth Century* (London, 1992); A. T. Q. Stewart, *A Deeper Silence: The Hidden Origins of the United Irishmen* (London, 1993); I. R. McBride, ' "When Ulster Joined Ireland": Anti-Popery, Presbyterian Radicalism and Irish Republicanism in the 1790s', *Past and Present*, 157 (1997), pp. 63–93; McDowell, *Ireland in the Age of Imperialism and Revolution*, chs 9–14; Evans, *Pitt the Younger*, pp. 62–65.

2. Ehrman, *Pitt*, vol. 2, pp. 221–22, 421–27, 430–40; McDowell, *Ireland in the Age of Imperialism and Revolution*, chs 13, 15, 16; Jupp, *Journal of Canning*, pp. 221, 225–26; Evans, *Pitt the Younger*, pp. 65–66.

3. Ehrman, *Pitt*, vol. 3, pp. 158–70; Stanhope, *Life of Pitt*, vol. 3, pp. 5–10, 67–69,

95–125, 145–57; Holland Rose, *Great War*, ch. 16; Evans, *Pitt the Younger*, pp. 67–68; Emsley, *British Society*, pp. 57, 68–69, 76–77; Reilly, *Pitt the Younger*, pp. 269–70; *Bathurst Manuscripts*, p. 21; Aspinall and Smith, *English Historical Documents*, pp. 892–93; Aspinall, *Later Correspondence of George III*, vol. 3, pp. 68–69, 70–71, 73–74, 75 n. 4, 76–78, 81–82, 86, 88–89, 104; Blanning, *French Revolutionary Wars*, pp. 203–5; Elliott, *Partners in Revolution*, chs 6–8; Wells, *Insurrection*, chs 7–8; McDowell, *Ireland in the Age of Imperialism and Revolution*, ch. 17; A. Jackson, *Ireland, 1798–1998* (Oxford, 1999), pp. 10–22.

4. *Speeches of Pitt*, vol. 3, pp. 347–60; *Wellesley Papers*, vol. 1, pp. 142–43; Wilkinson, 'Fitzwilliam Episode', p. 339 n. 108; Duffy, *Younger Pitt*, pp. 195–96; Ehrman, *Pitt*, vol. 3, pp. 170–78; Stanhope, *Life of Pitt*, vol. 3, pp. 158–62, 168–82, 222–31; Reilly, *Pitt the Younger*, pp. 270–73; Holland Rose, *Great War*, pp. 389–407; McDowell, *Ireland in the Age of Imperialism and Revolution*, chs 18–19.

5. McDowell, *Ireland in the Age of Imperialism and Revolution*, p. 678; Aspinall, *Later Correspondence of George III*, vol. 3, pp. 68 n. 1, 78 n. 2; *Fortescue Manuscripts*, vol. 4, pp. 344, 458; Stanhope, *Life of Pitt*, vol. 3, appendix p. xxvi.

6. Ehrman, *Pitt*, vol. 3, pp. 170–94; Stanhope, *Life of Pitt*, vol. 3, pp. 179–80, 222–31; *Speeches of Pitt*, vol. 3, pp. 361–403, vol. 4, pp. 70–92; Evans, *Pitt the Younger*, pp. 68–70, and idem, *Forging of the Modern State*, ch. 11; Aspinall, *Later Correspondence of George III*, vol. 3, pp. 158, 171–72; Buckingham and Chandos, *Memoirs*, vol. 2, pp. 429–31; D. Wilkinson, '"How Did They Pass the Union?" Secret Service Expenditure in Ireland, 1799–1804', *History*, 82 (1997), pp. 223–51; Gregory and Stevenson, *Britain in the Eighteenth Century*, pp. 160–61; *Parliamentary Debates*, XXXIV (London, 1819), 208–515, 657–981, XXXV (London, 1819), 37–198; Holland Rose, *Great War*, pp. 407–30; G. C. Bolton, *The Passing of the Irish Act of Union* (Oxford, 1966); Jackson, *Ireland*, pp. 23–29; Aspinall and Smith, *English Historical Documents*, pp. 197–203, 262–63.

7. P. Jupp, 'Britain and the Union, 1797–1801', *Transactions of the Royal Historical Society*, 6th series, 10 (2000), pp. 197–219.

8. *Fortescue Manuscripts*, vol. 4, p. 443, vol. 5, p. 27; Aspinall, *Later Correspondence of George III*, vol. 3, p. 78 n. 4; Holland Rose, *Pitt and Napoleon*, p. 243; Ehrman, *Pitt*, vol. 3, ch. 15; Stanhope, *Life of Pitt*, vol. 3, pp. 262–72; Barnes, *George III and Pitt*, ch. 8; Hibbert, *George III*, pp. 312–13; S. Ayling, *George the Third* (London, 1972), pp. 404–18; Brooke, *George III*, pp. 365–69; Gregory and Stevenson, *Britain in the Eighteenth Century*, pp. 60, 77. On the Catholic question see also U. Henriques, *Religious Toleration in England, 1787–1833* (London, 1961), pp. 136–58. In 'The Catholics and the Union', *Transactions of the Royal Historical Society*, 6th series, 10 (2000), pp. 243–58, Patrick Geoghegan argues that Catholic bishops and prominent laymen in Ireland could have prevented union, but chose not to, seeing it as their best hope for civil rights. They turned against the union, once it was implemented, because it was not accompanied by emancipation.

9. See Lord Camden's memorandum, printed in R. E. Willis, 'William Pitt's Resignation in 1801: Re-Examination and Document', *Bulletin of the Institute of Historical Research*, 44 (1971), pp. 239–57, especially p. 250.

10. Gregory and Stevenson, *England in the Eighteenth Century*, p. 160; Duffy, *Younger Pitt*, pp. 207–8; Willis, 'Pitt's Resignation', pp. 249–50; Jupp, *Journal of Canning*, pp. 97–100; Bickley, *Glenbervie*, vol. 1, p. 36; Ehrman, *Pitt*, vol. 2, p. 66, vol. 3, pp. 175–92; 496–97; Stanhope, *Life of Pitt*, vol. 3, pp. 268–74.

11. Stanhope, *Life of Pitt*, vol. 3, pp. 269–70, appendix pp. xxv–xxvi; Buckingham and Chandos, *Memoirs*, vol. 3, pp. 128–31; *Fortescue Manuscripts*, vol. 6, pp. 5–8, 10–11, 20–21, 86–89, 190–92, 197, 316, 435–36; Holland Rose, *Great War*, pp. 431–35; Jupp, *Grenville*, pp. 272, 277. Grenville had for some time been working on measures to reform the church. He backed the union with Ireland and hoped that it could be implemented quickly – not because he was much concerned about the condition of Ireland, but because he wanted to remove inconveniences that were affecting the war effort. He came to agree with Pitt that Catholic emancipation ought to accompany legislative union, though Grenville's main tasks at this time lay elsewhere: war strategy and mobilizing the Second Coalition against France.

12. Duffy, *Younger Pitt*, p. 208; Aspinall and Smith, *English Historical Documents*, pp. 158–59, 678; Willis, 'Pitt's Resignation', p. 250; Stanhope, *Life of Pitt*, vol. 2, appendix p. xxv, vol. 3, appendix p. xvi; Aspinall, *Later Correspondence of George III*, vol. 3, p. 186 n. 2; Ehrman, *Pitt*, vol. 3, pp. 497–502.

13. Aspinall, *Later Correspondence of George III*, vol. 3, pp. 476–77, 486–88; Malmesbury, *Diaries*, vol. 4, pp. 1–2; Harcourt, *Rose*, vol. 1, p. 308; Willis, 'Pitt's Resignation', pp. 250–54; Duffy, *Younger Pitt*, pp. 209–10; Pellew, *Sidmouth*, vol. 1, pp. 278–87, 500–12; P. Zeigler, *Addington: A Life of Henry Addington, first Viscout Sidmouth* (London, 1965), pp. 90–94; Ehrman, *Pitt*, vol. 3, pp. 501–6; Stanhope, *Life of Pitt*, vol. 3, pp. 266–69, 271, 273–75; Holland Rose, *Great War*, pp. 434–37.

14. Aspinall and Smith, *English Historical Documents*, pp. 176–77; Aspinall, *Later Correspondence of George III*, vol. 3, pp. xv–xvi, 383 n. 1, 476–77; Ehrman, *Pitt*, vol. 3, pp. 498–501, 504–5; Holland Rose, *Great War*, ch. 20; Evans, *Pitt the Younger*, pp. 39–40, 70; Hibbert, *George III*, pp. 312–14; Barnes, *George III and Pitt*, pp. 365–71; Brooke, *George III*, pp. 367–68.

15. Englefield, Seaton and White, *Prime Ministers*, pp. 79, 86; Pellew, *Sidmouth*, vol. 1, ch. 10; Ziegler, *Addington*, pp. 84–96; Aspinall, *Later Correspondence of George III*, vol. 3, pp. 476–77, 486–87; Malmesbury, *Diaries*, vol. 4, pp. 1–5; Stanhope, *Life of Pitt*, vol. 3, pp. 274–309; Ehrman, *Pitt*, vol. 3, pp. 495–96, 506–9, 523–33; Reilly, *Pitt the Younger*, pp. 299–301; Holland Rose, *Great War*, pp. 437–48.

16. Gregory and Stevenson, *Britain in the Eighteenth Century*, p. 61; Stanhope, *Life of Pitt*, vol. 3, pp. 276–77, 282–83, 289; Ehrman, *Pitt*, vol. 3, p. 610; Jupp, *Grenville*, ch. 6; Fry, *Dundas*, pp. 238–39, 242–43; *Windham Papers*, vol. 2, pp. 169–72; Ziegler, *Addington*, pp. 132–33, 137, 181; Mitchell, *Fox*, pp. 194–97; Smith, *Grey*, pp. 67, 78–82; Thorne, *House of Commons*, vol. 5, pp. 385–86.

17. Fry, *Dundas*, p. 243; Jupp, *Grenville*, p. 287; *Fortescue Manuscripts*, vol. 6, pp. 434–37, 445; Ehrman, *Pitt*, vol. 3, pp. 523–33; Stanhope, *Life of Pitt*, vol. 3,

pp. 276, 281–309; Aspinall, *Later Correspondence of George III*, vol. 3, p. xix; Barnes, *George III and Pitt*, pp. 382–84; Malmesbury, *Diaries*, vol. 4, pp. 31–32; Harcourt, *Rose*, vol. 1, p. 360; Holland Rose, *Great War*, pp. 446–49; Hibbert, *George III*, pp. 315–21.

18. Aspinall and Smith, *English Historical Documents*, pp. 163–65; Holland Rose, *Great War*, pp. 448–49.

19. Ehrman, *Pitt*, vol. 3, pp. 517–18; Holland Rose, *Great War*, chs 12, 15, 17; Aspinall, *Later Correspondence of George III*, vol. 3, pp. xiv–xv; Hibbert, *George III*, pp. 308–12; Jupp, *Grenville*, chs 4–5; Fry, *Dundas*, ch. 6; *Windham Papers*, vol. 2, pp. 94–148; Aspinall and Smith, *English Historical Documents*, pp. 104–5, 110–11, 280–81.

20. Duffy, *Younger Pitt*, pp. 211–12; Ehrman, *Pitt*, vol. 3, pp. 506–16; Holland Rose, *Great War*, pp. 437–39; Barnes, *George III and Pitt*, pp. 372–80; Pellew, *Sidmouth*, vol. 1, pp. 287–94; Ziegler, *Addington*, ch. 4; *Fortescue Manuscripts*, vol. 6, p. 434; Willis, 'Pitt's Resignation', pp. 254–55; Harcourt, *Rose*, vol. 1, pp. 286–309; Stanhope, *Life of Pitt*, vol. 3, appendix pp. xxiii–xxxii; Malmesbury, *Diaries*, vol. 4, pp. 4–5, 78; Aspinall and Smith, *English Historical Documents*, pp. 115–16, 159–63. On the change of ministers see also *Parliamentary Debates*, XXXV, 943–48.

21. Ehrman, *Pitt*, vol. 3, pp. 509–33; Stanhope, *Life of Pitt*, vol. 3, pp. 309–13; Holland Rose, *Great War*, ch. 20.

22. Fry, *Dundas*, pp. 225–26, 238; Jupp, *Grenville*, pp. 279–80; Sack, *Grenvillites*, pp. 49–50; Malmesbury, *Diaries*, vol. 4, p. 8; Aspinall, *Later Correspondence of George III*, vol. 3, p. 499; Ziegler, *Addington*, pp. 107–9.

23. Ehrman, *Pitt*, vol. 3, p. 530; Mackesy, *War without Victory*, ch. 9; C. J. Fedorak, 'Catholic Emancipation and the Resignation of William Pitt in 1801', *Albion*, 24 (1992), pp. 49–64; Willis, 'Pitt's Resignation', pp. 239–47.

24. Pellew, *Sidmouth*, vol. 1, chs 10–11; Ziegler, *Addington*, chs 4–5; Ehrman, *Pitt*, vol. 3, p. 842; Reilly, *Pitt the Younger*, pp. 301–5.

25. Englefield, Seaton and White, *Prime Ministers*, p. 79; Ehrman, *Pitt*, vol. 3, ch. 3; Duffy, *Younger Pitt*, p. 202; Stanhope, *Life of Pitt*, vol. 1, pp. 313–15, 367–68, vol. 2, p. 295, vol. 3, pp. 1–4, 62–64; Reilly, *Pitt the Younger*, pp. 251–60; Jupp, *Journal of Canning*, p. 77; Holland Rose, *Great War*, pp. 299–304, 325, 457–58; Wilberforce, *Life*, vol. 1, ch. 7, pp. 369–70, vol. 2, ch. 11, pp. 234, 236, 270.

26. Fry, *Dundas*, pp. 207–9, 238–39, 243; Jupp, *Grenville*, pp. 280–87; Sack, *Grenvillites*, pp. 14–15; Baring, *Windham Diary*, p. 406; Stanhope, *Life of Pitt*, vol. 3, p. 243; Ehrman, *Pitt*, vol. 3, p. 357; Duffy, *Younger Pitt*, p. 203; Englefield, Seaton and White, *Prime Ministers*, pp. 76, 79, 82, 91, 93, 97.

27. Jupp, *Grenville*, pp. 240–42, 248–52, 304; Fry, *Dundas*, pp. 208–9, 210, 213–14, 215, 224–25, 228; Aspinall, *Later Correspondence of George III*, vol. 3, p. xv; *Fortescue Manuscripts*, vol. 6, p. 242; *Windham Papers*, vol. 2, pp. 45, 64–67; Mackesy, *War without Victory*, pp. 176–77; Duffy, *Younger Pitt*, p. 203; Ehrman, *Pitt*, vol. 3, pp. 247, 356–57, 450–51, 517; Holland Rose, *Great War*, ch. 17.

28. Stanhope, *Life of Pitt*, vol. 2, p. 317, vol. 3, pp. 64, 129–34, 135–39, 246; Ehrman,

Pitt, vol. 3, pp. 79–83, 172, 232, 379, 517; Duffy, *Younger Pitt*, p. 204; Englefield, Seaton and White, *Prime Ministers*, pp. 79, 89; Mackesy, *War without Victory*, pp. 168, 174–75; Reilly, *Pitt the Younger*, pp. 276–81, 284; Holland Rose, *Great War*, pp. 334–35, 435, ch. 14; Pellew, *Sidmouth*, vol. 1, pp. 213–15, 263, 266–67; Ziegler, *Addington*, p. 89; *Wellesley Papers*, vol. 1, p. 129.

29. Duffy, *Younger Pitt*, pp. 204–5; Pellew, *Sidmouth*, vol. 1, pp. 152–53; Garlick, Macintyre and Cave, *Farington*, vol. 9, p. 3458.

30. Ehrman, *Pitt*, vol. 3, pp. 266–72, 279–85, 290–93; *Fortescue Manuscripts*, vol. 6, p. 373; *Parliamentary Debates*, XXXV, 454–63; Aspinall and Smith, *English Historical Documents*, pp. 104–5, 280–81.

31. Englefield, Seaton and White, *Prime Ministers*, p. 79; Aspinall, *Later Correspondence of George III*, vol. 3, p. 308; *Speeches of Pitt*, vol. 4, pp. 1–57; *Parliamentary Debates*, XXXIV, 1242–1397; Ehrman, *Pitt*, vol. 3, pp. 332–45; Stanhope, *Life of Pitt*, vol. 3, pp. 210–14; Holland Rose, *Great War*, pp. 384–86; Reilly, *Pitt the Younger*, pp. 292–93.

32. Bickley, *Glenbervie*, vol. 1, pp. 159–60; Duffy, *Younger Pitt*, pp. 205–6; Gregory and Stevenson, *Britain in the Eighteenth Century*, p. 191; Mackesy, *War without Victory*, ch. 7; Aspinall, *Later Correspondence of George III*, vol. 3, p. xv; Fry, *Dundas*, pp. 213–14, 221, 224–26; Stanhope, *Life of Pitt*, vol. 3, pp. 234–38, 336–38, 339, 340; Ehrman, *Pitt*, vol. 3, pp. 401–11; Holland Rose, *Great War*, pp. 387–88; Aspinall and Smith, *English Historical Documents*, pp. 893–95.

33. Emsley, *British Society*, pp. 85–88; *Parliamentary Debates*, XXXIV, 1489–1505, 1548–51, XXXV, 454–63, 777–854; Ehrman, *Pitt*, vol. 3, ch. 10; Duffy, *Younger Pitt*, p. 206; Ziegler, *Addington*, pp. 88–89; Pellew, *Sidmouth*, vol. 1, p. 263; Stanhope, *Life of Pitt*, vol. 3, pp. 243–50; Wells, *Wretched Faces*, part 3, especially pp. 247–48.

34. Ehrman, *Pitt*, vol. 3, pp. 34–35, 369–70, 427, 492, 521–22; Barnes, *George III and Pitt*, ch. 7; Hibbert, *George III*, p. 363; Duffy, *Younger Pitt*, pp. 206–7; *Wellesley Papers*, vol. 1, p. 129; Mackesy, *War without Victory*, pp. 112, 120, 127–33, 139–40, 167–68; Aspinall, *Later Correspondence of George III*, vol. 3, pp. xv–xvi, 376, 382–87, 424; Malmesbury, *Diaries*, vol. 4, pp. 24–25; *Windham Papers*, vol. 2, p. 160; Baring, *Windham*, p. 431.

35. Malmesbury, *Diaries*, vol. 4, p. 4.

36. Aspinall and Smith, *English Historical Documents*, pp. 124–25; Ziegler, *Addington*, pp. 95–96, 110, 157–58; Pellew, *Sidmouth*, vol. 1, ch. 11; Stanhope, *Life of Pitt*, vol. 3, pp. 384–85; Ehrman, *Pitt*, vol. 3, p. 554; Evans, *Pitt the Younger*, pp. 71–75; Jupp, *Grenville*, pp. 306–15; Sack, *Grenvillites*, pp. 50–51, 54–56; Mitchell, *Fox*, pp. 197–201; Smith, *Grey*, p. 88; *Wellesley Papers*, vol. 1, pp. 147–48.

37. Ziegler, *Addington*, pp. 116–27, 142–47; Evans, *Forging of the Modern State*, pp. 84–85, and idem, *Pitt the Younger*, pp. 72–73; Hinde, *Canning*, pp. 105–6; Aspinall and Smith, *English Historical Documents*, p. 177; Aspinall, *Later Correspondence of George III*, vol. 3, pp. 612–13, 614–15, 616–17, vol. 4, pp. ix, 16, 20; Ayling, *George the Third*, pp. 422–23; *Parliamentary Debates*, XXXVI, 86–140, 163–71; *Windham Papers*, vol. 2, p. 173; Baring, *Windham*, pp. 436–37; *Fortescue*

Manuscripts, vol. 7, pp. 30–33, 53, 55–60; Jupp, *Grenville*, pp. 309, 315–17; Sack, *Grenvillites*, pp. 54–60; Blanning, *French Revolutionary Wars*, p. 260; Mackesy, *War without Victory*, p. 209; Malmesbury, *Diaries*, vol. 4, pp. 65, 72; Ehrman, *Pitt*, vol. 3, pp. 557–68; Reilly, *Pitt the Younger*, pp. 309–11.

38. Aspinall and Smith, *English Historical Documents*, pp. 895–900; Mackesy, *War without Victory*, ch. 10; Englefield, Seaton and White, *Prime Ministers*, pp. 80, 86; Duffy, *Younger Pitt*, pp. 214–15; Gregory and Stevenson, *Britain in the Eighteenth Century*, p. 143; *Speeches of Pitt*, vol. 4, pp. 197–213; *Parliamentary Debates*, XXXVI, 25–28, 29–191, 557–97, 659–828; *Bathurst Manuscripts*, pp. 25–29; Malmesbury, *Diaries*, vol. 4, pp. 59, 61–66, 67–77; *Windham Papers*, vol. 2, pp. 184–87; Ziegler, *Addington*, pp. 126–27; Pellew, *Sidmouth*, vol. 1, pp. 447–62, vol. 2, pp. 1–55; Harcourt, *Rose*, vol. 1, pp. 429–30; Ehrman, *Pitt*, vol. 3, pp. 561–64; Stanhope, *Life of Pitt*, vol. 3, pp. 351–56, 358–62, 372–75; Reilly, *Pitt the Younger*, ch. 27; Holland Rose, *Great War*, pp. 468–71, 477–78.

39. Mitchell, *Fox*, pp. 171–77, 200–2, 218–19, 227–30; *Parliamentary Debates*, XXXVI, 72–83.

40. Parliamentary Debates, XXXVI, 321–50, 372–406, 445–62, 540–65, 889–913; Pellew, *Sidmouth*, vol. 2, pp. 56–72; Ziegler, *Addington*, pp. 148–50, 152–55, 158–60; Ehrman, *Pitt*, vol. 3, pp. 570, 574; Holland Rose, *Great War*, pp. 472–73, 480–81; Engleman, Seaton and White, *Prime Ministers*, pp. 77, 85; Gregory and Stevenson, *Britain in the Eighteenth Century*, pp. 108–9. The election results are reckoned to have been 467 seats to the government, 150 to the opposition, with 42 'independents' and others.

41. Stanhope, *Life of Pitt*, vol. 3, pp. 366–67, 375, 428–35, vol. 4, pp. 20–30, 32–39; Ehrman, *Pitt*, vol. 3, pp. 576–92, 596–97; Ziegler, *Addington*, pp. 174–82; Pellew, *Sidmouth*, vol. 2, pp. 106–9, 111–36; *Fortescue Manuscripts*, vol. 7, pp. 150–62; Malmesbury, *Diaries*, vol. 4, pp. 163–92; Aspinall and Smith, *English Historical Documents*, p. 125; Reilly, *Pitt the Younger*, pp. 316–19; Fry, *Dundas*, pp. 248–49, 254–55; Smith, *Grey*, pp. 87–92; Hinde, *Canning*, pp. 100–16; Jupp, *Grenville*, pp. 306–26; Sack, *Grenvillites*, pp. 54–75; Aspinall, *Later Correspondence of George III*, vol. 4, pp. xii–xiv; Harcourt, *Rose*, vol. 1, pp. 431–518; vol. 2, pp. 27–40; Holland Rose, *Great War*, pp. 481–87.

42. Englefield, Seaton and White, *Prime Ministers*, pp. 80, 83; Duffy, *Younger Pitt*, p. 213; Ziegler, *Addington*, pp. 43–45, 46–49, 51–58, 69–71, 95–96, 137–39, 161–64, 171–73; Pellew, *Sidmouth*, vol. 1, pp. 330–41, vol. 2, pp. 106–8; Ehrman, *Pitt*, vol. 3, pp. 46–50, 89–90, 525, 528–32, 564–65, 571–72, 576, 589 n., 596–97; Harcourt, *Rose*, vol. 1, pp. 335, 360, 426–28; Colchester, *Diary*, vol. 1, pp. 258–59; Malmesbury, *Diaries*, vol. 4, pp. 36–39, 77–88; Stanhope, *Life of Pitt*, vol. 3, pp. 302–8, 378–81, appendix p. xxxii; Aspinall, *Later Correspondence of George III*, vol. 3, pp. xiii, 487 n. 1; Holland Rose, *Great War*, pp. 450, 477–82, 471–72; Reilly, *Pitt the Younger*, pp. 313–19; Evans, *Pitt the Younger*, p. 73.

43. Malmesbury, *Diaries*, vol. 4, p. 78.

44. Pellew, *Sidmouth*, vol. 2, pp. 86–87, 149–53; Ziegler, *Addington*, pp. 165–67, 182–84; Englefield, Seaton and White, *Prime Ministers*, p. 86; Ehrman, *Pitt*,

vol. 3, pp. 567–68, 574–76; Stanhope, *Life of Pitt*, vol. 3, pp. 396–98, vol. 4, pp. 13–14; Reilly, *Pitt the Younger*, pp. 315, 320–21.

45. Stanhope, *Life of Pitt*, vol. 3, pp. 368–71, 426–27, vol. 4, pp. 20–30, 32–39; Ehrman, *Pitt*, vol. 3, pp. 553, 569–70, 579–80, 580–93, 630–31; Reilly, *Pitt the Younger*, pp. 317–19; Duffy, *Younger Pitt*, p. 215; Holland Rose, *Great War*, pp. 481–87; Aspinall, *Later Correspondence of George III*, vol. 4, pp. xii–xiv; Harcourt, *Rose*, vol. 1, p. 517, vol. 2, pp. 22–23, 27–28, 30–40; Ziegler, *Addington*, pp. 137–39, 163, 168–70, 173, 174–82; Pellew, *Sidmouth*, vol. 1, pp. 486–92, vol. 2, pp. 74–75, 111–36; Wilberforce, *Life*, vol. 3, p. 219; Fry, *Dundas*, pp. 249–54; Jupp, *Grenville*, pp. 322–24; Sack, *Grenvillites*, pp. 65–68; *Fortescue Manuscripts*, vol. 7, pp. 158–61.

46. Gregory and Stevenson, *Britain in the Eighteenth Century*, pp. 61, 108–9; Englefield, Seaton and White, *Prime Ministers*, pp. 77, 79, 80, 85; Harcourt, *Rose*, vol. 2, p. 40; Reilly, *Pitt the Younger*, ch. 27; Stanhope, *Life of Pitt*, vol. 3, ch. 33, vol. 4, pp. 1–10, 17–30, 32–39; Duffy, *Younger Pitt*, p. 216; Holland Rose, *Great War*, p. 487; Ehrman, *Pitt*, vol. 3, pp. 583–98.

47. Ziegler, *Addington*, p. 180; *Fortescue Manuscripts*, vol. 7, pp. 159–61; Aspinall, *Later Correspondence of George III*, vol. 4, pp. xiii–xiv.

48. Jupp, *Grenville*, pp. 304, 315–32; Sack, *Grenvillites*, pp. 69–78; Stanhope, *Life of Pitt*, vol. 3, pp. 305–6; Harcourt, *Rose*, vol. 4, p. 67; Ehrman, *Pitt*, vol. 3, pp. 592–602, 611–17; Holland Rose, *Great War*, pp. 469–70, 495–96; Evans, *Pitt the Younger*, pp. 73–74; Mitchell, *Fox*, pp. 202–7.

49. *Parliamentary Debates*, XXXVI, 1162–97, 1258–1514, 1517–79, 1594–1602, 1603–71; Emsley, *British Society*, ch. 6; Stanhope, *Life of Pitt*, vol. 4, pp. 41–44, 60–69; Reilly, *Pitt the Younger*, pp. 322, 324–25; *Windham Papers*, vol. 2, pp. 208–25; D. Gates, *The Napoleonic Wars, 1803–15* (London, 1997), pp. 16–17; Ziegler, *Addington*, pp. 182–94, 198–202; Pellew, *Sidmouth*, vol. 2, pp. 193–205, 148–87.

50. Mitchell, *Fox*, pp. 194, 201–11; Jupp, *Grenville*, pp. 326–36; Sack, *Grenvillites*, chs 3–4; Smith, *Grey*, pp. 90–92; *Fortescue Manuscripts*, vol. 7, p. 197; Ehrman, *Pitt*, vol. 3, pp. 607–14; Evans, *Pitt the Younger*, pp. 74–75.

51. *Parliamentary Debates*, XXXVI, 1385–1493, 1533–71, 1662–70; Malmesbury, *Diaries*, vol. 4, pp. 256, 260, 262, 266; Hinde, *Canning*, pp. 117–18; Reilly, *Pitt the Younger*, pp. 322–23; Sack, *Grenvillites*, pp. 69–70; *Fortescue Manuscripts*, vol. 7, p. 169; Aspinall, *Later Correspondence of George III*, vol. 4, pp. 102–4; *Speeches of Pitt*, vol. 4, pp. 221–40; Duffy, *Younger Pitt*, p. 216; Englefield, Seaton and White, *Prime Ministers*, pp. 80, 86; Holland Rose, *Great War*, pp. 487–88; Ehrman, *Pitt*, vol. 3, pp. 604–7; Stanhope, *Life of Pitt*, vol. 4, pp. 43–57, 61, 63–65; Ziegler, *Addington*, pp. 185–87; Pellew, *Sidmouth*, vol. 2, pp. 134–44, 182–86, 195–202.

52. Stanhope, *Life of Pitt*, vol. 4, pp. 61, 63–65; Colchester, *Diary*, vol. 1, p. 432.

53. Aspinall and Smith, *English Historical Documents*, pp. 900–1; Wilberforce, *Life*, vol. 3, pp. 110, 146–47; *Fortescue Manuscripts*, vol. 7, p. 210; Duffy, *Younger Pitt*, p. 217; Ehrman, *Pitt*, vol. 3, pp. 607–19, 623; Stanhope, *Life of Pitt*, vol. 4,

pp. 18–21, 76–83, 113–17, 120–23; Holland Rose, *Great War*, pp. 495–97; Reilly, *Pitt the Younger*, ch. 28.

54. Engleman, Seaton and White, *Prime Ministers*, pp. 80, 86–87; Duffy, *Younger Pitt*, p. 217; Ayling, *George the Third*, pp. 426–31; Hibbert, *George III*, pp. 339–50; Barnes, *George III and Pitt*, pp. 421–22; Aspinall, *Later Correspondence of George III*, vol. 4, pp. xvii–xx, 156; *Speeches of Pitt*, vol. 4, pp. 305–40; *Parliamentary Debates*, first series, II (London, 1804), 132–41, 182–251, 265–320; *Fortescue Manuscripts*, vol. 7, pp. 211–14, 217–19, 220; Stanhope, *Life of Pitt*, vol. 4, ch. 37; Aspinall and Smith, *English Historical Documents*, pp. 152–53; *Bathurst Manuscripts*, pp. 31–33; Malmesbury, *Diaries*, vol. 4, pp. 292–93, 300–5; Holland Rose, *Great War*, pp. 496–99; Evans, *Pitt the Younger*, p. 74; Ehrman, *Pitt*, vol. 3, pp. 623–53; Reilly, *Pitt the Younger*, pp. 325–28; Hinde, *Canning*, pp. 120–24; Ziegler, *Addington*, pp. 207–21; Pellew, *Sidmouth*, vol. 2, pp. 246–81.

55. Sack, *Grenvillites*, pp. 65–78; Jupp, *Grenville*, pp. 328–36; Mitchell, *Fox*, pp. 207–11; Smith, *Grey*, pp. 91–94; *Windham Papers*, vol. 2, pp. 226–33; Ziegler, *Addington*, pp. 210–16, 223; Malmesbury, *Diaries*, vol. 4, pp. 291–92, 294–99; Ehrman, *Pitt*, vol. 3, ch. 18; Reilly, *Pitt the Younger*, ch. 28; Buckingham and Chandos, *Memoirs*, vol. 3, pp. 282–90.

56. Aspinall and Smith, *English Historical Documents*, pp. 146–48, 165–67, 303–4; Stanhope, *Life of Pitt*, vol. 4, ch. 38, appendix pp. iv, x–xiii; Harcourt, *Rose*, vol. 2, pp. 100–10, 113–36; Sack, *Grenvillites*, pp. 70–78; Mitchell, *Fox*, pp. 207–8, 211–19; Jupp, *Grenville*, pp. 332–44; Smith, *Grey*, pp. 89–94; *Bathurst Manuscripts*, pp. 39–41, 43–44; Malmesbury, *Diaries*, vol. 4, pp. 302–15; Barnes, *George III and Pitt*, pp. 421–43; Holland Rose, *Great War*, pp. 499–504; Reilly, *Pitt the Younger*, pp. 326–28; Ehrman, *Pitt*, vol. 3, pp. 646, 653–62, 713–14; Buckingham and Chandos, *Memoirs*, vol. 3, pp. 352–53; *Fortescue Manuscripts*, vol. 7, pp. 222–23; Aspinall, *Later Correspondence of George III*, vol. 4, pp. xix–xxi, 156–66.

57. Olson, *Radical Duke*, pp. 230–32.

58. Englefield, Seaton and White, *Prime Ministers*, pp. 79–80, 81, 86; Duffy, *Younger Pitt*, p. 214; Pellew, *Sidmouth*, vol. 1, pp. 498–99; Ehrman, *Pitt*, vol. 3, ch. 16; Tolstoy, *Half Mad Lord*, pp. 90–94, 146, 148, 150–57; Harcourt, *Rose*, vol. 1, pp. 402–29; Stanhope, *Life of Pitt*, vol. 3, pp. 340–49, vol. 4, pp. 85–87; Reilly, *Pitt the Younger*, pp. 323–24; Holland Rose, *Great War*, ch. 21, pp. 490–95; Ziegler, *Addington*, pp. 141–42; Hinde, *Canning*, p. 116.

59. *Fortescue Manuscripts*, vol. 7, p. 223.

60. Ziegler, *Addington*, pp. 226–28; Pellew, *Sidmouth*, vol. 2, pp. 316–19, 350–53; Twiss, *Eldon*, vol. 1, ch. 19; Watson, *Reign of George III*, p. 581; Duffy, *Younger Pitt*, pp. 219–20; Harcourt, *Rose*, vol. 2, pp. 119–20, 144–46, 153–54; Hinde, *Canning*, pp. 124–29; Jupp, *Grenville*, p. 335; Smith, *Grey*, p. 93; Malmesbury, *Diaries*, vol. 4, pp. 311–14, 328–32; *Bathurst Manuscripts*, pp. 23–24, 41–42; *The Creevey Papers*, ed. H. Maxwell (2 vols, London, 1903), vol. 1, pp. 28–29; Stanhope, *Life of Pitt*, vol. 4, ch. 38, pp. 205–11, 259–63; Ehrman, *Pitt*, vol. 3, pp. 665–76, 708–11, 717–18; Evans, *Pitt the Younger*, pp. 75–76; Holland Rose, *Great War*, pp. 499–502, 509–10, 518; *Parliamentary Debates*, first series, II,

483–512, 562–608, 614–47, 663, 672–80, 683–97, 698–755, 757–71, III (London, 1805), 723–86, IV (London, 1805), 72–85, 112–28, 134–42, 160–61, 171–78; Aspinall, *Later Correspondence of George III*, vol. 4, pp. xx–xxii, 195–98; *Speeches of Pitt*, vol. 4, pp. 341–65, 403–20.

61. Ehrman, *Pitt*, vol. 3, pp. 715–16, 720; Stanhope, *Life of Pitt*, vol. 4, pp. 165–66, 226–29, appendix pp. x–xii; Holland Rose, *Great War*, pp. 499–500, 507–8; Duffy, *Younger Pitt*, p. 218; Ayling, *George the Third*, pp. 432–33; Hibbert, *George III*, pp. 322–57; Twiss, *Eldon*, vol. 1, pp. 460–64, 472–83; *Bathurst Manuscripts*, pp. 34–43; Aspinall and Smith, *English Historical Documents*, pp. 146–48, 166–67, 178, 287; Harcourt, *Rose*, vol. 2, pp. 113–29, 167–72; Aspinall, *Later Correspondence of George III*, vol. 4, pp. xxii, 231n., 266, 268–69; Olson, *Radical Duke*, p. 231; Aspinall, *Correspondence of George Prince of Wales*, vol. 5, pp. 6–11; *Fortescue Manuscripts*, vol. 7, pp. 228–33.

62. Englefield, Seaton and White, *Prime Ministers*, p. 80; Reilly, *Pitt the Younger*, p. 231; Maxwell, *Creevey*, vol. 1, pp. 14–15; Ehrman, *Pitt*, vol. 3, chs 16, 19; Holland Rose, *Great War*, p. 500; Duffy, *Younger Pitt*, pp. 220–21; Harcourt, *Rose*, vol. 2, pp. 126–28; Barnes, *George III and Pitt*, p. 444; Wilberforce, *Life*, vol. 3, pp. 187, 219–20; Garlick, Macintyre and Cave, *Farington*, vol. 6, p. 2436; *Windham Papers*, vol. 2, p. 264; Twiss, *Eldon*, vol. 1, p. 449.

63. Ehrman, *Pitt*, vol. 3, pp. 665–76; Stanhope, *Life of Pitt*, vol. 4, p. 207; *Speeches of Pitt*, vol. 4, p. 364; Hinde, *Canning*, pp. 129–31.

64. Ehrman, *Pitt*, vol. 3, pp. 676–706, 710, 726–46; Stanhope, *Life of Pitt*, vol. 4, pp. 205–11, 217–22, 259–63; Aspinall, *Later Correspondence of George III*, vol. 4, pp. 257–58, 259, 290, 292–93, 298; *Parliamentary Debates*, first series, III, 3, 57–58, 142–44, 149–55, 224–47, 289–306, 365–409, 410–68, 626, 785, V (London, 1805), 12–14, 460–82, 490–532, 535–47; Harvey, *Britain in the Early Nineteenth Century*, part 3, chs 2–3; Duffy, *Younger Pitt*, pp. 194, 221–22; Roseveare, *The Treasury*, pp. 154–57; Gregory and Stevenson, *Britain in the Eighteenth Century*, pp. 61–62; Englefield, Seaton and White, *Prime Ministers*, pp. 80, 86; J. M. Sherwig, *Guineas and Gunpowder: British Foreign Aid in the Wars with France, 1793–1815* (Cambridge, MA, 1969), ch. 7; Holland Rose, *Great War*, pp. 513–16, 522–25; Reilly, *Pitt the Younger*, pp. 328–29, 334–37; *Speeches of Pitt*, vol. 4, pp. 370–402; Schroeder, *European Politics*, pp. 257–64; *British Diplomacy, 1813–1815*, ed. C. K. Webster (London, 1921), pp. 389–94; Aspinall and Smith, *English Historical Documents*, pp. 901–4. Mulgrave may have had more influence over the shaping of Pitt's security plan than has often been recognized, though this is doubted by both Ehrman and Duffy. In E. Ingram, 'Lord Mulgrave's Proposals for the Reconstruction of Europe in 1804', *Historical Journal*, 19 (1976), pp. 511–20, Mulgrave emerges as a promoter of the European balance of power whose goal was to enable Britain to withdraw from continental commitments (hence the idea that it should be left to Austria and Prussia to check France in Europe). In terms of the strategic debates of the 1790s, Mulgrave preferred the focus on colonial warfare, as championed by Dundas, to Grenville's policy of fuller continental involvement.

65. Englefield, Seaton and White, *Prime Ministers*, p. 80; Malmesbury, *Diaries*, vol. 4, pp. 345–46; *Bathurst Manuscripts*, pp. 45–48; Aspinall, *Later Correspondence of George III*, vol. 4, pp. 310–12, 313–14, 315–16, 317–18, 320–21, 324; *Fortescue Manuscripts*, vol. 7, pp. 255–62, 273–74, 275–78; *Speeches of Pitt*, vol. 4, pp. 420–35, 446–71; Stanhope, *Life of Pitt*, vol. 4, pp. 270–86, 290–97, 308–12; Ehrman, *Pitt*, vol. 3, pp. 752–63; Evans, *Pitt the Younger*, p. 76; Duffy, *Younger Pitt*, p. 224; Holland Rose, *Great War*, pp. 519–21; Reilly, *Pitt the Younger*, pp. 332–33; Hinde, *Canning*, pp. 131–33; Jupp, *Grenville*, p. 338; Sack, *Grenvillites*, pp. 83–84; Smith, *Grey*, pp. 94–96; Fry, *Dundas*, pp. 261–76; Ziegler, *Addington*, pp. 235–40; Pellew, *Sidmouth*, vol. 2, pp. 349–50, 354–56, 367–70; Brown, 'Scotland under Dundas and Pitt', pp. 265–79; Wilberforce, *Life*, vol. 3, pp. 217–30; Baring, *Windham*, p. 449; *Windham Papers*, vol. 2, pp. 252–53. The Melville affair can also be followed in *Parliamentary Debates*, first series, IV and V.

66. Harling, *Waning of Old Corruption*, pp. 82–88; *Windham Papers*, vol. 2, p. 264.

67. Ehrman, *Pitt*, vol. 3, pp. 764, 774–75; Holland Rose, *Great War*, pp. 518–19; *Fortescue Manuscripts*, vol. 7, pp. 263–70; Aspinall, *Later Correspondence of George III*, vol. 4, pp. 328–29; *Windham Papers*, vol. 2, pp. 253–54; Mitchell, *Fox*, pp. 216–17; Smith, *Grey*, pp. 96–97; Jupp, *Grenville*, p. 338; Sack, *Grenvillites*, p. 71; Stanhope, *Life of Pitt*, vol. 4, pp. 297–303, 312–13; *Speeches of Pitt*, vol. 4, pp. 435–46; *Parliamentary Debates*, first series, IV, 651–729, 742–843, (different pagination) 833–950, 951–1060.

68. Aspinall and Smith, *English Historical Documents*, p. 304; *Fortescue Manuscripts*, vol. 7, pp. 237–46; Harcourt, *Rose*, vol. 2, pp. 92–100, 197; Malmesbury, *Diaries*, vol. 4, pp. 345–46; Mitchell, *Fox*, pp. 211–16; Jupp, *Grenville*, pp. 332–34, 336–37, 339–40; Hinde, *Canning*, pp. 130–31, 133–34, 135; Aspinall, *Later Correspondence of George III*, vol. 4, pp. xxii–xxiii, xxiv–xxv, 259, 260–62, 263–64, 265–66, 278; Ehrman, *Pitt*, vol. 3, pp. 720–25, 745–49, 763–66; Holland Rose, *Great War*, pp. 517–18; Reilly, *Pitt the Younger*, pp. 329–30, 332–34; Stanhope, *Life of Pitt*, vol. 4, pp. 135–44, 190, 235–50, appendix pp. xx–xxi; Evans, *Pitt the Younger*, pp. 76–77; Ziegler, *Addington*, pp. 229–40; Pellew, *Sidmouth*, vol. 2, pp. 324–48, 356–60, 369–71.

69. Gregory and Stevenson, *Britain in the Eighteenth Century*, p. 237; Aspinall and Smith, *English Historical Documents*, pp. 177–78; *Fortescue Manuscripts*, vol. 7, p. 252; Harcourt, *Rose*, vol. 2, pp. 82–90; Duffy, *Younger Pitt*, pp. 222–23; Ehrman, *Pitt*, vol. 3, pp. 745–63; Hibbert, *George III*, pp. 375–76; Barnes, *George III and Pitt*, p. 472; Ayling, *George the Third*, pp. 187–88; Aspinall, *Later Correspondence of George III*, vol. 4, pp. 282, 283–84, 285–86; Reilly, *Pitt the Younger*, pp. 331–34; Holland Rose, *Great War*, pp. 477, 517–18; Stanhope, *Life of Pitt*, vol. 4, pp. 252–53.

70. Aspinall and Smith, *English Historical Documents*, pp. 113–14, 254–55; *Bathurst Manuscripts*, pp. 44–45; Ziegler, *Addington*, pp. 233–34; Hinde, *Canning*, p. 130; Harcourt, *Rose*, vol. 2, p. 197; Aspinall, *Later Correspondence of George III*, vol. 4, p. xxv; Duffy, *Younger Pitt*, pp. 107, 223; Stanhope, *Life of Pitt*, vol. 4, pp. 235–50; Sack, *Grenvillites*, p. 81; Ehrman, *Pitt*, vol. 3, pp. 746–49; Thorne, *House of Commons*, vol. 4, pp. 460, 462, vol. 5, p. 455.

71. Melville, *Huskisson Papers*, pp. 53–54.

72. *Windham Papers*, vol. 2, p. 251; Baring, *Windham*, p. 445.

73. Ehrman, *Pitt*, vol. 3, pp. 763–66; Holland Rose, *Great War*, pp. 521–22, 530; Duffy, *Younger Pitt*, p. 224; Evans, *Pitt the Younger*, p. 77; Hinde, *Canning*, pp. 133–34; Smith, *Grey*, p. 96; Ziegler, *Addington*, pp. 240–44; Pellew, *Sidmouth*, vol. 2, pp. 369–77; Aspinall and Smith, *English Historical Documents*, p. 97; Aspinall, *Later Correspondence of George III*, vol. 4, p. 340 n. 2; *Bathurst Manuscripts*, pp. 45–48; *Fortescue Manuscripts*, vol. 7, pp. 278–90, 292.

74. *Fortescue Manuscripts*, vol. 7, pp. 287–90, 293–308; Buckingham and Chandos, *Memoirs*, vol. 3, pp. 427–30; *Bathurst Manuscripts*, pp. 48–49; Aspinall and Smith, *English Historical Documents*, p. 255; Russell, *Memorials and Correspondence of Fox*, vol. 4, p. 97; *Windham Papers*, vol. 2, pp. 241, 259, 264; Harcourt, *Rose*, vol. 2, pp. 198–201; Aspinall, *Later Correspondence of George III*, vol. 4, pp. xxv–xxvi; Barnes, *George III and Pitt*, pp. 461–64; Ayling, *George the Third*, p. 436; Sack, *Grenvillites*, pp. 78–84; Jupp, *Grenville*, p. 340; Mitchell, *Fox*, pp. 213–16; Smith, *Grey*, pp. 97–99; Reilly, *Pitt the Younger*, pp. 333–34, 337–38; Ehrman, *Pitt*, vol. 3, pp. 767–70, 802–5; Stanhope, *Life of Pitt*, vol. 4, pp. 286–90, 312–15, 333–36.

75. Duffy, *Younger Pitt*, pp. 107, 223; Colchester, *Diary*, vol. 1, p. 544; Stanhope, *Life of Pitt*, vol. 4, pp. 239–42; Thorne, *House of Commons*, vol. 5, p. 455; Ehrman, *Pitt*, vol. 3, pp. 746–47; Sack, *Grenvillites*, pp. 81–82.

76. Ehrman, *Pitt*, vol. 3, chs 19–20; Holland Rose, *Great War*, ch. 23; Reilly, *Pitt the Younger*, ch. 29; Duffy, *Younger Pitt*, p. 112; Brooke, *George III*, pp. 378–79; Aspinall and Smith, *English Historical Documents*, pp. 98, 264, 281, 287–88.

77. Stanhope, *Life of Pitt*, vol. 4, pp. 333–36, 352–53, 359–61; Ehrman, *Pitt*, vol. 3, pp. 802–5, 819–20; Holland Rose, *Great War*, pp. 530, 547; Duffy, *Younger Pitt*, p. 224; Hinde, *Canning*, pp. 134–36; Thorne, *House of Commons*, vol. 3, p. 386, vol. 5, pp. 668–69; Harcourt, *Rose*, vol. 2, pp. 198–201, 249–50; *Fortescue Manuscripts*, vol. 7, pp. 300–7, 311; Malmesbury, *Diaries*, vol. 4, p. 351; Aspinall, *Later Correspondence of George III*, vol. 4, pp. xxv–xxvi; *Bathurst Manuscripts*, pp. 48–50.

78. Gregory and Stevenson, *Britain in the Eighteenth Century*, p. 144; Malmesbury, *Diaries*, vol. 4, pp. 346–47; C. D. Hall, *British Strategy in the Napoleonic War, 1803–15* (Manchester, 1992), pp. 8, 115–26; Schroeder, *European Politics*, pp. 257–76, especially pp. 263–64; *Fortescue Manuscripts*, vol. 7, p. 233; Ehrman, *Pitt*, vol. 3, pp. 708–13, 726–45, 780–87; Stanhope, *Life of Pitt*, vol. 4, pp. 205–10, 259–63, 303–8, 317–20; Holland Rose, *Great War*, pp. 509–10, 522–30; Duffy, *Younger Pitt*, pp. 224–25; Cookson, *British Armed Nation*, ch. 4, especially pp. 114–16; R. Glover, *Peninsular Preparation: The Reform of the British Army, 1795–1809* (Cambridge, 1988), ch. 9.

79. Ehrman, *Pitt*, vol. 3, pp. 796–802; Stanhope, *Life of Pitt*, vol. 4, pp. 350–51, 366–67; Malmesbury, *Diaries*, vol. 4, p. 354 n.

80. E.g. Grenville to Windham, 5 November 1805, in *Windham Papers*, vol. 2, p. 275; Windham to Huskisson, 29 December 1805, in Melville, *Huskisson Papers*, p. 59.

81. Hinde, *Canning*, pp. 137–38; Ehrman, *Pitt*, vol. 3, pp. 805–18; Stanhope, *Life of Pitt*, vol. 4, pp. 339–46, 350–51, 357–67; Holland Rose, *Great War*, pp. 534–47; Reilly, *Pitt the Younger*, pp. 336–39; Duffy, *Younger Pitt*, p. 226; Evans, *Pitt the Younger*, pp. 77–78; Schroeder, *European Politics*, pp. 276–86; Aspinall, *Later Correspondence of George III*, vol. 4, pp. 367–70, 371, 375–79; *Bathurst Manuscripts*, pp. 50–51; Malmesbury, *Diaries*, vol. 4, pp. 347–52, 354 n.

82. Mitchell, *Fox*, p. 219; Smith, *Grey*, pp. 89–99; Sack, *Grenvillites*, pp. 83–84; Jupp, *Grenville*, pp. 341–42; *Wellesley Papers*, vol. 1, pp. 187–88.

83. Stanhope, *Life of Pitt*, vol. 4, ch. 43, p. 374; Ehrman, *Pitt*, vol. 3, pp. 549–51, 772–73, 819–22; Duffy, *Younger Pitt*, pp. 227–28; Wilberforce, *Life*, vol. 3, pp. 244–54; Harcourt, *Rose*, vol. 2, pp. 91, 199–201; Malmesbury, *Diaries*, vol. 4, pp. 352–57.

84. Melville, *Huskisson Papers*, p. 59; *Wellesley Papers*, vol. 1, p. 189; *Bathurst Manuscripts*, pp. 29–30; Wilberforce, *Life*, vol. 3, p. 251; Harcourt, *Rose*, vol. 2, pp. 222–35; *Fortescue Manuscripts*, vol. 7, pp. 327–32; Malmesbury, *Diaries*, vol. 4, pp. 352–57; Englefield, Seaton and White, *Prime Ministers*, pp. 76, 80; Duffy, *Younger Pitt*, p. 228; Stanhope, *Life of Pitt*, vol. 4, pp. 369–85; Ehrman, *Pitt*, vol. 3, ch. 22; Reilly, *Pitt the Younger*, ch. 30; Holland Rose, *Great War*, pp. 547–58; Ziegler, *Addington*, pp. 246–48.

85. Evans, *Forging of the Modern State*, p. 66; Aspinall and Smith, *English Historical Documents*, p. 99; Hibbert, *George III*, pp. 387–88; Malmesbury, *Diaries*, vol. 4, p. 357; Aspinall, *Later Correspondence of George III*, vol. 4, pp. 380–83, 386–87; Ehrman, *Pitt*, vol. 3, pp. 838–41; Stanhope, *Life of Pitt*, vol. 4, pp. 386–91, 395–97; Hinde, *Canning*, pp. 142–44; Sack, *Grenvillites*, pp. 85–101; Jupp, *Grenville*, pp. 345–46; Mitchell, *Fox*, pp. 220–22; Smith, *Grey*, pp. 99–103; Gates, *Napoleonic Wars*, p. 35; Hall, *British Strategy*, p. 126.

Notes to Chapter 8: Achievement

1. *Fortescue Manuscripts*, vol. 1, pp. 215–16; Rose, *National Revival*, pp. 134–35.

2. This is the basic line of argument presented in S. I. Davis, *Leadership in Conflict: The Lessons of History* (Basingstoke, 1995).

3. Anecdotes tend to illuminate and reinforce what we think we know about Pitt's personality, and for all the evidence of his aloofness and reserve it is also clear that he had a healthy sense of humour. On 21 September 1786, for instance, he underwent an operation to remove a facial cyst and chided the surgeon, John Hunter, because the procedure was expected to take six minutes and Hunter ran over by thirty seconds. There are also examples of Pitt's witty repartee, as when he met the Duchess of Gordon (who had been the government's main hostess in Downing Street during the 1780s) some years after they had last seen each other. 'Well, Mr Pitt, do you talk as much nonsense now as you used to do when you lived with me?' asked the duchess, to which Pitt replied: 'I do not know, madam, whether I talk so much nonsense, but I certainly do not hear as much.' Englefield, Seaton and White, *Prime Ministers*, p. 81.

4. Michael Duffy claims that 'in both what he attempted and what he actually achieved, Pitt was by far the most "improving" premier of the eighteenth century'. Duffy, *Younger Pitt*, p. 95.

5. Evans, *Pitt the Younger*, p. 87.

6. Barnes, *George III and Pitt*, p. 266.

7. Harcourt, *Rose*, vol. 1, pp. 402–27; Stanhope, *Life of Pitt*, vol. 3, pp. 1–4, 341–49; Englefield, Seaton and White, *Prime Ministers*, p. 81; Evans, *Pitt the Younger*, pp. 3–4, 85–86; Wilberforce, *Life*, vol. 3, pp. 245–49.

8. Pitt served as chancellor of the exchequer from 13 July 1782 to 5 April 1783, 27 December 1783 to 21 March 1801, and 10 May 1804 to 23 January 1806. He was first lord of the treasury and leader of the Commons from 19 December 1783 to 17 March 1801 and 10 May 1804 to 23 January 1806.

9. Melville, *Huskisson*, p. 59.

10. E.g. Evans, *Pitt the Younger*, pp. 2, 43, 86.

Index